America's
'Special R

This unique volume offers an original collection of essays on the theme of America's 'special relationships'. It interrogates, in an original and provocative manner, the distinctive character of America's interactions with an array of allies and clients, both international and domestic.

The essays vary in their focus; some are primarily historical, some are more contemporary. All consider the quality of 'specialness' in the context of America's relationship with particular countries, including the United Kingdom, Canada, Australia, New Zealand, Holland, Russia, Iran and Israel. The collection also concerns the relationship between the American state and key 'special' foreign policy interests, notably ethnic lobbies and religious groups.

Bringing together a wide range of experts, this timely collection provides a valuable addition to the debates surrounding US foreign policy, and will be of great interest to students and scholars of American politics, American history and international relations.

John Dumbrell is Professor of Government at Durham University. He specializes in the study of US foreign policy. He is the author of *President Lyndon Johnson and Soviet Communism* (2004), *A Special Relationship: Anglo–American Relations from the Cold War to Iraq* (2006) and *Clinton's Foreign Policy: Between the Bushes* (2009).

Axel R. Schäfer is Senior Lecturer in US History and Director of the David Bruce Centre for American Studies at Keele University. His main research interests are in US intellectual and political history. He is the author of *American Progressives and German Social Reform, 1875–1920* (2000) and *The Cold War State, Religion, and the Resurgence of Evangelicalism, 1942–1990* (forthcoming).

Routledge studies in US foreign policy

Edited by:

Inderjeet Parmar
University of Manchester

John Dumbrell
University of Durham

This new series sets out to publish high-quality works by leading and emerging scholars critically engaging with US Foreign Policy. The series welcomes a variety of approaches to the subject and draws on scholarship from international relations, security studies, international political economy, foreign policy analysis and contemporary international history.

Subjects covered include the role of administrations and institutions; the media, think-tanks, ideologues and intellectuals; elites, transnational corporations, public opinion and pressure groups in shaping foreign policy; US relations with individual nations, with global regions and global institutions; and America's evolving strategic and military policies.

The series aims to provide a range of books – from individual research monographs and edited collections to textbooks and supplemental reading for scholars, researchers, policy analysts and students.

United States Foreign Policy and National Identity in the 21st Century
Edited by Kenneth Christie

New Directions in US Foreign Policy
Edited by Inderjeet Parmar, Linda B. Miller and Mark Ledwidge

America's 'Special Relationships'
Foreign and domestic aspects of the politics of alliance
Edited by John Dumbrell and Axel R. Schäfer

America's 'Special Relationships'

Foreign and domestic aspects of the politics of alliance

Edited by
John Dumbrell and
Axel R. Schäfer

LONDON AND NEW YORK

First published 2009
by Routledge
2 Park Square, Milton Park, Abingdon, Oxon OX14 4RN

Simultaneously published in the USA and Canada
by Routledge
270 Madison Ave, New York, NY 10016

Routledge is an imprint of the Taylor & Francis Group, an Informa business

© 2009 Editorial selection and matter, John Dumbrell and
Axel R. Schäfer; individual chapters, the contributors

Typeset in Times New Roman by Keyword Group Ltd
Printed and bound in Great Britain by CPI Antony Rowe,
Chippenham, Wiltshire

British Library Cataloguing in Publication Data
A catalogue record for this book is available
from the British Library

Library of Congress Cataloging in Publication Data
America's special relationships' : foreign and domestic aspects of the
politics of alliance / edited by John Dumbrell and Axel R. Schäfer.
p. cm. — (Routledge studies in US foreign policy)
ISBN 978-0-415-48376-6 (hardbound) — ISBN 978-0-415-48375-9
(pbk.) — ISBN 978-0-203-87270-3 (e-book) 1. United States — Foreign
relations—1989- 2. Alliances. I. Dumbrell, John, 1950- II. Schäfer, Axel R.
JZ1480.A9836 2009
327.73—dc22   2009006220

ISBN13: 978-0-415-48376-6 (hbk)
ISBN13: 978-0-415-48375-9 (pbk)
ISBN13: 978-0-203-87270-3 (ebk)

Contents

List of contributors   vii

Acknowledgements   x

Introduction: The politics of special relationships   1
JOHN DUMBRELL AND AXEL R. SCHÄFER

1   **Model nations: US allies and partners in the
    modernizing imagination**   7
    NICK CULLATHER

2   **Old world, new world: Great Britain and America
    from the beginning**   24
    KATHLEEN BURK

3   **Hating Bush, supporting Washington: George W. Bush,
    anti-Americanism and the US–UK special relationship**   45
    JOHN DUMBRELL

4   **The US–Canada relationship: How 'special' is America's
    oldest unbroken alliance?**   60
    DAVID G. HAGLUND

5   **Australia, the United States and the unassailable alliance**   76
    MARK BEESON

6   **Yearning and spurning: New Zealand's special relationships
    with Britain and the United States**   93
    DOLORES E. JANIEWSKI

7   **Testing the limits of a special relationship: US unilateralism
    and Dutch multilateralism in the twenty-first century**   115
    GILES SCOTT-SMITH

8   **An aborted special relationship: US–Russia relations in the post-Cold War world: 1989–2007**   132
ALEX MARSHALL AND J. SIMON ROFE

9   **The ecstasy and the agony: The rise and fall of US–Iran relations**   152
DONETTE MURRAY

10   **America's Israel/ Israel's America**   173
IAN J. BICKERTON

11   **US–Israel relations: A special friendship**   191
LEE MARSDEN

12   **The death of a peculiar special relationship: Myron Taylor and the religious roots of America's Cold War**   208
ANDREW PRESTON

13   **'What Marx, Lenin, and Stalin needed was . . . to be born again': Evangelicals and the special relationship between church and state in US Cold War foreign policy**   223
AXEL R. SCHÄFER

Index   242

List of contributors

Mark Beeson is Professor of International Politics in the Department of Political Science and International Studies at the University of Birmingham. His most recent publications are *Regionalism, Globalization and East Asia: Politics, Security and Economic Development* (2007), *Securing Southeast Asia: The Politics of Security Sector Reform* (with Alex Bellamy, 2008) and *Institutions of the Asia-Pacific: ASEAN, APEC and Beyond* (2009).

Ian J. Bickerton completed his PhD at the Claremont Graduate School, California. He is a member of the School of History at the University of New South Wales. His publications include *Forty-Three Days: The Gulf War* (1991), *Contested Spaces: The Historiography of the Arab–Israeli Conflict* (2005), *A History of the Arab–Israeli Conflict* (2007) and, most recently, *Unintended Consequences: The United States at War* (with Kenneth Hagan, 2008).

Kathleen Burk is Professor of Modern and Contemporary History at University College London. Author of a number of books on Anglo–American relations, her most recent is *Old World, New World: The Story of Britain and America*, published in the United Kingdom in 2007 and the United States in 2008.

Nick Cullather, a historian of US foreign relations, received his PhD from the University of Virginia and has taught at Indiana University for 16 years. He is author of two books on nation-building, *Illusions of Influence* (1994), a study of US–Philippines relations, and *Secret History* (1999 and 2006), a history of the CIA's overthrow of the Guatemalan government in 1954. He is currently at work on *Calories and Cold War: America's Quest to Feed the World*.

John Dumbrell is Professor of Government at Durham University. He is the author of several books on American foreign policy, including *President Lyndon Johnson and Soviet Communism* (winner of the 2004 Richard E. Neustadt book prize) and *A Special Relationship: Anglo-American Relations from the Cold War to Iraq* (2006). His latest book is *Clinton's Foreign Policy: Between the Bushes* (2009).

David G. Haglund is Professor of Political Studies at Queen's University, Kingston, Ontario. His research focuses on transatlantic security and on Canadian and American international security policy. He co-edits the *International Journal*. Among his books are *Latin America and the Transformation of U.S. Strategic Thought, 1936–1940* (1984) and *Over Here and Over There: Canada–US Defence Cooperation in an Era of Interoperability* (2001).

Dolores E. Janiewski is an Associate Professor of History at Victoria University of Wellington in the School of History, Philosophy, Politics and International Relations, specializing in US History. She is currently working on a book on conservatism and US foreign policy under the working title *Righteous Empire and Republican Virtues: U.S. Conservatives and the Long Cold War, 1871–2001.* She co-authored *New Rights, New Zealand: Myths, Moralities and Markets* (2005).

Lee Marsden is a Lecturer in International Relations at the University of East Anglia. He is the author of *Lessons from Russia: Clinton and US Democracy Promotion* (2005) and *For God's Sake: The Christian Right and US Foreign Policy* (2008).

Alex Marshall is a Lecturer at the Scottish Centre for War Studies at the University of Glasgow. His publications include *The Russian General Staff and Asia, 1800–1917* (2006) and *Soviet Rule in the Caucasus* (forthcoming).

Donette Murray is a Senior Lecturer in the Department of Defence and International Affairs at the Royal Military Academy Sandhurst. Her most recent book is *US Foreign Policy and Iran: American–Iranian Relations since the Revolution* (Routledge, 2009).

Andrew Preston is Lecturer in History at Cambridge University, where he is a Fellow of Clare College. He is the author of *The War Council: McGeorge Bundy, the NSC, and Vietnam* (2006) and co-editor of *Nixon in the World: American Foreign Relations, 1969–1977* (2008).

J. Simon Rofe is a Lecturer in the Department of Politics and International Relations at the University of Leicester. His research interests focus on US foreign relations and diplomacy in the twentieth century, with a specific focus on presidential post-war planning. Amongst his most recent publications is *Franklin Roosevelt's Foreign Policy and the Welles Mission* (2007).

Axel R. Schäfer is a Senior Lecturer in US History and Director of the David Bruce Centre for American Studies at Keele University. His main research interests are in US intellectual and political history, with a particular focus on the Progressive Era and on Cold War America. He is the author of *American Progressives and German Social Reform, 1875–1920* (2000) and has just completed a monograph titled *The Cold War State, Religion, and the Resurgence of Evangelicalism, 1942–1990*.

Giles Scott-Smith is Senior Researcher with the Roosevelt Study Center and Associate Professor in International Relations with the Roosevelt Academy, both in Middelburg, in the Netherlands. From 2009, he also occupies the Ernst van der Beugel Chair in the Diplomatic History of Transatlantic Cooperation, Leiden University.

Acknowledgements

This collection of essays grew out of an international colloquium on *Allies and Clients: America's 'Special Relationships'* organized by the David Bruce Centre for American Studies at Keele University in April 2007. The volume primarily brings together edited versions of the best papers produced for the colloquium. The editors would like to thank the David Bruce Centre for funding the conference and for providing administrative support in the editing of this volume.

Introduction
The politics of special relationships

John Dumbrell and Axel R. Schäfer

Since the end of the Cold War, and especially since the later 1990s, journalistic and academic commentary on the United States has been preoccupied with the nature and sheer extent of American international power. The United States has been variously described as the global hegemon, the lone superpower, the indispensable nation, the hyperpower and the Überpower.[1] By the close of the twentieth century, American global pre-eminence, rooted in the triad of military, economic and political/cultural 'soft power', was widely recognized as having assumed extraordinary proportions, to a degree arguably unparalleled in human history. In turn, a major academic industry developed to explain, denounce and unravel the story of America's rise.

One aspect of this recent preoccupation with American hegemony – its roots, its impact, its possible supercession – has been a new concern with the politics of alliance. How have 'friends' of the United States – allies or clients of the hegemon – adapted to the realities of American global power? The policies of the Bush administration of 2001–9, especially in the three or four years following 9/11, set the tone for this contemporary sharpening of interest in the politics of alliance. Ever since the close of World War II, America's alliances have been characterized by a radical asymmetry of power. However, the early twenty-first century saw a confluence of vast, hegemonic power with a newly imperial style. Chris Patten recalled the effect on US–European relations: 'Even for a senior foreign official dealing with the US administration, you are aware of your role as a tributary: however courteous your hosts, you come as a subordinate bearing goodwill and hoping to depart with a blessing on your endeavours'.[2]

As a result, the Bush administration will be recalled in historical memory as, especially in terms of its foreign policy, one of the most controversial in American history. President Bush himself was reviled outside the United States to a degree unknown in recent history. European perspectives on the Bush administration were shaped by two concepts which, between them, came almost to define the politics of alliance in the early twenty-first century: the concepts of unilateralism and of imperialism.

The pre-2005 penchant for unilateralism, and the willingness of Bush appointees to embrace it, grew from neo-conservative thinking about the nature and purpose of American international power. It also grew from the logic of the post-Cold War international system: from the extent to which the United States had become so unlike other countries that it seemed to have no need to work with other countries on a basis of mutual respect and recognition. The multilateral alliance structures of the Cold War era seemed to have served their purpose; they would have to adapt to a world of unvarnished American eminence, or simply join other relics of the Cold War in the dustbin of history. Bilateral patron–client relationships seemed increasingly to be replacing the older system of relatively stable multilateral alliances.

Unilateralism, however, was never the 'official' policy of the Bush administration. The day before the 9/11 terror attacks on New York City and Washington D.C., Secretary of State Colin Powell told *Time* magazine that unilateralism was not an option for the United States: 'The world is too complicated'.[3] Even as the United States invaded Iraq without United Nations backing, the United States retained a commitment to multilateral solutions to many global issues, such as nuclear negotiations with North Korea. The foreign policy of the second George W. Bush administration (2005–9) was significantly less committed to unilateral action – not least via *ad hoc* coalitions – than was its predecessor.

The post-1995 era also brought new talk of American imperialism: not just from the Marxist left, but also from the many other points on the political spectrum. Chalmers Johnson noted in 2002: 'Not since the jingoists of the Spanish–American War have so many Americans openly called for abandoning even a semblance of constitutional and democratic foreign policy and endorsed imperialism'.[4] Just as surely, commentators, encouraged by the apparent policy failures of the administration of President George W. Bush, soon began to speculate on the degree to which American hegemony held the seeds of its own destruction: the extent to which American 'over-reaching' was actually ushering in a new, 'post-American' order – whether one characterized by global multipolarity, a new global regionalism or even by an age of Chinese power.[5]

President George W. Bush himself regularly denied any imperialist, or even unilateralist, intent. Nonetheless, the unilateralist and imperialist thrust of his policy remains a force to be reckoned with, even after his departure from office. During the 2008 election campaign Barack Obama condemned the ideological and hubristic foreign policy stances of the Bush administration, yet he stopped well short of advocating a thoroughgoing and unshakeable commitment to multilateralism. In April 2007, for example, he declared: 'No President should ever hesitate to use force – unilaterally if necessary – to protect ourselves and our vital interest when we are attacked or imminently threatened. But when we use force in situations other than self-defense, we should make every effort to garner the clear support and participation of others – the kind of burden-sharing and support President George H. W. Bush mustered before he launched Operation Desert Storm'.[6] During a debate in early 2008 with Hillary Clinton, Obama argued: 'I think we should always cooperate with our allies and sovereign nations in making sure that we are rooting out terrorist organizations, but if they are planning attacks on Americans, like what happened in 9/11, it is my job – it will be my job as president to make sure that we are hunting them down'.[7] And when

Barack Obama began the process of making appointments to his new administration in late 2008, he signalled a clear eagerness to establish continuity with the post-2004 Bush policies.

These debates over American hegemony and its implications, and over the imperialist and unilateralist tendencies of the younger Bush's foreign policy, form the immediate backdrop to our collection of essays on American 'special relationships'. Academic discussion has primarily focused on the various strategies open to smaller powers, notably 'bandwagoning', 'taming' and 'rebalancing'.[8] Alongside recent writing on alliance politics, there is also a substantial academic literature on special relations in US foreign policy. At its most incisive, this literature interrogates the very notion of 'specialness'.[9] To the British, of course, the US–UK alliance is *the* special relationship. It draws on history, language and culture, as well as on military and intelligence cooperation, rooted in perceptions of shared interest as well as in London's desire to bask in Washington's reflected glory. To other nations, the US–UK relationship evokes suspicion of conspiratorial Anglo-Saxonism, recently extended in the form of an 'Anglosphere' which includes Australia, Canada and New Zealand.[10] The Mexican ambassador to the United Nations, Adolfo Aguilar Zinser, announced in 2003 that Washington's commitment to London would always be stronger than towards its southern neighbour. America's relations with Mexico were, in comparison with the British alliance, '*un noviazgo de fin de semana*' ('a casual weekend fling').[11]

There are important essays in this book on America's relationship with Britain and with other English-speaking countries. Yet, this collection goes much further. In considering other alliances, the authors raise important questions, both for historians and for contemporary policymakers. What exactly does make a particular bilateral relationship with the United States 'special'? Judging merely by book and article titles, the United States would appear to have had special relations with countries as various as China, Israel, Germany and Canada.[12] According to David Schoenbaum, since the American Revolution, the United States has 'entertained, cultivated, endured, and suffered special relationships' with, among others, Canada, Panama, France, Germany, Russia, South Korea, 'one Vietnam and two Chinas', Guatemala, Nicaragua and El Salvador.[13] As (still) the global hegemon, the United States has, in some sense, 'special relations' with every country in the world. America is the only country to which every other country, no matter how small or how regionally oriented, has to develop a policy.

Stretched too far, of course, the term 'special relations' ceases to have any meaning. Perhaps, therefore, it is appropriate to reserve the term, after all, for the US–UK relationship, with its peculiar mixture of historical, cultural, military and intelligence interlinkages? Are all bilateral relationships with the United States unique, or do they have important dimensions and features in common? What strategies have various countries adopted in order to come to terms with American power, either in the Cold War or in the post-Cold War years? What strategies *should* they adopt? Is there some kind of dynamic of 'special relations' – some dialectic of intimacy, illusion and disillusion? How do special relations relate to the universalizing dynamic of American exceptionalism?

In addressing these and other questions, the present collection is not designed to provide a comprehensive overview of the state of America's various special relationships. Rather, the book aims to consider the concept of specialness from a variety of angles, including international relations and domestic politics. Collectively, the essays suggest that the notion of specialness, both in the word's comparative and normative senses (as 'different' and as 'better'), remains at the heart of US foreign policy. Foreign policy in a democratic polity relies upon popular appeal that derives in part from constructions of cultural similarity, a sense of historical ties and a level of emotional identification. While purely utilitarian *Realpolitik* does play a role, the powerful perceptions, images, projections and legitimations that underlie the special relationship narrative can determine relations beyond pragmatic interest or the personal chemistry between political leaders. Indeed, as a number of essays suggest, religious imagery and the 'modernizing imagination' are two master narratives of American politics and culture that, imposed upon a global scene, define the relevance or irrelevance of particular international relationships. Likewise, many of the essays invoke the language of familial and emotional ties. They discuss specialness in terms of child–parent relationships, loyalty and betrayal, agony and ecstasy, and yearning and spurning – dimensions that go beyond self-interest, personal diplomacy or even soft power.

In short, foreign relations cannot be divorced from the myopic perspectives imposed by powerful specialness frameworks. Our first, keynote, essay by Nick Cullather is a poignant reminder of this. Based on original research, Cullather shows that US relations with Mexico in the 1930s and 1940s and with India in the 1950s entered the policy orbit only when US politicians, bureaucrats and social scientists selected these countries as 'models'. They projected an idealized story of American 'development' onto these two nations in ways that depicted them as reliable bearers of democratic, capitalist American ideals into the future. Being defined as 'special' in this way translated directly into aid. Moreover, these alliances, built upon projected notions of replicated experience, provided templates for approaches to other international contexts. The 'modernizing imagination' that underlay relations with Mexico, for example, also provided the model for post-war reconstruction in Europe and Asia.

Our two essays on the US–UK relationship, by Kathleen Burk and by John Dumbrell, analyse how the special relationship narrative is constructed and reconstructed both in times of placid relations and in times of transatlantic tension. They focus particularly on how the two sides to the relationship have seen, and continue to see, each other. Kathleen Burk offers a wide-ranging *tour de force* surveying the entire historical relationship. John Dumbrell considers the extraordinary British reception of the presidency of George W. Bush, locating in it some of the key symbols and themes of the Anglo-American story as analysed by Burk.

Six case studies follow on a number of both familiar and unfamiliar candidates for specialness. They highlight that, within the special relationship narrative, America's allies and clients had leeway and leverage, but that when relations turned sour, the mantle of specialness could easily turn into a straightjacket. David Haglund starts off by examining how images of specialness were utilized for political purposes in the North American political discourse. In this context, he argues for the unique closeness of the US–Canada alliance, deriving from the Kingston dispensation of 1938 that set Canada and the United States on a distinctly different plane from any of the linkages America has with its transoceanic allies. Mark Beeson considers the US–Australian alliance in the era of 9/11 and of American hegemony. He argues that Canberra has misjudged Australian interests and has paid too high a price for the alliance, and that the politics of alliance can be simultaneously politically beneficial and economically deleterious. Dolores Janiewski, reviewing the experience of New Zealand primarily from the peace movement perspective, looks at the strategic calculation of small states in relation to global American power. She maintains that small nations are able to follow their own path and can reject ties to the hegemon.

The remaining three essays in this section examine relations beyond the 'Anglosphere'. In his chapter, Giles Scott-Smith considers the contemporary relationship between Washington and the Netherlands, focusing particularly on those elements in Dutch history that have tended to encourage pro-American policies and attitudes. He suggests that quasi-instinctive alliance sentiments meant that questioning transatlantic ties became a domestic no-go area. Simon Rofe and Alex Marshall review the possibility of a special relationship between the United States and Russia emerging in the 1990s. They relate their discussion to the trajectory and history of US–Russian relations, and trace the breakdown of the US–Russian 'strategic partnership'. In parallel with the Rofe and Marshall piece, Donette Murray employs original historical scholarship to trace US policy during the upheavals in US–Iran relations in the 1970s, when 'special' closeness gave way to disastrous estrangement. Her essay suggests that the hegemon can be beholden to the client to his own detriment. While specialness imposes a powerful narrative of similarity that helps deepen relations, it can also depict the former ally as the civilizational other once the special ties have been severed.

The third set of essays highlights that contemporary academic enquiry into American alliances and special relations does not begin at the water's edge. It is not confined to the international sphere. A considerable literature has now emerged on specialness in a different sense: on the role of domestic entities, including religious and citizen groups, seeking to influence, even to 'capture', elements of US foreign policy.[14] Indeed, one theme that runs through many of the essays of this volume is that the discursive dominance of the specialness narrative in its many forms, from 'model nations' to 'regional influentials', relies upon the ability of domestic actors to maintain the relationship's political and cultural salience. The foreign policy influence of US ethnic groups, of course, has long been the subject of intense examination in this regard. Our collection contains two accounts of the most well known of all foreign policy ethnic lobbies: the Jewish-American lobby. Ian Bickerton and Lee Marsden offer strikingly different interpretations of Jewish-American lobby influence over American Middle Eastern policy. Their contributions relate importantly to the debate stimulated by John Mearsheimer and Stephen Walt's study of AIPAC (the American Israeli Public Affairs Committee) and its influence over policy towards the region.[15]

Similarly, the final two of our essays link directly into debates about the historical role of domestic religious groups in forming foreign policy. Although religious imagery and pressure groups have become the focus of much political analysis in the aftermath of the rise of the Christian Right and the declaration of the War on Terror, the historical transformation of US church–state relations during the Cold War has been largely ignored. Our penultimate essay by Andrew Preston discusses the American state's relationship with religious groups in the early stages of the Cold War. He suggests that the activities of anti-communist religionists in positions of political power helped scupper the prospects for convergence and collaboration between the United States and the Soviet Union after World War II. The final piece by Axel Schäfer maintains that Cold War administrative needs, especially in the foreign aid arena, engineered new ties between evangelicals and the federal government. These new political and institutional inroads provided opportunities for asserting a 'baptized' foreign policy agenda and influenced the patterns of evangelicalism's conservative political mobilization.

Notes

1 See Josef Joffe, *Überpower: The Imperial Temptations of America*, New York: W. W. Norton, 2006.
2 Christopher Patten, *Not Quite the Diplomat: Home Truths about World Affairs*, London: Allen Lane, 2005, p. 229.
3 Colin Powell, 'The Only Voice I Listen To', *Time*, 10 September 2001, p. 15.
4 Chalmers Johnson, *Blowback*, New York: Time Warner, 2002, p. 43.
5 See Fareed Zakaria, *The Post-American World*, London: Allen Lane, 2008.
6 Remarks of Senator Barack Obama to the Chicago Council on Global Affairs, 23 April 2007, <http:my.barackobama.com/page/content/fpccga/> (accessed 2 February 2008).
7 Democratic Debate Transcript, Cleveland, Ohio, 26 February 2008, p. 9, <http://www.cfr.org/publication/15604/> (accessed 2 April 2008).
8 See P. H. Gordon and J. Shapiro, *Allies at War: America, Europe, and the Crisis over Iraq*, New York: McGraw-Hill, 2004; Stephen M. Walt, *The Taming of American Power: The Global Response to US Primacy*, New York: W. W. Norton, 2005.
9 See Alex Danchev, *On Specialness: Essays in Anglo-American Relations*, Basingstoke: Macmillan, 1998.
10 See J. Bennett, *Anglosphere: The Future of the English-Speaking Nations*, Lanham: Rowman and Littlefield, 2004.
11 Quoted in *The Economist*, 18 June 2005, p. 91.
12 See H. Gatzke, *Germany and the United States: A 'Special Relationship'?* Cambridge: Cambridge University Press, 1980; M. H. Hunt, *The Making of a Special Relationship: The United States and China to 1914*, New York: Columbia University Press, 1983; D. Little, 'The Making of a Special Relationship: The United States and Israel, 1957–68', *International Journal of Middle East Studies*, 1993, vol. 25, pp. 563–85; P. Morici, *A New Special Relationship: US–Canada Economic Relations in the 1990s*, Ottawa: IRPE, 1991.
13 David Schoenbaum, 'Commentary: Special Relationships', *Diplomatic History*, 1998, vol. 22, pp. 273–84.
14 See Hugh Wilford and Helen Laville (eds) *The US Government, Citizen Groups and the Cold War: The State–Private Network*, London and New York: Routledge, 2006.
15 See John J. Mearsheimer and S. M. Walt, *The Israel Lobby and US Foreign Policy*, London: Penguin, 2008.

1 Model nations
US allies and partners in the modernizing imagination

Nick Cullather

As John F. Kennedy pledged in his inaugural address to support any friend and oppose any foe, he stipulated that while foes were all of one type, friends came in three varieties, each entailing a different obligation. Addressing himself first to 'those old allies whose cultural and spiritual origins we share' he promised unity and cooperation. To 'our sister republics south of our border' he offered an Alliance for Progress. His most vivid words were reserved for a third category. To 'those new states whom we welcome to the ranks of the free . . . those peoples in the huts and villages across the globe struggling to break the bonds of mass misery', he offered the vaguest but most quotable promises, namely to prevail in their long twilight struggle, to ameliorate poverty and to help them help themselves. Among allies and clients, there were crucial distinctions of wealth, geography and, especially, time. Kennedy's speech located the United States at a historic juncture in the present moment ('let the word go forth from this time and place') from which he looked forward and backward at America's partners, some as cultural forebears, others as inheritors of an American legacy.[1]

Classifying nations into 'old' and 'new' is a recurring theme in American rhetoric. Woodrow Wilson, on returning from the Paris Peace Conference, contrasted the old and powerful nations of Europe with the 'new nations' anxious to construct an age of cooperation and justice.[2] In 2003, Defence Secretary Donald Rumsfeld outraged France and Germany by relegating them into an 'old Europe' whose centre of gravity was shifting to the East. Implicit in the rhetoric of Wilson, Kennedy and Rumsfeld was an invitation for all nations to break free of their antiquity and join ranks of the new, but for many it was a difficult invitation to accept. Mexico's ambassador to India in the 1960s, Octavio Paz, explained that countries clung to their former selves for reasons the United States did not understand because it 'was not founded on a common tradition, as has been the case elsewhere, but on the notion of creating a common future. For modern India, as it is for Mexico, the national project, the future to be realized, implies a critique of the past'[3] However, with history, as with finances and roads, American advisers lent valuable assistance to Mexico, India and other clients by constructing narratives to explain their journey forward.

When historians use the term 'special relationship', most often they refer to affinities of language, geography or heritage. There were also partnerships of destiny, however. The United States exercised global power in the post-war years through a form of welfare imperialism usually known as development, nation building or modernization.[4] This strategy gave considerable scope for projecting the American ego into imagined futures. It is often said that Americans sought to copy themselves, to recreate other nations in their own image, but this actually understates the modernizing ambition. In Frank Lloyd Wright's 1958 blueprint for Greater Baghdad, in the neoclassical capital built by the Americans in Manila, or in the privatization of government services in Iraq during the 2003 occupation, there is evidence of grander aspirations, a search for heights unachieved in the original.[5]

By the mid-twentieth century, American nation-builders already saw the United States as too encumbered by habit and politics to live up to its own true character. The authentic America could only be built elsewhere. The historian Perry Miller, who participated in the post-war occupation of Japan, observed that General Douglas MacArthur wanted 'to make of Japan a new Middle West – not, of course, the Middle West as it is, or in fact ever was – but how it perpetually dreams of being'.[6] There was a tension inherent in the enterprise, as he implied, since the dreams cast abroad were idiosyncratic. MacArthur's Japan might differ from Truman's, and there might be a different Japan for each political complexion, each claiming to represent the essence of the American way.

Walt W. Rostow, probably the most eminent modernization theorist, observed that Kennedy came to office amid a mood of 'romantic hope about the developing nations [prevailing] in the early 1960s – a hope that they, coming late to modernity and the arena of power, would be wiser than the old states of Europe. Perhaps they could avoid pedestrian and bloody struggles for real estate and glory and lead the whole community of nations to stable peace'.[7] Kennedy was immune to these illusions, Rostow insisted, but both he and his predecessor, Dwight Eisenhower, believed the bar was set higher for the new nations. They would have to overcome burdens of tradition, overpopulation and colonial involution that the United States never faced, and their breakthrough to modernity would be a correspondingly greater triumph.

The power of the Soviet and Chinese examples was that they unfolded in the punishing social environment of Asia. China's struggle to overcome immemorial poverty and backwardness was, Walter Lippmann wrote shortly before Kennedy's inaugural address, 'a terrible and awe-inspiring spectacle'. Comparisons to America's achievements only stoked the communist propaganda mill because they had come too easily. 'Our system, which grew up on a rich and empty continent, cannot be duplicated in Asia'. For that reason, the United States needed a surrogate, a crowded, destitute, tradition-bound country in which to demonstrate that American principles could conquer poverty. 'We are NOT an example that backward peoples can follow, and unless we manage to create an example which they *can* follow, we shall almost certainly lose the Cold War in Asia, and Africa, and perhaps elsewhere'.[8]

Hardheaded realists, as well as softhearted idealists, had a stake in creating showcases of American progress around the world. This project became urgent at the same time that mathematical modelling, the technique that revealed the inner workings of the atom, began to be widely used to analyse complex social systems. Joseph Schumpeter's models of business fluctuations, Wassily Leontief's simulations of organizational structures and John von Neumann's and Oskar Morgenstern's mathematical maps of multiplayer games lent a new scientific credibility to sociology, economics and political science in the 1940s and 1950s. Perhaps inevitably, 'model' joined the vocabulary of development, referring to a loose, descriptive analogue pairing a nation with a strategy – the Taiwan model of export-led growth or the Chilean model of monetary reform – encapsulating a country's economic or political history as a sequence of strategic moves open to imitation.[9]

Timothy Mitchell notes that in this usage 'the nation-state appears to be a functional unit – something akin to a refrigerator or a pump – that can be compared with and used as a model for improving other such units'.[10] All models are seen as elaborations on some aspect of the American template, but each is different. They reflect the strategic or economic priorities of a given moment, as well as varying opinions on the image that best represents modernity, and choices about what other nations can and will imitate. Barbara Ward, a journalist and popularizer of modernization theory, wrote that much depended on discovering 'the version of our society which is appreciable to the backward peoples of Asia'.[11]

This essay will examine two models: Mexico in the 1930s and 1940s became a model for post-war reconstruction and the revitalization of agriculture, and India in the 1950s came to be seen as the West's contender in a race for modernization against China. In each case, the politics of representation became the principal dynamic in a bilateral relationship with the United States. As nations, each provoked ambivalence or antagonism in Washington, but as models, they became partners in global strategy.

Mexican President Lázaro Cárdenas earned the nickname *el FDR mexicano*, partly because his time in office (1934–40) roughly coincided with Franklin Roosevelt's first two terms, but also because his social experiment, involving reforms of health care, trade, labour and agriculture, came to be seen as the first real application of the New Deal outside the United States. His most impressive breakthrough was in agriculture. Scientific techniques and village outreach combined to produce a boom in staple crops. By 1950, Mexico was recognized as 'a blueprint for hungry nations', a prototype for the US government's Point IV initiative and for Ford and Rockefeller Foundation projects in Asia. India's food ministry announced in 1964 that 'if Mexico can do it, so can India'.[12]

Cárdenas had little to do with making his country a model. American tourists, social scientists, image-makers and politicians did most of the work. In 1935, the *Sunset Limited* began daily rail service between Los Angeles and Mexico City. The following year, the Pan American Highway was completed from Nuevo Laredo to the capital, and 10,000 American tourists a year descended on Mexico. A popular guidebook reassured travellers that there was no need to cross an ocean to find the attractions 'of the cold north and the lower tropics; of Persia, India, Arabia, Spain, and the Holy Land'.[13] Mexico was better than Europe, Katherine dos Passos noted, 'because the country is not standardized or touristed'.[14] Its untouched villages lured sociologists such as Robert Redfield, eager to study the workings of a preindustrial community, social critics such as John Steinbeck, and filmmakers such as John Huston.

Hollywood found in Mexico, according to Richard Slotkin, 'a mythic space par excellence' into which it could project America's struggle to build a civilization. This was the glory era of the Mexican western. *Viva Villa!* (1933), *Juarez* (1939), *The Fugitive* (1947), and Huston's *Treasure of the Sierra Madre* (1948) – all had political themes.[15] Malcolm Lowry, whose novel *Under the Volcano* was also filmed by Huston, sketched this figurative landscape: 'The scene is Mexico, the meeting place, according to some, of mankind itself . . . the age-old arena of racial and political conflicts of every nature', he told his publisher. 'We can see it as a kind of timeless symbol of the world on which we can place the Garden of Eden, the Tower of Babel and indeed anything else we please'.[16]

Americans discovered in Mexico a baseline against which to gauge their modernity. As Texas State Highway 96 turned south onto the Pan American Highway, Ernest Gruening, editor of *The Nation*, noticed that 'the swift-moving mechanized patter of a modern society gives way to a simple, less regulated, earlier stage of development'. Downshifting for the ascent into the Sierra Madre, the motorist travelled 'backward also, through the long reaches of the past'. The indigenous inhabitants, he explained, were 'original Americans' preserving traditions 'rejected and neglected by us'.[17] Academic and popular interest in Mexico revealed a discontent with the barrenness and uncertainty of modern life. For those unable to make the trip, Abby Rockefeller sponsored travelling folk art exhibits, giving Depression-weary Americans a glimpse of a simpler time. Stuart Chase, the economist who gave the New Deal its name, penned a bestselling travel account that contrasted the United States, 'the outstanding exhibit of the power age', against Mexico, 'the outstanding exhibit of the handicraft age'. Mexico's pueblos, he estimated, stood roughly 100 years behind Muncie, Indiana, but Americans could nonetheless envy the villagers' self-reliant indifference to the laws of supply and demand. An ultimate solution to the ravages of the business cycle, he proposed, might be found in a merger of old and new cultures.[18]

Cárdenas's experiment with autonomous village communes (*ejidos*) fascinated intellectuals who saw in urban slums and rural 'dust bowls' evidence that industrial economies had become dangerously unbalanced. Redford, Steinbeck, Lewis Mumford and other critics argued that wealth, population and knowledge had become overly concentrated in cities. Eyler N. Simpson, dean of arts and sciences at the University of Chicago, studied the *ejido* system and admired Mexico's policy of sending young, urban doctors, teachers and technicians to help build self-sufficient rural villages. In *The Ejido: Mexico's Way Out*, he portrayed Mexico as a neutral terrain ideal for social experimentation, a 'clear and unencumbered' ground without the 'vested interests and antiquated institutional structures' that bedevilled planning in the United States. Like Chase, he sought a middle way between urban congestion and bucolic poverty. He predicted that *ejidos* would grow into balanced farming and manufacturing villages interlinked by highways and power lines, creating an economy both spiritually and materially enriching. It was a way out not just for Mexico, but for Americans, too.[19]

When he came into office, Roosevelt attributed the Depression to 'the dislocation of a proper balance between urban and rural life'. As farm groups were felling telephone polls to block roads into the cities and the Oklahoma and Nebraska breadbaskets were engulfed in massive dust storms, Roosevelt saw the economic catastrophe facing industry and natural disasters in the countryside as symptoms. Rebalancing the vital functions of modern life called for 'something deeper and far more important' than Herbert Hoover's emergency measures – 'in other words state planning'.[20] Domestic concerns gave New Dealers an interest in Cárdenas's experiment, but liberals watched Mexico for other reasons too. Gruening, Chase, Simpson, Frank Tannenbaum of the *New York Times* and other observers argued that a social revolution was underway throughout the rural world, and that Mexico offered 'a moderate answer to the radical solutions unfolding in Russia and Spain'. Agriculture Secretary Henry Wallace and Josephus Daniels, the US ambassador to Mexico, urged Roosevelt to send aid and advisers to prevent Mexico from becoming 'another Spain'.[21]

These voices were counterbalanced by conservatives who saw Mexico as a renegade nation. Cárdenas's redistribution of US-owned lands and his 1938 nationalization of oil and railroad properties outraged the American financial community almost as much as his aid to the Republican side in Spain's civil war offended anti-communists. To Sumner Welles and Cordell Hull in the State Department, *Cárdenismo* was not far removed from Bolshevism. The United States imposed sanctions and demanded restitution for expropriated property at terms Mexico was unwilling to accept. Pro-Mexican New Dealers urged lifting the sanctions, but the issue of restitution proved unresolvable because each side spoke of a different Mexico. Conservatives demanded that Mexico perform on its obligations as a nation, while liberals valued Mexico for its example to other nations. The term had not yet come into diplomatic parlance, but they saw it as a model.[22]

Ultimately, the approach of war and the realization that Mexico's resources would be vital to US defence decided the issue. Shortly after FDR's third inauguration in 1940, he dispatched Wallace, now vice president, to Mexico with offers of agricultural aid. He offered guaranteed prices for Mexican commodities, particularly rubber and other tropical goods cut off by the Japanese. Wallace personally asked the Rockefeller Foundation to begin an agricultural research program. The Foundation decided Mexico represented an ideal testing ground for strategies for the post-war revitalization of Europe and Asia, and the Mexican Agricultural Program soon became the foundation's largest venture.[23]

In a series of speeches in 1942, Wallace presented a vision of prosperity, freedom from hunger and entitlement to health that, he said, was already unfolding in Mexico. Isaiah Berlin, an astute reporter for the British embassy, noted that within months of the Japanese attack on Pearl Harbor, Washington had split into two factions on the crucial issue of post-war reconstruction: 'The Willkie–Welles–Luce group . . . see the world as a vast market for the American producer, industrialist, and trader. They are believers in the American Century, energetic technicians and businessmen filled with romantic, self-confident, economic imperialism'. A second 'group of self-confident, country-bred liberal reformers' offered blueprints for redistributive economic reform. This group had an apocalyptic vision of 'the culture of Palestine, Rome, and Britain brought to final fruition', and viewed the 'New Deal as the New Islam, divinely inspired to save the world, a faith of which Wallace is the leading exponent'.[24]

Recast as prototype of the international New Deal, Mexico changed from pariah nation to poster child. Nelson Rockefeller arranged for a triumphal tour for the retired Cárdenas, assuring propaganda coverage of his stops at New Deal monuments – housing projects, the TVA and aircraft factories. Rockefeller kept the theme of the visit focused on the *ejido* system as a 'solution for the world-wide agrarian problem'.[25] The Rockefeller Foundation's Mexican Agricultural Program (MAP) gave rise to the set of strategies known as the 'Green Revolution', a combination of genetic engineering, chemicalization and mechanization that made a tremendous impact on agriculture in Asia, Europe and even the United States. American agronomists found in Mexico a freedom to experiment with procedures and technologies that would have been resisted in the United States. They could take over experiment stations, go directly to farmers and have the state fix prices and tell farmers what to grow and how. They created a style of outreach modelled on ideal practices, not American agriculture as it was, but as it dreamed of being.[26]

As early as 1946, before the MAP had made any significant accomplishments, the Rockefeller Foundation and the US government both promoted it around the world as a model worthy of imitation by other countries. This focus on the far horizons had a crucial effect on the outcome of Mexico's agrarian experiment. The Foundation had been invited to Mexico to provide technical support for the *ejido* program, but the ultimate effect was to create a commercial agriculture heavily dependent on the US market and vulnerable to the business cycle. Instead of revitalizing the countryside, it diverted incomes and jobs towards the city. As the US–Mexican partnership grew in the 1950s, the *ejido* experiment quietly died. When American agronomist and green revolution pioneer Norman Borlaug won the 1970 Nobel Peace Prize for his work in Mexico, Mexican writers noted that the Foundation's success had come at the cost of Cárdenas's vision. Borlaug, however, explained that the critics had missed the point: The payoff for the Mexican model was not in Mexico, but in India.[27]

Within a few years, Mexico went from pariah to paragon. The misunderstanding over expropriation was quietly shelved, and diplomats emphasized the close friendship that had always existed between the two countries. In 1953, John Foster Dulles cited Mexico's agricultural program as 'the type of thing' that the United States could use in nation building in Indochina.[28] 'Mexico and India are alike in many ways', especially 'in their determination to develop into modern societies', Borlaug told Indian officials. Mexico's threefold increase in wheat output was the cornerstone of an economic success story in which 'success' was measured in productivity rather than equity.[29] The agricultural breakthrough had been a symptom, rather than a cause of improving relations, but it provided a narrative that explained Mexico's place in the larger scheme of US global strategy. It had become a model of the benefits of US guidance. However, a model nation's status is fleeting. It is inevitably discarded in favour of a newer, thinner model, and as the Cold War shifted from Europe to the east, Asian models came into vogue.

In 1947, Harry S. Truman could not imagine that 'anyone thought [India] was important'. He pictured a country 'jammed with poor people and cows wandering around streets, witch doctors, and people sitting on hot coals and bathing in the Ganges', and he was far from alone in this impression. The National Security Council (NSC), in its first evaluation of India's strategic weight in 1949, concluded that an alliance with 300 million Indians living near the 'margins of subsistence' would encumber rather than bolster US defences. It was essential, the Council emphasized, not to give the new nation any firm assurances, and to 'scrupulously avoid responsibility for raising Asiatic living standards'.[30]

Only a decade later, Senator John F. Kennedy put forward a radically different appraisal of the value of India, and the strategic meaning of poverty. The sheer scale of India's deprivation, he argued, made it the decisive ideological battleground, and 'a world power with a world audience' in its own right.[31] Walter Lippmann agreed: to win over 'the submerged masses in the old imperial lands' the West needed the right surrogate, 'a very big and very poor country' in which to demonstrate a 'take-off from the ancient stagnant poverty of Asia toward a progressive, independent, modern economy'. India was the best and only contender.[32]

India became strategically important to American leaders only after they came to see it as a model of development with Western characteristics. The debates over aid to India coincided with the emergence of economics as a policy language. As the Cold War shifted from Europe to Asia, the terminology of alliances, iron curtains and armaments gave way to a language of take-offs, 5-year plans and growth rates. In the minds of American planners, India's position at the centre of a line of containment, as well as its stance as a non-aligned nation, were superseded by its more crucial function as an 'answer to the Communist argument', a living example of rapid development without revolution. However, for India to represent a democratic alternative, its development had to be packaged in a way that differentiated it from the Soviet and Chinese experience. This ambition – to mark off India as a developmental model that was both effective and distinctly Western – inspired aid officials, economists and the press first to create the 'problem' of hunger and then make solving it an international goal.

Prior to the Korean War, India did not measure up, either as an ally or a supplicant, in Washington's calculus of Cold War strategy. In its original version, the containment concept centred on holding defensible lines and securing bases, strategic ports and industrial assets, none of which could be found in India. The problem of what to do with large populations caught between the defended perimeters and the communist advance troubled military officials, but tight post-war budgets precluded alternatives. Although the first two US ambassadors, Henry Grady and

Loy Henderson, cabled persistent and imaginative appeals for aid to India, the Truman administration demurred.[33]

Aid officials concluded that the immensity of South Asia's poverty would rapidly exhaust the limited sums available. Despite the public attention given to the Point IV programme, the 1949 foreign aid budget amounted to less than $40 million. While Prime Minister Jawaharlal Nehru complained of American plans to 'buy up countries and continents', Washington was sure India was one it could not afford. The descriptor most frequently applied to India's condition was 'chronic'. Its economy was characterized, according to intelligence officials, by 'the predominance of an underdeveloped agriculture' with an unbroken record of 'chronic stagnation'. Government economists warned that aid to India would become a 'chronic affair in view of the frequent recurrence of famines'.[34]

If the sheer scale of India's needs justified dodging a commitment before 1950, the Chinese revolution and the North Korean attack on the South reversed Washington's calculations. Reformulating containment in the wake of these setbacks, the NSC stressed that pervasive poverty offered communists a 'springboard for a further incursion' into Asia. The power of the peasantry – demonstrated by Mao's 'Big Push' offensive which expelled the nationalists from the mainland – confirmed the danger of allowing large, ideologically vulnerable populations to slip. The notion of a linear defence running through a chain of islands along Asia's coast gave way to a strategic concept emphasizing control of population and resources. Intelligence officials foresaw a struggle in which each superpower gathered 'those elements of human and material power in the Far East which will ultimately help weigh a world balance in their favor'.[35]

The new doctrine attached greater strategic value to both South Asia and foreign aid. State Department officials presented India and Pakistan as frontline states, reservoirs of military manpower and raw materials that could be won over by showcase development programmes that produced 'early and obvious results'. In a picture essay in *Life* magazine, former diplomat William Bullitt conjured an image of India as half treasure house, half slum, 'an immense country' with 'enormous natural resources and superb fighting men' where millions survived on 'fewer calories and vitamins a day than even the Chinese'. Its tiny corps of civil servants, British-trained 'men of striking ability', were engaged in a unique experiment to transform an illiterate peasantry, a fifth of humanity, into citizens of a new Asia. In the spring of 1951, Truman authorized the first wheat loan to cover shortages caused by droughts in Madras and Bihar, and went to Capitol Hill to lobby in person for an additional $8.5 billion in aid, including $50 million for India's community development scheme. It was vital, he argued, to prevent 'more of the peaceful millions of the East' from turning 'into armies to be used as pawns of the Kremlin'.[36]

Despite strongly favourable public opinion, aid to India remained a tough sell in Congress owing to lawmakers' indignant and mystified response to Nehru's public persona. Legislators took notice of his unflattering remarks on the American character, but his disapproval of US efforts to defend his continent provoked a more acute reaction. After initially supporting the introduction of American troops in Korea, the Indian prime minister denounced MacArthur's decision to carry the war past the 38th parallel and went on to condemn US actions in Taiwan, Indochina and the United Nations. His statements nearly derailed the aid programme as congressional leaders lashed out at India's betrayal. Merciless editorials labelled him a fellow traveller who lent 'aid and comfort to the enemy' while 'playing us for suckers'. The prime minister shot back that his sympathy for exploited nations would naturally not appeal to 'great powers who directly or indirectly share in that exploitation'.[37] He made a deal for Soviet and Chinese grain, raising the political temperature another notch.

The offence of Nehru's neutrality was aggravated by his open admiration for Soviet economic methods. The new government's plans to exclude foreign investment, assert control over of key sectors, and launch an industrialization drive modelled on Stalin's 5-year plans drew fire from the business press and a Republican congressional majority bent on rolling back the New Deal at home and communism abroad. Convinced that only planned development would reverse the distortions of the colonial economy, Nehru and his chief planner Prasanta Mahalanobis set their sights on a rapid build-up in heavy industries, such as machine tools, steel, electricity, chemicals and mining. Food aid would underwrite the growth of the state sector; government warehouses would sell American wheat and deposit the earnings in rupees into a 'counterpart' fund to be used for development. Apart from ideological reservations, the Truman administration opposed the industrial focus on strategic grounds. War planners envisioned the Indian economy as an 'Asiatic production and supply base in the event of general war' with food and agricultural products as its primary assets. The difference could be papered over – Indian planners were happy to steer US aid toward agriculture while diverting other resources into manufacturing – but disagreement over means and ends built a tension into the aid relationship.[38] When ships containing two million tons of American wheat berthed in Bombay in August 1951, both nations toasted a new era of friendship, but US officials had already begun to lean toward Pakistan as a more tractable partner.

The fiscally orthodox Eisenhower administration assumed a still more sceptical stance toward aid and India. The president's 'New Look' policies merged Point IV into the military aid programme and categorically rejected public disbursements as a cure for the 'chronic malady' of underdevelopment. A formal alliance with Pakistan, sealed in 1954, and Congress's determination to deny assistance to neutrals 'not clearly aligned with the free world' left John Foster Dulles, the secretary of state, in a quandary. Extending the program would be difficult, but terminating it would place him in 'the rather untenable position of believing [the] increased stability of India as very much to our interest but not being able to do anything about it'.[39] He held aid to current levels while funnelling revenue to India through the backdoor, in the form of food shipments and secret trade in atomic materials. Meanwhile, congressional Democrats, including Senators Hubert Humphrey and John F. Kennedy, exhibited the administration's alienation of India and defeats in Indochina as symptoms of a flawed Asia policy.

For most of the 1950s, the debate on aid to India teetered between images of a downtrodden, dependent nation grateful for American attention, and a rising, defiant, socialistic state personified by Nehru. As with Mexico, the work of remaking this image began with travel writers. James Michener, Norman Cousins and other writers accounted for the paradox of India's nonconformity in developmental terms as the brashness of an immature society yearning for the trappings of success.[40] 'No one likes a rich uncle who flaunts his wealth in the face of your poverty', Eleanor Roosevelt explained. Supreme Court Justice William O. Douglas likened India's leaders to America's founding fathers, equally sensitive to the fragility of their hard-won independence. Nehru, according to Margaret Bourke-White, 'represents a maturing Asia, growing out of feudalism and entering into modern industrial civilization, learning to dispense with European masters and teachers'. An informal India lobby, comprised of liberal academics, politicians and journalists, took up these themes, arguing that democratic India was America's natural ally. A partnership in modernization could dispel communism's ideological pretensions, Henry Steele Commager observed, but only if the United States could sustain the commitment despite the invective issuing from Delhi and Capitol Hill; this would be an 'acid test for the American character'.[41]

The lobby recast India as the free world's contender against China in a fateful race to set the course of the developing world. In an influential 1951 feature in the *New York Times*, journalist Barbara Ward sketched an image of South America, Africa and Asia watching the emergence of two giants. India and China had launched their 5-year plans simultaneously, juxtaposing systems so similar 'in tradition, in structure, in problems, and in resources that the contrast in their methods takes on an almost clinical accuracy'. Two methods of national development would 'in the next decade be pursued side by side'. Editorials and congressional testimony embellished the picture. 'The future of Asia, and eventually the world balance of power', US ambassador to India Chester Bowles asserted, hinged on 'the competition between democratic India' and China. The United States Information Agency (USIA) asked readers to imagine 'a beam-scale set across the Himalayas' with its vast pans balancing 'two ancient peoples hard at work transforming their economically underdeveloped countries into industrialized nations'. Symbolism soon morphed into strategic reality. Washington, according Rostow, closely tracked the rivalry, regarding it as 'a kind of pure ideological test of great significance'.[42] Until then, India had played its own game outside the superpower sandbox, but now it was on a track, running a development race parallel to the arms race and the space race – the second heat in a Cold War triple crown.

Bipartisan adoption of the race allegory marked a further evolution of India's position in US strategic thinking, namely its conversion into symbol. From 1954 through the 1960s, every NSC position paper on the region echoed the thesis that 'the outcome of the competition' would produce a 'profound effect throughout Asia'. India's 'war potential' remained negligible next to its real significance as an answer to the 'Communist argument'. The Federal Reserve Board, which oversaw US and World Bank loans, dropped its categorical objections to India's

5-year plan in light of 'the inevitable comparison' to China 'which is bound to be drawn throughout the world'.[43] The parable enabled security planners to regain a sense of movement, to bypass the deadlock of containment and nuclear standoff. 'For several years', Henry Kissinger wrote in 1956, 'we have been groping for a concept to deal with the transformation of the Cold War from an effort to build defensive barriers into a contest for the allegiance of humanity'. The race for modernization furnished the summary narrative into which all other images of India's struggle were scripted.[44]

The race was a wholly Western construction. India refused to be drawn, even rhetorically, into a new version of the Great Game. However, more fundamentally, Nehru challenged the very notion of models, contending that development followed no one track, and neither India nor China could stand in for a system. 'There may be different ways of progress' he argued, 'truth is not confined to one country or one people; . . . each country and each people if they are true to themselves, have to find out their path themselves'.[45]

Congress was also inclined to judge India by actions rather than symbols. North Dakota Republican congressman Usher Burdick allowed that 'Red China and India under Nehru are the same breed of cats'. However, the concept of a race captured the Eisenhower administration's ambivalence, allowing it to acknowledge the urgency of India's need, while continuing to disown Nehru and neutralism. As with Mexico, symbolism did not match performance, but increasingly symbolism became the determining factor. Beset by a chorus of congressional objections, US ambassador to India George V. Allen conceded that all points were valid, but nonetheless 'a lot of attention is being paid to whether China is going to make progress faster than India' and cutting aid would 'assume the attitude that India is finished'.[46]

In March 1958, Senator John F. Kennedy proposed a radical increase in aid to India. His legislation, the Kennedy–Cooper resolution, became the centrepiece of a liberal critique of the New Look. Underscoring the attitudinal realities behind the mirage of military power, he argued that armaments and alliances left no trace on the 'fluid pattern of events in the uncommitted world'. The vital challenge was to dispel the 'glamour' of communism's 'answer to the overwhelming problems of economic mobilization and takeoff'. He exhorted Congress to shake off the self-doubt induced by nuclear deadlock and join India in the 'shared adventure' of modernization.[47]

Rarely does a bill land in the legislative hopper just as the public mood inclines decisively in its favour. Kennedy–Cooper initially garnered the routine scepticism accorded to aid handouts, but in October, while it languished in committee, the *Saturday Evening Post* began serializing William J. Lederer's and Eugene Burdick's fictional interpretation of the dynamics of communist subversion. The next month, *The Ugly American* hit the top of the bestseller list where it remained for 72 weeks. More allegorical than factual, it dramatically revised the broad narrative premise of the Cold War encounter. Sputnik, the arms race and the iron curtain were sideshows, the authors argued. The communists were winning the decisive contest 'in the rice fields of Asia'.[48]

Contrary to standard depictions of an Asia neglected by the West, *The Ugly American* portrayed a continent thick with projects and personnel. Rounding up by a million or so, the authors claimed the United States supported 'a horde of 1,500,000 Americans' lodged in luxury enclaves and occupied in erecting 'huge technical complexes' designed to win allies among the populace. However, while Americans alienated their clients with grandiose engineering, communist propagandists cunningly pitched their appeals around the rustic concerns of average Asians. 'Powdered milk and cattle are part of politics, and therefore part of history', a Maoist insurgent explains, 'America had its chance and it missed'. The plot consisted of a series of vignettes contrasting stock careerists – striped-pants diplomats, slick admen, and gold-digging secretaries – against the dedicated minority of 'ugly' Americans, mainly mechanics and agronomists willing to 'get into the countryside' and meet Asians on their own terms. Despite its tone of alarm, the novel offered a reassuring moral. Americans could win hearts and minds by remembering their own rural past, working with their hands, and rallying allies with a programme that could be understood in 'farmyard English'. In the countryside, Americans and Asians were natural partners sharing a common past and a vision for the future.[49]

Recast as a summons to join in a mythic enterprise, foreign aid experienced a groundswell of public support. A bare majority of Americans approved of continuing aid in February 1958, but by the end of the year, over 60 per cent wanted to expand the programme.[50] Shortly after his inauguration in January 1961, Kennedy declared the 1960s the 'Development Decade' and presented aid bills that made India the cornerstone of a plan to win over new nations 'from Casablanca to Djakarta'. Indian officials could feel the political wind shifting in their favour. The new cabinet was filled with 'friends of India', Ambassador B. K. Nehru realized. 'The press too was supportive. The *Washington Post* was fully with us; so were *The New York Times*, the *Christian Science Monitor*, and *The Baltimore Sun*'. European countries put up $1 billion in aid. It was time, Kennedy said, for the old nations to come to the aid of the new: 'India today represents as great a hope and challenge to the future of liberal democracy as Western Europe did in 1947'.[51]

However, this came with a cost. As Mexico showed, symbolism had imperatives, too, and it was as crucial for American modernizers to differentiate India's development from China's as it was to make it a success. A premium was placed on new, identifiably Western approaches, and this clashed with India's vision of growth on a 'socialist pattern'. India's planning board, led by chief statistician Prasanta Mahalanobis, had blueprints for an industrial drive emphasizing steel, machine tools, hydroelectric dams and chemicals. The 'Mahalanobis model' envisioned a regional economy in which industrial India would exchange manufactured goods for rice from Southeast Asia, providing factory jobs for the burgeoning population and solving the food shortage through trade.[52]

To US officials, this sounded too much like the Soviet model, and they recognized that the Chinese challenge arose from its reputation for agricultural reform. In his 1956 article 'Marx Was a City Boy', Rostow argued that agriculture was communism's real weakness. Shortages of food handicapped Chinese industry, and the Soviet Union appeared unable to grow enough wheat. Redrawing the finish line in the developmental race, Rostow claimed that victory would be marked not by the rise of factories or steel mills but when 'chronic starvation' dispelled the notion that 'Communism holds the key to rapid economic growth'. *The Ugly American* underscored this orientation. When the Great Leap famine hit China just after the 1961 inauguration, Rostow told Kennedy that this was 'the hinge on which his administration would turn'.[53]

The horse race analogy is an apt one for models. They are in their prime as yearlings, all expectancy and unfulfilled potential. They exist in the present tense for three minutes of geopolitical time, whereupon, succeed or fail, they go into the record books. India had its moment in 1968, when the Green Revolution made it, briefly, self-sufficient in food. The Green Revolution strategy fell out of favour almost immediately after its greatest success; its vision of American science uniting with Asian peasants to dominate nature lost plausibility in the wake of Earth Day and the Tet Offensive. The India–US relationship also hit the skids. By 1976, Lucian Pye was writing about the development race as if it had all been imagined:

> At one time, the United States did think that it was helping India in a race against China which would test the relative merits of democracy and communism. With China no longer a threat, it was possible to ask in much more realistic terms what had been accomplished in India as a result of nearly $10 billion of American assistance.[54]

The United States does not accord model nations the kind of 'special' relationship that certain allies have, but neither does it relegate them to the status of client states. They constitute a third category of friendship and obligation with three distinctive features. Firstly, models rest on a narrative written by Americans for domestic consumption. India and Mexico each came to represent a formula policymakers wanted other nations to follow, but since neither had a hand in crafting the narrative, their actual policies and positions were often at odds with the image they represented. Secondly, the gap between image and reality gives the model a measure of freedom. During the phase of early enthusiasm, the model is exempt from obligations expected of friendly nations. Mexico's expropriation of oil properties barely dampened liberal support for the *Cárdenista* experiment; and Indira Gandhi's Soviet overtures and criticisms of Vietnam policy only seemed to endear her to Lyndon Johnson all the more. 'I want to help that little girl', he told Ambassador B. K. Nehru in the run-up to the 1967 elections, 'You tell me what to do. Send her food? Attack her? I'll do whatever you say?'[55] Finally, models claim a level of importance and attention far out of line with their practical or strategic significance, but only for a short span of time. It is difficult now to recall how much attention Taiwan received during the Reagan years. Memory fades because 'export-led' strategies have fallen from fashion, and to policymakers Taiwan represents an entirely different set of problems. A country holds on to its status only so long as it has a compelling story. As American supermodel Tyra Banks once remarked, 'you can't be a model forever'.

Notes

1 'Text of President Kennedy's Inaugural Address', *Washington Post*, 21 January 1961, p. A1.
2 'Challenge to His Critics', *New York Times*, 25 February 1919, p. 1.
3 BBC News, 'Outrage at "Old Europe" Remarks', 23 January 2003, <http://news.bbc.co.uk/2/hi/europe/2687403.stm> (accessed 7 July 2008); Octavio Paz, *In Light of India*, New York: Harcourt Brace, 1995, p. 79.
4 C. Vann Woodward, *Thinking Back: The Perils of Writing History*, Baton Rouge: Louisiana State University Press, 1986, p. 103.
5 Frank Lloyd Wright, 'Frank Lloyd Wright Designs for Baghdad', *The Architectural Forum*, 1958, vol. 108, pp. 89–101; James B. Goodno, 'Burnham's Manila', *Planning*, 2004, vol. 70, pp. 30–34; Stephen Holmes, 'Milton Friedman in Baghdad', *London Review of Books*, 8 May 2008, pp. 7–9.
6 Quoted in Michael Schaller, *Altered States: The United States and Japan Since the Occupation*, New York: Oxford, 1997, p. 10.
7 W. W. Rostow, *The Diffusion of Power*, New York: Macmillan, 1972, p. 407.
8 Walter Lippmann, 'India, the Glorious Gamble', *Ladies Home Journal*, August 1959, pp. 48–49.
9 Joseph A. Schumpeter, *Business Cycles*, New York: McGraw Hill, 1939; Wassily Leontief, *The Structure of American Economy, 1919–1929*, Cambridge, Mass.: Harvard, 1941; John Louis von Neumann and Oskar Morgenstern, *Theory of Games and Economic Behavior*, Princeton: Princeton University Press, 1944. On modelling see Max Black, *Models and Metaphors: Studies in Language and Philosophy*, Ithaca: Cornell University Press, 1962; Harold D. Lasswell, 'The Semantics of Political Science – A Discussion', *American Political Science Review*, 1950, vol. 44, pp. 422–25; Ron Robin, *The Making of the Cold War Enemy: Culture and Politics in the Military Intellectual Complex*, Princeton: Princeton University Press, 2001, pp. 59–71; and Albert O. Hirschman, 'The Search for Paradigms as a Hindrance to Understanding', *World Politics*, 1970, vol. 22, p. 335.
10 Tim Mitchell, 'America's Egypt: Discourses of the Development Industry', *Middle East Report*, 1991, vol. 21, pp. 29–30.
11 Barbara Ward, 'A Crusading Faith to Counter Communism', *New York Times Magazine*, 16 July 1950, p. 32.
12 George W. Gray, 'Blueprint for Hungry Nations', *New York Times Magazine*, 1 January 1950, pp. 93–99; Ford Foundation, 'Study of the Ford Foundation on Policy and Program [Gaither Report]', January 1950, Ford Foundation Archives, New York; Sharada Prasad, 'Story of a Giant and a Dwarf', *Yojana*, 29 March 1964, p. 2.
13 Jeffrey Paul, 'All Mexico Prepares for Tourist Invasion', *Washington Post*, 10 May 1936, p. B7; T. Philip Terry, *Terry's Guide to Mexico*, Boston: Houghton Mifflin, 1935, p. iii. 'Going to Mexico', said former US ambassador Dwight Morrow, offering a minor revision, 'is like making a visit to Spain, Italy, Egypt, and India all at one time'. Pablo C. de Gante, 'Mexico as a Tourist Resort', *Banker's Magazine*, January 1936, p. 75.
14 Dos Passos quoted in Helen Delpar, *The Enormous Vogue of Things Mexican*, Tuscaloosa: University of Alabama Press, 1992, p. 58; Hubert Herring, 'Mexico On the March', *New York Times Book Review*, 16 April 1939, p. 8.
15 Richard Slotkin, *Gunfighter Nation: The Myth of the Frontier in Twentieth Century America*, New York: Harper Perennial, 1992, p. 311.

16 Malcolm Lowry, *Selected Letters of Malcolm Lowry*, Philadelphia: J. B. Lippincott, 1965, p. 67.
17 Ernest Gruening, 'The Meaning of Mexico', in Hubert Herring (ed.) *Renascent Mexico*, New York: Covici Freide, 1935, pp. 1–8.
18 Stuart Chase, 'Machineless Men', *Forum and Century*, December 1930, p. 379.
19 Eyler N. Simpson, *The Ejido: Mexico's Way Out*, Chapel Hill: University of North Carolina Press, 1937, esp. pp. 496–501, 558–81.
20 'New Leadership is Urged', *New York Times*, 3 June 1931, p. 1; Sarah T. Phillips, 'Acres Fit and Unfit: Conservation and Rural Rehabilitation in the New Deal Era', PhD dissertation, Boston University, 2004, pp. 22, 88–89.
21 'Trouble in Mexico', *New Republic*, 25 May 1938, p. 62; Ralph Bates, 'The Future of Mexico', *New Republic*, 19 October 1938, p. 298; Deborah Fitzgerald, 'Exporting American Agriculture: The Rockefeller Foundation in Mexico, 1943–53', *Social Studies of Science*, 1986, vol. 16, p. 462.
22 Clayton Koppes, 'The Good Neighbor Policy and the Nationalization of Mexican Oil', *Journal of American History*, 1982, vol. 69, p. 69. Friedrich E. Schuler, *Mexico Between Hitler and Roosevelt*, Albuquerque: University of New Mexico Press, 1998, p. 133; Charles S. Maier, 'The Politics of Productivity: Foundations of American International Economic Policy After World War II', *International Organization*, 1977, vol. 31, pp. 607–33; Harold B. Hinton, *Cordell Hull: A Biography*, Garden City: Doubleday, 1942, p. 287; Michael A. Butler, *Cautious Visionary: Cordell Hull and Trade Reform, 1933–1937*, Kent, Ohio: Kent State University Press, 1998, pp. 83–84.
23 Fitzgerald, 'Exporting American Agriculture', p. 463; John C. Culver and John Hyde, *American Dreamer: The Life and Times of Henry Wallace*, New York: Norton, 2000, p. 128.
24 Isaiah Berlin, *Washington Despatches, 1941–1945*, ed. by H. G. Nicholas, Chicago: University of Chicago Press, 1981, pp. 39–47.
25 Nelson Rockefeller, 'A Cárdenas Trip to the United States', 15 April 1943, State Department decimal files, 812.001, RG 59, box 4113, National Archives (hereafter NA), Washington.
26 Leon Hesser, *The Man Who Fed the World*, Dallas: Durban House, 2006, pp. 41–66.
27 Norman Borlaug, 'A Review by Norman E. Borlaug of the Report: The Social and Economic Implications of Large Scale Introductions of New Varieties of Food Grain', 17 September 1975, Borlaug Papers, box 7, University of Minnesota Library.
28 Edward E. Bomar, 'Indo-China Grants Due to Increase', *Washington Post*, 13 April 1953, p. 2.
29 Prasad, 'Giant and a Dwarf', pp. 1–4.
30 Robert L. Beisner, *Dean Acheson: A Life in the Cold War*, New York: Oxford University Press, 2006, p. 507; National Security Council, 'NSC-48, The Position of the United States With Respect to Asia', 30 December 1949, in Thomas E. Etzold and John Lewis Gaddis (eds) *Containment: Documents on American Policy and Strategy*, New York: Columbia University Press, 1978, p. 265.
31 W. W. Rostow, *Eisenhower, Kennedy, and Foreign Aid*, Austin: University of Texas Press, 1986, pp. 8–9; John F. Kennedy, 'If India Falls', *The Progressive*, January 1958, pp. 8–11.
32 Michael Latham, *Modernization as Ideology*, Chapel Hill: University of North Carolina Press, 2000, pp. 86–87; Nils Gilman, *Mandarins of the Future*, Baltimore: Johns Hopkins University Press, 2003, pp. 44–45; Walter Lippmann, 'India, The Glorious Gamble', *Ladies Home Journal*, August 1959, pp. 48–49.
33 CIA, 'Analysis of Possible Political Developments of Strategic Significance that May Occur Between 1951 and 1954', 28 February 1950, *Declassified Documents Reference System* (hereafter DDRS), item CK3100296001, <http://www.gale.com>

(accessed 7 July 2008); Gary R. Hess, *America Encounters India, 1941–1947*, Baltimore: Johns Hopkins University Press, 1971, pp. 162–72; H. W. Brands, *India and the United States: The Cold Peace*, Boston: Twayne, 1990, p. 42; 'JSPC 814/3, December 11, 1947', in Etzold and Gaddis (eds) *Containment*, p. 296.

34 Andrew Rotter, *Comrades at Odds: The United States and India, 1947–1964*, Ithaca: Cornell University Press, 2000, p. 32; Office of Intelligence and Research, South Asia Branch, 'The Need for and Possibility of Economic Development in India', 2 March 1951, Far East Program Division, South Asia Country Subject Files, 195–52, India, box 13, RG 469, NA, College Park, Md.; Milton Katz to Richard Bissell, 21 April 1951, Office of the Deputy Administrator, Country Files, 1950–51, box 2, RG 469, NA.

35 CIA, 'Comprehensive Plan of Requirements for Production of National Intelligence on the Far East', 15 June 1950, CIA-RDP79, CREST, NA.

36 William C. Bullitt, 'The Old Ills of Modern India', *Life*, 1 October 1951, pp. 111–12; Dennis Merrill, *Bread and the Ballot: The United States and India's Economic Development, 1947–1963*, Chapel Hill: University of North Carolina Press, 1990, p. 55; Acheson to Truman, 'Indian Request for Food Grains', 2 February 1951, DDRS, CK3100407683; Ferdinand Kuhn, 'Truman Asks Foreign Grant of $8.5 Billion', *Washington Post*, 25 May 1951, p. 1.

37 Robert J. McMahon, *The Cold War on the Periphery: The United States, India, and Pakistan*, New York: Columbia University Press, 1994, p. 107; 'GOP Demands India Vow Aid Against Russia', *Chicago Tribune*, 24 May 1951, p. D6; Willard Edwards, 'Denounce Bill to Give India Grain as "Phony"', *Chicago Tribune*, 7 March 1951, p. 5; 'How Real is India's Famine?', *Chicago Tribune*, 19 February 1951, p. 16; M. J. Akbar, *Nehru: The Making of India*, New Delhi: Roli Books, 2002, p. 491.

38 Jawaharlal Nehru, *The Discovery of India*, New York: Doubleday, 1960, p. 386; India Planning Commission, *Our Plan*, Delhi: GOI Publications Division, 1953, pp. 27–29; Harlan Cleveland to William C. Foster and Richard Bissell, 'Aid to India', 19 January 1951, Records of the US Foreign Assistance Agencies, RG 469, Country files, Box 1, NA.

39 Oscar Calvo-Gonzalez, 'Neither a Carrot nor a Stick: American Foreign Aid and Economic Policymaking in Spain During the 1950s', *Diplomatic History*, 2006, vol. 30, pp. 409–38; Senate Committee on Foreign Relations, *Development of Technical Assistance Programs: Background Information and Documents*, 83rd Cong., 2nd sess., 1954, p. 60; George V. Allen to Dulles, 26 July 1953, *Foreign Relations of the United States, 1952–1954* (hereafter *FRUS*), Washington: Government Printing Office, 1986, 9:1699; Dulles to Allen, 3 September 1953, *FRUS, 1952–1954*, 9: 1717.

40 James Michener, 'The Riddle of Pandit Nehru', *Reader's Digest*, July 1956, pp. 96–102; Norman Cousins, 'What About Nehru?' *Saturday Review*, 10 April 1954, p. 24.

41 Eleanor Roosevelt, *India and the Awakening East*, New York: Harper and Brothers, 1953, pp. 113–14; W. O. Douglas, 'Way to Win in the East', *Rotarian*, June 1951, pp. 6–53; Margaret Bourke-White, *Interview With India*, London: The Travel Book Club, 1950, p. 175; Henry Steele Commager, 'Acid Test for the American Character', *New York Times Magazine*, 29 April 1951, p. 8.

42 Barbara Ward, 'The Fateful Race Between China and India', *New York Times Magazine*, 20 September 1953, pp. 9–67; Chester Bowles, 'New India', *Foreign Affairs*, 1952, vol. 31, p. 80; Yuan-li Wu and Robert C. North, 'China and India: Two Paths to Industrialization', *Problems of Communism*, 1955, vol. 4, pp. 13–19; Rostow, *Diffusion of Power*, p. 104.

43 NSC 5409, 'United States Policy Toward South Asia', 19 February 1954, *FRUS, 1952–1954*, 11: 1098; NSC 5701, 'Statement of Policy on US Policy Toward South Asia', 10 January 1957, *FRUS, 1955, 1957*, 8: 31; Yves Moroni, 'India's Second Five Year Plan', 22 May 1956, Records of the Federal Reserve, country

files, Asia, Australia, and New Zealand, general, Federal Reserve Board Archives, Washington, D.C.

44 Kissinger, 'Reflections on American Diplomacy', *Foreign Affairs*, 1956, vol. 35, p. 37; on images of Indians as economic actors, see Rotter, *Comrades at Odds*, pp. 77–115.

45 For the text of the *Panchsheel*, see G. V. Ambekar, *Documents on China's Relations with South and South-East Asia*, Bombay: Allied Publishers, 1964, pp. 7–8; Nehru, 'The Concept of Panchsheel', 17 September 1955, in *India's Foreign Policy*, Delhi: Ministry of Information, 1961, p. 100; Judith M. Brown, *Nehru: A Political Life*, New Haven: Yale University Press, 2003, p. 269.

46 *Congressional Record*, 84th Congress, 1st sess., 29 June 1955, p. 9536; *Congressional Record*, 84th Cong., 1st sess., 11 July 1953, p. 10234.

47 *Congressional Record*, 85th Cong., 2nd sess., 25 March 1958, pp. 5246–53.

48 William J. Lederer and Eugene Burdick, 'The Ugly American, Part 1', *Saturday Evening Post*, 4 October 1958, pp. 19–20, 108–13.

49 William J. Lederer and Eugene Burdick, *The Ugly American*, New York: W. W. Norton, 1958, pp. 24, 284. For a rundown of the novel's factual errors, see Thomas W. Wilson Jr., 'How to Make a Movie Out of The Ugly American', *Harper's*, June 1959, p. 16; and for why facts were beside the point, see Slotkin, *Gunfighter Nation*, pp. 447–53; Jonathan Nashel, 'The Road to Vietnam: Modernization Theory in Fact and Fiction', in C. Appy (ed.) *Cold War Constructions: The Political Culture of United States Imperialism, 1945–1966*, Amherst: University of Massachusetts Press, 2000, pp. 132–54.

50 George Gallup, 'Gallup Finds Majority for Foreign Aid', *Los Angeles Times*, 30 March 1958, p. 27; Willard Johnson, 'Foreign Aid Cut Opposed', *Washington Post*, 17 April 1960, p. E8.

51 'To World of Peace, Text of the Address', *Washington Post*, 26 September 1961, p. A1; 'Text of Kennedy's Message to Congress', *New York Times*, 23 March 1961, p. 14; B. K. Nehru, *Nice Guys Finish Second*, Delhi: Viking, 1997, p. 334.

52 On Indian planning, see Sunil Khilnani, *The Idea of India*, New York: Farrar Straus, 1997, pp. 61–106; Ramachandra Guha, *India After Gandhi*, New York: Harper Collins, 2007, pp. 214–29.

53 W. W. Rostow, 'Marx Was a City Boy or, Why Communism May Fail', *Harper's Magazine*, February 1955, p. 26–29; Thomas P. Bernstein, 'Mao Zedong and the Famine of 1959–60: A Study of Willfulness', *China Quarterly*, 2006, vol. 186, pp. 421–45; Matthew S. Young, 'When Your Enemy Hungers: The Kennedy Administration, Public Opinion, and the Famine in China, 1961–62', PhD dissertation, Bowling Green State University, 2000, pp. 109, 124–25.

54 Lucian W. Pye, 'Foreign Aid and America's Involvement in the Developing World', in Anthony Lake (ed.) *The Vietnam Legacy*, New York: New York University Press, 1976, p. 379.

55 Quoted in Inder Malhotra's, *Indira Gandhi: A Personal and Political Biography*, London: Hodder and Stoughton, 1989, p. 96.

2 Old world, new world
Great Britain and America from the beginning

Kathleen Burk

The concept of a 'special relationship' is very problematic, in that, in general, it is the weaker power which needs it: the stronger power tends to get what it wants without such supplication. When the stronger power – the United States, say – does refer to having a special relationship with another country, it is generally for one of two reasons. It can actually need the help of the other power, such as that of the United Kingdom in the Iraq crisis; or it can be acting in a kindly fashion towards that power's leadership. In this context, it is useful to recall the incident chronicled by Raymond Seitz, American ambassador to the United Kingdom from 1991 to 1994, in his memoir, *Over Here*: 'As was the custom, [Prime Minister] John Major went to Washington a few weeks after the President's inauguration. I preceded him by a couple of days in order to scout out the tricky political terrain. . . . Just before the Prime Minister arrived at the White House, Clinton was sitting with a few aides in the Oval Office. "Don't forget to say 'special relationship' when the press comes in", one of them joked – a little like "don't forget to put out the cat". "Oh, yes", Clinton said. "How could I forget? The 'special relationship'!" And he threw back his head and laughed'.[1]

The whole idea of an Anglo-American 'special relationship' is extraordinarily complicated, in a manner which cannot be claimed by any other country. It is not just the language, which can be claimed by several other candidates; it is not just the history; it is not just the military alliance; it is not just the shared cultures of various sorts. It is all of these tangled up together, and it is the intention in this essay to sort out some of these strands, whilst giving an overview of this relationship.

England began to colonize North America in the late sixteenth century, with the first permanent colony being established at Jamestown in Virginia in 1607. Over the succeeding century and a half, other colonies were established up and down the Atlantic seaboard and the Caribbean: by the eighteenth century, Great Britain had 23 colonies in the Western Hemisphere.[2] It is with the central 13 colonies that this essay is concerned. One strong point which must be made is that, overwhelmingly, the colonists were proud of being part of the British Empire. On the whole, people were conservative and the decision to change one's traditional loyalty to Great Britain would not have been an easy one to take. Fundamentally, as Pauline Maier has written, 'Americans took particular pride in being governed under Britain's unwritten constitution, which they considered the most perfect form of government ever invented "by the wit of man"'.[3] For many, it was not obvious that they would be better off outside of the Empire.

Great Britain herself drove the colonies to declare independence by unilateral changes she made in their relationships after her victory over France in the Seven Years' War of 1756–63. First of all, she attempted to change the tax regime. It had always been accepted that the Crown-in-Parliament had the right to impose duties in order to direct trade – e.g., to tax a product produced by a French West Indian island to encourage its purchase from a British West Indian island; what the colonists refused to accept was the British claim that London could impose so-called 'internal' taxes, such as on stamps, without the colonial legislatures having voted on it. And, secondly, the huge increase in the territory of the British Empire – she took Quebec and a large chunk of India from France, for example – led to London's attempts to re-organize the administration and defence of the Empire. As a result, London seems to have changed its view as to how the American colonies ought to be treated, even though they were 'settler colonies', not colonies acquired by conquest.[4] Many American colonists saw themselves as provincial Englishmen, as Englishmen who happened to live rather far away from the home islands, not as 'colonists';[5] according to Stephen Conway, London increasingly saw and treated them as part of the dependent empire, colonists who had to obey London's decisions without question, not as fellow-Englishmen over the ocean.[6] Following on decades of benign neglect, this was not acceptable to increasing numbers of Americans. Before 1763, most were content to remain as Englishmen across the sea: 13 years later, a plurality wished for independence. By 1783, the colonies were independent, and by 1815, after the War of 1812 – called by some the Second War of Independence[7] – Great Britain finally accepted the finality of American nationhood.

It is undeniable that the fact that the United States had to fight for her independence from the Empire, to become the first new nation, seared the collective American memory and stamped Great Britain as the hereditary enemy: after all, it was only with the Korean War that the two had fought together against a common foe more often than they had fought each other. Certainly during the nineteenth century, the relationship was very complicated. Politically and diplomatically, they were now separated. There were numerous conflicts between them during the century, particularly over the boundary with Canada – especially in the Oregon Territory[8] – and over British actions during the American Civil War,[9] and war between them actually threatened more than once. The relationship was between two, theoretically equal, countries. In reality, of course, it was between the world's supreme global power, whose Royal Navy and currency dominated, and a power whose primary focus was on extending her dominion over the continent and perhaps further south, but whose international clout was relatively weak. This relationship would only begin to change near the end of the century.

Perhaps of more interest during the nineteenth century were the private relationships. First of all, the British were intensely curious about Americans and America, about what they were like and what the new country was like: as the

French writer J. Hector St John de Crèvecoeur asked in his *Letters from an American Farmer*, 'what then is the American, this new man?'[10] Visitors from England (and elsewhere) began to arrive soon after the Revolution, but it was the period after 1815 that saw a steady increase in the flow. Although they did not all write books about their experiences, according to the historian C. Vann Woodward, over 200 British visitors did publish books about their travels to the United States between just 1835 and 1860.[11] Most of them dripped with condescension. Some liked America and Americans, but rather more found serious flaws – slavery was a notable example. Harriet Martineau, the writer on political economy, visited America in the mid-1830s and then wrote about her experiences in a two-volume work, *Society in America*. She was broadly favourable, slavery always excepted, but a comment published in 1837 would have been agreed to by most: 'It is an absorbing thing to watch the process of world-making – both the formation of the natural and the conventional world. I witnessed both in America; and when I look back upon it now, it seems as if I had been in another planet'.[12]

Others deeply disliked what they found. Mrs Fanny Trollope, mother of the more famous Anthony Trollope, visited the United States from 1827 to 1831; she then published one of the most famous of these accounts, *Domestic Manners of the Americans*, in 1832. After referring to 'one of the most remarkable traits in the national character of the Americans; namely, their exquisite sensitiveness and soreness respecting everything said or written concerning them',[13] she then proceeded to make them intensely sore. Her premise was that it was better to be governed by the few than by the many, and she found, she thought, ample evidence to support her conviction. What she really hated most was the lack of deference, the assumption of equality. She was mortified at having to share a coach; she disliked shopkeepers dressing and acting as though they were aristocrats at a ball; she found the rude indifference of American children repellent; she hated the constant spitting everywhere, which frequently landed on her skirt; and she hated what she considered the lack of refinement, which she decided was the greatest difference between England and the United States. She emphasized what she considered the unbridled and ignorant nature of religion.[14] But it was American politics that called forth her most memorable comment. As she wrote, with mounting hostility, 'I speak not of these, but of the population generally, as seen in town and country, among the rich and the poor, in the slave states and the free states. I do not like them. I do not like their principles, I do not like their manners, I do not like their opinions'. She then adds, 'Both as a woman, and as a stranger, it might be unseemly for me to say that I do not like their government, and therefore I will not say so'.[15] The book sold thousands on both sides of the Atlantic. For many Britons, it confirmed their suspicions that, by winning independence from the Mother Country, the Americans had gone astray. The Americans hated this implication, and, just possibly, they hated the fact that in many cases chronicled in her book, she was telling the truth.

Charles Dickens was a visitor who left England expecting to like America, and, as he said later, his 'young enthusiasm' was 'anything but prepared' for what he found and for his subsequent disillusion.[16] In 1842, he was 29 and handsome, the writer of five novels in 5 years, and, as an ardent radical at home, he expected to find that the poor were better off in the United States than in England. He also wanted to be lionized – 'Washington Irving writes to me that if I went, it would be such a triumph from one end of the States to the other, as was never known in any other Nation'[17] – and to make lots of money. He was profoundly disappointed in what he found – tobacco-chewing and spitting, mentioned by almost all British visitors, disgusted him. He particularly disliked those aspects of America that he attributed to money-grasping. He was enraged, for example, by the fact that although Americans in their tens of thousands read his novels, they read American pirated editions, and Dickens himself received not a penny.[18] Americans, Dickens wrote, admired a man who was 'smart', who got ahead whether or not he did it honestly. An American, he concluded, was basically an economic animal.[19] He chronicled this disappointment in his *American Notes*, which also formed the basis of his novel *Martin Chuzzlewit*, and Americans could hardly decide which they hated the more.

As with many other visitors, Dickens liked the theory of democracy but hated many of its products. Most disliked the oft-stated assumptions of Americans that they could do as they liked because they were free; also disliked were the invasive nature of American curiosity, the truly horrible nature of the newspapers, and the uniformity of American culture – as Matthew Arnold put it in 1888 in his *Civilization in the United States*, 'what really dissatisfies in American civilization is the want of the *interesting*'.[20]

Americans also visited Great Britain, although in fewer numbers. Many went preparing to like what they saw, especially visitors from New England. One example was Harriet Beecher Stowe, the author of *Uncle Tom's Cabin*, who wrote that 'Say what you will, an American, particularly a New Englander, can never approach the old country without a kind of thrill and pulsation of kindred . . . Our very life-blood is English life-blood. It is Anglo-Saxon vigor that is spreading our country from Atlantic to Pacific'.[21] Others found that the class system stuck in their craw. This was the case even with those who liked England, of whom Mark Twain was one. He loved England and the English, and he spent long periods there. He had many English friends; indeed, when he received an honorary degree from Oxford, he received a standing ovation from the assembled Oxford Fellows.[22] Yet, his contempt for the aristocratic system appears in neon lights in his novel *A Yankee at the Court of King Arthur*, published in London in 1890: 'It is enough to make a body ashamed of his race to think of the sort of froth that has always occupied its thrones without shadow of right or reason, and the seventh-rate people that have figured as its aristocracies – a company of monarchs and nobles who, as a rule, would have achieved only poverty and obscurity if left, like their betters, to their own exertions'.[23] The existence of this system of inequality was an important reason for American dislike of and contempt for Great Britain.

Another visitor was the New England philosopher and essayist Ralph Waldo Emerson, an Anglophile whose primary concern was to visit literary men, but who also wished to learn about Great Britain. He liked what he saw: 'A wise traveller will naturally choose to visit the best of actual nations; and an American has more reasons than another to draw him to Britain. In all that is done or begun by the Americans towards right thinking or practice, we are met by a civilization already settled and overpowering. The culture of the day, the thoughts and aims of men, are English thoughts and aims. . . . The practical common-sense of modern society, the utilitarian directions which labor, laws, opinion, religion take, is the natural genius of the British mind'.[24] Yet, he was an American first, and he drew a conclusion which increasingly became a dominating idea in the United States. As he wrote in his book *English Traits*, published in 1856, 'I saw everywhere [in England] proofs of sense and spirit, and success of every sort: I like the people: they are as good as they are handsome; they have everything, and can do every-thing; but meantime, I surely know, that, as soon as I return to Massachusetts, I shall lapse at once into the feeling, which the geography of America inevitably inspires, that we play the game with immense advantage; that there and not here is the seat and center of the British race; and that no skill or activity can long compete with the prodigious natural advantages of that country, in the hands of the same race; and that England, an old and exhausted island, must one day be contented, like other parents, to be strong only in her children'. 'But', he added, 'this is a proposition which no Englishman of whatever condition can easily entertain'.[25]

If one looks at culture in the United States during this period, it is clear that even though she was politically independent of Great Britain, she remained something of a social and intellectual colony. Whilst she was part of the Empire, American culture, not very surprisingly, was 'a steady, resolute, instinctive repro-duction of contemporary English culture'.[26] Samuel Richardson's novel *Pamela, or Virtue Rewarded*, published in 1742 and the first novel published in America, was a success there as in England. With independence, little changed. Indeed, Americans insisted that they had every right to claim for their own any authors published before the Revolution, such as Shakespeare and Milton. However, the War of 1812 unleashed a tide of frenzied nationalism, and an independent coun-try obviously required an independent literature. There was a great deal of brag-ging about American literary output, which excited – again – British contempt, in the so-called 'Paper War'. Sydney Smith, in a piece in the *Edinburgh Review* of January 1820, brought this particular war to a peak: 'In the four quarters of the globe, who reads an American book? Or goes to an American play? Or looks at an American picture or statue? . . . When these questions are fairly and favourably answered, their laudatory epithets may be allowed: But, till that can be done, we would seriously advise them to keep clear of superlatives'.[27]

It was the sentence 'In the four quarters of the globe, who reads an American book?' which was the most piercing and the resentment about which was the longest-lasting. It did not help that, over the century, thousands of English books were published in the United States, with many fewer American ones. Partly, it was the lack of copyright protection, which caused incandescent rage in Dickens and other English authors, who received nothing but fame from the sale of thousands of their books in the United States. However, this meant that because publishers could publish English books very cheaply, they had little incentive to pay American authors. (This could work both ways: Mark Twain's *The Adventures of Huckleberry Finn* was first published in London, in December 1884, because of copyright concerns; being published first in Britain, it would receive British copyright protection.) American publishers also appreciated that their ability to read the reviews of English books before deciding whether or not to publish meant that the hazard of publication was lessened.[28] And it was not just authors: according to Alexis de Tocqueville in his *Democracy in America*, 'Citizens of the United States themselves seem so convinced that books are not published for them, that before settling on the merit of one of their writers, they ordinarily wait for him to have been sampled in England. . . . The inhabitants of the United States, therefore, still do not have a literature, properly speaking'.[29] A number of American authors went to England to be published, partly for copyright protection (as with Twain), but also because publishers would take a chance on them. Furthermore, they were often more highly regarded in London than at home: Herman Melville found that his *Moby Dick; or, The Whale* received its most searching praise from British critics, whilst the London publication of *Leaves of Grass* (as *Poems by Walt Whitman*) was a turning point in Whitman's struggle for recognition.[30]

The balance of literary power would not change until the twentieth century. In 1908, the young poet Ezra Pound went to London, when, as he later recollected, the United States was 'still a colony of London so far as culture was concerned', and 'Henry James, Whitman and myself all had to come to the metropolis, to the capital of the US, so far as arts and letters were concerned'.[31] London would ineluctably lose this status over the first half of the century, as British wealth and power declined. British literary influence in general would also decline, but it would not be an easy battle for the Americans to win: in 1901, when the US College Entrance Exams selected 16 books as essential reading when preparing for the literature exams, 13 of the authors were British.[32]

What was already beginning to change, however, was the geopolitical balance of power between the two countries. Partly, it was the change in economic circumstances. This was not so much the relative decline of Great Britain, as relative ascension by the United States in comparison with every other country in the world. Take just one example, that of steel, then the foundation of military power. In a table comparing the steel production of the Great Powers from 1850 to 1914, the United States does not even appear until 1880, when she produces 1.3 million tons, the same as Great Britain. By 1914, in comparison to Britain's output of 6.5 million tons, the United States produced 32 million: this was more than all of Europe combined.[33] However, it was not just the United States' growing economic might that brought her increasingly to the notice of British statesmen: it was the darkening of the international scene and Britain's worrying isolation within it.

Turning to the United States was also encouraged by the changing perceptions of the United States after 1870: in books by British visitors, one begins to see terms such as W.G. Adams's 'our American cousins',[34] Anthony Trollope's 'these children of our own',[35] and Matthew Arnold's 'the English people on the other side of the Atlantic'.[36] Even Sherlock Holmes got in on the act: 'It is always a joy to me to meet an American, Mr Moulton, for I am one of those who believe that the folly of a monarch and the blundering of a Minister in fargone years will not prevent our children from being some day citizens of the same worldwide country under a flag which shall be a quartering of the Union Jack with the Stars and Stripes'.[37] In newspapers as well as books, there were celebrations of the two countries as united in an Anglo-Saxon race which was self-evidently the fittest – after all, look at the economic power of both, or at the British Empire, which at the turn of the century covered 20 per cent of the globe and incorporated 25 per cent of the world's population. They came, commentators said, from the same stock, they were both liberal democracies and they had the same approaches to the world – although this last claim was not necessarily accepted by most Americans. In short, war between the two was highly unlikely: according to the British Prime Minister A. J. Balfour, in 1896, 'the idea of a war with the United States of America carries with it something of the unnatural horror of civil war'.[38] Therefore, if Britain needed a colleague, the United States was the most likely candidate.

Great Britain embarked, at the turn of the century, on a pattern of settling outstanding imperial problems. Partly, it was to lessen the dangers of war with France and Russia, particularly after the Fashoda Crisis with France in 1898, when the two nearly fought over control of the headwaters of the Nile; partly, it was to free ships of the Royal Navy from patrolling the Western Hemisphere and China Waters for re-deployment against newly threatening countries; and partly, it was to free resources elsewhere in order to face a growing German threat. What role was the United States to play in this? The hope of the British Government was that the United States would support Britain if trouble arose, or that at least she would not support Britain's enemies. This would eventually be the case, but not before there was a crucial test of power between the two countries over primacy in the Western Hemisphere.

In 1895–96, there was an Anglo-American crisis over a boundary between Venezuela and the British colony of Guinea, during which the United States claimed to be defending the Monroe Doctrine against a British scheme to increase the size of her colony at the expense of Venezuela. (The 1823 Monroe Doctrine stated that territory in the Western Hemisphere was no longer open for colonization or re-colonization.) She also claimed hegemony over the Western Hemisphere. As Richard Olney, the secretary of state, warned in a despatch to the foreign secretary and prime minister, Lord Salisbury, 'Today the United States is practically sovereign on this continent, and its fiat is law upon the subjects to which it confines its interposition. Why? It is not because of the pure friendship or goodwill felt for it. It is not simply by reason of its high character as a civilized state, nor because wisdom and justice and equity are the invariable characteristics of the dealings of the United States. It is because, in addition to all other grounds, its infinite resources combined with its isolated position render it master of the situation and practically invulnerable as against any or all other powers'.[39] Known as the Olney Doctrine, this came very close to maintaining that might makes right.

Salisbury ignored the American demarche for some months, and then sent a despatch heavy with gravitas and ripe with the very sort of *de haut en bas* tone that the Foreign Office did so well and which might have been calculated to raise the hackles of the Americans. Essentially, the despatch stated that the relationship between Great Britain, its colony and Venezuela was not the business of the United States: the 'British Empire and the Republic of Venezuela are neighbours, and they have differed for some time past, and continue to differ, as to the line by which their dominions are separated. It is a controversy with which the United States have no apparent practical concern. . . . It is simply the determination of the frontier of a British possession which belonged to the Throne of England long before the Republic of Venezuela came into existence'.[40] In response, on 17 December, President Grover Cleveland sent a message to Congress that threatened war. Salisbury wanted to hold out against this threat, but his Cabinet, alarmed by other international threats – over South Africa, the Ottoman Empire and China, from France, Russia, and Germany – did not support him.[41] The United States, therefore, won, and the implication, at least to the Americans, was that Britain had thereby surrendered her own claims to dominance in the hemisphere.

The fact that, alone of the European powers, Britain supported the United States in the Spanish–American War of 1898; and the fact that, alone of all of the powers, the US government, although not American public opinion, supported Britain in the Boer War of 1899–1902, encouraged closer relations. This made it, if not easier, at least more acceptable for Britain to settle outstanding points of conflict with the United States, in every case in favour of the United States. She agreed to a new treaty giving the United States control of an isthmian canal, whenever it might be built; she sacrificed the Canadians – as far as the Canadians were concerned – once again, over a boundary dispute with the United States; and she withdrew almost the entire American Squadron of the Royal Navy from the Caribbean and the northern Atlantic seaboard, effectively turning over her naval base at Halifax to the Canadians. For the United States, this was recognition by Great Britain that the Caribbean was now an American lake. For the British government, however, convinced as she was that the United States and the United Kingdom shared the same interests in peace and in maintaining the international status quo, she had turned over to the United States the responsibility for the Western Hemisphere, effectively incorporating the United States into her own defence strategy.[42]

With the twentieth century, the story becomes much better known. It is a mistake to see the United States and Britain as firm allies: the United States did not join World War I until she was torpedoed into it in April 1917, and even then she refused any closer relationship than as an Associate. However, the Great War is crucial to the Anglo-American relationship for one overwhelmingly important reason: the financial relationship. During the war, Britain guaranteed the purchases in the United States not only of herself, but also of France, Belgium,

Italy, Russia, Greece and Romania, and the effort nearly destroyed her financial system. It certainly began the destruction of the role of the pound, although this was not obvious for some years. To finance these purchases, Britain borrowed huge sums of money in the United States, both from the private sector and from the American government, the latter the genesis of the war debts. Over the course of the summer of 1917, it is almost possible to track, day by day in the offices of the US Treasury, the passing of financial hegemony from Britain to the United States, and by the end of the war, the two countries had changed positions, irrevocably as it turned out, as supreme international financial power.[43] This had significant implications for the ability of both to wield power. Not only does a country need wealth to run foreign and defence policies, but Britain had traditionally (and the United States would soon) financed, through subsidies and other aid, the fighting capabilities of other countries, as well as encouraging their support in other ways.

During the interwar period, the financial relations of the two countries were intermittently fraught. On the one hand, there was conflict over the war debts: briefly, Washington wanted them repaid whilst Britain wanted them cancelled. The British had suffered roughly 947,000 deaths, the United States roughly 115,000; Britain had lost fifteen per cent of her prewar wealth, primarily American and other foreign securities, and had borrowed massively – by 1928, fully forty per cent of government expenditure would be spent on servicing war debts[44] – whilst the United States had become a huge economic power. The United States refused. If not always expressed with the crudity of President Calvin Coolidge – 'they hired the money, didn't they?' – there were few in the United States who did not believe that Britain, the great international financial power, could not pay; it seemed obvious to many that Britain was just trying to take advantage of the United States. The upshot was that not only did Britain agree to pay, but the United States insisted that she pay a higher rate of interest than the other debtor countries.[45]

Importantly, although there was huge competition for business, their financial communities were able to work closely together during this period of so-called 'bankers' diplomacy'. European states, including the 'successor states' of the old empires, and especially of the Austro-Hungarian Empire, had to be reconstructed, and the support had to come from the private sector. For the United States, 'foreign aid' from the government during peacetime was a concept that emerged from World War II, and not World War I. Therefore, the money came by means of loans from the private sector, and Wall Street and the City of London worked closely together.[46]

On the other hand, the two navies were locked together in nonviolent combat over their respective sizes, a conflict which caused 'the worst level of Anglo-American hostility in the twentieth century'.[47] The US Navy, and many politicians, wanted parity with the Royal Navy if not supremacy over it, and threatened to outbuild the Royal Navy. Great Britain knew that the United States could indeed do this. Even the First Lord of the Admiralty admitted that if the United States 'chose to put all of their resources into the provision of a larger Navy the competition between us would be impossible, and we should in the end be beaten from the point of view merely of finance'.[48] However, many doubted that the American public would provide the money to increase the number of American ships. The two countries fought over the types and sizes of the ships which could make up their respective navies,[49] to the extent that in 1928, the Foreign Office, in an urgent paper for the Cabinet, wrote that 'war is *not* unthinkable between the two countries. On the contrary, there are present all the factors which in the past have made for wars between States'.[50] The problem was settled in 1930 by means of an ingenuous compromise suggested by the US president, Herbert Hoover.[51]

However, what really frustrated the British government during the interwar period was that the United States wanted international power without assuming the associated international responsibilities. It became nearly a mantra in British political and diplomatic circles that the United States would never respond to a crisis with force; instead, she would respond with words: Stanley Baldwin, then lord president of the Council, in 1931, burst out to a friend, 'You will get nothing out of Washington but words, big words, but only words';[52] in 1932, Sir Robert Vansittart, the permanent undersecretary at the Foreign Office, minuted that 'It is universally assumed that the United States will never use force';[53] and in 1935, Sir Neville Chamberlain, the prime minister, wrote to his sister that 'It is always best and safest to count on nothing from the Americans except words'.[54] Neither the US government nor American public opinion wished to become involved again in international affairs, believing that having done so in 1917 had been a mistake.[55] As events in the 1930s marched to their conclusion, Britain could only hope that the US government would change its mind. If they did not, she was probably doomed.

The coming of World War II signals the beginning of the period when the term 'special relationship' began to be used. In one sense, the former German chancellor, Otto von Bismarck, had foreseen this: when asked just before his death in 1898 what he considered to be the most important factor in the modern world, his answer was 'The fact that the North Americans speak English'.[56] For a special relationship, this may be necessary, or at least useful, but it is not sufficient. Words can be weapons. Roosevelt used words to humiliate Churchill publicly at the Teheran Conference in November 1943 in order to emphasize to Stalin that the United States was eschewing a close relationship with the United Kingdom in favour of a close relationship with the USSR.[57] On the other hand, Churchill used words even more powerfully in his speech at Fulton, Missouri, on 5 March 1946, when he proclaimed that 'From Stettin in the Baltic to Trieste in the Adriatic, an iron curtain has descended across the Continent'. Furthermore, 'in a great number of countries, far from the Russian frontiers and throughout the world, Communist fifth columns are established and work in complete unity and absolute obedience to the directions they receive from the Communist centre'. The only sure defence, Churchill stated, was 'the fraternal association of the English-speaking peoples. This means a special relationship between the British Commonwealth and Empire and the United States'.[58]

As special relationships go, it has been repeatedly and severely tested since 1945.[59] Undoubtedly, World War II saw the closest military alliance in history, with the combined chiefs of staffs, the combined economic and supply boards, and the innovation of all armed forces in a given theatre being under the command of one man. To some extent, this alliance, based on habits, closely linked personnel, and a mostly common view of the international scene, extended into the post-War world for a decade. The United Kingdom worked fiercely for this, the government believing that it needed to co-opt American power for the safety of the realm. As a committee of high British officials, gathered for an informal discussion on European co-operation in January 1949 during the negotiations over NATO, reaffirmed, 'Since post-war planning began, our policy has been to secure close political, military and economic co-operation with USA. This has been necessary to get economic aid. It will always be decisive for our security. . . . We hope to secure a special relationship with USA and Canada . . . for in the last resort we cannot rely upon the European countries'.[60]

However, this worked both ways. A year earlier, in a State Department policy statement of 11 June 1948, it was affirmed that 'The policies and actions of no other country in the world, with the possible exception of the USSR, are of greater importance to us'. Continuing, 'British friendship and cooperation . . . is necessary for American defence. The United Kingdom, the Dominions, Colonies and Dependencies, form a worldwide network of strategically located territories of great military value, which have served as defensive outposts and as bridgeheads for operations. Subject to our general policy of favoring eventual self-determination of peoples, it is our objective that the integrity of the area be maintained'.[61] (Or, as it was later put by Frank Wisner, head of covert operations for the CIA, in a conversation with Foreign Office official and Soviet spy Kim Philby, 'whenever there is somewhere we want to destabilize, the British have an island nearby'.[62]) After 2 years, in a statement for the Department of State, it was reaffirmed that 'No other country has the same qualifications for being our principal ally and partner as the United Kingdom. It has internal political strength and important capabilities in the political, economic and military fields throughout the world. Most important, the British share our fundamental objectives and standards of conduct . . . . To achieve our foreign policy objectives we must have the cooperation of our allies and friends. The British and with them the rest of the Commonwealth, particularly the older dominions, are our most reliable and useful allies, with whom a special relationship should exist. This relationship is not an end in itself but must be used as an instrument of achieving common objectives. We cannot afford to permit a deterioration in our relationship with the British'.[63]

The nuclear relationship during this period was distinctly non-special, with the United States, through the 1946 McMahon Act, cutting the United Kingdom off from all sharing of scientific knowledge or technology. This was in spite of the Hyde Park aide-mémoire of September 1944, Clause 2 of which stated that 'Full collaboration between the United States and the British Government in developing tube alloys [the code name for atomic research] for military and commercial purposes should continue after the defeat of Japan unless and until terminated by joint agreement'.[64] To the British, the abrupt withdrawal of co-operation came as a shock. After the shock came anger, and after the anger came a determination to build their own bomb. As Ernest Bevin, the foreign secretary, stated to the House of Commons on 16 May 1947, 'His Majesty's Government do not accept the view . . . that we have ceased to be a Great Power',[65] and the mark now of this status was to be a nuclear power. However, there were other reasons, too. Prime Minister Clement Attlee later recalled that this was before NATO, and 'there was always the possibility of their [the United States'] withdrawing and becoming isolationist again. The manufacture of a British bomb was therefore at that stage essential for our defence'.[66] Furthermore, as a medium-sized country, she had to depend on her scientific and technological superiority for her defence against the USSR – the Cabinet believed that only British possession of the bomb would deter a nuclear-armed enemy.[67] However, it must be said that the British wanted the bomb not only as a defence against an enemy but also as defence against a friend – the United States. Partly, it was because they felt cheated by the United States, a sentiment that was, in fact, shared by former secretary of state Dean Acheson and former president Dwight D. Eisenhower.[68] However, of overwhelming importance was the conviction of the Cabinet that if Britain did not possess the bomb, the United States would pay no attention to British wishes in foreign policy. As Bevin emphasized, 'We could not afford to acquiesce in an American monopoly of this new development . . . we must develop it ourselves'. And, therefore, at a meeting of the War Cabinet on 8 January 1947, the decision was taken to build the bomb,[69] which was tested on 3 October 1952 on the Australian island of Monte Bello.

By then, however, research had moved on; in 1952 and 1953 the Americans and the Soviets tested their thermonuclear bombs, the hydrogen (or H–) bomb. In July 1954, the Cabinet decided that the United Kingdom had to have a comparable weapon, with Churchill, then prime minister, arguing that 'we could not expect to maintain our influence as a world power unless we possessed the most up-to-date nuclear weapons'.[70] She successfully tested her own H–bomb on Christmas Island in the Pacific in May 1957. President Dwight D. Eisenhower believed that closer co-operation with the United Kingdom would be beneficial to the United States, a situation which suddenly grew more attractive to the Americans when in October 1957 the Soviets launched Sputnik, the world's first satellite. Because the United States had held aloof, the United Kingdom had developed her own bombs, both atomic and hydrogen. In the other area of research, the peaceful use of atomic energy, she was considerably ahead of the United States: in 1955, the first of the so-called 'Magnox reactors', which produced both electricity for commercial use and plutonium for bombs, came on stream at Calder Hall. With these demonstrations that the United Kingdom had something to contribute, the United States passed the 1958 Atomic Energy Act. This enabled the two countries to sign the US–UK Mutual Defence Agreement, by which both information and materials are transferred between the two countries.

The growing intelligence relationship had its ups and downs. For roughly the first half of the century, the United Kingdom was the dominant power.

The United States had virtually no intelligence capability before World War I, and little more by its end, although the intelligence services of the two allies worked together very well on the Western Front.[71] During the interwar period, the State Department's encrypting and decrypting unit, the Black Chamber, was shut down in 1931, although military and naval efforts continued, with their focus on Japan.[72] The United Kingdom retained this lead during World War II, although the United States rapidly caught up, taking responsibility for the Japanese codes whilst the United Kingdom concentrated on the German.[73] But after the war the United States had vastly superior resources, and thus is overwhelmingly dominant in signals intelligence; the United Kingdom, however, retains a substantial position in human intelligence (i.e., spies). The intelligence relationship is rather less unequal than is the nuclear one. Nevertheless, it sometimes contributed almost as much anxiety as reassurance, particularly in the early 1950s when the United Kingdom feared that the CIA was out of control and as likely to cause a war with the USSR as to prevent one. Early on, the organization began to devote itself to covert activities rather than to intelligence-gathering. Not the least of the strains in the alliance was that caused by growing British apprehension that the United States would push the USSR beyond endurance by her series of covert activities around the Soviet perimeter.[74]

It was the Suez crisis that destroyed the Anglo-American special relationship based on the wartime alliance, thereby eliminating much of the associated sentimentality. As Sir Harold Caccia, the British ambassador to Washington, wrote in late December 1956, 'something has ended, and, in my view, three things: first, the sentimental attachment, in the Administration, created by our wartime experience as crusaders in arms; second, the innate trust in our longer experience in international affairs and our reputation for dependability; third, our largely unquestioned right to a special position . . . Now the position is different'.[75] The relationship in some sense was re-built, but the weight was now overwhelmingly on the American side, and the period of the 1960s and 1970s was largely a nadir. There was the Empire, for example – or, rather, the lack of it. The United States appreciated that British control of chunks of the globe eliminated the need for US involvement, but Suez and other crises, such as Iran in the early 1950s, led the United States to take over increasing responsibility for the defence of the West against what was perceived as global communism. By this period, with hardly any useful bits of land left, an economy spiralling down, a steep decline in the size of her armed forces, and a turbulent domestic political and economic scene, Britain's value as an ally faded away, as other countries, and particularly Germany, replaced her in the American government's assessment of allied usefulness.[76]

It seems clear that what reversed the situation was the impressive British performance in the Falklands War. The United States sacrificed considerable Latin American interests to aid British. The intention was to ensure a British victory, and in particular to keep in power the Conservative Government under Mrs Thatcher, the bulwark against a possible anti-NATO, anti-Europe and anti-nuclear left-wing Labour Government. The credibility of NATO was also at stake. The demonstration of British military prowess in the Falklands, and her willingness to fight and fight impressively well in the First Gulf War, ensured her popularity in the Pentagon, never mind the Oval Office.[77]

The mention of Mrs Thatcher is also a reminder of the importance of personal relationships between leaders, and here the front row includes Macmillan and Kennedy, Thatcher and Reagan, Blair and Clinton, although this was less important than it seemed at the time, and Blair and Bush. A close relationship will seldom cause a huge sacrifice of a national interest in favour of the comrade – although one might argue about Macmillan, Kennedy and Polaris – but it can certainly facilitate.[78] The most important element is to walk the line between playing hard to get and throwing oneself at the lover. It is as dangerous for a leader as for a country to be taken too much for granted.

And, finally, and briefly, there are the cultural relationships. A significant proportion of this essay was devoted to the nineteenth century because this is relatively unknown territory compared to the twentieth. Most people are aware of the influence of Hollywood in the United Kingdom; fewer may recall the so-called Second British Invasion of 1964 when British music, and pre-eminently the Beatles, appeared for a time to dominate the American music scene, with the group making the cover of *Life* magazine. An issue of *Time* magazine in 1966 celebrated 'swinging London'. There was the fear of 'Americanization', a constant complaint in the United Kingdom amongst the chattering classes, with 'Dallas' and McDonald's as agents of America's foreign cultural policy. Brains drain back and forth, American banks are a towering presence in the City, the British frequently edit the important American fashion magazines, such as *Vogue*, and shows from the West End are often a major presence on Broadway. To the extent that Americans know that any place outside of the United States exists, they love Britain. This affection is not always reciprocated, because the constant, even if low-key, British anti-Americanism can rapidly grow to full-blown mode, as it did over the 2003 invasion of Iraq.

Therefore, to what extent is there an Anglo-American 'special relationship'? The bones are the nuclear and intelligence relationships, which continue as other elements falter. The diplomatic corps work closely together, as do the armed forces and particularly the two navies. In an international crisis, the United Kingdom always turns to the United States; depending on the region, the United States will probably turn to the United Kingdom. After all – and here is language again – the United States has to have someone dependable with whom to talk. As long as each government has something important to contribute, and each believes that it benefits enough, the close links will continue. In cultural and social terms, in attitudes and assumptions, the two countries, whilst not the same, resemble each other enough to be comfortable together. In political institutions and in political cultures, the two countries are wildly different, but this seems to attract rather than to repel interest. Indeed, it is the interest of each country in the other, at private or public level, that is special, and that will help to ensure that the links between the two remain in the turbulent years ahead.

Notes

1 Raymond Seitz, *Over Here*, London: Weidenfeld & Nicolson, 1998, p. 322.
2 For a more detailed overview and references, see Kathleen Burk, *Old World, New World: The Story of Britain and America*, London: Little, Brown, 2007, pp. 23–88.
3 Pauline Maier, *American Scripture: Making the Declaration of Independence*, New York: Vintage, 1998, p. 29.
4 Ian K. Steele, 'The Anointed, the Appointed, and the Elected: Governance of the British Empire, 1689–1784', in Peter Marshall (ed.) *The Oxford History of the British Empire, Volume II: The Eighteenth Century*, Oxford: Oxford University Press, 1998, p. 121; Stephen Conway, 'From Fellow-Nationals to Foreigners: British Perceptions of the Americans, *circa* 1739–83', *William and Mary Quarterly*, 2002, vol. 59, pp. 82–83; Jack P. Greene, *Peripheries and Center: Constitutional Development in the Extended Politics of the British Empire and the United States, 1607–1788*, Athens: University of Georgia Press, 1986, pp. 57–58.
5 Ned Landsman, *From Colonials to Provincials: American Thought and Culture 1680–1760*, Ithaca: Cornell University Press, 1997, pp. 3–47.
6 Conway, 'From Fellow-Nationals to Foreigners', pp. 82–83.
7 Bradford Perkins, *Prologue to War: England and the United States, 1805–1812*, Berkeley: University of California Press, 1968, p. 377, and Francis D. Cogliano, *Revolutionary America 1763–1815: A Political History*, London: Routledge, 2000, p. 180. The term was also used by, for example, Senator James Henry Hammond in a speech to the Senate on 4 March 1858, <www.sewanee.edu/faculty/Willis/Civil_War/documents/HammondCotton.html> (accessed 19 January 2008).
8 Negotiations took place in 1818, 1825–26, 1841–42, 1845–46 and 1903. Kenneth Bourne, *Britain and the Balance of Power in North America 1815–1908*, Berkeley: University of California Press, 1967, pp. 9, 70, 79–81, 86–97, 147–61; C. P. Stacey, 'The Myth of the Unguarded Frontier', *American Historical Review*, 1950, vol. 56, pp. 4–9; Bradford Perkins, *Castlereagh and Adams: England and the United States, 1812–1823*, Berkeley: University of California Press, 1964, pp. 240–44; Bradford Perkins, *The Cambridge History of American Foreign Relations, Volume I: The Creation of a Republican Empire, 1776–1865*, Cambridge: Cambridge University Press, 1995, pp. 207–17; R. B. Mowat, *The Diplomatic Relations of Great Britain and the United States*, London: Edward Arnold, 1925, pp. 78, 212–16; Richard Rush, *Memoranda of a Residence at the Court of London*, Philadelphia: Carey, Lea & Blanchard, 1833, pp. 345, 353, 363–64, 380, 409–10; Richard Rush, *Memoranda of a Residence at the Court of London, Comprising Incidents Official and Personal from 1819–1825. Including Negotiations on the Oregon Question, and Other Unsettled Questions between the United States and Great Britain*, Philadelphia: Lea & Blanchard, 1845, pp. 469–72, 507–10; Frederick Merk, *The Oregon Question: Essays in Anglo-American Diplomacy and Politics*, Cambridge, Mass.: Harvard University Press, 1967, pp. 33–43, 193, 408–13; Howard Jones, 'The *Caroline* Affair', *Historian*, 1976, vol. 38, pp. 485–502; Francis M. Carroll, *A Good and Wise Measure: The Search for the Canadian–American Boundary, 1783–1842*, Toronto: University of Toronto Press, 2001, passim; John O. Geiger, 'A Scholar Meets John Bull: Edward Everett as United States Minister to England, 1841–45', *New England Quarterly*, 1976, vol. 49, pp. 582–86; George J. Gill, 'Edward Everett and the North-eastern Boundary Controversy', *New England Quarterly*, 1969, vol. 42, pp. 201–13; Wilbur Devereux Jones, *The American Problem in British Diplomacy, 1841–1861*, London: Macmillan, 1974, pp. 38–46; M. M. Quaife (ed.) *The Diary of James K. Polk during His Presidency, 1845–1849, Now First Printed from the Original Manuscript in the Collections of the Chicago Historical Society*, Chicago: A.C. McClurg, 1910, I, p. 241; John Seigenthaler, *James K. Polk*, New York: Henry Holt, 2003, pp. 122–28; Kinley Brauer, 'The United States and British Imperial Expansion, 1815–60', *Diplomatic History*, 1988, vol. 12, pp. 31–32;

Rush to Adams, 4 Feb. 1818, No. 6 and 14 Feb. 1818, No. 7, both M30/18, Despatches from Ministers to Great Britain, 1791–1906, Record Group 59 (State Department Papers), US National Archives, Washington, D.C., Microfilm Series 30, Roll 18 (hereafter cited as, e.g., M30/18); Rush to Adams, 25 July 1818, No. 30 and Gallatin and Rush to Adams, 20 Oct. 1818, both M30/19; Everett to Webster, 21 Feb. 1842, No. 5, enclosing Everett to Aberdeen, 21 Feb. 18 1842, M30/45; Everett to Buchanan, 16 April 1845, No. 302, and 3 March 1845, both M30/51; McLane to Buchanan, 3 Feb. 1845, No. 34, 3 Feb. 1845, No. 35, 18 May 1846, No. 44, and 3 July 1846, No. 58, all M30/52; Aaron L. Friedberg, *The Weary Titan: Britain and the Experience of Relative Decline, 1895–1905*, Princeton: Princeton University Press, 1988, pp. 196–99; Allan Nevins, *Henry White: Thirty Years of American Diplomacy*, New York: Harper & Brothers, 1930, p. 146; Kenton J. Clymer, *John Hay: The Gentleman as Diplomat*, Ann Arbor: University of Michigan Press, 1975, p. 176; David G. Haglund and Tudor Onea, 'Victory Without Triumph? Theodore Roosevelt, Honour, and the Alaska Panhandle Boundary Dispute', *Diplomacy and Statecraft*, 2008, vol. 19, pp. 20–41; Bradford Perkins, *The Great Rapprochement: England and the United States, 1895–1914*, London: Gollancz, 1969, pp. 161–72. Burk, *Old World, New World*, pp. 191, 257–60, 263–68 and 422–24.

9 John Stuart Mill, *Autobiography*, London: Longmans, Green, Reader, and Dyer, 1873, p. 270; Lord Stanley to Lady Stanley, 6 December 1861, in Nancy Mitford (ed.) *The Stanleys of Alderley: Their Letters Between the Years 1851–1865*, London: Hamish Hamilton, 1968, p. 272; Bourne, *Balance of Power*, pp. 219–28, 245–51; Adams to Seward, 12 December 1861, No. 88, 3 December 1861, No. 82, and 6 December 1861, No. 84, all M30/74; Palmerston to the Queen, 5 December 1861, quoted in James Chambers, *Palmerston: 'The Peoples' Darling'*, London: John Murray, 2005, pp. 487–92; Perkins, *Republican Empire*, pp. 225–27; Adams to Seward, 10 October 1862, No. 237 and 17 October 1862, No. 243, both M30/76; Martin B. Duberman, *Charles Francis Adams 1807–1886*, Boston: Houghton Mifflin, 1961, pp. 293–94; James D. Bulloch, *The Secret Service of the Confederate States in Europe or, How the Confederate Cruisers Were Equipped*, New York: Random House, 2001, 1st pub. 1884, pp. 162–79; Mowat, *Diplomatic Relations*, pp. 186–89, 206–9, 216–20; Lord Tenterden, 'Relations with the United States', 21 November 1870, FO 5/1331, Foreign Office Papers, UK National Archive, Kew, London (hereafter cited as FO); John Morley, *The Life of William Ewart Gladstone*, 3 vols, London: Macmillan, 1903, I, p. 401; Walter LaFeber, *The Cambridge History of American Foreign Relations, Volume II: The American Search for Opportunity, 1865–1913*, Cambridge: Cambridge University Press, 1993, p. 61.

10 J. Hector St John de Crèvecoeur, *Letters from an American Farmer*, Harmondsworth: Penguin, 1997, pp. 43–44.

11 C. Vann Woodward, *The Old World's New World*, New York: Oxford University Press, 1991, p. xvi. For an overview, see Burk, *Old World, New World*, Chapter 4.

12 Harriet Martineau, *Society in America*, 2 vols, 4th edn., New York: Saunders and Otley, 1877, I, p. 156.

13 Frances Trollope, *Domestic Manners of the Americans*, 5th edn., London: Richard Bentley, 1839, 1st pub. 1832, p. 295.

14 Ibid., Preface to the 4th edn., n.p., pp. 12, 14, 94, 61, 84, 157, 117, 166, 194.

15 Ibid., p. 336.

16 Philip Collins, 'Charles Dickens 1812–70', in Marc Pachter and Frances Wein (eds) *Abroad in America: Visitors to the New Nation 1776–1914*, Reading, Mass.: Addison-Wesley for the National Portrait Gallery, 1976, p. 84.

17 Dickens to John Forster, 13 Sept. 1841, in Benjamin Lease, *Anglo-American Encounters: England and the Rise of American Literature*, Cambridge: Cambridge University Press, 1981, p. 88.

18 Charles Dickens, *Martin Chuzzlewit and American Notes*, 2 vols, Boston: Houghton Mifflin, 1894, I [*Martin Chuzzlewit*], pp. 463–64.

19 Ibid., II [*American Notes*], p. 598.

20 Matthew Arnold, *Civilization in the United States: First and Last Impressions of America*, Boston: Cupples and Hurd, 1888, p. 190.

21 Harriet Beecher Stowe, *Sunny Memories of Foreign Lands*, 2 vols, Boston: Phillips, Sampson, 1854, I, pp. 14, 18.

22 Lease, *Anglo-American Encounters*, pp. 255–57.

23 Mark Twain, *A Yankee at the Court of King Arthur*, London: Chatto & Windus, 1890, p. 77.

24 Ralph Waldo Emerson, *English Traits*, Boston: Phillips, Sampson, 1856, pp. 41–42.

25 Ibid., pp. 274–75.

26 William Reitzel, 'The Purchasing of English Books in Philadelphia, 1790–1800', *Modern Philology*, 1937, vol. 35, p. 159.

27 Sydney Smith, review of Adam Seybert, *Statistical Annals of the United States of America*, *Edinburgh Review*, January 1820, vol. 33, pp. 79–80; Burk, *Old World, New World*, pp. 353–55.

28 James Fenimore Cooper, *Notions of the Americans: Picked Up by a Travelling Bachelor*, 2 vols, Philadelphia: Carey, Lea & Carey, 1833, II, pp. 106–7; Philip V. Allingham, 'Dickens' 1842 Reading Tour: Launching the Copyright Question in Tempestuous Seas', <http://www.victorianweb.org/authors/dickens/pva/pva75.html> (accessed 19 January 2008); Alexis de Tocqueville, *Democracy in America*, trans. and ed. by Harvey C. Mansfield and Delba Winthrop, Chicago: University of Chicago Press, 2000, II, part 1, Chapter 13, p. 446.

29 De Tocqueville, *Democracy in America*, II, part 1, Chapter 21, p. 446.

30 Lease, *Anglo-American Encounters*, pp. 144, 237, 199, 255; Burk, *Old World, New World*, pp. 356–58.

31 Stephen Spender, *Love–Hate Relations: A Study of Anglo-American Sensibilities*, London: Hamish Hamilton, 1974, p. 146; Burk, *Old World, New World*, pp. 364–68.

32 Perkins, *The Great Rapprochement*, p. 137.

33 A. J. P. Taylor, *The Struggle for Mastery in Europe, 1848–1918*, Oxford: Oxford University Press, 1954, preface p. xxx , Table IX; US Bureau of the Budget, *Historical Abstracts of the United States: Colonial Times to 1957*, Washington: US Government Printing Office, 1960, p. 418. In 1871, US steel production was 73, 214 long tons, Ibid., p. 417.

34 W.E. Adams, *Our American Cousins: Being Personal Impressions of the People and Institutions of the United States*, London: Walter Scott, 1883, p. iv.

35 Anthony Trollope, *North America*, 2 vols, London: Chapman & Hall, 1862, II, p. 462.

36 Arnold, *Civilization in the United States*, p. 71.

37 From 'The Adventures of the Noble Bachelor', first published in *Strand* magazine in 1892, in Sir Arthur Conan Doyle, *Sherlock Holmes: His Adventures, Memoirs, Return, His Last Bow and The Casebook: The Complete Short Stories*, London: John Murray, 1928, p. 246.

38 W. T. Stead, *The Americanisation of the World, On the Trend of the Twentieth Century: The Review of Reviews Annual*, New York: Horace Markley, 1902, p. 14.

39 Olney to Bayard, 20 July 1995, No. 222, fols 305–6, M77/90.

40 Salisbury to Pauncefote, 26 Nov. 1895, No. 15, *Parliamentary Papers* [Blue Book], Cmmd Paper United States, No. 1, 'Correspondence Respecting the Question of the Boundary of British Guinea', February 1896.

41 J. F. Watts and Fred L. Israel (eds) *Presidential Documents: The Speeches, Proclamations, and Policies that Have Shaped a Nation from Washington to Clinton*, London: Routledge, 2000, pp. 181–84; Zara S. Steiner, *The Foreign Office and Foreign Policy, 1898–1914*, Cambridge: Cambridge University Press, 1969, p. 24; Burk, *Old World, New World*, pp. 403–9.

42 Burk, *Old World, New World*, pp. 411–36.

43 Kathleen Burk, *Britain, America and the Sinews of War 1914–1918*, London: George Allen & Unwin, 1985, passim.

44 'Since the war [the British people] have been carrying a burden of indebtedness amounting to approximately £8,000,000 (40,000,000 dollars) or £178 (850 dollars) per head of their population, about one fifth of which represents war loans made to allied governments'. R. C. Lindsay, British ambassador to the United States, to Cordell Hull, 4 June 1934, and passed on to Roosevelt, File War Debts, Box 190, p. 4, President's Secretary's Files, Franklin D. Roosevelt Papers, Franklin D. Roosevelt Presidential Library, Hyde Park, New York.

45 Britain paid 3.3 per cent, France 1.6 per cent and Italy 0.4 per cent. Burk, *Old World, New World*, pp. 462.

46 Kathleen Burk, 'Money and Power: The Shift from Great Britain to the United States', in Youssef Cassis (ed.) *Finance and Financiers in European History, 1880–1960*, Cambridge: Cambridge University Press, 1992, pp. 363–64; Paul Einzig, *The Fight for Financial Supremacy*, London: Macmillan, 1931, p. 52; Kathleen Burk, 'The House of Morgan in Financial Diplomacy', in B. J. C. McKercher (ed.) *Anglo-American Relations in the 1920s: The Struggle for Supremacy*, London: Macmillan, 1991, pp. 125–57.

47 Phillips Payson O'Brien, *British and American Naval Power: Politics and Policy, 1900–1936*, Westport, Conn.: Praeger, 1998, p. 5.

48 Long to Lloyd George, 16 February 1919, F/33/2, David Lloyd George Papers, House of Lords Record Office, London. In 1917, the Admiralty estimated that the United States spent $240 million (about £11,420,000) on new construction alone, an amount greater than the total Royal Navy budget. O'Brien, *British and American Naval Power*, p. 152.

49 Paul Kennedy, *The Rise and Fall of British Naval Mastery*, London: Macmillan, 1983, p. 263; John R. Ferris, 'The Symbol and Substance of Seapower: Great Britain, the United States, and the One-Power Standard, 1919–21', in McKercher (ed.) *Anglo-American Relations in the 1920s*, pp. 56–72; Stephen Roskill, *Naval Policy Between the Wars, Volume I: The Period of Anglo-American Antagonism 1919–1929*, New York: Walker, 1968, pp. 225–26, 302, 310–28, 498–502; O'Brien, *British and American Naval Power*, 166–99; Akira Iriye, *The Cambridge History of American Foreign Relations: The Globalizing of America, 1913–1945*, Cambridge: Cambridge University Press, 1993, p. 82; B. J. C. McKercher, '"The Deep and Latent Distrust": The British Official Mind and the United States, 1919–29', in McKercher (ed.) *Anglo-American Relations in the 1920s*, p. 223; B. J. C. McKercher, *The Second Baldwin Government and the United States, 1924–1929: Attitudes and Diplomacy*, Cambridge: Cambridge University Press, 1984, pp. 65–71; Winston Churchill, 'Reduction and Limitation of Armaments: The Naval Conference', 29 June 1927, CAB 24/187, fols. 189–90, Cabinet Papers, UK National Archive, Kew, London (hereafter cited as CAB); Diary, June–August 1927, in Philip Williamson (ed.) *The Modernisation of Conservative Politics: The Diaries and Letters of William Bridgeman, 1904–1936* [First Lord of the Admiralty], London: The Historians' Press, 1988; Burk, *Old World, New World*, pp. 464–73.

50 'Outstanding Problems Affecting Anglo-American Relations', 12 November 1928, FO 371/12812.

51 O'Brien, *British and American Naval Power*, pp. 210–15.

52 Thomas Jones, *A Diary With Letters 1931–1950*, London: Oxford University Press, 1954, p. 30.

53 Minute on Sir J. Pratt, 'The Shanghai Situation', 1 February 1932, Rohan Butler, in Douglas Dakin and M. E. Lambert (eds) *Documents on British Foreign Policy 1919–1939*, 2nd Series, vol. 9, no. 238, p. 282.

54 B. J. C. McKercher, *Transition of Power: Britain's Loss of Global Pre-eminence to the United States 1930–1945*, Cambridge: Cambridge University Press, 1999, p. 248.

55 Kathleen Burk, 'The Lineaments of Foreign Policy: The United States and a "New World Order", 1919–39', *Journal of American Studies*, 1992, vol. 26, p. 380.

56 Winston Churchill, *News of the World*, 22 May 1938. Churchill is attributing this to Bismarck, not quoting him.

57 Mark A. Stoler, *Allies in War: Britain and America against the Axis Powers 1940–1945*, London: Hodder Arnold, 2005, pp. 140–42; David Dilks (ed.), *The Diaries of Sir Alexander Cadogan O.M., 1938–1945*, New York, G.P. Putnam's Sons, 1972, p. 582.

58 John Baylis, *Anglo-American Defence Relations 1939–1984*, 2nd edn., London: Macmillan, 1984, Document 2.2, pp. 42–43.

59 Burk, *Old World, New World*, Chapter 8.

60 Sir Richard Clarke, 'Policy in Europe', in Alec Cairncross (ed.), *Anglo-American Economic Collaboration in War and Peace 1942–1949*, Oxford: Oxford University Press, 1982, pp. 175–86. Those attending were Sir Edward Bridges, Permanent Secretary to the Treasury; Sir Henry Wilson-Smith, Head of the Overseas Finance Division of the Treasury; F. G. Lee (later Sir Frank Lee, Permanent Secretary to the Treasury); D. H. F. Rickett (later Sir Denis Rickett, Second Permanent Secretary to the Treasury); R. W. B. Clarke (later Sir Richard 'Otto' Clarke, Second Permanent Secretary to the Treasury); Roger Makins, Deputy Under Secretary at the Foreign Office (later British Ambassador to the United States and Lord Sherfield); Sir Percivale Liesching, Under Secretary of State at the Dominions Office; Sir John Henry Woods, Permanent Secretary to the Board of Trade; and Sir Edwin (later Lord) Plowden, Chief Planning Officer of the British Government.

61 'Department of State Policy Statement: Great Britain', 11 June 1948, Department of State, *Foreign Relations of the United States* (hereafter *FRUS*), *1948, Volume III: Western Europe*, Washington, D.C.: US Government Printing Office, 1974, quotations on pp.1092 and 1091.

62 Kim Philby, *Silent War*, p. 117, quoted in Richard J. Aldrich, *The Hidden Hand: Britain, America and Cold War Secret Intelligence*, London: John Murray, 2001, p. 305.

63 Paper prepared for the Department of State, 19 April 1950, *FRUS, 1950, Volume III: Western Europe*, Washington, D.C.: US Government Printing Office, 1977, pp. 870–79.

64 Baylis, *Anglo-American Defence Relations*, Appendix 3, p. 136.

65 Hansard, *Parliamentary Debates, House of Commons*, 437 H.C. Deb. 1965.

66 Francis Williams, *Twilight of Empire: Memoirs of Prime Minister Clement Attlee, as Set Down by Francis Williams*, Westport, Conn.: Greenwood Press, 1978, p. 119.

67 Margaret Gowing, *Independence and Deterrence: Britain and Atomic Energy, Volume I: Policy Making*, London: UK Atomic Energy Authority and Macmillan, 1974, p. 174.

68 Acheson, a man with *Realpolitik* in his bones, later wrote: 'During the winter of 1945–46 I learned about a matter which was to disturb me for some years to come, for with knowledge came the belief that our Government, having made an agreement from which it had gained immeasurably, was not keeping its word and performing its obligations. Like all great issues it was not simple. Grave consequences might follow upon keeping our word, but the idea of not keeping it was repulsive to me. The analogy of a nation to a person is not sound in all matters of moral conduct; in this case, however, it seemed to me pretty close. Even in *Realpolitik* a reputation for probity carries its own pragmatic rewards'. Dean Acheson, *Present at the Creation: My Years in the State Department*, New York: W. W. Norton, 1969, p. 164; as for Eisenhower, he told Harold Macmillan in 1957 that the McMahon Act was 'one of the most deplorable incidents in American history, of which he personally felt ashamed'. Harold Macmillan, *Riding the Storm 1956–1959*, New York: Harper & Row, 1971, p. 324.

69 Confidential Annex, Minute 1, Research in Atomic Weapons, GEN. 163/1st meeting, CAB 130/16. Bevin's comment is on p. 1.

70 Ian Clark and Nicholas J. Wheeler, *The British Origins of Nuclear Strategy, 1945–1955*, Oxford: Oxford University Press, 1989, p. 214.

71 Christopher Andrew, *Secret Service: The Making of the British Intelligence Community*, London: Heinemann, 1985, passim; Christopher Andrew, *For the President's Eyes Only: Secret Intelligence and the American Presidency from Washington to Bush*, London: HarperCollins, 1995, pp. 34–47, 78; James Thurber, 'Exhibit X', *Alarms and Diversions*, New York: Harper & Brothers, [1957], pp. 117–22; Arthur S. Link, *Wilson: Campaigns for Progressivism and Peace, 1916–1917*, Princeton: Princeton University Press, 1965, pp. 354–57; Jim Beach, 'Origins of the Special Intelligence Relationship? Anglo-American Intelligence Co-operation on the Western Front, 1917–18', *Intelligence and National Security*, 2007, vol. 22, pp. 229–49; Burk, *Old World, New World*, pp. 449–54.

72 Robert G. Angevine, 'Gentlemen Do Read Each Other's Mail: American Intelligence in the Interwar Era', *Intelligence and National Security*, 1992, vol. 7, pp. 1–29.

73 Christopher Andrew, 'Anglo–American–Soviet Intelligence Relations', in Ann Lane and Howard Temperley (eds) *The Rise and Fall of the Grand Alliance, 1941–45*, London: Macmillan, 1995, passim; John Chapman, 'Signals Intelligence Warfare', I. C. B. Dear (ed.) *The Oxford Companion to the Second World War*, Oxford: Oxford University Press, 1995, p. 1005; Jeffrey T. Richelson and Desmond Ball, *The Ties That Bind*, 2nd edn., Boston: Unwin Hyman, 1990, pp. 4–7.

74 See Aldrich, *The Hidden Hand*; Burk, *Old World, New World*, pp. 594–95.

75 Caccia to Lloyd, 'The Present State of Anglo–United States Relations', 28 December 1956, pp. 4–5, PREM 11/2189, Prime Ministers' Papers, The National Archive, Kew.

76 Jonathan Colman, *A 'Special Relationship?': Harold Wilson, Lyndon B. Johnson and Anglo-American Relations 'at the Summit'*, Manchester: Manchester University Press, 2004, p. 114; Jeffrey Pickering, *Britain's Withdrawal from East of Suez: The Politics of Retrenchment*, London: Macmillan, 1998, pp. 168–86; John Freeman, 'United States Review for 1970. Mr Freeman's Farewell Despatch', 8 January 1971, FCO 42/82, Foreign and Commonwealth Office Papers, the UK National Archive, Kew, London (hereafter cited as FCO); Cromer to Douglas Home, 'The Middle East War and US/UK Relations', 9 January 1974, FCO 82/304; Kathleen Burk and Alex Cairncross, *'Good-bye Great Britain': The 1976 IMF Crisis*, London: Yale University Press, 1992, passim; Burk, *Old World, New World*, pp. 615–30.

77 Louise Richardson, *When Allies Differ: Anglo-American Relations During the Suez and Falklands Crises*, New York: St Martin's Press, 1996, pp. 113–39, 202; Sir Henry Leach, in 1982 the First Sea Lord and Chief of Naval Staff, 'The Falklands War', 5 June 2002, Centre for Contemporary British History seminar, <http://www.icbh. ac.uk/witness/falklands/> (accessed 19 January 2008); Admiral Harry D. Train, in 1982 the US Commander in Chief, Atlantic Command, 'Falklands Roundtable', Presidential Oral History Program, Miller Center of Public Affairs, University of Virginia, 15–16 May 2003, <http://millercenter.virginia.edu/index.php/academic/ oral-history/projects/special/falklands> (accessed 19 January 2008); Sir Lawrence Freedman, *The Official History of the Falklands Campaign, Volume I: The Origins of the Falklands War*, London: Routledge, 2005, pp. 172–90; Dr Jeane Kirkpatrick, 'Falklands Roundtable'; Nicholas Henderson, *Mandarin: The Diaries of an Ambassador 1969–1982*, London: Weidenfeld and Nicolson, 1994, pp. 448–53; Michael Charlton, *The Little Platoon: Diplomacy and the Falklands Dispute*, Oxford: Basil Blackwell, 1989, pp. 168, 176; Alexander Haig, *Caveat: Realism, Reagan, and Foreign Policy*, London: Weidenfeld & Nicolson, 1984, p. 266; D. George Boyce, *The Falklands War*, London: Palgrave, 2005, p. 57; General Paul Gorman, in 1982 assistant to the Chair, Joint Chiefs of Staff, and David Gompert, deputy to the Under

Secretary for Political Affairs and part of Secretary Haig's mediation team, both 'Falklands Roundtable'; Nicholas Henderson, *Channels and Tunnels: Reflections on Britain and Abroad*, London: Weidenfeld & Nicolson, 1987, p. 107; Caspar Weinberger, *Fighting for Peace: Seven Critical Years in the Pentagon*, New York: Warner Books, 1990, p. 205; Duncan Anderson, *The Falklands War 1982*, Oxford: Osprey, 2002, pp. 43, 92; Freedman, *The Official History of the Falklands Campaign, Volume II: War and Diplomacy*, pp. 516–17; Henry Brandon, *Special Relationships: A Foreign Correspondent's Memoirs from Roosevelt to Reagan*, London: Macmillan, 1988, p. 392; George P. Shultz, *Turmoil and Triumph: My Years as Secretary of State*, New York: Charles Scribner's Sons, 1993, p. 152; John Nott, *Here Today, Gone Tomorrow: Recollections of an Errant Politician*, London: Politico's, 2002, pp. 242–43; Robin Renwick, *Fighting with Allies: America and Britain in Peace and War*, Houndmills: Macmillan, 1996, pp. 258–70; Lawrence Freedman and Efraim Karsh, *The Gulf Conflict 1990–1991: Diplomacy and War in the New World Order*, London: Faber and Faber, 1994, pp. 42–47, 346–47, 409, Table 16; Margaret Thatcher, *The Downing Street Years*, London: HarperCollins, 1993, pp. 817–24; John Dumbrell, *A Special Relationship: Anglo-American Relations from the Cold War to Iraq*, 2nd edn., London: Palgrave, 2006, pp. 206–7; James Baker, *The Politics of Diplomacy: Revolution, War and Peace 1989–1992*, New York: G.P. Putnam's Sons, 1995, pp. 278–79; Peter de la Billière, *Storm Command*, London: HarperCollins, 1992, pp. 26, 39–40, 123–24, 304–5; Norman Schwarzkopf, *It Doesn't Take a Hero*, London: Bantam Press, 1993, p. 478; Burk, *Old World, New World*, pp. 630–43.

78 Burk, *Old World, New World*, pp. 656–58, 609–15.

3 Hating Bush, supporting Washington
George W. Bush, anti-Americanism and the US–UK special relationship

John Dumbrell

That the United Kingdom was a close and supportive ally of the United States in the various incarnations of the Global War on Terror during the presidency of George W. Bush is scarcely a matter of dispute. When President Bush visited London in June 2008, Prime Minister Gordon Brown spoke of 'the special partnership' between the United States and the United Kingdom, 'a partnership not just of governments but of peoples . . . driven forward not simply by mutual interests, but by our shared values'. Bush responded: 'First thing about Gordon Brown, he's tough on terror, and I appreciate it'.[1] The 2008 visit, though it generated some street protest, stood in fairly vivid contrast to Bush's state visit of November, 2003, when shops ran out of rubber Bush masks, and the idea of a presidential speech to parliament was rejected in face of the likelihood of a protest by MPs.[2]

Especially between the middle of 2002 and the early part of his second term, President Bush was the object of an extraordinary degree of derision, extending into blind hatred, among important sections of the population of the United Kingdom. Rather than a 'partnership not just of governments but of peoples', the US–UK special relationship resembled rather a shotgun marriage, with much of the British population apparently forced into union with a country whose leader they hated and despised. Oona King, Labour MP and a supporter of the war in Iraq, declared that 'the fact that Bush could be in agreement with me on anything is enough to make me reach for a bucket to puke into'.[3] As late as May 2008, a YouGov poll for *The Daily Telegraph* reported 35 per cent of respondents as seeing the United States as a 'force for evil' in the world; a month later, *The Economist* described George W. Bush as 'a near universal figure of fun'.[4]

The purpose of this chapter is to investigate further the phenomenon of British Bush-hatred, situating it within the traditions and iconography of the special relationship. We begin with a brief exploration of elite attitudes, including some striking literary representations of, and contributions to, the febrile transatlantic politics associated with Bush's War on Terror, and especially with the Iraq invasion of 2003.

Literary Bush-haters

In what has become almost a set text of the British liberal intelligentsia's response to the invasion of Iraq, English novelist Margaret Drabble wrote in 2003: 'My anti-Americanism has become almost uncontrollable . . . I now loathe the United States and what it has done to Iraq and the rest of the world . . . I detest Disneyfication, I detest Coca-Cola, I detest burgers, I detest sentimental and violent Hollywood movies that tell lies about history'.[5] Before commenting on Drabble's hate-list, let us note a few further related comments in the literature and literary thought of the period. In his Nobel Prize address of 2005, Harold Pinter mockingly composed a short television address for George Bush: 'I possess moral authority. You see this fist? This is my moral authority. And don't you forget it'.[6] Moving from self-advertising Bush-haters to writers who sought to express the 2002–5 mood in works of fiction, David Hare, in his 2004 play *Stuff Happens*, offered his audience the figure of the 'Brit in New York'. 'On September 11th, America changed. Yes, it got much stupider', proclaimed this character, 'the infantile psycho-babble of popular culture is grafted opportunistically onto America's politics. The language of childish entitlement becomes the lethal rhetoric of global wealth and privilege'.[7] Ian McEwan's 2005 novel *Saturday* was actually set on 15 February 2003, the day of the huge London protest march against the invasion of Iraq. Daisy Perowne tells her father that this is a war of imperial conquest: 'You know very well these extremists, the Neo-cons, have taken over America'.[8] The February 2003 London march also featured in a telephonic rant by an English character – Rachel, estranged wife of the Dutch narrator – in the 2008 novel *Netherland*, by Irish writer Joseph O'Neill. Rachel describes for the narrator's benefit how their infant son carried a 'NOT IN MY NAME' placard in the march. She verbally attacked an America that was in the hands of 'the fanatical evangelical Christian movement'. President 'Bush wants to attack Iraq as part of a right-wing plan to destroy international law and order as we know it and replace it with the global rule of American force'. Rachel vows to keep her son in London rather than return him to New York: 'You want him to grow up with an American perspective? You want him not to be able to point to Britain on a map?'[9]

It should be emphasized that, while Drabble and Pinter presented themselves as fairly unmediated Bush-haters, the fictional representations in the works by Hare, McEwan and O'Neill were just that: fictional representations of what are presented as fairly stock British attitudes of the time – attitudes with which the author may or may not have sympathy. McEwan's central character, Henry Perowne, appreciates the complexity of the debates surrounding the Iraq invasion. He knows that 'when a powerful imperium – Assyrian, Roman, American – makes war and claims just cause, history will not be impressed'; but he 'can't feel, as the marchers themselves probably can, that they can have an exclusive hold on moral discernment'.[10] David Hare's own sympathies were squarely anti-Bush, but *Stuff Happens* – the title, of course, derived from remarks made by Secretary of Defence Donald Rumsfeld about the post-invasion disorder in Baghdad – incorporated a wide range of pro- and anti-invasion viewpoints. O'Neill's narrator feels bewildered by all the talk of 'the menace of the neoconservative cabal'.[11] The various literary extracts do, however, present some important features of British thinking and feeling about the United States around the time of the Iraq invasion: the supposed link (clear in Drabble's anti-American 'confession') between American culture and American power; the perceived hypocrisy and childish assertiveness of President Bush as depicted by Pinter; the American 'stupidity' and fickle childishness proclaimed by Hare's character; the fear and hatred of American neoconservatives, referred to in both the McEwan and the O'Neill pieces; the role of Christian fundamentalism, the American power-fixation and ignorant parochialism discussed by Rachel in *Netherland*; and – especially in the Drabble article – the very nature and acknowledgement of anti-Americanism (including its relationship to anti-Bushism).

Taking these features one by one, the tendency to conceive American power in terms of its cultural products represents a kind of 'soft power' in reverse. America's ability to sell itself to the world in the form of its cultural production is frequently cited as an important offset and complement to 'hard' military, or even direct economic, power.[12] However, in Drabble's formulation, cultural products – from Coca-Cola to Hollywood films – simply provide more scope for an increasingly expansive hatred. These products are hated because they emanate from the land of Bush.

The parent–child theme, of course, has been central to Anglo-American interactions ever since the two nations parted company in 1776. D. H. Lawrence interpreted American literary culture in terms of a child's rebellion 'against the old parenthood of Europe'.[13] American rebellion was balanced by British resentment at the errant child who, over time, grows more powerful and richer than its parents. If Graham Greene's *The Quiet American*[14] offered a paradigmatic type of adolescent American earnestness, perceptions of George Bush evinced another Anglo-American paradigm: that of the spoiled child. Around the time of the Iraq invasion, President Bush was widely perceived less as the well-meaning adolescent, more as the wilful, childish hypocrite portrayed in Harold Pinter's address. An inherent tension emerged here between Bush the simpleton, who actually *believed* in the mutually supporting co-existence of American morality and American power, and Bush the hypocrite who talked morality and thought oil. The Bush-as-child theme has a strong resonance, not only in terms of the parent–child provenance of US–UK relations, but also in the widespread and genuine perception that the president thought and acted in childish ways. British journalist Matt Frei in 2008 referred to 'dozens of stories of the commander-in-chief's childishness': his habit of giving nicknames to his associates, his 'playing peek-a-boo with the media on his campaign jet', his embarrassing routine staged at the post-invasion White House correspondents' dinner: 'A giant screen showed him and the First Dog, Barney, looking for WMD under the desks and behind the sofas of the Oval Office. George Bush was addressing Barney: "Have ya found those darned weapons yet, Barney?"'.[15]

In October 2001, President Bush made a famous outburst against the 'vitriolic hatred' of the United States. Bush declared himself 'amazed that there is such misunderstanding of what our country is about, that people would hate us . . . like most Americans, I just can't believe it. Because I know how good we are'.[16] Considering these comments of Bush in the context of our discussion of British Bush-hatred, a few observations come to mind. Bush's remarks were linked directly to Islamic terrorism, and were not directed at European critics of the subsequent War on Terror. They have nevertheless frequently been cited as indic- ative of Bush's blinkered, petulant childishness. Bush's attitude towards liberal critiques of US foreign policy is probably better encapsulated in his comment to Tony Blair and Alastair Campbell regarding Downing Street's wars with the BBC: 'Hey, congratulations, you took on the bastards, and you did great'.[17] Bush's October 2001 comments were primarily aimed at the 9/11 bombers. They might, however, have been equally directed to the school of British commentary exemplified by Mary Beard in the *London Review of Books*: 'However tactfully you dress it up, the United States had it coming. That is, of course, what many people openly or privately think'.[18] Leaving aside Beard's personal opinions, she was undoubtedly correct. Many people, including many prominent British intellectuals, indeed did think the United States had it coming (presumably, had it coming for its overweening self-satisfaction, its neglect of developmental and environmental issues, its sheer international power, its support for Israel – for what *exactly*, few Bush/America-haters would have found it easy to say). Bush's 'Why do they hate us?' outburst, in this context, was not unreasonable, even if it gave more ammunition to his enemies. It leads us back to the tension between Bush-as-child and Bush-as-cynic. George W. Bush clearly *does* believe in simple American verities in a way that Europeans find easy to interpret as childish and petulant. However, the assumption of the American cloak of innocence is a ploy as old as the republic itself. President John Adams eschewed the wicked ways of international diplomacy, denying 'any notion of cheating anybody'.[19] Woodrow Wilson stood in Adams's footsteps when he confronted European lead- ers at Versailles, as did President Clinton when he presented his straightforward 'parameters' for solving the complex problems of the Middle East at the Camp David summit in 2000. Bush's outburst about American innocence both exempli- fied and drew on this venerable tradition.

The fear of neoconservatism, exemplified in Daisy Perowne's outburst, perme- ated British popular and literary discussion of the post-2001 foreign policy. It frequently proceeded with no coherent understanding of the nature of American neoconservatism, beyond a vague notion that neocons wished to create a new American empire as a way of safeguarding the security of Israel. As in the telephonic debate in O'Neill's novel, this interpretation of the neocons was often yoked to the view that Bush's policies were simultaneously the product of Christian evangelical thinking and influence: that the old looking glass world of communism *versus* liberal capitalism had been replaced by (a similarly morally equivalent) world of competing fundamentalisms, Christian and Islamic. The parochialism and naive 'stupidity' ascribed to Bush also had echoes in the

Anglo-American traditions of parent and child, cosmopolitan and backwoods-man. As in the earlier identified tension between Bush the naive moralist and Bush the oil-obsessed Machiavel, hostile commentary found it difficult to acknowledge that Bush was actually capable of devising his own world-domination plan. Daisy Perowne's solution was to portray him as the inert dupe of the shadowy and malevolent neocons. Andrew O'Hagan, Scottish novelist and author of trenchant essays on transatlantic relations, went so far as to cast Tony Blair in this role. Often criticized for lending the inarticulate Bush the cover of his own rhetorical and imaginative skill, Blair was attacked by O'Hagan in 2008 for actually pushing America forward: 'Blair's version of brotherhood cost America dearly. He can say what he likes, and so can those soulless people who stood silent to save their jobs, but Britain was the bad brother that goaded its sibling into psychosis'.[20]

Beside the parent/child trope, we can easily discern in these various depictions of Bush the shadows of Athens and Rome. Let us remind ourselves of Harold Macmillan's formulation of the Anglo-American 'Greeks and Romans' doctrine. Macmillan told the young Richard Crossman in 1943 that the British must act to the new American imperialists 'as the Greek slaves ran the operations of the Emperor Claudius'.[21] In his diary, Macmillan wrote of the need to 'guide' Washington away from the extremes of 'isolation' and 'a pathetic desire to solve in few months by the most childish and amateurish means problems that have baffled statesmen for many centuries'.[22] Greeks, it might be recalled, were often regarded by Roman commentators as superior, sly and inherently parasitic: equivalents, in other words, to Peter Fallow, the archetypal sponging Englishman from Tom Wolfe's novel, *The Bonfire of the Vanities*.[23] John Bolton, Bush's former ambassador to the United Nations, fumed in his memoirs: 'Many Brits believed that their role in life was to play Athens to America's Rome, lending us the benefit of their superior suaveness, and smoothing off our regrettable colonial rough edges'. He recalled a 2006 speech by Mark Malloch Brown (then chief of staff to UN Secretary General Kofi Annan and later appointed by Gordon Brown as minister for Africa, Asia and the UN) in the following terms: 'He essentially criticized not just the Bush administration, but the American people for getting their news only from Fox (News) and Rush Limbaugh, which was a typically elitist, left-wing view of the slobs in "flyover country"'.[24] According to the account given in the Alastair Campbell diaries, the Labour Cabinet in 2002–3 actually did see itself as in the business of trying to smooth out Washington's rough edges. A cabinet meeting of 23 September 2002 apparently focused – in true Macmillan style – 'on the idea that we were having to deal with a mad America and (Tony Blair) keeping them on the straight and narrow'.[25] It is a measure of the intensity of feeling and debate during this period, that Andrew O'Hagan was actually prepared to go further – effectively accusing Blair of positively roughing up Bush's regrettable colonial edges!

Clearly, some of George W. Bush's personal characteristics *did* play rather easily into familiar Anglo-American tropes such as parent and child, and Athens/Rome. After all, as Daisy Perowne might argue, President Bush wore his Yale education rather lightly. He was a mangler of the English language. Many 'Bushisms' – the economic pie getting higher, the president losing no sleep in thinking up ways to damage America – are genuine, just as many are apocryphal. Some jokes about America's 43rd president both rang true and were genuinely amusing. Here is a fictional President Bush excoriating French culture: 'They don't even have a word for entrepreneur'.[26] We may also point to Bush's personal impatience, another characteristic imputed by Macmillan to the *arriviste* American imperialists. Matt Frei describes the president arriving for an interview: 'This is clearly a man in a hurry who would look more comfortable if he was about to receive root-canal surgery'.[27] Accounts of Bush's personal like-ability, relaxed humour, graciousness to staff and so on, are often very credible, but sometimes take on the aspect (as in the words of Cherie Blair) of someone deliberately setting out to defend the indefensible.[28]

Let us consider a little further the imagined case of a Daisy Perowne: that President Bush really *was* as stupid, naive, graceless and so on, as he appeared to many in the United Kingdom. One riposte to such an assertion is that it is itself little more than naive essentialism. For one thing, the imagined Daisy Perowne outburst ignores the modish, primarily youthful, in-group character of much British anti-Bushism. The daughter of McEwan's protagonist in *Saturday* herself asked: 'Why is it that the few people I've met who aren't against this crappy war are all over forty?'[29] Chris Martin, singer with the rock group Coldplay, used the occasion of the Brit music awards in February 2003 to announce that 'we are all going to die when George Bush has his way'.[30] A second point is that Bush actually is very well educated, at least if we believe that formal qualifica-tions mean anything. He was actually the first US president to have a Master's degree in Business Administration – arguably a fine accreditation for a national chief executive. He was certainly capable of making some fine public addresses, as in post-9/11 speeches to the US Congress. By the same token, he was also capable of making some acutely embarrassing and ill-conceived ones – most memorably what Martin Amis calls his 'mortifying appearance in the flight suit on the aircraft carrier *USS Abraham Lincoln*' to announce 'mission accom-plished' in Iraq; in Amis's words, 'every dash and comma in his body language betrayed the unscrupulous confidence of the power surge'.[31] Recognition of some weaknesses and inconsistencies in the simple 'Bush is stupid' slogan, however, simply re-opens for confirmed Bush-haters the familiar tension between Bush as simpleton and Bush as Machiavel. George Bush in a sense *is* what his haters see: a Texan oilman, a pro-business conservative, a failed baseball manager, an evan-gelical Christian with profound family-related hang-ups, a reformed alcoholic. However, 'a slob from "flyover country"', he surely is not. He is the grandson of liberal Republican Connecticut senator Prescott Bush, the son of a presiden-tial father (who was also an enemy of the English language but had a pragmatic foreign policy), and the possessor of an elite Yale/Skull and Bones background. Perhaps it was the younger Bush's unique achievement to be hated both for being a 'slob from "flyover country"' *and* for being a privileged, educated (and inevitably hypocritical) elitist.

Before we leave the imagined objections of a Daisy Perowne to any line of argument that might possibly be construed as mildly pro-Bush, let us consider the interplay between personality, policy and the Iraq invasion. In retrospect, the invasion of Iraq appears reckless and arrogant. It was certainly very poorly prepared and woefully ill-conceived. It bore the impression of Bush's impetuosity, of Rumsfeld's failure to appreciate the limits of the Revolution in Military Affairs, and of neoconservative naivety about the prospects for democracy in Iraq.[32] It breached most reasonable interpretations of international law. It had its honourable opponents and its honourable defenders – on the left as well as on the right of the British political spectrum.[33] However, reasonable and principled opposition to the war was undermined and weakened by crass anti-Bushism. Moreover, some aspects of the Bush record did not really fit with the preconceptions of the Bush-haters. The Bush legislative record, essentially a contribution to big-government conservatism, embraced Medicare extension and the No Child Left Behind education reform, famously passed with the support of Senator Ted Kennedy. Liberal (pro-business) policies on immigration, support for increased aid to Africa, pragmatic multilateralism in Asia: these were also part of the repertoire of the toxic Texan. Aesthetically unpleasing though he may have been to many British left-liberals, George W. Bush was the democratically elected president of the United States. He had, after all, stolen the 2000 presidential election fair and square.

British anti-Americanism

European anti-Americanism, in general, has generated a significant body of literature. The philosophical roots of, especially, continental European anti-Americanism are complex and embrace the notion of the New World counter-colonizing the Old with its hyper-democratic materialist anti-intellectualism.[34] Anti-Americanism among European intellectuals is also frequently linked to status anxiety: to the fear of mass society and the loss of intellectual leadership.[35] Rob Kroes juxtaposes American and European sensibilities as follows: American spatial 'flatness' *versus* European hierarchy; American 'making it new' *versus* European reverence for tradition; American cultural fragmentation *versus* European holism.[36] Such intellectual, historical and cultural currents do feed into differing perceptions and, ultimately, into European anti-Americanism. What is central here is, of course, how we define 'anti-Americanism'. According to Barry and Joyce Rubin, anti-Americans are people whose 'antagonism to the United States is systemic, seeing it as completely and inevitably evil'.[37] Few even of the more extreme 2002–5 British Bush-haters would probably acknowledge such a description of their attitudes. Yet, the tendency to extrapolate from the perceived failings of the president – arrogance, ignorance, insensitivity – to the supposed failings of the American people as a whole would seem to meet a test of anti-Americanism even more persuasive than that offered by the Rubins: the denial of the ultimate and defining characteristic of the American population, its diversity.

Like the tag, 'isolationist', the accusation of anti-Americanism often is unfair and tends to be used to stifle and shout off debate, rather than to encourage it. Andrew O'Hagan sees himself as defending 'the America once imagined by Scott Fitzgerald' – 'idealistic, generous, open': 'Let the lazy snipers seize their opportunity and call those of us appalled by Dick Cheney and Donald Rumsfeld anti-American, for they know nothing of America that is worth defending'.[38] Margaret Drabble was, in fact, very unusual in accepting the 'anti-American' label. Her defence was that the very extremism of the Bush distortion of 'America' had pushed her over the brink. It is not the intention here to bandy around the 'anti-American' label as a way of censoring debate. Criticism of the Bush administration is certainly not intrinsically anti-American. Peter Kilfoyle, junior defence minister during the onset of the Iraq conflict, made a reasonable point to his former boss: 'No Mr Blair, it is not knee-jerk anti-Americanism which holds sway in the United Kingdom. It is the reaction of one old friend to another when the latter is acting wholly unreasonably and unacceptably'.[39] My point, rather, is that anti-Americanism, defined primarily in terms of denying American diversity, but also in terms of the Rubins's notion of ascribing necessary 'systemic evil' to the United States, does exist. That policy-specific (even person-specific) criticism can slide over into a foolish and counter-productive anti-Americanism was evident from the experience of British attitudes to the United States in the Bush years.

British anti-Americanism has at least three major variants: leftist (hostility to the United States as standard-bearer for globalizing capitalism); nationalist (resentment at the apparent infringement of British freedom of action supposedly inherent in US–UK 'special relations'); and cultural (the 'defence' of British/European elite culture against the perceived incursions of mass American consumerist, homogenized cultural production).[40] It should be emphasized that each variant has reasonable, policy-specific and detail-specific arguments associated with it; each, however, has the potential to descend into a generalized, American diversity-denying anti-Americanism. George W. Bush and his administration provided particularly fertile ground for each variety to flourish. Bill Clinton had been the 'globalization president' but had not celebrated the capitalist ethic of inequality with quite such gusto as his successor. During the transatlantic interchanges that preceded the invasion of Iraq, Blair seems to have been treated variously as a valued ally and as a sanctimonious nuisance.[41] The Bush-haters could indeed be forgiven for concluding that this was not a great time for British sovereignty and independence. As for culture: well . . . in Condoleezza Rice, first-term national security adviser and second-term secretary of state, the administration had a concert-level-trained classical pianist. It also had Donald Rumsfeld, whose (actually rather witty) response to a question about his opinion of a performance of modern dance and poetry, which he had witnessed while attending a NATO summit in Prague, was: 'I'm from Chicago'.[42]

Perusal of the set-piece House of Commons debate of 18 March 2003 on British involvement in the Iraq invasion reveals a common desire to avoid the 'anti-American' label. Conservative MP Douglas Hogg denied that he was 'indulging in anti-Americanism' by indicating Washington's apparent 'delight in stressing their disdain for international opinion and in asserting their right to determine not only the target but the means and timetable (for action on Iraq), their gratuitous actions apparently designed to make a common voice impossible, not least here in Europe'. Even supporters of the Blair line on the war were keen to disassociate themselves from the despised Bush. Thus, Labour MP Bruce George (Walsall, South) made clear that he was 'not standing for election for the Walsall chapter of his fan club'. Contumely was actually poured on France – for apparently threatening to veto any UN Security Council resolution on Iraq that was supported by the United States – as much as on America. Prime Minister Blair acknowledged 'resentment of US predominance' and 'fear of American unilateralism', but (implicitly) excoriated Paris for losing sight of an important rule of transatlantic relations: 'Partners are not servants, but neither are they rivals'. Labour member John McDonnell felt that France, 'the traditional enemy', rather than America, the real villain and progenitor of the 'international atrocity' of invasion, was being blamed unfairly: 'Any criticism of the Bush regime is pounced on as anti-American'. Tony Banks (London Labour MP) maintained that the real problem was that 'we in this country are now trapped between a bunch of right-wing religious bigots in the White House and Islamic terrorists in the Middle East'. Blair had been 'a restraining influence', but Bush 'desperately needs that war for his own domestic agenda'. Using 'that old Texan cowboy cliche', the British 'have been led into a box canyon'. Some members happily accepted the 'anti-American' tag. Ronnie Campbell (Labour, Blyth Valley) declared: 'Other Members have had a good bash at the French this evening, and I am going to have a go at the Americans'. This was a war about oil. The exasperation expressed by Welsh MP Chris Ruane reflected many other contributions to the debate: 'The UK, along with dozens of other nations, stood shoulder to shoulder with the US over Afghanistan and now Iraq', he declared, 'That loyalty has been rewarded by the Bush administration with the imposition of steel tariffs, the withdrawal from test ban treaties, the introduction of farm subsidies in America, and contempt for the International Criminal Court'. Bush 'rubbished and reneged on the Kyoto and Johannesburg treaties, and scuppered my hon. friend's [Tony Blair's] attempts to open dialogue with the Palestinians in January'.[43]

Much of this exasperation was justified. The administration's assumption of the right to take unilateral action – for example in Paul Wolfowitz's address to the Munich security conference in February 2002 – left the clear impression that NATO and the US–UK special relationship were expendable in the higher cause of protecting American security.[44] Such assertions were, at one level, simple statements of the realities of power in a unipolar order. They were, however, atrocious public diplomacy and a hindrance to Blair's efforts to win British elite and public opinion for the cause of supporting Washington. Chris Ruane's list of grievances, however, revealed a rather common attribution of excessive authority and autonomy to President Bush. Some of his complaints referred to actions inaugurated under the Clinton rather than the Bush presidency. The US Senate actually rejected the Comprehensive Test Ban Treaty in 1999. Bush supported

American nuclear testing, but acceptance or rejection of treaties is primarily a Senate matter. Trade policies, and certainly the award of farm subsidies, are areas where the Congress, not the White House, dominates. British exasperation at Washington's attitudes towards international cooperation, particularly in the first Bush term, was entirely reasonable. My point here, however, is that such exasperation often took the characteristic (and in this sense authentically 'anti-American') form of denying the fragmentary nature of the US system of separated power, while according Bush a degree of domestic authority to advance his villainy that he did not, in fact, possess.

By the end of the second Bush term, much of the bile of the period 2002–5 had disappeared. More Ozymandias than Tamburlaine, Bush in 2008 was a president with a 26 per cent approval rating, a Democratic Congress and an expressed regret that he was likely to be remembered as a warmonger. The 2008 election, beginning with the intense fight for the Democratic nomination, did much to remind Britain that the United States contained liberals as well as conservatives. A glance through some of the journalism and other writing from the pre-2006 period, however, will serve to remind us of the intensity of the earlier hatred and disdain for Bush's America. Gerald Kaufman, the senior Labour figure and Manchester MP, declared in 2002: 'Bush, himself the most intellectually backward American president of my political lifetime, is surrounded by advisers whose bellicosity is exceeded only by their political, military and diplomatic illiteracy'.[45] A leader in *The New Statesman* in November 2003 announced: 'Nobody should apologise for being anti-American; if you don't like what America does, wear the badge with pride'.[46] Even more alarming was a September 2003 *Guardian* piece by Michael Meacher, minister for the environment from 1997 to 2003, entitled 'This War on Terrorism is Bogus'. Meacher echoed conspiracy theories usually associated with Michael Moore, whose film *Fahrenheit 9/11* and books offered the 'true' interpretation of 9/11 and its links to the invasion. Meacher noted that 'the US authorities did little or nothing to pre-empt the events of 9/11'. He raised the possibility that US air security operations had been deliberately stood down on that day and asserted that no 'serious attempt has ever been made to catch Bin Laden'. The 9/11 incident offered 'an extremely convenient pretext to put' the neoconservative plan to invade Iraq in order to 'secure energy supplies' into action.[47]

Hating Bush, supporting Washington

To assert that British left-liberal-leaning elites around the time of the Iraq invasion despised the American president, and that such feelings frequently melded into a more general anti-Americanism is, in view of some of the opinions quoted above, hardly controversial. Yet, the British government *did* support Washington in the 2003 invasion. Blair was re-elected in 2005. How surprising is this? After all, novelists, playwrights and journalists do not make policy. In any case, there were counter-elites, standing apart from the Polly Toynbees or the Margaret Drabbles. Against the anti-Bush opinions cited earlier, it would be possible to quote the pro-war views of an Andrew Roberts or a Frederick Forsyth. The Conservative Party was prepared to support the Iraq invasion, though several Tory MPs took critical, anti-Bush positions in the 18 March House of Commons debate. Yet, this was a Labour government, and thus presumably not entirely oblivious to the views of left-leaning elites and opinion-formers, most of whom voted Labour and some of whom were even Labour MPs. Many critics of the American administration, however, were prepared to give Blair the benefit of the doubt. 'Only' a minority of Labour MPs, 139 in number, opposed Blair's position on the floor of the Commons in the 18 March vote. In November 2003, David Marquand announced the 'end of the (Anglo-American) affair' and berated Blair for his 'Iraq follies'. Yet, Marquand, a former right-leaning Labour MP and early convert to the Social Democratic Party in the early 1980s, acknowledged that Blair had 'argued his case with a fervour unequalled by any prime minister since Gladstone'. He also acknowledged the core of Blair's pro-American case 'that the cause of multilateral global governance would suffer more if the US acted alone than if it could be prevailed upon to lead a coalition, to which it would necessarily have to make concessions . . .'.[48] Such views certainly diluted the policy impact of the anti-Bush temper that we have been considering.

Hatred, suspicion and fear of America and its leader, however, was not – particularly in the crucial period beginning about a year following 9/11 – the exclusive preserve of any elite, liberal or otherwise. A poll in 2002 by the Pew organization revealed that less than half of British respondents held a favourable view of America, a significant drop from 2000.[49] In early 2004, 58 per cent of British respondents said that the Iraq invasion had damaged their faith in America's trustworthiness. Britain shared in the general international negativity towards Bush, metaphorically voting overwhelmingly for John Kerry in 2004, as for Barack Obama over John McCain in 2008. The public mood after 9/11 mixed sympathy for the dead with anxiety about the possibility of America hitting out indiscriminately, and dragging Britain into its wars of revenge. Salman Rushdie wrote about his conversations with Londoners in 2002: 'Night after night, I have found myself listening to Londoners' diatribes against the sheer weirdness of the American citizenry. The [9/11] attacks on America are routinely discounted ("Americans care only about their own dead")'.[50] A *Sunday Times* poll, published a month before the invasion, saw approximately equal numbers of respondents citing George W. Bush and Saddam Hussein as the 'greatest threat to world peace'.[51] The polling evidence relating to British public opinion also had implications for social cohesion. Polls in general tended to show women as particularly negatively disposed to US foreign policy. British Muslim opinion in particular was distinguished by consistent and intense anti-Americanism.[52]

The state of British public opinion at the start of the major commitment to war in Iraq was, at least on the surface, markedly non-bellicose and significantly anti-American. The leader of the country's major ally seems to have been viewed more or less on a par with the leader of the country being invaded. It may be possible to provide some historical parallels, but possible candidates (such as Suez or the Boer conflicts) are scarcely comparable. The Suez commitment was made (as was to some degree the case in the Falklands) in the face of

American opposition. The Korean War was fought in alliance with an American president (Harry Truman) who was the object of a degree of derision in Britain, though less than was the case with George W. Bush. Both Korea and the 1991 Gulf War, of course, were – unlike the 2003 Iraq invasion – fought under United Nations auspices. There were some parallels between the Clinton wars – the bombing of Iraq and Kosovo, and the 2003 invasion. In the case of Desert Fox, the air campaign against Iraq, the United Kingdom was, in effect, America's sole ally. However, neither in Desert Fox, nor (just) in Kosovo, were UK ground troops deployed in openly hostile conditions. The simple fact is that Tony Blair took the United Kingdom to war in 2003 against a rather extraordinary background of elite and mass opposition.

The phenomenon of Britain simultaneously hating Bush *and* continuing to act as America's closest ally prompts a number of observations and possible explanations. Firstly, the common view that British anti-Americanism is not as deeply seated as its continental West European equivalent is probably true. Pew Research Center findings in June 2007 revealed 30 per cent of Germans with a positive view of the United States, compared to 51 per cent in the United Kingdom. Of the French population, 60 per cent disliked America, as did a majority in Spain. Eastern European opinion was more positive, though even there hostility to the United States had increased since 2002.[53] The French reputation for anti-Americanism was somewhat dented by the famous *Le Monde* headline of 12 September 2001 that read 'Nous Sommes tous Americains'. However, the same newspaper was soon referring to 'le cretinisation' of US foreign policy.[54]

A second point relates to the structures and uniqueness of the US–UK special relationship. Though swathed in the kind of emotionalism embodied in Gordon Brown's June 2008 address (quoted at the beginning of this chapter), the special relationship has a tough and resilient centre. It is rooted in defence cooperation and intelligence sharing. The structures of defence and intelligence cooperation entered a period of crisis with the termination of the Cold War. They weakened somewhat in the 1990s, but failed to succumb to pressure for European defence and intelligence institutions to supplant transatlantic ones. The defence and intelligence relationship between London and Washington was revived as Tony Blair took it upon himself to act as a leading international diplomatist and apologist for the Bush administration's response to 9/11. The institutionalized special relationship did not make it impossible for Blair to oppose the invasion of Iraq. After all, Prime Minister Harold Wilson, in the mid-1960s, refused to send British troops to Vietnam, despite the strong defence and intelligence interlinkages which existed at that time. The institutionalized special relationship, however, inclined London to support Washington in 2003, and eased Blair's way in defying widespread elite and public dislike of President Bush.[55]

Lastly, it is difficult to avoid the conclusion that many in Britain very much enjoyed hating Bush. Condescension towards the leader of the United States became almost a force for national unity. The American president reinforced comforting stereotypes and invited Britain to come into its own, acting as a parent would act towards a wayward child: not cutting off support for the child, but rather educating the infant in the ways of moderation, civilized behaviour and decorum. The phenomenon of hating Bush while supporting America exemplified the paradoxes and contradictions of the Macmillan theory of Greeks and Romans. It rested, at least at one level, on an unrealistic analysis of Britain's importance to the United States. Far from embodying a healthy spirit of national independence, Bush-hatred partook of a strange sense that the American president is somehow also the president of the United Kingdom: a figure whose behaviour should somehow always be acceptable to, and cognisant of, prevailing British cultural preferences.

The British public response to the election of Barack Obama in November 2008 was almost as extraordinary as the phenomenon of Bush-hatred itself. A Populus poll for the *Times* reported an increase of 22 per cent, compared to June 2006, in the proportion of respondents believing it 'is important for Britain's long-term security that we have a close and special relationship with the US' (80 per cent in November 2008, compared to 58 per cent in June 2006). In June 2006, 62 per cent wanted the next prime minister to be 'less close to George Bush than Tony Blair' had been. In November 2008, 61 per cent wanted Gordon Brown to be 'as close to Barack Obama as Tony Blair was to George Bush'.[56] Britain shared much of the world's joy at Obama's election. The turnaround in opinion appeared to be based on a generally positive perception of the new US president and on relief at the imminent departure of his predecessor. The new mood ignored possible problems – such as Obama's ambivalent attitude towards protectionist pressures in the United States, and his commitment to securing further European engagement in Afghanistan – for the future of transatlantic relations. It seemed to confirm the view of the Bush-haters that the American president is not merely a national leader, but rather a kind of alternative British leader – to be judged by his ability to respond positively to *British* expectations and preferences. Such a perspective tells us much about British attitudes to the United States, but it does violence to the fundamentally asymmetrical structure of the special relationship.

Notes

1 'Remarks by President Bush and United Kingdom Prime Minister Brown in Joint Press Availability', 16 June 2008, <http://london.usembassy.gov/potus08/potus08_014.html> (accessed 20 June 2008).
2 James Naughtie, *The Accidental American: Tony Blair and the Presidency*, London: Macmillan, 2004, p. 101.
3 Michael Mosbacher and Digby Anderson, 'Recent trends in British Anti-Americanism', in Paul Hollander (ed.) *Understanding Anti-Americanism: Its Origins and Impact at Home and Abroad*, Chicago: Ivan Dee, 2004, pp. 84–104, 85.
4 'Americans Abroad: Not For Much Longer', *The Economist*, 28 June 2008, p. 42.
5 Margaret Drabble, 'I Loathe America and What It Has Done to the Rest of the World', *The Daily Telegraph*, 8 May 2003; Barry and Joyce C. Rubin, *Hating America: A History*, New York: Oxford University Press, 2004, p. 215; Nick Cohen, *What's Left? How Liberals Lost Their Way*, London: Fourth Estate, 2007, p. 263; Justin Webb, *Have a Nice Day*, London: Short Books, 2008, p. 9; Bronwen Maddox, *In Defence of America*, London: Duckworth, 2008, p. 19.

6   Nobel Lecture, 'Art, Truth and Politics', 7 December 2005, <http://nobelprize.org/nobel_prizes/literature/laureates/2005/pinter-lecture.html> (accessed 26 June 2008).

7   David Hare, *Stuff Happens*, London: Faber and Faber, 2004, p. 92–93.

8   Ian McEwan, *Saturday*, London: Jonathan Cape, 2005, p. 190.

9   Joseph O'Neill, *Netherland*, London: Fourth Estate, 2008, pp. 94–95.

10 McEwan, *Saturday*, p. 73.

11 O'Neill, *Netherland*, p. 96.

12 Joseph S. Nye, *Soft Power: The Means to Success in World Politics*, New York: Public Affairs, 2004.

13 D. H. Lawrence, *Studies in Classic American Literature*, London: Penguin, 1977, p. 4.

14 Graham Greene, *The Quiet American*, London: Penguin, 1977.

15 Matt Frei, *Only in America: Inside the Mind and Under the Skin of the Nation Everyone Loves to Hate*, London: Fourth Estate, 2008, p. 102.

16 Quoted in Stephen M. Walt, *Taming American Power: The Global Response to American Primacy*, New York: W. W. Norton, 2005, p. 62.

17 See Alastair Campbell and Richard Stott (eds) *The Blair Years: Extracts from the Campbell Diaries*, London: Hutchinson, 2007, p. 722 (17 July 2003).

18 Quoted in Robert McCrum, 'Up Pompeii with the Roguish Don', *The Observer*, August 24, 2008, p. 22.

19 C. F. Adams (ed.) *The Works of John Adams*, Boston: Little Brown, 1853, p. 178.

20 Andrew O'Hagan, *The Atlantic Ocean: Essays on Britain and America*, London: Faber and Faber, 2008, p. 4.

21 See Alex Danchev, 'On Specialness', *International Affairs*, 1996, vol. 72, pp. 737–51, 740.

22 Harold Macmillan, *War Diaries*, New York: St Martin's Press, 1984, p. 446.

23 See Tom Wolfe, *The Bonfire of the Vanities*, New York: Farrar, Straus, Giroux, 1987.

24 John Bolton, *Surrender Is Not an Option: Defending America at the United Nations and Abroad*, New York: Simon and Schuster, 2007, pp. 210, 281.

25 Campbell and Stott (eds) *The Blair Years*, p. 640.

26 Webb, *Have a Nice Day*, p. 12.

27 Frei, *Only in America*, p. 311.

28 Cherie Blair, *Speaking for Myself: The Autobiography*, Boston: Little, Brown, 2008, p. 313.

29 McEwan, *Saturday*, p. 121.

30 KR Washington Bureau, 'Bush's Image in Europe Takes Sharply Negative Turn', press release, 24 February 2003.

31 Martin Amis, *The Second Plane: September 11: 2001–2007*, London: Jonathan Cape, 2008, p. 82.

32 John Dumbrell, 'The Neo-conservative Roots of the War in Iraq', in James Pfiffner and Mark Phythian (eds) *Intelligence and National Security Policymaking on Iraq*, Manchester: Manchester University Press, 2008, pp. 19–39.

33 See Cohen, *What's Left;* Thomas Cushman (ed.) *A Matter of Principle*, Berkeley and London: University of California Press, 2005; Oliver Kamm, *Anti-Totalitarianism: The Left-Wing Case for a Neoconservative Foreign Policy*, London: The Social Affairs Unit, 2005; Douglas Murray, *Neoconservatism: Why We Need It*, London: The Social Affairs Unit, 2005.

34 James Ceaser, 'The Philosophical Origins of Anti-Americanism in Europe', in Paul Hollander (ed.) *Understanding Anti-Americanism: Its Origins at Home and Abroad*, Chicago: Ivan Dee, 2004, pp. 37–51.

35 See Richard Pells, *Not Like Us: How Europeans Have Loved, Hated and Transformed America*, New York: Basic Books, 1997.

36 Rob Kroes, 'Commentary: World Wars and Watersheds', *Diplomatic History*, 1999, vol. 23, pp. 71–77.

37 Rubin and Rubin, *Hating America*, p. ix.
38 O'Hagan, *The Atlantic Ocean*, p. 4.
39 Peter Kilfoyle, 'US and Them', *The Guardian*, 18 November 2003, p. 18.
40 John Dumbrell, *A Special Relationship: Anglo-American Relations from the Cold War to Iraq*, Basingstoke: Palgrave, 2006.
41 See Con Coughlin, *American Ally: Tony Blair and the War on Terror*, London: Politico's, 2006
42 Quoted in Ben Macintyre, 'When Rimbaud Meets Rambo', *The Times*, 4 June 2005, p. 16.
43 House of Commons Hansard Debates (online), 18–19 March 2003.
44 See Elizabeth Pond, 'The Dynamics of the Feud over Iraq', in D. M. Andrews (ed.) *The Atlantic Alliance under Stress: US–European Relations after Iraq*, Cambridge: Cambridge University Press, 2005, pp. 54–81.
45 William Shawcross, *Allies: The United States, Britain, Europe and the War in Iraq*, London: Atlantic Books, 2003, p. 48.
46 'Proud to be Anti-American?', *New Statesman*, 17 November 2003, pp. 6–7.
47 Michael Meacher, 'This War on Terrorism Is Bogus', *The Guardian*, 6 September 2003, p. 21.
48 David Marquand, 'The End of the Affair', *New Statesman*, 24 November 2003, pp. 18–20.
49 See B. Stokes and M. McIntosh, 'How They See Us', *National Journal*, 21 December 2002, pp. 3720–26; A. Applebaum, 'In Search of Pro-Americanism', *Foreign Policy*, 2005, vol. 149, pp. 32–35, 37–39; S. Kull, 'It's Lonely at the Top', *Foreign Policy*, 2005, vol. 149, pp. 36–37.
50 Quoted in Richard Crockatt, *America Embattled: September 11, Anti-Americanism and the Global Order*, London: Routledge, 2003, pp. 61–62.
51 *The Sunday Times*, 16 February 2003, p. 1.
52 See Applebaum, 'In Search of Pro-Americanism', p. 39; Michael Gove, *Celsius 7/7*, London: Phoenix, 2006, p. 93.
53 Maddox, *In Defence of America*, pp. 17–18.
54 Shawcross, *Allies*, p. 40.
55 See Dumbrell, *A Special Relationship*.
56 See Peter Riddell, 'In a Week, Britain Learns to Love America Again', *The Times*, 12 November 2008, p. 20.

4 The US–Canada relationship
How 'special' is America's oldest unbroken alliance?

David G. Haglund

Imagined communities: Lake Wobegon and animal farm

Fans of Minnesota Public Radio's *Prairie Home Companion* are certainly familiar with a place where 'all the women are strong, all the men are good looking, and all the children are above average'. It is called Lake Wobegon, and exists only in their imagination, as well as that of host Garrison Keillor, whose weekly tales from this fictional community are punctuated with the words quoted above. For legions of analysts of American foreign policy, there is another locale not unlike Lake Wobegon that also fills the imagination. It is called America's alliance network, and it too is a place in which 'above-average' entities abound. These entities are known as 'special relationships', the most commented among them, of course, being the one between the United States and the United Kingdom, the direct or indirect subject of several of this volume's chapters.

Yet, as many of the other chapters make clear, the US–UK tandem hardly represents the sole special relationship said to connect America with an ally in a noteworthy manner. This is so even in the transatlantic arena. Not too many years ago, around the time that its pending reunification was prompting the first President Bush to imagine that Germany was bound to emerge as America's 'partner in leadership', it was becoming easy for some to imagine the bond between Bonn and Washington eclipsing the more celebrated London–Washington one, and doing so on the presumption that an enlarging Germany must become more influential in transatlantic, and by extension global, security matters.[1] Nor was it only Germany that could get invoked in such a context. For a few observers of transatlantic relations, it was even possible to imagine that France (!) and the United States might be forging a special relationship, an assertion made by no less an expert on France–American interaction than Jean-Baptiste Duroselle, who concluded his *magnum opus* on the bilateral relationship by noting that it, too, was special, because it was predicated upon 'the old fund of affection' between the two countries.[2]

This chapter is about a special relationship that, while clearly within the Atlantic community, is not *per se* a transatlantic linkage. It is a North American relationship, albeit one crafted by two states that have often claimed to be 'European' powers, and have backed up their claim by substantial military and other commitments to European security. Still, what makes the Canada–US relationship so interesting, in the context of this volume, inheres more in its continental than in its transoceanic setting.

Accordingly, I am going to be drawing inspiration in this chapter from another imagined community, the one conjured up in George Orwell's satire on revolutionary dictatorships. For, as it was with *Animal Farm*, so it is with America's alliance network: all the allies may be equal, but some allies are more equal than others.[3] I will argue, in a nutshell, that the Canada–US relationship is, by dint of geography, economics and history, more 'special' than any of America's other special relationships. In so doing, I will primarily focus upon one line of enquiry, which takes us into the comparative 'specialness' of our couple, albeit paying heed to the distinction between client and ally relations.[4] However, there is a second line of enquiry, to which I will briefly advert in the chapter's closing pages, which relates to the manner in which the image of 'special relationship' can and does get utilized for the political purposes of state or societal actors. Thus, for the most part, I will seek to explain what it is that has made the Canada–US relationship qualitatively different from America's other special relationships, though I will also have a word or two to say about the way in which images of 'specialness' figure (or, more to the point, do *not* figure) in North American political discourse.

In most dictionaries, 'special' is defined in two principal ways. It can be construed as referring to a particular quality that sets whatever is being assessed apart from other cases, including from some that might initially have been taken to be reasonably comparable; here, the emphasis is placed on observable empirical differences among cases. Alternatively, 'special' can be understood as conveying a normative judgement. This is usually a positive judgement (as in, 'he is my "special" – i.e., "best" – friend'), though at times the normative value being connoted by the distinction can be a negative one. Both senses of 'special' are implicated in discussing the Canada–US relationship, but its 'Orwellian' aspects relate more to the empirical than the normative side of the ledger.

By this, I mean that, in the realm of security and defence, the Canada–US relationship really does have a claim to noteworthiness and even, in some respects, to uniqueness. There are three reasons for stating this. Firstly, the two countries were either the first, or among the first, Western neighbouring countries to forge between themselves what would come to be called a 'security community'. Secondly, the alliance that followed, though not necessarily prefigured by, the formation of this security community happens to be America's longest-running unbroken alliance. And, thirdly, Canada has, by dint of geography, demography and economic interdependence, a role in the US homeland security agenda that no other Western ally of America can claim. I discuss each of these points in the following text.

The North American security community and 'specialness'

A recent report of a high-level task force commissioned to study the community-building prospects of Canada, the United States and Mexico contained, among its series of recommendations, one major proposal: that the three countries establish, by 2010, a 'North American economic and security community'.[5] The chairs of this 31-member task force were John Manley, William Weld and Pedro Aspe, from Canada, the United States and Mexico, respectively. Manley was a veteran Liberal who had been Canada's minister of foreign affairs as well as deputy prime minister; Aspe had served as finance minister of Mexico; and Weld was a former Republican governor of Massachusetts. Their work was sponsored by the New York-based Council on Foreign Relations, in conjunction with the Canadian Council of Chief Executives and the Consejo Mexicano de Asuntos Internacionales. Not surprisingly, given the ambitious nature of many of the report's recommendations, some of the task force's members were moved to append a dissenting, or otherwise modifying, view to the set of proposals.[6] What is surprising, however, is that none challenged the contention that the three countries should be working towards the *construction* of a security community.

The reason why this is surprising is that it really misstates the problem, at least in the realm of security. Despite some sceptical voices, it is generally conceded that, for nearly three-quarters of a century, Canada, the United States and Mexico *have* constituted a security community. By 'security community' is meant an order in which the use of force as a means of conflict resolution between members of the group has simply become inconceivable. They neither go to war against one another nor even consider doing so. Instead, whatever problems arise between them, they undertake to resolve peacefully. With neither organized armed conflict nor the threat of such conflict playing a part in the resolution of intra-group problems, policymakers and other policy elites are able to entertain 'dependable expectations' that peaceful change will be the only kind of change that occurs.[7]

As noted above, some dissent to the contention that there already exists a North American security community can be encountered, usually in the case of the US–Mexican dyad.[8] Moreover, in respect of the Canada–US tandem, one also confronts occasional scepticism on the part of those who really do believe that organized armed force might be employed by one country against the other. For instance, one Kingston (Ontario)-based peace activist (an American expatriate from Maine) managed to publish a book during the first Clinton administration purporting that the choice of the nearby Fort Drum in upstate New York as the base of the US Army's 10th Mountain Division bespoke of aggressive designs on Canada![9] Even prior to the Clinton administration, there had been some in Canada who worried about an American invasion, one perhaps motivated by a desire to snatch oil or some other precious commodity, and at least one Canadian novelist dined out fairly regularly on this thesis during the early 1970s.[10]

Today, a few policy analysts, including one prominent member of a recent Liberal government, can be found fretting that an American siphoning off of Canadian water has the potential to disturb continental peace; while others (Conservatives, this time) imagine that the disagreement over whether or not the Northwest Passage constitutes an international strait could escalate into armed conflict.[11] This last prospect managed to figure in the rhetoric of the recent federal election campaign, when Conservative leader and later prime minister Stephen Harper promised, on 22 December 2005, to use military means, if necessary, to defend Canada's claims to sovereignty in the Arctic. As one observer wryly commented at the time, taking this pledge seriously could possibly result in the 'insanity' of Canada's having to launch depth charges from an icebreaker onto an *American* nuclear-powered submarine![12]

Needless to say, should what Franklyn Griffiths brands as 'insanity' come to pass, then we can all safely consign the Canada–US security community to the dustbin of history. Fortunately, the prospect of Canada–US armed conflict in the far north remains what it has been for many years: an absurdity, and thus an effective impossibility in a world in which 'rationality' is still said to provide the basis of state action. Therefore, even if it should one day transpire that the Canada–US security community proves not to have been completely idiotproof, for the moment it is hard to gainsay that this security community looks amazingly stable.[13]

Yet, it is not so much its stability as its *longevity* that renders the Canada–US security community so noteworthy, for one can imagine equally stable security communities elsewhere in the transatlantic community, and not only within the European Union. The Canada–US security community is thought by many to be special because it is often held to be the first pluralistic security community ever to have come into existence between neighbours. There may be reason to doubt this assertion of pioneering status, for some will tell you that the original Western security community arose not in North America but in Scandinavia, pursuant to the peaceful, if not completely frictionless separation of Norway from Sweden in 1905. It is probably wisest to conclude that the two security communities arose more or less simultaneously, and did so independently of each other.[14]

To be sure, if the absence of war is taken as the litmus test for a security community's coming into being, then it is possible to stretch the origins of the Canada–US one back to the last time they engaged in armed conflict against each other: 1814. However, if the test is a widespread absence of credible *suspicions* that intra-group armed conflict might erupt, then one could date the community's origins from, perhaps, the Washington treaty of 1871 resolving Civil War controversies between the United States and the United Kingdom, or possibly from the immediate aftermath of the Alaska Panhandle boundary dispute of 1903, a span of years characterized as the 'slate-cleaning' moment in Canada–US relations.[15] Further, and not to put too fine a point on the matter, if the test is the cancellation of war plans envisioning military action against a member of the group, then we could certainly date the onset of the Canada–US security community from the interwar period, a time when both Ottawa and Washington discontinued such planning.

Interestingly, if this latter is the appropriate measure for dating the origins of the security community, then it appears as if the Scandinavians attained the status a few years ahead of the North Americans, as the 1920s were the decade in which Oslo and Stockholm abandoned planning for military contingencies against each other.[16] They did not, however, manage to sustain the security community unbroken over the years, for the Nazi conquest of Norway in April 1940 did suspend, for a time, the latter's sovereign status, effectively placing into suspension as well the Scandinavian security community.

In North America, it initially took a bit longer for the practice of planning military contingencies against the neighbour to cease, with Canada being the first to give up the habit, at the start of the 1920s, while in the United States it would not be until 1937 that the War and Navy departments would officially replace the obsolete RED plans (red being the colour code for the British commonwealth and empire) with the new RAINBOW plans directed at Germany, Italy or Japan, or all three together.[17] Ever since then, the Canada–US security community has remained intact.

The creation of the Canada–US alliance

Less shrouded in ambiguity than the starting date of the Canada–US security community is the identity of the partner with which America has maintained its longest unbroken alliance. That partner is Canada. Such a statement might seem bizarre, even insulting, to those who believe that they already know the identity of America's 'oldest' ally: France. However, what often gets forgotten by those who accurately remember the 1778 alliance between America and France, which did so much to safeguard the departure of nearly all of the English-speaking North American colonies from the British Empire, is how short-lived this alliance turned out to be.[18] The reality is that Washington and Paris would only briefly be allied, first because their collective defence agreement had become a dead letter by as early as the Paris Peace Conference of 1783, when American negotiators 'double-crossed', in Walter McDougall's apt term, the French and negotiated a separate peace with Britain.[19] Secondly, in the following decade, the two erstwhile 'allies' were even for a time engaged in an undeclared naval war against each other.[20] Finally, and for good measure, the 1778 alliance was *officially* put out of existence with the 1800 treaty of Mortefontaine – and it would not be until 1949 that the two 'oldest allies' would once more become formally linked in a collective defence pact, with the Washington Treaty and the formation of NATO.

France is so often, if inaccurately, recalled as being America's oldest *continuous* ally that it is easy to lose sight of who actually has occupied that status. The problem is compounded by the tendency of many to assume that alliances must always be summoned forth by treaties, and must above all be formalized arrangements with permanent institutional structures. For those who regard alliances in this manner, NATO fills the bill admirably, given that it has both treaty-based status and the necessary institutional accoutrements (a headquarters, an integrated military command structure, a secretary general, even a bit of common infrastructure). And if NATO is the standard against which to measure claims of longevity as an American ally, then the status must be one shared among the 11 states that joined the United States in signing the Washington (or North Atlantic) Treaty in April 1949.[21]

However, alliances, as Stephen Walt argues, can and do take shape independently of treaties. They can even exist 'informally', though assuredly in reality they often are every bit as meaningful as more formal pacts: the operative notion is that these be effective instances of reciprocated defence collaboration.[22] In the case of the Canada–US alliance, the starting point is generally considered to have been a formal accord, albeit not a treaty. This was the agreement struck by President Franklin D. Roosevelt and Prime Minister Mackenzie King in the upstate New York town of Ogdensburg in mid-August 1940.[23] This accord led directly to the creation of the first of what would be a long line of binational defence arrangements, the Permanent Joint Board on Defence (PJBD), which set to work planning a series of measures to enhance continental security.[24]

In time, the PJBD would be supplemented with, and to an extent even eclipsed by, newer institutional means of strengthening North American defence cooperation. Among the most important of these were the Military Cooperation Committee (MCC) of 1946, the North American Air (now Aerospace) Defence Command (NORAD) of 1958, and, most recently, the Binational Planning Group (BPG) of 2003.[25] To these must be added a thick network of other accords, committees and arrangements pertaining to North American defence, whose numbers are no easy matter to keep count of, but which run into the several hundreds.[26] Thus, in a manner distinctly different from most of America's transatlantic relations, the United States and Canada were solidly allied well before the formation of NATO, and would almost certainly still be allied, had the latter organization never come into existence.

Only one other of America's alliances comes close to matching this longevity of the North American alliance, and that is the US–UK alliance. This alliance also took shape outside of a formal treaty, and did so at nearly the same time and for much the same reason as the US alliance with Canada. If the North American alliance began in the middle of August 1940, the transatlantic one that would effectively bind America to British fortunes formed 2 weeks later, on 2 September 1940, with the completion and announcement of the 'destroyers-for-bases' deal. This impending 'exchange of benefits' (Stephen Walt) had been adumbrated on 20 August 1940, when Prime Minister Winston Churchill announced in the House of Commons that a final agreement was near, concerning the leasing of British New World bases to the armed forces of the United States. Churchill conceded, in a very approving manner, that 'undoubtedly this process means that these two great organizations of the English-speaking democracies, the British Empire and the United States, will have to be somewhat mixed up together in some of their affairs for mutual and general advantage'.[27]

In fact, the prime minister was announcing the onset of the US alliance with Britain, though he could not say so in those words at the time. Nor could he say anything about the *American* quid pro quo. Though it had been decided at the president's cabinet meeting on 2 August, it had not yet been made public. However, that *quid pro quo* was huge, for in agreeing to transfer part of its fleet to a belligerent power, neutral America was engaging in the most flagrant breach of international law, since the Hague Convention of 1907 explicitly prohibited neutrals from transferring part of their forces-in-being to belligerents, though neutrals could, legally, sell munitions to both sides in a conflict.[28] Much more importantly, the arrangement breached America's Neutrality Acts and its policy of isolation from the European balance of power.[29]

From that point on, it was going to be increasingly likely that the United States would enter the war – American public opinion to the contrary notwithstanding – for the initial decision to underwrite British security with the transfer of destroyers would be followed, in early 1941, by Lend–Lease, a policy measure that would enable cash-strapped Britain to purchase war material in North America with US assistance. This measure would culminate in the necessity of the American navy convoying war supplies halfway across the Atlantic. Convoying, in turn, resulted in German U-boats engaging in combat against American destroyers. By mid-1941, whatever the American public might have thought or desired, the US Navy was taking part in a real, albeit 'undeclared' war against Germany, and it was doing so alongside its new British and Canadian allies.[30] Seen in this light, Pearl Harbor was epiphenomenal. America would have entered World War II, officially, for the same reasons it had entered the First: as a result of a German submarine offensive in the Atlantic.

The 'Kingston dispensation' and homeland security

There is a third noteworthy aspect of the Canada–US relationship, the most special of all. We can refer to it as the 'Kingston dispensation', and in so many ways it does set the alliance relationship between the two North American coun-tries on a distinctly different plane from any of the defence and security linkages that America has with its transoceanic allies. It does so because it establishes the boundary conditions for Canadian participation in American 'homeland security'. It is a normative arrangement that predates the founding of the US alliance with Canada by 2 years, and constituted an attempt to resolve a security challenge stemming from what were, at the time, the North American neighbours' radically different approaches to the deteriorating security environment in Europe. Should war come to that continent, Canada was almost certain to join in, because Britain would have. In contrast, America remained firmly set against participation, despite the appearance of occasional denunciations at home of an isolationist grand strategy that could look more cowardly than coherent.[31]

In August 1938, during the height of the Sudetenland crisis and at a moment when war in Europe seemed imminent, President Roosevelt told an audience at Queen's University in Kingston, Ontario, that America would 'not stand idly by' if the physical security of Canada were threatened by a European adversary as a consequence of the country's participation in a European war. Nor could the United States stand by in any such event, for Canada's participation would be bound to have an impact on American grand strategy, because if things were to go badly in Europe for the Allies, who could say what consequences might unfold in the Western hemisphere, and what the implications would be for the Monroe Doctrine? For his part, Prime Minister King, speaking a few days later, made a reciprocal commitment. He pledged that Canada would ensure that nothing it did would jeopardize the physical security of the United States. Taken together, the two leaders' remarks reflected a new dispensation that would come to shape the unalterable normative core of North American security: henceforth, each country understood that it had a 'neighbourly' obligation to the other not only to refrain from any activities that might imperil the security of the other, but also to demonstrate nearly as much solicitude for the other's physical security needs as for its own.[32]

The Kingston dispensation was not quite an alliance, but it would only take 2 years more before a bilateral alliance did get forged in North America. Significantly, the Kingston dispensation implies a level of reciprocal obligation that exceeds those that define either a security community or an alliance; for in the case of the former, the obligation is that one does not make or threaten armed conflict against one's neighbour, while in the case of the latter, if NATO's Article 5 is taken as a guide, the obligation extends to treating armed attack upon an ally as tantamount to an armed attack upon oneself, but does not entail any particular response on the allies' part – i.e., it is a rhetorical more than a binding commitment.[33]

For nearly seven decades, the Kingston dispensation has remained the most important constitutive norm in the realm of Canada–US defence and security cooperation. During most of that time, much of the countries' most significant defence cooperation has taken place far from North American shores, and usually within a multilateral 'internationalist' context. In Joel Sokolsky's apt assessment of the bilateral defence relationship during the latter half of the 1990s, Canada–US defence cooperation was increasingly going on 'over there', within the context of NATO conflict management operations, rather than 'over here' on the North American landmass.[34] Yet, while Canada was becoming more engaged operationally with NATO, changes were underway in the international threat environment, suggesting that American strategists might soon be paying more attention to physical security interests within the North American heartland. This theatre of operations had tumbled into deep eclipse as a result of the advent of the era of intercontinental ballistic missiles by the late 1950s, since there was no defence against a massive attack involving ICBMs. As the latter threat waned, it was possible once again to contemplate meaningful continental defence measures.

Thus, even before the attacks on Washington and New York on 11 September 2001, there were signs that the structural basis of Canada–US defence and security cooperation was shifting in ways that put a premium once more on territory in the Western hemisphere, and especially on the North American landmass. Some interpreted the signs as evidence that America might again be turning inward. During the early rounds of the Canadian debate over national missile defence (NMD), it was not uncommon to encounter such claims, with more than a few Canadian observers wondering whether a new era of American isolationism was at hand, one whose arrival was being heralded by the novel concept of 'homeland defence' (subsequently expanded to 'homeland security' by early 2001). There was, of course, an alternative interpretation of homeland defence and its associated menu of policies, including NMD. According to this view, the concept and its policies represented a necessary condition for the maintenance of American global engagement, and thus were more consistent with 'international-ism' than with its doctrinal antithesis. This tended to be an interpretation held only by a few Canadian observers, but as the current wars in Iraq and Afghanistan testify, it likely will turn out to have been the more reliable of the two readings of homeland defence/security.

For a variety of reasons, including the Kingston dispensation, Canada felt the impact of the attacks on New York and Washington more intensely than any country other than the United States itself. There were three reasons in addition to the Kingston dispensation that account for this, stemming from both emotional ('subjective') and structural ('objective') considerations. The first was simply a function of geography: no other foreign country is as close to 'ground zero' as Canada, and, indeed, a greater percentage of its population than of America's own population lives within a 500-mile radius of New York City. In an all-too-literal sense, the attack on the United States hit home for Canadians, even if it is true that many more British than Canadian citizens perished in the inferno of the World Trade Center.

The second reason why it hit home was owing to the social–psychological tendency of Canadians to identify with Americans in times of acute crisis – even though, at most other times, the impulse to differentiate from Americans takes priority. Perhaps it would be going too far to endow this crisis-generated sentiment with the attributes of 'collective identity', for this is a much-disputed concept in social science, and especially in the discipline of international relations, where states, borders and the different identities that are associated with these categories are said still to possess the power to vitiate any generalizable and enduring sense of empathy.[35] Nevertheless, in the immediate aftermath of the attacks, Canadians strongly rallied to America's side. Though it may not be entirely accurate to call this 'civilization rallying' (Samuel Huntington), it certainly did display the hallmarks of in-group solidarity at a moment of crisis.[36] For, notwithstanding the myriad policy disputes in which the two countries are routinely embroiled, most Canadians knew that the attack on American institutions and values was an attack on theirs as well, and that the challenge to be faced was not just America's, but Canada's too. The country's minister of foreign affairs and later deputy prime minister, John Manley, captured the mood of the Canadian public – at least the public in English Canada[37] – at a time in mid-September 2001 when the Canadian *government* was still struggling to frame Canada's response to the attacks:

> Let's make no mistake about it. Canada does not have a history as a pacifist or neutralist country. Canada has soldiers that are buried all over Europe because we fought in defence of liberty. And we're not about to back away from a challenge now because we think somebody might get hurt.[38]

The third reason for the differential impact on Canada as opposed to other foreign countries had to do with economics. It included not only the desire to keep vital trade links with the United States as open as possible in the circumstances – critically important for a country with a trade surplus of more than C\$70 billion a year in its commerce with its neighbour to the South – but also efforts to ensure that the country would remain attractive to offshore foreign investors tempted to set up shop in Canada so as to serve the wider North American market. On an average day, some C\$2 billion worth of trade crosses the Canada–US border in both directions. Canada is especially sensitive to anything that could slow down the volume of traffic southward, as happened with the dramatic, if temporary, impact in the immediate wake of the attacks, and again at the start of the war with Iraq.

Canadian exports go mainly to the United States, the market for more than 87 per cent of Canada's foreign sales. Because Canada's economy is much more trade-dependent than America's, more than 35 per cent of the country's GDP is accounted for by exports to the United States alone. In addition, while the relative importance of trade with Canada for its own economy is much less, the United States too has a major economic interest in keeping commerce flowing as smoothly as possible with Canada, its largest trading partner.[39] Consider, for instance, that the state of Georgia by itself trades more with Canada than all of the United States does with France and Italy. Not only is Canada the leading market for 38 American states, but one Canadian province on its own, Ontario, would rank as America's fifth-largest trading partner, trailing in importance only Canada itself, Japan, Mexico and China. It is no wonder that one prominent Canadian economist can state that the 'most important policy issue facing Canada today is our relationship with the United States'.[40]

Does 'special' mean 'better'?

As noted earlier, there are two principal ways in which we might understand the meaning of 'special'. So far, I have been analysing the Canada–US security and defence relationship from the perspective of what sets it apart from the constellation of reasonably comparable cases. In this section, I enquire into the second connotation of our word, and ask whether, from the point of view of either North American ally, their ties to each other are normatively superior to bonds they might have with other Western allies.

What was suggested in the preceding section on the Kingston dispensation is *not* that Canada must follow in lockstep every twist and turn in American foreign and security policy, as some analysts who adopt a perspective on Canada as a 'satellite' of the United States appear to believe. In fact, Canada possesses a surprising degree of latitude when it comes to deviating from, even frankly opposing, certain US initiatives abroad. This was the case at the time of the Vietnam War, and much more recently with the Iraq war of 2003. What *is* suggested, however, is that there are understood requirements that both Canada and the United States must meet in the pursuit of North American security, and that these are the very same requirements acknowledged by the two countries' leaders back in 1938.

In Canada, the obligation is sometimes couched in terms of a 'loyalty test'.[41] However, if it is such a test, then it is so only in part, given that Canada can and does choose to opt out of participation in a variety of American undertakings, from which many American allies situated elsewhere would not necessarily wish to absent themselves. Partly, Canada's margin of manoeuvre in alliance commitments inheres in a generalizable characteristic of life in the 'democratic alliance', namely that the very normative basis of liberal–democratic security interdependence imposes a powerful check on the ability of an alliance leader to elicit compliance with its agenda from its less powerful allies. It knows, and more to the point, *they* know, that beyond a certain amount of scolding, there is little that the great power heading the democratic alliance can or will do to compel cooperation.[42]

However, if the liberal–democratic nature of the transatlantic alliance can be said to reduce the cost of disagreeing with the alliance leader, there is something else at play that further diminishes any prospect of Canada being compelled to undertake some kinds of military commitments in selected parts of the world: geography. The very same binding conditions established in the Kingston dispensation that ensure tight cooperation in matters of homeland security ironically grant Canada a certain freedom from alliance constraint beyond the North American continent, for the Kingston dispensation testifies to the existence of what has been termed an American 'involuntary' (sometimes 'automatic') guarantee of Canada's own physical security. This guarantee can be perceived in a minatory way by some Canadians who enjoy remarking that the United States is 'our best friend, whether we like it or not', and who ponder the cost – political and also economic – of securing for the country 'defence against help'.[43]

Notwithstanding its alleged menacing aspects, the American guarantee does provide a temptation for Canadian leaders, no matter what their political stripe, to seek to spend less on defence than would be the case in the absence of the guarantee. The temptation is a powerful one, and it proves all too easy for sentient policymakers to succumb to it. Who can blame them, if political decisions are supposed to be a function of 'rational' action, with rationality construed in terms of a sustainable match between the ends and means of policy? For, if the end be that of defending Canada against attack by the United States, no imaginable means could be conjured forth to attain it; conversely, if the United States can be counted upon to safeguard Canada's physical security against anyone else, there exists an incentive to do no more than what is minimally required to satisfy the Americans that Canada is pulling its weight.

Joel Sokolsky has cogently summarized the ongoing challenge faced by Canadian leaders pondering which level of commitment is sufficient to keep Washington minimally satisfied. 'The current policy', he wrote, at a time when the Liberals were in power in Ottawa, 'is very much in the Canadian tradition of asking *not* "How much is enough?" but rather, "How much is just enough?"'[44] That amount is easier to determine when it concerns North American security, but harder to assess when global security is in question, for the good reason that Canadians, unlike geographically distant American allies, do not have to ask themselves, in the way for instance that Australians do, whether support for a

US overseas endeavour might make sense as a means of purchasing insurance for some future contingency, when an American reciprocal gesture would come in more than handy.[45]

Nor is the Australian case exceptional; many other American allies want, if at all possible, to participate alongside their protector in parts of the world in which, objectively, they may have no obvious interests at stake. Polish officials, for instance, make no secret of the rationale underlying their commitments in both Iraq and Afghanistan, which has much less to do with promoting the democratization of the Greater Middle East than with promoting the principle of 'solidarity'. It is hardly necessary for them to specify the context in which they might wish to call upon that principle. Thus, even though only 17 per cent of the Polish public might think sending a battalion to Afghanistan, as Warsaw is currently doing, makes sense, policymakers understand it to be emphatically in the national interest to do this.[46] The examples could be multiplied, for the same logic drove the decision of many of America's and Britain's allies who agreed to deploy forces in Iraq back in 2003 in a 'coalition of the willing' that counted a couple of dozen states among its membership.

So does special mean 'better' in the case of Canada as an ally of the United States? Apparently not, at least not from Washington's point of view, insofar as interventions beyond the shores of North America are concerned. It does not follow, however, that Canada is a 'bad' ally, as many rightwing talk-show hosts on American AM radio seem to believe, even if the American public remains convinced that Canada, along with Britain, ranks as their country's 'best' ally.[47] Even less does it follow that Canada is somehow a 'security threat to the United States', because of its opposition to American policy on a range of diplomatic fronts in recent years.[48] The point is that while Washington clearly would prefer Canadian support abroad, such as it currently enjoys in Afghanistan (though less so in Iraq), the litmus test of Canada–US alliance solidarity will remain the geographically circumscribed one established so long ago: the North American continent. And, even here, Canada's freedom to say 'no' is greater than some imagine – witness the bizarre decision of the previous federal government headed by Paul Martin to 'decline' participation in National Missile Defence in early 2005, although this selfsame government had agreed, a half-year earlier, to allow NORAD to serve as the detection system for the missile defence batteries currently being deployed in Alaska and California.

For many reasons, but most of all because of the huge power disparity separating the two North American neighbours, their alliance will always be a matter of greater interest to the Canadians than to the Americans. The latter will assume the alliance to be (a) naturally beneficial to both countries, and (b) normally problem free except for those issues that domestic political pressures in Canada cause to rise to the fore. In respect of this latter point, there had been a tendency in recent federal election campaigns for some politicians (usually Liberals) to try to convince voters that they are running not against their Canadian opponents but against George W. Bush, a president whose popularity in Canada (as elsewhere) was at an unusually low ebb.[49]

In contrast, for Canada, the relationship with the United States is and will remain something conditioned not only by security concerns, but also by identity issues. No American would seek to understand who he or she 'is' by conjuring up a Canadian 'other' to serve as referent for his or her own sense of identity. Very few Canadians are immune from the psychological need to construct an American 'other' so as to know not only who they are, but to buttress that knowledge with the conviction that they must be better than their neighbours. Hence, the iron law of Canadian politics is this: one must always avoid drawing 'too close' to the United States (for, if so, many appear to think, What need is there for a separate Canadian existence in North America?); yet, by the same token, one must always ensure that relations between the two countries are never allowed to deteriorate to such a degree that Canada's prosperity and survival might be placed in jeopardy by American wrath. Thus, what Frank Underhill wrote nearly half a century ago seems to be no less relevant today than it was then: 'Americans are benevolently ignorant about Canada, whereas Canadians are malevolently informed about the United States'.[50]

Conclusion: Goodbye Mr. Chip?

If the quote that closed the previous section demonstrates that Canadians as well as other Western publics might be swept up in a kind of 'friendly fire anti-Americanism' (Julia Sweig), there is and will remain something special about their ever-complex and psychologically interesting relationship with the United States.[51] In this chapter, I have made two arguments: first, that there are important empirical differences that so distinguish Canada's alliance with the United States as to warrant the Orwellian allusion to its being 'more special' than other bilateral alliances America has developed; and second, that it does not follow from these empirical differences that the Canada–US alliance is particularly special in the normative sense of their being 'better' allies of each other than they are of anyone else. In closing, I wish to return to a point raised at the outset – namely, the manner in which images of 'specialness' get injected into policy discussions by state or societal actors. Here, what stands out is how little political gain is to be had, in North America, from emphasizing the special qualities of this alliance. In the United States, not enough people care – thus, there is little point in drawing attention to the alliance; while in Canada, too many care – thus there will always be some risk associated with the emphasizing. Because this is a volume whose inspiration is, in large measure, owing to work done earlier on the Western world's most celebrated special relationship, namely that between America and Britain, allow me to conclude this chapter by referring to that relationship.

Illustratively, and notwithstanding its empirical 'specialness', there is something about the North American alliance that, from the social–psychological perspective, is quite familiar to those who study the transatlantic relationship. It concerns the impact that power differentials can have upon relations between peoples who share more or less the same political values, and even speak (more or less) the same language. Briefly put, it required, a shift in the relative capabilities as between themselves and the British for Americans finally to abandon their previous habit of 'tweaking the lion's tail' and, through so doing, establish their sense of 'identity' and importance, not so much in the world's as in their own eyes. Because, for so many years, Britain was *the* standard against which Americans measured their own worth, we sometimes forget why and how the measuring could work against the two constructing a more 'healthy' relationship. In a word, America outgrew Britain, and in so doing, could outgrow its earlier practice of walking around with a geopolitical chip conspicuously balanced on its shoulder. It is hard to imagine, North American power differentials being what they are (and will remain), the Canadian chip similarly disappearing.

Notes

1 K.-D. Mensel, 'The United States and the United Germany: Partners in Leadership?' in D. G. Haglund (ed.) *Can America Remain Committed? US Security Horizons in the 1990s*, Boulder: Westview, 1992, pp. 81–109.

2 J.-B. Duroselle, *France and the United States: From the Beginnings to the Present*, trans. Derek Coltman, Chicago: University of Chicago Press, 1978, pp. 252–53.

3 G. Orwell, *Animal Farm: A Fairy Story*, Harmondsworth: Penguin Books, 1951, p. 114.

4 A. Danchev, 'On Specialness', *International Affairs*, 1996, vol. 72, pp. 737–50.

5 R. N. Haass, 'Foreword' to *Building a North American Community*, Independent Task Force Report no. 53, New York: Council on Foreign Relations, 2005, p. xvii

6 Ibid., 'Additional and Dissenting Views', pp. 33–39.

7 E. Adler and M. N. Barnett, 'Governing Anarchy: A Research Agenda for the Study of Security Communities', *Ethics & International Affairs*, 1996, vol. 10, p. 73; K. W. Deutsch et al., *Political Community and the North Atlantic Area: International Organization in the Light of Historical Experience*. Princeton: Princeton University Press, 1957.

8 G. González and S. Haggard, 'The United States and Mexico: A Pluralistic Security Community?' in E. Adler and M. Barnett (eds) *Security Communities*, Cambridge: Cambridge University Press, 1998, pp. 295–332.

9 F. W. Rudmin, *Bordering on Aggression: Evidence of US Military Preparations against Canada*, Hull: Voyageur, 1993.

10 R. Rohmer, *Ultimatum*, Toronto: Clark Irwin, 1973; R. Rohmer, *Exxoneration*, Toronto: McClelland and Stewart, 1974.

11 A. Charron, 'The Northwest Passage: Is Canada's Sovereignty Floating Away?' *International Journal*, 2005, vol. 60, pp. 831–48.

12 F. Griffiths, 'Breaking the Ice on Canada–US Arctic Cooperation', *Globe and Mail* (Toronto), 22 February 2006, p. A21.

13 S. Roussel, *The North American Democratic Peace: Absence of War and Security Institution-Building in Canada–US Relations, 1867–1958*, Montreal and Kingston: McGill-Queen's University Press, 2004.

14 R. N. Lebow, 'The Long Peace, the End of the Cold War, and the Failure of Realism', *International Organization*, 1994, vol. 48, pp. 249–77; M. Stolleis, 'The Dissolution of the Union between Norway and Sweden in 1905: A Century Later', in O. Mestad and D. Michalsen (eds) *Rett, nasjon, union – Den svensk-norske unionens rettslige historie 1814–1905*, Oslo: Universitetsforlaget, 2005, pp. 35–48.

15 J. L. Granatstein and N. Hillmer, *For Better or for Worse: Canada and the United States to the 1990s*, Toronto: Copp Clark Pitman, 1991, pp. 39–40.

16 M. Ericson, 'A Realist Stable Peace: Power, Threat, and the Development of a Shared Norwegian–Swedish Democratic Security Identity 1905–40', unpublished thesis, Lund University, 2000.

17 L. Morton, 'Germany First: The Basic Concept of Allied Strategy in World War II', in K. R. Greenfield (ed.) *Command Decisions*, Washington: Office of the Chief of Military History, Department of the Army, 1960, pp. 12–22.

18 M. R. Zahniser, *Uncertain Friendship: American–French Diplomatic Relations Through the Cold War*, New York: John Wiley & Sons, 1975, p. 70.

19 W. A. McDougall, *Promised Land, Crusader State: The American Encounter with the World Since 1776*, Boston: Houghton Mifflin, 1997, p. 25.

20 G. W. Allen, *Our Naval War with France*, Boston: Houghton Mifflin, 1909; A. De Conde, *The Quasi War: The Politics and Diplomacy of the Undeclared War with France, 1797–1801*, New York: Scribner, 1966.

21 NATO Office of Information and Press, *The NATO Handbook: Fiftieth Anniversary Edition, 1949–1999*, Brussels: NATO Office of Information and Press, 1998, p. 26.

22 S. M. Walt, *The Origins of Alliances*, Ithaca: Cornell University Press, 1987, p. 1.

23 F. W. Gibson and J. G. Rossie (eds) *The Road to Ogdensburg: The Queen's/St. Lawrence Conferences on Canadian–American Affairs, 1935–1941*, East Lansing: Michigan State University Press, 1993.

24 C. Conliffe, 'The Permanent Joint Board on Defense, 1940–88', in D. G. Haglund and J. J. Sokolsky (eds) *The US–Canada Security Relationship: The Politics, Strategy, and Technology of Defense*, Boulder: Westview, 1989, pp. 146–65.

25 D. N. Mason, 'The Canadian–American North American Defence Alliance in 2005', *International Journal*, 2005, vol. 60, pp. 385–96.

26 Bi-National Planning Group, *The Final Report on Canada and the United States (CANUS) Enhanced Military Cooperation*, Peterson AFB (CO), 13 March 2006, Appendix G.

27 C. Eade (comp.), *The War Speeches of the Rt. Hon. Winston S. Churchill*, vol. 1, London: Cassell's, 1951, p. 244.

28 A. A. Offner, *The Origins of the Second World War: American Foreign Policy and World Politics, 1917–1941*, New York: Praeger, 1975, p 182.

29 J. R. Leutze, *Bargaining for Supremacy: Anglo-American Naval Collaboration, 1937–1941*. Chapel Hill: University of North Carolina Press, 1977; P. Goodhart, *Fifty Ships that Saved the World: The Foundation of the Anglo-American Alliance*, Garden City, NY: Doubleday, 1965.

30 T. A. Bailey and P. B. Ryan, *Hitler vs. Roosevelt: The Undeclared Naval War*. New York: Free Press/Macmillan, 1979.

31 L. Hartley, *Is America Afraid? A New Foreign Policy for the United States*, New York: Prentice-Hall, 1937.

32 J. MacCormac, *Canada: America's Problem*, New York: Viking Press, 1940.

33 The wording of article 5 is instructive, for it obliges each ally to 'assist the Party or Parties so attacked by taking forthwith, individually and in concert with the other Parties, such action as it deems necessary'. NATO Office of Information and Press, *NATO Handbook*, p. 396.

34 J. J. Sokolsky, 'Over There With Uncle Sam: Peacekeeping, the "Trans-European Bargain", and the Canadian Forces', in D. G. Haglund (ed.) *What NATO for Canada?* Martello Papers 23, Kingston: Queen's University Centre for International Relations, 2000, pp. 15–36.

35 J. Mercer, 'Identity and Anarchy', *International Organization*, 1995, vol. 49, pp. 229–52.

36 S. P. Huntington, 'The Clash of Civilizations?', *Foreign Affairs*, 1993, vol. 72, pp. 22–49.

37 For French-speaking Canada, Québec in particular does of late seem to have taken a differing perspective to the United States. See D. G. Haglund, 'Québec's "America Problem": Differential Threat Perception in the North American Security Community', *American Review of Canadian Studies*, 2006, vol. 36, pp. 552–67.

38 Quoted in R. Boswell, 'A Life's Journey', *Ottawa Citizen*, 2 February 2002, p. B1.

39 J. D. Phillips, 'Improving Border Management', *International Journal*, 2005, vol. 60, pp. 407–15.

40 W. Dobson, 'Trade Can Brush in a New Border', *Globe and Mail*, 21 January 2003, p. A15.

41 S. Roussel, 'Pearl Harbor et le World Trade Center: Le Canada face aux États-Unis en période de crise', *Études internationales*, 2002, vol. 33, p. 685.

42 D. G. Haglund and S. Roussel, 'Is the Democratic Alliance a Ticket to (Free) Ride? Canada's "Imperial Commitments", from the Interwar Period to the Present', *Journal of Transatlantic Studies*, 2007, vol. 5, pp. 1–24.

43 N. Ørvik, 'Canadian Security and "Defence Against Help"', *Survival*, 1984, vol. 42, pp. 26–31.

44 J. J. Sokolsky, 'Over There With Uncle Sam', p. 31.

45 J. C. Blaxland, *Strategic Cousins: Australian and Canadian Expeditionary Forces and the British and American Empires*, Montréal and Kingston: McGill-Queen's University Press, 2006.

46 Poland is currently completing the deployment of 1200 soldiers to Afghanistan, in a commitment to NATO intended to last until mid 2010. Poland also deployed some 2500 troops to Iraq in the period 2003–5.

47 P. Koring, 'Iran Seen as Worst Enemy of US, Poll Shows', *Globe and Mail*, 24 February 2006, p. A17.

48 H. M. Sapolsky, 'Canada: Crossing the Line', *Breakthroughs*, 2005, vol. 14, p. 31.

49 The temptation to run against Bush was on display during the 2005 federal campaign, when Paul Martin began improbably to sound like Hugo Chávez, eliciting a public rebuke from the US ambassador to Canada, David Wilkins, who warned that such electoral opportunism could take the bilateral relationship onto a 'slippery slope', with potentially ominous consequences. Said the ambassador, '[i]t may be smart election-year politics to thump your chest and constantly criticize your friend and your No. 1 trading partner. But it is a slippery slope, and all of us should hope that it doesn't have a long-term impact on the relationship'. Quoted in D. Leblanc and G. Galloway, 'Washington Scolds Ottawa', *Globe and Mail*, 14 December 2005, pp. A1, A12.

50 F. H. Underhill, 'Canada and the North Atlantic Triangle', in Underhill (comp.) *In Search of Canadian Liberalism*, Toronto: Macmillan of Canada, 1961, p. 255.

51 J. E. Sweig, *Friendly Fire: Losing Friends and Making Enemies in the Anti-American Century*, New York: Public Affairs, 2006.

5 Australia, the United States and the unassailable alliance

Mark Beeson

Australia may not be the most important ally of the United States, but few could claim to be closer or more unequivocal in their support. No other country has participated as regularly as Australia in the major conflicts that the United States has found itself involved in since it became a hegemonic power in the aftermath of World War II. In Korea, Vietnam, Afghanistan and both wars with Iraq, Australia has played an important supporting role, albeit one of little material importance. Yet, the very fact that Australia's participation in these conflicts was essentially symbolic tells us something important about the nature of contemporary American hegemony and the role played by valued allies such as Australia. It also sheds a revealing light on the motivations of such allies: although Australia's circumstances are unique and the dynamics of the alliance relationship are contingent and historically determined, the Australian experience has a wider significance in the context of post-Cold War geopolitics. Indeed, surprisingly and somewhat paradoxically, even in an era in which ideological issues are routinely considered to have less purchase, and when a reconfigured international order might have been expected to confer a greater degree of autonomy on client states, the alliance with the United States remains the universally supported centre-piece of Australia's foreign policies. The ideational construction of the bilateral relationship in Australia ensures that, despite the purported benefits of the relationship being less clear and more contentious, there is little chance of it being downgraded in the immediate future, despite the election of a new government in Australia and a commitment to withdraw its tokenistic presence in Iraq. Indeed, it is significant that Kevin Rudd, the Australian Labor Party (ALP) prime minister elected in November 2007, made a point in his post-election victory speech of reassuring the United States that his commitment to the alliance remained undiminished.[1]

To explain this apparent paradox, in which Australian support for the United States has largely remained undiminished despite the sometimes negative impact that the alliance has had on 'Australian' political and economic interests, we need to examine the specific historical circumstances that have shaped Australian foreign policy, and the way in which the alliance relationship has been discursively constructed by Australian policymakers and commentators. Consequently, after providing a brief outline of the development of the increasingly close ties that have characterized contemporary Australia–US relations, I suggest that the alliance remains unassailable because of an underlying ideational consensus about its merits that persists despite major changes in the international order, growing doubts about the conduct and efficacy of the American foreign policies with which Australia is so closely aligned, and growing evidence of the deleterious impact of such policies on more narrowly conceived 'Australian' interests. The discussion of the Australian case is preceded by a brief theoretical introduction that provides a framework with which to understand the complex nature of American hegemony and the way it has affected other states. One of the central claims in what follows is that hegemony has differential effects on other states, and that its overall impact is mediated and ultimately determined as much by friend or foe, as it is by the hegemon itself. In other words, while the United States may still be 'hegemonic' and the central foreign policy reality with which other less-powerful states must contend, the precise nature of this interaction and the role played by other states will be determined largely by the subordinate states themselves. Although there has recently been a change of government in Australia, it is too soon to judge what impact this may have on the alliance. Consequently, most attention is given to the Howard government, which has dominated Australian foreign policy for over a decade.

Living with hegemons

Australia's history as an independent nation has been distinguished by a reliance on what former Liberal prime minister Robert Menzies famously called 'great and powerful friends'. These days, we might describe such powers more prosaically as hegemonic. It is, however, important to remember that Menzies' principal allegiance was to Britain, the former colonial power, and that Britain's attraction for Menzies was as much emotional and normative as it was material and pragmatic. It would take the exigencies of war and the installation of an ALP prime minister – John Curtin – to make the decisive shift from a declining to a rising hegemon. However, before considering the implications of this transformation in Australian foreign policy in any detail, it is useful to consider, albeit briefly, the nature of hegemonic power at a theoretical level, as this helps to explain both Australia's distinctive relationship with the United States and its willingness pragmatically to abandon colonial ties.[2]

The first point to emphasize about hegemonic power and the response of other countries to it is that it has major 'structural' components. It is not necessary to accept the entire Realist corpus – particularly its assumptions about the presumed inevitability of conflict and hegemonic cyclical change[3] – to recognize that material power matters. World War II unambiguously revealed the extent of Britain's decline and America's rise. As a result, the fall of Singapore was a pivotal moment in Australian history and an apparent confirmation of deeply held fears about isolation and insecurity.[4] It was clear that only the United States had the capacity to play the sort of global hegemonic role formerly associated with Britain. With Britain clearly unable to underwrite Australian security, Curtin pragmatically observed that 'Australia looks to America, free of any pangs as to our traditional links or kinship with the United Kingdom'. Yet, despite the fact that Curtin had – prophetically and heretically – already expressed misgivings about the reliability of Britain as a security guarantor even before World War II, it took the War itself and the threat of Japanese invasion to dilute the hitherto powerful emotional bonds with Britain.[5]

Significant shifts in Australian foreign policy would thus seem to require major transformations in the external order before they can occur. Without such a stimulus, the requisite domestic reconfiguration is unlikely. There is, of course, a substantial literature that emphasizes the durability of institutional and ideational orders,[6] and the possible importance of crises in puncturing extant equilibria.[7] However, what is striking in Australia's case is the persistence of earlier patterns of allegiance and identification, even when the circumstances that generated such behaviours appear to have substantially changed. While it may be unsurprising that Australia became closely aligned to the United States at the height of World War II, or that such an allegiance was consolidated during the Cold War when Australian politics was dominated by the conservative figure of Bob Menzies, it is rather more surprising that such underlying relations persist in the aftermath of major, interconnected transformations in the international system and in the nature of American hegemony.

There have been a number of changes in Australia's external environment that might have been expected to bring about a reassessment of ties with the United States. Most fundamentally, perhaps, the end of the Cold War, and the breakdown of the bipolarity with which it was associated, completely transformed the wider geopolitical order that had apparently provided the rationale for close ties with the United States. The resultant 'unipolar' international order was not simply almost entirely unforeseen, but prepared the ground for the subsequent transformation of American foreign policy and the rise of the so-called neoconservatives and an increasingly unilateral application of American power.[8] Although we now know that such ambitions have proved largely unachievable, this should not obscure the fact that they initially enjoyed widespread support amongst Australian policymakers.

It is important to note that the most conventional International Relations (IR) theory offered little guidance about likely state behaviour in such circumstances. On the contrary, some of the most influential strands of IR theorizing suggested that other states might be expected to 'balance' against, rather than 'bandwagon' with America's unipolar power.[9] Clearly, Australian foreign policy – and that of many other states – has been driven by something more that a simple reflexive recalibration of 'the national interest' in the face of a major re-structuring of the international order. As a result, materially based explanations of state behaviour can only take us so far. To develop a more complete picture of state behaviour, especially of the Australian state, we need to consider the impact of non-material, ideational forces and the way apparently universal forces such as hegemonic powers have been meditated by contingent, discursively realized, domestic factors.

Making sense of hegemony

One striking, widely noted feature of American hegemony has been its ideational component.[10] Not only has the United States had the world's largest economy and its most imposing military capacity, but it has also had an unparalleled ability to promote a particular worldview, as well as quite specific economic and political practices. True, not all countries have subscribed to this normative order as closely as the Americans might like, but even those countries that were less enthusiastic about adopting the United States' liberal values were often prepared to support its dominance, since they stood to benefit from the existence of a stable, predictable, rules-based international order.[11] The institutionalization of American power in the post-war period, which culminated in the creation of the Bretton Woods institutions, helped to legitimize and entrench US hegemony in ways that go beyond simple material pre-eminence. Indeed, for countries like Australia, there was an even deeper affinity with the United States: because there was generally a normative congruity and sympathy with the rhetoric of American foreign policy, there has tended to be relatively little ideological opposition to American dominance in Australia.

Yet, the very different responses that the George W. Bush administration's foreign policies generated amongst allies and possible opponents remind us of the potentially decisive role that contingent national factors play in determining the impact of hegemony. In this context, Australia's early, prominent place in the 'coalition of the willing' in Iraq contrasted strikingly with countries such as New Zealand and Canada, which took no part, or with a number of European countries, such as France and Germany, which were actively hostile to American intervention.[12] The recognition that state behaviour is not a simple reflection of structural change in the overarching international system, but dependent on the way policymakers understand their own circumstances and relations with other states has led to some important theoretical innovations. At its most ambitious, the sort of constructivist reading of inter-state behaviour developed by Alexander Wendt claims that 'the character of international life is determined by the beliefs and expectations that states have about each other, and these are constituted largely by social rather than material structures'.[13] Put differently, state behaviour reflects the institutionalized patterns of belief and behaviour that have become historically entrenched in particular polities.[14] Such behaviours not only reflect earlier patterns of domestic and international interaction, but they also help to shape current policy.

The other non-material feature of inter-state behaviour that merits emphasis is the response of non-hegemonic states to changes in American policy and the nature of its hegemonic power. The construction of the highly institutionalized, multilateral order inaugurated at Bretton Woods marked a distinctive phase and form of American hegemony,[15] one from which Australia was potentially well-placed to benefit. When American policymakers chose to undermine, if not abandon, this regime in favour of a more unilateral or bilateral approach to international relations[16] – one that was potentially much less likely to further

'Australian' interests – then we might have expected a cooling of Australia–US relations as a consequence. That they have not is something of a problem for much conventional IR theorizing, and suggests that, when attempting to understand why Australia's policymaking elites remain so closely tied to the United States, we need to consider the way that generations of policymakers in Australia have understood the relationship. Crucially, we need to analyse the way in which the costs and benefits of the relationship have been calculated, and recognize the impact of a wider array of domestic factors in shaping this calculus. In Australia's case, it seems possible that, not only have ideas about Australia's relationship with the United States been different and distinctive from other countries as a consequence of its unique historical circumstances, but such conceptions of the relationship may have led to a general policy paradigm that has not always worked in Australia's 'national interest', no matter how this imprecise and ideologically loaded notion is actually defined.

The evolution of Australia's strategic relationship with the United States

There is one aspect of Australia's unique historical circumstances that arguably has played a bigger role in shaping its subsequent international orientation than any other. Former prime minister John Howard liked to argue that Australia does not have to choose between its geography and history in deciding policy priorities.[17] In other words, Australia could accept the reality of its location adjacent to Asia without sacrificing 'traditional' ties to Britain and latterly the United States. Nevertheless, brute geography *has* played a large part in the way Australia's foreign relations have developed. Being a long way from Europe and close to the populous nations of the East Asian region to its north induced a permanent sense of anxiety amongst generations of Australian policymakers.[18] Australia was, for much of its history, an outpost of European colonialism, and its demographic profile and policy orientation reflected this. For many years, this made relations with its Asian neighbours inherently problematic, characterized as they frequently were by mutual incomprehension. While relations with the region have generally improved beyond recognition over the last 30 or 40 years, a lingering sense of anxiety, especially in strategic terms, continues to influence policymaking.

Even though Australia's sense of identity was not with its immediate neighbourhood (or even with Australia itself, initially),[19] its policy orientation was not immutably fixed on Europe generally or Britain in particular either. On the contrary, when faced with the prospect of isolation and possible invasion, Australian policymakers rapidly and pragmatically shifted their principal allegiance and strategic ties from Britain to the United States. However, in the immediate aftermath of World War II, it became clear that Australia was destined to play the role of supplicant in this relationship. Australian policymakers were generally unhappy about the 'soft' peace that American policymakers offered to Japan, but were willing to go along with it as the price that had to be paid for securing a formal security agreement with the United States.[20] Whatever the merits of the Australian position, from the outset, the resultant compromise established a pattern in which Australian policymakers went along with US preferences in the hope of satisfying their own.

Much has been written about the subsequent ANZUS Treaty between Australia, the United States and New Zealand that emerged from this period. Its admirers argue that it has been the backbone of Australia's security for more than 50 years, and cite common 'cultural and normative factors' as central components of its success[21] – despite the fact that New Zealand is no longer a member, following its refusal to allow American nuclear-armed or nuclear-powered vessels to use its ports. Nevertheless, there is clearly something in the claim that factors other than a simple calculation of material capacities and strategic obligations have been at work, and this helps explain the Treaty's noteworthy durability. This longevity is even more remarkable, given the famously imprecise and ambiguous nature of the document itself: the signatories are obliged to do little more than 'consult' in the event that any of them is attacked by another power. The only occasion on which the Treaty has actually been invoked was by John Howard in the aftermath of the September 11 attacks on the United States. At one level, the gesture was essentially symbolic, as Australia's offer of assistance to the United States could have little material impact on American security or even on its subsequent efforts to conduct the 'War on Terror'. At another level, however, this gesture was entirely in keeping with a long-standing Australian tradition of attempting to curry favour with the dominant power of the era.

Although the former coalition government was understandably keen to emphasize the continuing importance of the alliance, given its prominent role in the 'coalition of the willing' in Iraq, when seen in a longer historical context, the arguments in its favour seem less compelling. Even the former head of the armed forces, General Peter Cosgrove, has now conceded that the major commitment that Australia made in Vietnam, for example, was not 'sensible' when seen in retrospect.[22] Even in the overheated, ideologically charged context of the Cold War, and in view of the apparent threat of communist expansion, it was never clear that Australia's vital strategic interests were threatened, or that its costly participation in Vietnam served any other function than reinforcing its reputation as a dependable ally. Precisely, the same sorts of debates were revisited in the context of Iraq, but this time they were canvassed, not by radical students or the political left, but by senior retired military figures, diplomats and prime ministers.[23]

In essence, the arguments put forward by domestic critics revolved around the claims that Howard's open-ended commitment to Iraq was misguided; that it fundamentally compromised Australian autonomy by binding it to unilateral and aggressive American policies; and that it was a betrayal of the Australian tradition of not being involved in unprovoked aggression. Even if such arguments about the supposedly different geopolitical constraints imposed by the Cold War are occasionally self-serving and revisionist, it is nonetheless remarkable that Malcolm Fraser, a former Liberal prime minister, would claim that 'the US has become a fundamentalist regime, believing fervently that what it judges to be right is in fact right, and that others do not have anything much worthwhile to contribute. Such an America will not make friends'.[24]

Such remarks stand in striking contrast to John Howard's line on the ANZUS Treaty, in particular, and the alliance relationship more generally. In contrast, Howard has argued that Australia and the United States are united by a 'common sense of values and common traditions'.[25] At its most extreme, this sort of thinking underpins the claim that the Anglo-Saxon countries – the United States, Australia, Canada, Britain and New Zealand – constitute an 'Anglosphere' of nations, with similar (and superior) political and economic practices that can act as a model for the world.[26] However, despite the importance that Howard, in particular, attached to distinctive values and cultural traditions, it is important to recognize that his government was politically shrewd enough to make a more practical case for the alliance's continuing relevance.

Calculating the benefits

Australia's former foreign minister Alexander Downer advanced four central arguments in defence of the ANZUS Treaty, in particular, and the alliance with the United States more generally. First, it 'provides a bedrock of certainty and security on which both Australia and the United States know they can always rely'. Second, it 'helps cement the United States into the security architecture of the region'. Third, it 'gives Australia much greater weight and relevance in regional and global security issues'. And, finally, it allows Australia to 'carry substantially more weight in Washington' than it would do otherwise.[27] It is worth considering all of these claims in more detail, as they are central to debates about the relationship's continuing importance.

Predictably enough, given Australian policymakers' historical preoccupation with security, the principal justification for the alliance is as a bedrock of certainty. And yet, the reality is that the United States has shown a conspicuous unwillingness to assist Australia when confronted with a series of security challenges in Timor and other parts of the so-called 'arc of instability' in the Pacific.[28] On the contrary, the United States has encouraged Australia to play a more prominent role in maintaining stability in the Asia-Pacific – something the Howard government attempted to do, in addition to maintaining a commitment in Iraq and elsewhere. Not only did this severely stretch Australia's limited military capacities, but it also led the Howard government into diplomatic difficulties that might have been avoided, had Australia not been encumbered by its alliance commitments.

The most egregious example of such difficulties occurred when Howard failed to repudiate the idea that Australia would play the role of 'deputy sheriff' to the United States in Southeast Asia and the Pacific.[29] This gaffe was compounded when the Howard government indicated that it reserved the right to follow America's unilateral lead and launch pre-emptive strikes in the region if the 'war on terror' made this necessary. Needless to say, such views did not impress some of Australia's neighbours and gave ammunition to some of Australia's regional critics who had long been sceptical about the Howard government's enthusiasm for 'Asian engagement'.[30] After all, Howard came to power in the mid-1990s promising to 'reinvigorate' the US relationship, which he claimed had been neglected as a consequence of successive Labor governments' 'obsession' with Asia.[31] Consequently, Downer's third major claim – that the alliance relationship gives Australia greater weight in regional affairs – looks contestable at best.

Tangible evidence of just how complicated the alliance could make Australia's regional relations was seen in the Howard government's initial refusal to sign the Association of Southeast Asian Nations' (ASEAN) Treaty of Amity and Cooperation. Although this Treaty obliged its signatories to do little other than commit themselves to pursuing peaceful relations in the region, the Howard government was concerned that this might conflict with its alliance commitments and marginalize the United States.[32] Eventually, Howard did sign up, as this was the price to be paid for a place at the East Asian Summit, which has the potential to define the region's future institutional architecture and intra-regional relations. The point to emphasize is that the privileging of the alliance with the United States made the conduct of independent relations in 'Australia's national interest' far more problematic than it might otherwise have been.

Downer's second major claim – that the alliance helps cement the United States into the security architecture of the region – looks more credible superficially; but, even here, calculating the benefits for Australia and the wider region is no straightforward task. The first point to make is that the United States would remain engaged with the region with or without the ANZUS Treaty. Not only does the United States have a number of other key allies, such as Japan, in the region, but, as a global power, it will inevitably remain deeply engaged with the region, whatever Australian policy may look like. Indeed, it is important to emphasize that the United States will necessarily have a very different view of the region and its importance, partly because it is not potentially 'of' the region in quite the same way as Australia, and partly because it adopts a global and hegemonic perspective. To expect that Australian and American perspectives would necessarily coincide, therefore, is to ignore the very different underlying histories and capacities that shape the foreign policies in the United States and Australia.[33]

The other, generally neglected, point to make is that not only will United States strategic engagement with the region occur independently of Australian policy, but it is not unambiguously clear that it is necessarily beneficial, whatever circumstances it occurs under. After all, the United States – and Australia, as a consequence of its alliance obligations – has been involved in all the major conflicts in the East Asian region since World War II, and has been at the centre of the continuing 'war on terror', which is causing such difficulties for a number of Southeast Asian countries.[34] The United States' long track record of violent intervention around the world makes claims about its supposedly indispensable stabilizing and pacific role contentious at best.[35] What is of potentially greatest significance in the long term, perhaps, is that there seems to be a growing recognition that the United States may not be the indispensable force for stability that some claim, that East Asians may be able to manage their intra-regional security relations without US help, and that China may actually play a stabilizing role in the future.[36]

From an Australian perspective, therefore, the danger is that East Asia will become increasingly independent on the United States, and develop self-reliant, institutionalized capacities from which Australia is either excluded or has little influence. There are, indeed, signs both that such processes are gathering momentum and that Australia is not a central part of them.[37] However, this might be less problematic if Downer's fourth claim – that Australia has significant influence in Washington – carries weight. Here, the evidence is less ambiguous: while there is much talk about a 'special relationship' and much praise heaped upon Australia as a reliable ally, as in Britain, evidence about Australia's ability to influence American policy is scant. On the contrary, not only is Australia arguably not benefiting from its strategic relationship, but it is suffering politically and economically as well.

The political, economic and strategic nexus

Although it is conventional to consider politics, economics and security separately, and to make a distinction between 'external' and 'internal' affairs, such academic niceties are becoming increasingly difficult to sustain. Political economists have long drawn attention to the mutually constitutive, interdependent nature of political and economic activity.[38] However, it is also clear that the wider geopolitical context within which such activities are embedded can have a profound impact upon the way they are realized within nationally demarcated arenas, and on the way the very idea of security is construed as a consequence.[39] In this context, it is important to recognize that recent changes in the conduct of American foreign policy, especially the self-conscious linking of formerly discrete economic and strategic goals, have been specifically designed to give its policymakers enhanced leverage over other states in pursuit of wider American policy objectives.[40] The potentially multidimensional impact of such a strategy on Australia's bilateral relationship with the United States can consequently be seen in a number of deeply interconnected areas.

The possibility that strategic issues might have direct political consequences is evident in the Australian case, although not in the manner that might intuitively be expected. In other countries such as Britain, for example, foreign policy, generally, and the conflict in Iraq were the centre of heated debate and the cause of much political pain for the Blair government. In Australia, in contrast, despite opinion polls showing extremely low levels of support for the war in Iraq,[41] and diminishing confidence in the United States to 'act responsibly' in international affairs, there has been less popular pressure on the government to change course – despite over 90 per cent of the population claiming to be at least 'interested' in foreign affairs.[42] This is all the more remarkable, given that it is possible to argue that Australia's overall security has actually been significantly *diminished* by its alliance with the United States: one of the motives for the series of attacks on Australians in Indonesia, according to some of the bombers themselves, was to punish Australia for its support of the United States.[43]

There are a number of possible explanations for the comparative lack of political pressure that was placed on the Howard government as a consequence of its participation in the Iraq conflict. First, the debate about Iraq was conducted primarily in elite policymaking circles and the opinion pages of Australia's limited number of broadsheets. Rupert Murdoch's *Australian* has been a strong supporter of American policy, and its influential foreign affairs editor Greg Sheridan remains a prominent advocate of American policy and the alliance.[44] Critics of American policy have tended to be dismissed as strategic illiterates at best, mindlessly anti-American at worst. This has become an acutely sensitive issue for the ALP as its recently deposed leader, Mark Latham, was one of the few political figures to question the conventional wisdom about the alliance. His depiction of George W. Bush as 'the most incompetent president in living memory'[45] may have been recently echoed in the United States,[46] but the intemperate nature of his language, and Latham's subsequent political demise, have made criticism of the alliance an extremely sensitive topic for the incoming ALP prime minister, Kevin Rudd.

Consequently, the ALP has been at pains to cast itself as a strong supporter of the alliance. While this is understandable, perhaps, it is still somewhat surprising for a number of reasons. First, one of the key benefits that both the government and the opposition use to justify the alliance is that Australia's defence is 'greatly enhanced' through security cooperation.[47] And yet, not only was access to US intelligence of little value as far as the attacks on Bali were concerned, but the United States has been unwilling to share sensitive operational information about weapons systems that Australia has committed to in line with the demands of 'inter-operability'.[48] This raises a further question about the necessity of acquiring such weapon systems at all. Plainly, the issue of how best to defend Australia reflects a judgement about the types of threat that the country faces and the best way of addressing them. The Howard government argued that 'Australian security interests are not defined by geography alone', and that 'by virtue of its effective integration into the global community, Australia has security interests far distant from its shores'.[49] Although the language is coy and imprecise, the reference to the 'global community' can be taken to imply that the defence of Australia involves much more than the protection of Australia itself and suggests participation alongside the United States, wherever that may lead.

As we have seen, such a stance is entirely in keeping with Australian policy since it shifted allegiance from Britain to the United States. There is little to suggest that Kevin Rudd's Labor government is likely to deviate significantly from this line. Although Rudd has committed himself to eventually withdrawing Australia's essentially tokenistic force in Iraq, the troops in Afghanistan are likely to remain, and he has been at pains to emphasize how important the overall alliance remains to Australia. Indeed, Rudd argues that 'despite Iraq, America is an overwhelming force for good in the world. It is time we sang that from the world's rooftops'.[50] There is plainly a recognition in Washington, too, that the

United States needs to come to terms with the new order in Australia and make the most of Kevin Rudd's ascendancy, as he is a long-time and enthusiastic supporter of the alliance.[51] There may also be some recognition in the United States of the need to make amends for the behaviour of former ambassador Tom Schieffer, who undertook unprecedented levels of political interference in Australia's domestic politics as the US government sought to discredit the Latham-led Labor Party and shore up support for the alliance.[52] Although American foreign policy, generally, and the alliance, in particular, have regularly spilled over into Australia's domestic political scene, both sides of politics in Australia have shown a remarkable willingness to support America's strategic ambitions. The Howard government was even willing to sacrifice 'Australia's' economic interests as well.

The political economy of alliance relations

One of the most telling indications of just how far the Howard government was prepared to go to secure the alliance, and of how much its policy autonomy had been constrained by the overarching geopolitical context in which it was embedded, was revealed in the negotiation of the 'free trade' deal with the United States. If ever there was a potentially unambiguous confirmation of Downer's claimed influence in Washington, and of the overall merits of close ties with the United States delivering advantageous political outcomes, this was it. In reality, the much-trumpeted agreement failed to serve 'Australian' interests. Given the importance of this agreement and its capacity to highlight the overall dynamics and consequences of the alliance, it is worth spelling out why.

At one level, Australian policymakers must contend with precisely the same sorts of difficulties that confront their counterparts everywhere: despite the rhetorical importance that the Howard government attached to the idea of 'the national interest',[53] in an increasingly transnationalized economic and political environment, where 'national' economies are less discrete and their management is reliant on international cooperation, defining – let alone pursuing – 'the national interest' is an inherently problematic exercise. Indeed, even the definition of national security objectives has become more complex as a wider range of factors and actors influences its discursive realization.[54] What has distinguished the Australian response to this dilemma of late, however, has been a single-minded privileging of the strategic aspects of the US–Australia relationship at the expense of economic considerations.

Three issues make this a contentious prioritization of policies. First, Australia is one of a relatively small number of countries that actually runs a trade deficit with the United States. Many Australian products like dairy, beef and sugar, and even sophisticated manufactured goods like fast ferries, compete directly with politically powerful economic sectors in the United States and consequently face a range of import barriers. In such circumstances, we might expect that the negotiation of a 'free trade' deal with the United States would offer an opportunity for overcoming such obstacles and allow Australian producers unfettered access to

America's domestic market. In reality, however, there is widespread agreement amongst most Australian economists and commentators that the agreement overwhelmingly reflects American priorities and has further opened the Australian market with few reciprocal concessions being won in return. Indeed, Australia's own professional trade officials and negotiators actually advised the Howard government not to sign such an unfavourable deal.[55] However, given the political capital that Howard had invested in the relationship, and the benefits he claimed were derived from it, his government was virtually obliged to sign any sort of agreement or risk undermining the legitimacy of the alliance more generally.

A second reason for expecting an Australian government to be leery of a bilateral trade deal is that the current fashion for bilateralism – which the United States has been largely responsible for encouraging[56] – is unlikely to work in favour of less powerful nations such as Australia. In bilateral negotiations between larger and smaller powers, it is almost inevitable that the more powerful player will succumb to the 'hegemonic temptation'[57] and use its superior leverage to secure deals that reflect an American conception of the national interest. In contrast, Australia – a country that is reliant on access to an open international economic system – has long championed multilateral approaches to trade negations, in particular. However, Australia's influential role in promoting bodies like the Cairns Group, the Asia Pacific Economic Cooperation forum and the WTO has been undermined by its participation in bilateral agreements.[58] In the period since the agreement was concluded, it has become clear that the fears of the sceptics are being realized: US exports to Australia grew by 4 per cent till 2006, while Australian exports to the United States actually *fell* by the same amount.[59] Even more importantly, perhaps, in addition to the damage inflicted on Australia's short-term economic position, American misgivings about the merits of international cooperation have been supported by Australia, something that has made tackling definitively global problems like climate change even more difficult. It is significant that Australia was initially the only other OECD country other than the United States to refuse to sign the Kyoto Agreement.[60] However, given that Australia has been one of the countries that has already been most adversely affected by climate change, the efficacy of such actions as far as Australia's more broadly conceived 'security' interests are concerned is debateable at best.[61]

A final reason for questioning the wisdom of Australia's consolidation of close ties with the United States through mechanisms such as the bilateral trade agreement is that most of Australia's major economic partners are located in East Asia, not North America.[62] Japan has long been Australia's single most important market, but the rise of China is likely to entrench the significance of the Asian region for Australia and further complicate its external relations. The Rudd government finds itself in the difficult position of having to balance the economic imperatives that flow from its complementary economic relationship with China and its seemingly insatiable appetite for Australian resources, and the obligations it feels flow from the strategic relationship with the United States. Compounding Australia's difficulties is the apparent willingness of the American government to apply direct bilateral pressure on Australia to align itself more closely and unambiguously with the United States. A key forum in which this pressure is being applied is through the Australia–US Ministerial Consultations, or 'AusMin' talks. In a familiar pattern, a mechanism that is routinely claimed as offering Australians unparalleled access to key American decision makers and a chance to influence US policy is, it seems, one more instrument with which the hegemon has been able to bind supplicant states to its overall agenda.[63]

Concluding remarks

Despite the recent transformation that has occurred in both the content of American foreign policy, and in the way such changes have been viewed by other states, Australian policymakers remain broadly supportive of the United States. Even though there has been a noticeable decline in the levels of public support in Australia for American foreign policy generally, and the war in Iraq in particular, support for the alliance and confidence about America's willingness to under-write Australia's defence remains undiminished.[64] Such apparent contradictions notwithstanding, continuing public confidence in the alliance is clearly one of the reasons why Australia's political class remains similarly wedded to the United States. Australia's unique history, in which strategic anxiety about the country's geographical location and a concomitant uncertainty about its place in the region have contributed to a sense of vulnerability among policy makers and the general public alike, has plainly contributed to the durability of the alliance.

Nevertheless, it is remarkable that discourses of danger and uncertainty have proved so enduring and resistant to change in Australia. While relations with the region to Australia's north have improved under both the ALP and the Liberal–National Party coalition government of John Howard, it is also evident that suspicions remain. If Australia does face a conventional threat against which an alliance with the United States might offer the promise of protection, then it must emanate from East Asia. Although Australian policymakers are understand-ably coy about naming names, the only even vaguely realistic possible threat is China. However, even if we put aside the limited nature of China's military capability,[65] considering China (or any of Australia's other neighbours) as a strategic threat would seem to overlook some key characteristics of the current international system and Australia's place in it. Not only is Australia naturally protected by its status as an island continent, but transformations in the 'logic' of the international political economy make the attractions of military conquest increasingly dubious.[66] In any case, the United States would be unlikely to view a Chinese (or any other nation, for that matter) takeover of the Australian mainland with equanimity. Given that even the Australian government concedes that such threats are now remote,[67] it begs the question of what purpose the alliance any longer serves and why Australian policymakers remain locked into it – despite its increasingly evident costs. This is an especially important consideration, given that Kevin Rudd has been keen to emphasize that China should be seen as the key to Australia's economic future, rather than as an inevitable strategic threat.[68]

Balancing relations between the United States and China in such circumstances will be one of the defining challenges for the new government.

Does any of this matter? Are the actions of a peripheral middle power of any great significance, either to the hegemon or to the general international order of which it is still such a central constitutive part?[69] No and yes. While the functioning of the hegemon is clearly not dependent on the actions of a minor ally like Australia, Australia's actions have given a fig leaf of legitimacy to American actions on occasion and saved it from international isolation. Even more importantly, perhaps, Australia has been complicit in encouraging a form of aggressive unilateralism that most observers consider to have been ill-advised and counter-productive, and which even its 'neocon' architects have sought to distance themselves from of late.[70] It is in this latter context that the actions of the Howard government, in particular, must be subjected to especially critical scrutiny: not only did the Howard government's actions arguably undermine Australia's overall strategic and environmental security, and disadvantage Australian-based economic actors, but they contributed to the erosion of the multilateral system that served 'Australian' interests so well and arguably contributed to the overall stability of the international system. Kevin Rudd's decision to make signing the Kyoto Protocol one of the first acts of his new government suggests that he recognizes that, for a country like Australia, multilateralism matters. One can only assume – and hope – that, as in Australia, the new American administration will adopt a similarly, more collaborative, internationally oriented stance than their predecessors have done.

Notes

1 P. Kelly, 'A Realistic Beginning', *The Australian*, December 2008.
2 For a more detailed discussion of the nature of hegemony, especially the American variety, see Mark Beeson, 'American Ascendancy: Conceptualising Contemporary Hegemony', in Mark Beeson (ed.) *Bush and Asia: America's Evolving Relations with East Asia*, London: Routledge, 2006, pp. 3–23.
3 One of the most influential statements of this position is provided by Robert Gilpin, *War and Change in World Politics*, Cambridge: Cambridge University Press, 1981.
4 For one of the best discussions of these fears and their impact on Australian foreign policy, see A. Burke, *In Fear of Security: Australia's Invasion Anxiety*, Sydney: Pluto Press, 2001.
5 C. Waters, 'War, decolonization and postwar security', in D. Goldsworthy (ed.) *A Century of Australian Engagement with Asia: Volume 1, 1901 to the 1970s*, Melbourne: Melbourne University Press, 2001, pp. 97–133.
6 See, for example, Judith Goldstein and Robert O. Keohane, 'Ideas and Foreign Policy: An Analytical Framework', in J. Goldstein and R. Keohane (eds) *Ideas and Foreign Policy: Beliefs, Institutions, and Political Change*, Ithaca: Cornell University Press, 1993, pp. 3–30; J. Mahoney, 'Path Dependence and Historical Sociology', *Theory and Society*, 2000, vol. 29, pp. 507–48.
7 S. Krasner, 'Approaches to the State: Alternative Conceptions and Historical Dynamics', *Comparative Politics*, 1984, vol. 16, pp. 223–46; Peter Gourevitch, *Politics in Hard Times: Comparative Responses to International Economic Crises*, Ithaca: Cornell University Press, 1986.

8 Ivo H. Daadler and James M Lindsay, *America Unbound: The Bush Revolution in Foreign Policy*, Washington D.C.: Brookings Institution, 2003; Mark Beeson, 'The Rise of the "Neocons" and the Evolution of American Foreign Policy', in Vedi Hadiz (ed.) *Empire, Neoliberalism, and Asia*, London: Routledge, 2006, pp. 69–82.

9 For a fuller explanation of this point, see Mark Beeson, 'The Declining Theoretical and Practical Utility of "Bandwagoning": American Hegemony in the Age of Terror', *British Journal of Politics and International Relations*, 2007, vol. 9, pp. 618–35.

10 Joseph S. Nye, *The Paradox of American Power*. Oxford: Oxford University Press, 2002.

11 This possibility is amply demonstrated in the 'Asia-Pacific' region, of which Australia is a part, where many East Asian countries benefited from US hegemony without necessarily subscribing to American-style economic and political practices. See R. Stubbs, *Rethinking Asia's Economic Miracle*, Basingstoke: Palgrave, 2005.

12 Beeson, 'The Declining Utility of "Bandwagoning"'; P. H. Gordon and J. Shapiro, *Allies at War: America, Europe, and the Crisis Over Iraq*, New York: McGraw-Hill, 2004.

13 Alexander Wendt, *Social Theory of International Politics*, Cambridge University Press, 1999, p 20.

14 See also P. A. Hall, 'Policy Paradigms, Social Learning, and the State: The Case of Economic Policymaking in Britain'. *Comparative Politics*, 1993, vol. 25, pp. 275–96.

15 Robert W. Cox, *Production, Power, and World Order*, New York: Columbia University Press, 1987; R. Latham, *The Liberal Moment: Modernity, Security, and the Making of Postwar International Order*, New York: Columbia University Press, 1997; Mark Beeson and Richard Higgott, 'Hegemony, Institutionalism and US Foreign Policy: Theory and Practice in Comparative Historical Perspective', *Third World Quarterly*, 2005, vol. 26, pp. 1173–88.

16 See C. Prestowitz, *Rogue Nation: American Unilateralism and the Failure of Good Intentions*, New York: Basic Books, 2003; C. Layne, 'The unipolar illusion revisited: The coming end of the United States' unipolar moment'. *International Security*, 1993, vol. 31, pp. 7–41.

17 John Howard, 'Australia's Links with Asia: Realising Opportunities in Our Region', the Fifth Asialink Lecture, 1995.

18 D. Walker, *Anxious Nation: Australia and the Rise of Asia 1850–1939*, St Lucia: University of Queensland Press, 1999.

19 R. Hughes, *The Fatal Shore: A History of the Transportation of Convicts to Australia, 1787–1868*, London: Collins Harvill, 1987.

20 See T. B. Millar, *Australia in Peace and War*, Canberra: Australian National University Press, 1978.

21 W. T. Tow and H. Albinski. 'ANZUS – Alive and Well after Fifty Years'. *Australian Journal of Politics and History*, 2002, vol. 48, pp. 153–73.

22 Mark Beeson, 'Australia's Relationship with the United States: The Case for Greater Independence', *Australian Journal of Political Science*, 2003, vol. 38, pp. 387–405.

23 P. Kelly, 'The "Group of 43" Is Right', *The Australian*, August 2004.

24 M. Fraser, 'The End of Our Independence?' *The Age*, 14 July 2004.

25 John Howard, 'Speech at the Launch of Documents on Australian Foreign Policy – the ANZUS Treaty 1951', Parliament House, Canberra, 29 August 2001.

26 J. C. Bennett, *The Anglosphere Challenge: Why the English Speaking Nations Will Lead the Way in the Twenty-First Century*, Lanham: Rowman & Littlefield, 2004.

27 Alexander Downer, 'Australia's Alliance with the United States: Maintaining the "Fabric of Peace"', unpublished paper presented to The Australia–United States Alliance and East Asian Security, University of Sydney, 29 June 2001.

28 R.Leaver, 'The Meanings, Origins and Implications of "the Howard Doctrine"', *The Pacific Review*, 2001, vol. 14, pp. 15–34.

29 A. Brantley, 'The Howard Defense Doctrine', *The Bulletin*, 28 September 2002, pp. 22–24.

30 T. Allard, 'Pre-emptive Strikes: PM Weighs UN Rules Change', *Sydney Morning Herald*, 6 December 2002. The Howard government was far less enthusiastic about 'engaging' with Asia, a process that had been pioneered by its Labor predecessors generally and former prime minister Paul Keating in particular. See Paul Keating, *Engagement: Australia Faces the Asia Pacific*, Sydney: Macmillan, 2000.

31 See Beeson, 'Australia's Relationship with the United States'.

32 D. Rowel, 'Treaty Another Way into East Asia', *Sydney Morning Herald* 15 April 2005.

33 Condoleezza Rice, 'Promoting the National Interest'. *Foreign Affairs*, 2000, vol. 79, pp. 45–62; Paul Trubowitz, *Defining the National Interest: Conflict and Change in American Foreign Policy*, Chicago: University of Chicago Press, 1998.

34 Jim Glassman, 'US Foreign Policy and the War on Terror in Southeast Asia', in Garry Rodan, Kevin Hewison, and Richard Robison (eds) *The Political Economy of South-East Asia: An Introduction*, 3rd edn., Melbourne: Oxford University Press, 2006, pp. 219–37.

35 See S. Kinzer, *Overthrow: America's Century of Regime Change from Hawaii to Iraq*, New York: Times Books, 2006.

36 See David C. Kang, 'Getting Asia Wrong: The Need for New Analytical Frameworks', *International Security*, 2003, vol. 27, pp. 57–85; Mark Beeson, *Regionalism, Globalization and East Asia: Politics, Security and Economic Development*, Basingstoke: Palgrave, 2007.

37 T. Terada, 'Constructing an "East Asia" Concept and Growing Regional Identity: From EAEC to ASEAN+3', *Pacific Review*, 2003, vol. 16, pp. 251–77.

38 For an overview of some of the most important contributions, see M. Watson, *Foundations of Political Economy,* Basingstoke: Palgrave, 2005.

39 Ian Clark, *Globalization and International Relations Theory*, Oxford: Oxford University Press, 1999.

40 G. John Ikenberry, 'Liberalism and Empire: Logics of Order in the American Unipolar Age', *Review of International Studies*, 2004, vol. 30, pp. 609–30; Richard Higgott, 'US Foreign Policy and the "Securitization" of Economic Globalization', *International Politics*, 2004, vol. 41, pp. 147–75.

41 P. Waters, '80 pc Believe Iraq War Has Failed', *The Australian*, 3 October 2006.

42 Not only is there growing scepticism about the merits of American foreign policy, but 69 per cent of respondents thought that America exercised 'too much' influence over Australian foreign policy. Paradoxically enough, however, 42 per cent thought the ANZUS alliance remained 'very important'. See I. Cook, *The Lowy Institute Poll 2006*, Lowy Institute: Sydney, 2006.

43 Beeson, 'Australia's relationship with the United States'.

44 For a recent example of a voluminous and remarkably consistent output, see G. Sheridan, 'US Shift Won't Hurt PM', *The Australian*, 16 November 2006.

45 P. Hartcher, 'It's a Bit Foreign to Latham, but Diplomacy Works', *Sydney Morning Herald*, 8 April 2004.

46 J. Borger, 'Neocons Turn on Bush for Incompetence Over Iraq War', *The Guardian*, 5 August 2006.

47 See Kevin Rudd, 'The Renewal of Australian Middle Power Diplomacy', Address to the Sydney Institute, 19 September 2006, p 2.

48 Despite the Australian government's willingness to spare no expense in making its force structure compatible with America's, the United States has refused to sell Australia its latest F-22 fighter planes on security grounds. See C. Stewart, 'US Rules out Deal on F-22', *The Australian*, 14 February 2007.

49 Commonwealth of Australia, *Australia's National Security: A Defence Update*, Canberra: Department of Defence, 2005.

50   Kevin Rudd, 'US is an Overwhelming Force for Good', *The Australian*, 24 August 2007.
51   'Bush Welcomes PM Kevin Rudd', *The Sunday Telegraph*, 25 November 2007.
52   L. Tingle, 'US Envoy Ignites Diplomatic Row', *Australian Financial Review*, 13 February 2003.
53   See, for example, Australia. Department of Foreign Affairs and Trade, *In the National Interest: Australia's Foreign and Trade Policy*, Canberra: DFAT, 1997.
54   J.-M. Guéhenno, 'The Impact of Globalisation on Strategy'. *Survival*, 1998–99, vol. 40, pp. 5–19.
55   Howard government officials were reportedly astounded by how little the Americans were prepared to concede to a supposedly valued ally – an indication of just how powerful domestic forces are in the construction of US foreign policy and how compartmentalised policymaking has become. See Christine Wallace, 'Bush Rebuff Stunned Negotiators', *The Australian*, 25 February 2004.
56   J. Ravenhill, 'The New Bilateralism in the Asia-Pacific', *Third World Quarterly*, 2003, vol. 24, pp. 299–317.
57   R. Rogowski, *Commerce and Coalitions: How Trade Affects Domestic Political Alignments*, New York: Princeton University Press, 1989.
58   For a fuller discussion of these issues, see A. Capling, *Australia and the Global Trading System*, Cambridge: Cambridge University Press, 2001.
59   Michael Costello, 'Done like a Dinner on Free Trade Deal', *The Australian*, 6 January 2006.
60   Equally significantly, Australia and the United States are the prime movers behind the 'Asia-Pacific Partnership on Clean Development and Climate'. Positioned as an alternative to Kyoto, the 'P6' countries are relying on the private sector and techno-logical change to promote change, rather than binding international agreements. See A. Hodge, 'The Third Way', *The Weekend Australian*, 14–15 January 2006.
61   Despite the dramatic impact that climate change is having on Australia, the Howard government remains closely aligned to the US position that resists multilateral agreements in favour of technological fixes. See Alexander Downer, 'The Impact of Energy Security on Australia's International Relations', 11 October 2006, <http://www.foreignminister.gov.au/speeches/2006/061011_es.html> (accessed 21 January 2009).
62   Commonwealth of Australia, *Trade 2006*, Canberra: CoA, 2006.
63   H. White, 'US May Play Hardball with Australia over China Ties', *Straits Times*, 16 April 2005.
64   A recent Lowy Institute poll suggested that a clear majority of Australians continue to regard the ANZUS alliance as 'very' or 'fairly' important. See A. Gyngell, *Lowy Institute Poll 2007: Australia and the World*, Sydney: Lowy Institute, 2007, p. 9.
65   D. Shambaugh, *Modernizing China's Military: Progress, Problems, and Prospects*, Berkeley: University of California Press, 2004.
66   E. Luttwak, *Turbo-Capitalism: Winners and Losers in the Global Economy*, London: Weidenfeld & Nicholson, 1998; R. Rosecrance, *The Rise of the Trading State: Commerce and Conquest in the Modern World*, New York: Basic Books, 1986.
67   Commonwealth of Australia, *Defence 2000: Our Future Defence Force*, Canberra: CoA, 2000.
68   Kevin Rudd, 'Don't Lock China Out', *The Age*, 14 March 2007.
69   S. Gill, 'New Constitutionalism, Democratisation and Global Political Economy', *Pacifica Review*, 1998, vol. 10, pp. 23–38.
70   D. Rose, 'Neo Culpa', *Vanity Fair*, 3 November 2006.

6 Yearning and spurning
New Zealand's special relationships with Britain and the United States

Dolores E. Janiewski

When a thoughtful observer reflected on New Zealand's position in the world in 1940, he saw Britain as the most important external relationship. Historian Frederick Wood had welcomed signs of 'rebellion against British dominance' after the election of the Labour government in 1935, but the declaration of war in September 1939 had reinvigorated New Zealand's imperial ties. History, according to Wood, had 'shaped New Zealanders into a people British in sentiment, tradition and economic interest', and history, once again, in the form of global war, had reinforced that identification. As a result, Wood predicted that New Zealand might someday achieve a 'modest independence in international affairs', but only as a 'small but not subservient member of the British Commonwealth', rather than a fully independent nation. Wood clearly regretted this state of 'psychological dependence on Britain', but reluctantly recognized the importance of New Zealand's 'special relationship' with Great Britain.[1]

New Zealand's declaration of war within an hour after the British declared war on Germany demonstrated its loyalty. Prime Minister Michael Joseph Savage paraphrased Ruth in the Old Testament as he pledged his country's devotion to Britain's cause. Motivated by 'gratitude for the past and with confidence in the future we range ourselves without fear beside Britain. Where she goes we go. Where she stands, we stand. We are only a small and young nation, but we are one and all a band of brothers'. Peter Fraser, the acting leader of the House during Savage's fatal illness, swore 'unshakeable loyalty to His Majesty, the King', the United Kingdom and the British Commonwealth.[2] Based upon the near-universal national assent to this decision to fight with Britain far away from New Zealand's shores, it was clear that a special relationship connected New Zealanders to monarchy, mother country and empire.

After 50 years, ex-Prime Minister David Lange mused about the Queen's arrival in New Zealand to celebrate the 150th anniversary of the Treaty of Waitangi. The Royal Yacht *Britannia* stayed away as a result of New Zealand's refusal to accept the 'neither to confirm nor deny' policy about the presence of nuclear weapons on British or American vessels. Lange pondered what he considered an absurd overreaction because the *Britannia* clearly carried only the Queen's shipboard necessities. 'I knew it wasn't me who'd taken leave of my senses', he wrote as he related the history of 'one small country' which 'found the political will to say no to nuclear weapons'. *Nuclear Free: The New Zealand Way* traced the 'difficult path' that had ended with the anti-nuclear actions that kept the *Britannia*, but not the Queen, from arriving in New Zealand.[3]

Between 1940 and 1990, New Zealand's two 'special relationships' flourished and then withered. This analysis offers insights into the strategic calculations and manoeuvres of a self-consciously 'small state' for whom the forging of such alliances required the ability to sense the larger partner's goals and vulnerabilities. It reveals the strength of a political movement ultimately able to force officials to witness the destruction of their prized connections to two great powers. New Zealand's history thus presents a parallax view of special relationships from the vantage point of a smaller partner. This makes it possible to examine the influence of nongovernmental actors on the conduct of foreign policy. Because the existing scholarship focuses primarily upon the role of diplomats and politicians in constructing special relationships, this analysis will include a focus on the peace movement and the anti-nuclear movement as they developed from marginalized and persecuted dissenters during the 1940s to a position of political influence in the 1980s.[4] Although some peace advocates initially viewed the 'American connection' as a betrayal of Britain, the peace and anti-nuclear movements eventually contributed to the construction of a post-imperial identity for New Zealand as independent, internationalist, moral and pacific in both the upper- and lower-case sense. It was the New Zealand for which Frederick Wood had yearned but never expected to witness.

As developed during World War II and the early Cold War, New Zealand's foreign policy combined three major elements: a special relationship with Britain, conceived as a mother–child relationship, but also a market for New Zealand products; a security-driven 'American connection' often framed as an 'alliance' or, more intimately, as a cousin relationship; and an internationalist dimension expressed through the Commonwealth and the United Nations. It was the task of diplomats, public officials and ministers to negotiate these complex identities and relationships. The official strategy based upon maintaining two special relationships retained its hold on public opinion through the 1960s. The Vietnam debacle and détente, and the subsequent revival of Cold War tensions, built support for the anti-nuclear movement. Simultaneously, the movement and its political allies gained adherents for their view of New Zealand as a Pacific nation seeking 'independence' in foreign policy. This study will trace the evolution of this vision and its consequences for New Zealand's existing allegiances and the foreign policy based upon them.

Focused on the conflict in Europe in 1940, Wood's assessment of New Zealand's position in the world did not predict the effects of the Pacific war. Already fearful of Japanese aggression, New Zealand officials began to work on the formation of a new security alliance. The same year, Wood's analysis appeared. Having become prime minister after the death of Savage, Fraser asked the British government for permission to send a minister to Washington to develop a closer relationship with the 'large powerful neighbour' across the Pacific. In June 1941, Fraser visited London to attend meetings of the War Cabinet, while a special envoy travelled to Washington to discuss security matters. After 2 months, Fraser made the same trip to confer with President Roosevelt and prepare the way for diplomatic relations.[5]

Even as they carefully nurtured a new special relationship, New Zealand's leaders maintained the 'British connection for solid reasons of self interest as well as of sentiment'. Located next to the British embassy in November 1941, New Zealand's official diplomatic presence in Washington began just as the Japanese attack brought the United States into the war. The decision to send Walter Nash, the deputy prime minister, signified the importance of this new relationship when he took up his new post in early 1942. The ties to Britain that kept New Zealand forces fighting in North Africa and Europe had engendered a greater need for American protection. The fall of Singapore in February increased that sense of vulnerability. One special relationship now required the formation of another one to provide the security it had once guaranteed.[6]

The peace movement found it impossible to break New Zealand's military alliance with Britain or prevent its new security relationship with the United States. The press, police and the government made strenuous efforts to suppress anti-war criticism. The police allowed mobs to attack anti-war meetings with impunity while the speakers faced arrest, fines and imprisonment. New Zealanders characterized as 'anti-war' became tagged as 'subversive'. The Wellington *Dominion* editorialized against 'our internal enemies', condemning those who sought to 'undermine our defences from within'. The editor urged the restoration of capital punishment and flogging as the 'most effective and salutary deterrents' to subversive and criminal elements. Public employees espousing pacifist sentiments, particularly those with communist affiliations, lost their positions. Legal constraints forced the leftist journal *Tomorrow* to cease publication. Marginalized by censorship, violence and severe punishments, the peace movement also faced internal divisions between religiously inspired pacifists, communists and other participants. Convinced of the need for American protection and loyalty to Britain , many New Zealanders cheered on the efforts to silence the critics of the war.[7]

Despite public hostility and legal pressure, peace activists continued to express their views. Christian pacifists did not waver in the face of adversity or the desertion by their communist allies after the German attack on the Soviet Union. The Reverend Alan Brash asked his fellow Presbyterians to 'serve as peacemakers in a war-stricken world', although only a handful of fellow believers agreed with his condemnation of 'war as incompatible with the mind and Spirit of Jesus'. One Methodist activist, after his arrest and his imprisonment, even found himself expelled from his church. Undeterred, pacifists criticized the bombing of civilians, the deliberate starvation inflicted upon children and other signs of the 'moral deterioration that has accompanied the struggle'. Lincoln Efford stood as a peace candidate in 1943, but his accusation that the Labour government had betrayed 'fundamental truths' went largely unheard. He received only 114 votes in the by-election, and 280 in the general election that was won later that year by Labour.[8] Despite the earnest efforts of peace campaigners, few New Zealanders questioned military alliances or calculated the humanitarian consequences of war tactics.

The allied victory enabled the leftist and Christian pacifists to reunite while the 'new terror' unleashed at Hiroshima and Nagasaki gave them a new cause. Efford organized the first Hiroshima Day March in 1946, a practice he continued until his death in 1962. Meanwhile, the rising tensions between the Soviet Union and the United States encouraged New Zealand communists to resume their peace efforts. The presence of communists in the peace movement at a time of heightened fear of subversion and popular acceptance of the need to look to the United States for protection deprived peace activists of broad-based support for their criticisms of nuclear weapons and the division of the world into hostile, armed camps.[9]

Although Fraser had acted on his commitment to internationalism and 'collective security' by playing a prominent role in founding the United Nations, the post-war atmosphere did not foster the internationalist strand in New Zealand's foreign policy. Carl Berendsen, who had taken up his post in Washington in 1944 as New Zealand's ambassador, described the situation in a letter to Alister McIntosh, the secretary of external affairs. Berendsen disliked the 'look of the world' in October 1945, but ruefully added, 'I don't see anything that I or New Zealand can do about it. Whether we like it or not it is going to be a "Great Power" world and a "Great Power" world in which the Great Powers will not agree'. He wrote to McIntosh that 'the United Nations was outdated the moment the atomic bomb appeared on the scene', because it placed 'decisive power in the hands of an aggressor'. Increasingly inclined to agree with the Truman administration that the Soviet Union was the likely aggressor, Berendsen prodded the New Zealand government to strengthen the American connection. As Wood described the situation, New Zealand now looked to the 'powerful American cousins who had replaced the ageing British parent' for leadership and security.[10]

New Zealand, 16 years after it had been enacted by the British Parliament, finally ratified the Statute of Westminster in 1947 to control its own foreign policy, but at the same time sought to maintain its special relationship with Britain and to strengthen its ties to the United States. The fear of a resurgent Japan propelled New Zealand and Australia to seek a post-war security alliance with the United States, which Berendsen now defined as the 'one bright spot' in the troubled world of 1947. A joint Australia–New Zealand campaign consumed 5 years of effort by diplomats and officials. Berendsen's visit to Wellington early in 1948, the year of the Czechoslovakian coup and the Berlin airlift, gave him the opportunity to persuade Wellington-based officials of the urgency of this goal in a bipolar world.[11] Back in Washington, Berendsen continued the campaign to transform a temporary wartime alliance into a permanent special relationship based upon military cooperation.

Blaming the Soviets for the failure of his vision of collective security under the auspices of the United Nations, Fraser agreed with Berendsen that New Zealand must take the American and British side in the Cold War. After the Commonwealth Conference in 1948, Fraser returned to New Zealand to campaign for peacetime conscription and universal military training. Despite opposition from the peace movement, Fraser won the referendum but lost the general election later that year. In a year when even a leftist New Zealand writer described himself as apprehensive that 'Uncle Sam and Uncle Joe' might soon 'come to blows', the ideological atmosphere favoured neither the peace movement, an internationalist foreign policy nor parties that could be portrayed as left-leaning.[12]

The National government steered New Zealand's foreign policy towards an even more aggressive anti-communism, which included a decision to close the diplomatic post in Moscow. When communists triumphed in China and war broke out in Korea, the Truman administration became convinced of the need to turn Japan into a bulwark against communist expansion. Sending military forces to Korea, New Zealand and Australia seized the opportunity to make assiduous efforts to gain the 'greatest gift that the most powerful country in the world can offer to a small and comparatively helpless group of people', a military alliance that would guarantee that Japan 'will not again become a menace to the peace and security of the world'. Despite British anxieties about the 'weakening of the bonds between the older dominions' and the United Kingdom, New Zealand and Australian diplomats used every chance to lobby for this 'gift'.[13] The newer special relationship must be strengthened even if it disturbed the senior partner in the older relationship.

Frederick Doidge, the New Zealand minister of external affairs, requested an explicit security guarantee against 'Asian expansionism' in a conversation with John Foster Dulles, then Truman's special representative. In Washington, Berendsen assured American officials that New Zealand stood 'with those whose continued support is essential to our own survival', earning praise from Dulles and others for his willingness to 'play this game with the Americans'. When the stalemate in Korea heightened American concern about the security situation in the Asia-Pacific region, New Zealand and Australian diplomats renewed their efforts. Although Dulles tried to fend them off by referring to British objections to a Pacific pact 'which excluded them', they could not be dissuaded.[14]

Finally, the Truman administration became convinced about the benefits of a tripartite pact to the 'defence of the free world' at a conference in Canberra attended by Dulles, Percy Spender of Australia and Doidge in February 1951. The New Zealand and Australian offer to endorse the peace treaty with Japan in tandem with a Pacific pact gave the Americans a *quid pro quo*. New Zealand officials sought to persuade the British government that the pact was 'complementary' to their existing relationship. To quieten suspicions that the 'flag of the United Kingdom was being struck in the Pacific' or that the 'United Kingdom was being unduly subservient to the United States', simultaneous statements from London, Washington, Canberra and Wellington portrayed the newly forming triangular arrangement as reinforcing existing relationships with Britain.[15]

On 1 September 1951, Australia, New Zealand and the United States signed what became known as the ANZUS agreement, in San Francisco, in a televised ceremony. Secretary of State Dean Acheson described the document as putting into 'words strong ties and purposes already in existence'. Australian ambassador

Spender claimed that the treaty was 'fashioned within the framework of the Charter of the United Nations' to produce 'peaceful security'. Berendsen stressed that the alliance was 'defensive in nature', but served 'notice' upon any 'evil-doer' of the risks of aggression. The tripartite security pact allowed New Zealand to 'play our part elsewhere in the global effort' to defend the 'free world'. ANZUS became 'a sort of talisman' for two generations of New Zealand officials who sought the protection of a more powerful partner. These same officials believed that New Zealand's political leaders did not fully appreciate its benefits. There was thus ample scope for what one official described as a 'serious non-meeting of minds' between diplomats and politicians about the value of the new special relationship forged in San Francisco.[16]

After 4 days, another San Francisco conference ratified the peace treaty with Japan. Berendsen enjoyed 'stonkering the Soviet's machinations' by ensuring that conference rules stymied Soviet goals. He received widespread praise in the American media for his role. Dulles celebrated the peace treaty as the result of the 'moral investment' that the United States had made in Japan. The eradication of Japanese 'militarism' allowed a 'peace of justice' to be signed. The next day, Berendsen interjected a more sceptical note into the proceedings. He warned that Japan might once more take the 'path of evil' in a forceful speech that attracted favourable comment. New Zealand had taken a 'risk' as a 'small country' in the hope that Japan would fulfil the trust symbolized by the treaty.[17] Implying that New Zealand had made the greater sacrifice, Berendsen concealed his own sense of triumph about having cajoled the United States into giving what it had been reluctant to grant.

The ANZUS treaty elicited approval from many New Zealanders, but also evoked disquiet about the exclusion of the United Kingdom. A National MP insisted that the negotiations with the United States 'have been made with the full knowledge and support of the United Kingdom' and that it did not 'affect our allegiance to the Mother-country' as he stressed the importance of ANZUS to combat the 'forces of evil'. Inside and outside Parliament, some New Zealanders remained unconvinced of the wisdom of a Cold War alliance with the United States. A student group angrily denounced an agreement that allowed 'the life of every young New Zealander' to hang 'on the whim of a bunch of trigger-happy hill-billies' and 'stand-over' men in a less than flattering description of Americans. As explained by a New Zealand writer, the critical reaction stemmed from a sense of 'helplessness to deflect the policies of a too-powerful friend—a friend without whom it would be impossible to get on at all, but alongside whom one might one day find oneself fighting in a last convulsive Armageddon'.[18] Conveying the irony that a security agreement evoked insecurity among some New Zealanders, these responses also pointed to the possibility that the anti-nuclear movement might gain traction if more New Zealanders came to share its fears of imminent destruction.

Seeking to silence the accusations of betrayal of the 'mother country', the National government vociferously declared its loyalty to Britain. After attending the Queen's coronation, Prime Minister Sidney Holland endorsed British views on international issues. That same year, the New Zealand Parliament passed the Royal Titles Act of 1953, designating the Queen as the monarch of New Zealand. The government organized an enormously popular royal tour in 1954 to reaffirm the 'fundamental strength of this country's attachment to the British connection'. Seeking to disguise the actual weakening of ties, this ritual expression of devotion to Queen and mother country remained a political imperative in a society where many continued to refer to Britain as 'home'. A National MP assured Parliament that the 'Commonwealth alliance is still the basis of our foreign policy'. Even as he spoke reassuring words about 'New Zealand's consistency', the same MP explained that New Zealand had 'been forced by a complex world situation to exercise greater maturity of judgment than heretofore'. He told his colleagues that 'the cornerstone of our Pacific defence' rested on the ANZUS agreement. New Zealand politicians began to speak of 'our American cousins' and 'our Commonwealth brothers' in a language that constructed both special relationships as compatible and mutually reinforcing, while also stressing the greater intimacy of the older imperial connection. This rhetorical effort to portray a stable triangular structure of two special relationships accompanied a foreign policy that increasingly relied upon the American connection.[19]

Criticisms from the leftist and European-oriented peace movement argued that the United States should be considered an 'unseemly ally'. In the pages of *Here and Now*, a journal dedicated to 'a peaceful world' and described by McIntosh as 'the magazine of the Left Wing Intellectuals', editors and contributors found little good to say about the United States or its New Zealand sympathizers. *Here and Now* described the 'police action' in Korea as a 'doubtful and dangerous cause' promoted by 'hysterical US generals and politicians'. The government decision to support this action earned a rebuke from a writer occupying the 'uneasy no man's land which lies between the two sides in the Cold War'. Another author criticized American foreign policy as 'steered by a map in which two-thirds or more of the globe is depicted as regions of darkness and contagion'. In early 1951, two contributors debated the feasibility of a security pact with the United States. One hoped that American help would be forthcoming against 'Russian-inspired aggression', while the other warned that a security alliance might 'interfere with the genuine aspirations of colonial peoples toward economic advance and self-government'. The editor suggested that Holland preferred 'the free-enterprising USA' instead of a 'Commonwealth led by a Labour government and including "fellow travellers" like Mr. Nehru'. *Here and Now* criticized Berendsen and Doidge for belonging to 'the all-out American party'.[20]

Among the objections in *Here and Now* to ANZUS lay a concern for the impact on British ties. A contributor asked, 'Should we lean toward the British policy of coming to an understanding with China or the American policy of hostility?' The editor warned about Dulles's aggressive rhetoric about liberating Eastern Europe, declaring that the 'British Commonwealth cannot afford participating in such a desperate adventure'. In the same issue, a correspondent complained that New Zealand had meekly acquiesced in 'the American refusal to permit British observers' at a recent ANZUS meeting. Using a pseudonym,

Bill Sutch described New Zealand as having been set 'completely adrift from British policy and interests in the Pacific' and having bound itself 'irrevocably to the US juggernaut'. A strong sense of British cultural and ideological superiority reinforced the suspicions expressed in *Here and Now* of a brash, reckless and imperious new ally.[21]

Ormond Wilson's essays in *Here and Now* displayed a more complicated mix of 'yearning' and 'spurning' that underlay his ambivalence towards the new partnership. Referring to the 'American colossus', Wilson claimed that it 'overwhelms us with its power but also tantalizes us with its luxury and fascinates us with its glamour'. New Zealanders faced pressures to 'conform to the American way of life' and to take the 'American line' on international issues. A few months later, he added a doleful prophecy: 'By accepting the inevitability of a world divided into hostile blocs we are helping to make war certain'. Wilson wanted the Americans put on notice 'that they cannot count on the unquestioning support of the "free world" in any dangerous adventures they care to embark on'; however, the New Zealand government continued to endorse United States policies.[22]

Some contributors to *Here and Now*, usually historians with an interest in Asia, imagined a future New Zealand free of imperial ties and ANZUS. Instead of forming a 'great, white Austral-Asian Power' with Australia and the United States, New Zealanders should 'develop the progressive mentality, the farsightedness, necessary for us to adopt a policy of working with Asia'. If New Zealand continued to cooperate with 'a calamitous anti-Asian policy', these authors warned about the dangers of involvement in 'dirty wars' in Indochina. Historian Keith Sinclair hoped that New Zealand might develop a foreign policy based on 'independence and morality' rather than follow Britain 'right or wrong' or share the 'American obsession' with communism. These authors sketched out the possibility of a non-aligned foreign policy oriented to Asia and the Pacific, rather than one reliant upon two special relationships with more powerful partners.[23]

For New Zealanders whose major objection to ANZUS was the British exclusion, events in 1954 offered a remedy. Dissatisfaction with the results of the Geneva conference that ended the French role in Vietnam persuaded the Eisenhower administration to negotiate a new security agreement covering Southeast Asia. New Zealand officials saw an opportunity to ensure 'respectable company' for any future 'collective action' in Indochina by pressing for British involvement. During the prolonged negotiations, Clifton Webb, the new minister of external affairs, made it clear that 'anti-red planning' could not advance without Britain. The formation of the Southeast Asia Treaty Organization (SEATO) with British membership thus delayed the cutting and tying of New Zealand's diplomatic umbilical cord to Britain. SEATO further enmeshed New Zealand in a Cold War security system through bilateral, trilateral and multilateral ties.[24]

Some New Zealanders worried about the risks of SEATO membership. According to Willis Airey, SEATO yoked New Zealand to undemocratic states and risked its involvement 'in the internal struggles of other peoples' under the 'cover of slogans about democracy and defending the free world'. He pointed to the inclusion of South Vietnam in a treaty protocol as potentially leading to an undesirable intervention. Diplomat Frank Corner mused about the contradictions between New Zealand's alliances and 'our geography'. Believing that a policy of neutrality might 'increase our security', he advised against making 'a commitment which places us under direct American command'. Disregarding such doubts, successive National governments operated on the assumption that 'our future safety is bound up with the safety of the great Western nations; more particularly, the United Kingdom and the United States of America'.[25] Non-alignment, thus, could not be countenanced by New Zealand's National Party and its leaders.

Even as New Zealand maintained ties to Britain through SEATO, the Malaya campaign and support for its intervention in Suez, nuclear testing in the Pacific created a new form of public opposition to this special relationship and the one with the United States. When the National government sent frigates to support a British H-bomb test at Christmas Island in 1957, a New Zealand newspaper expressed concern about 'using the Pacific as an atomic laboratory'. The testing of hydrogen bombs in the Pacific seemed to foretell the impending doom evocatively described in Australian Neville Shute's 1957 best-seller, *On the Beach*. In the last issue of *Here and Now* which appeared that same year, Robert Chapman, historian, political scientist and future mentor of Prime Minister Helen Clark, discussed the formation of an organization to advocate 'progressive disarmament' and 'move the Government to act' against nuclear testing.[26]

The Campaign for Nuclear Disarmament in Britain inspired anti-nuclear activists to organize the New Zealand Campaign for Nuclear Disarmament (NZCND) to advocate withdrawal from 'alliances such as SEATO and ANZUS which could make us a party to nuclear war'. NZCND urged New Zealand to join a 'neutral bloc' and participate through the UN in defending the 'security of all small nations'. Hiroshima and Easter marches, led in Christchurch by Efford and Brash, pamphlets, speeches and vigils sought to persuade New Zealanders that security alliances with nuclear powers produced the ultimate form of insecurity.[27]

In 1962, a 20-year-old David Lange witnessed the atmospheric effects of a nuclear test at distant Christmas Island. The blast caused the sky to be 'diffused with a ghastly brush of red'. As he later recalled, 'The sky that night haunted me as a vision of a man-made apocalypse' and a 'warning that a small country at the edge of the world' was no longer 'far enough away from the quarrels of the great powers to escape their consequences'. The still greater terrors of the Cuban Missile Crisis later in 1962 caused more New Zealanders to ponder the risks of special relationships that conjured up the danger of nuclear war. The anti-nuclear movement gained new recruits, and New Zealand attracted refugees from the United States and the United Kingdom, anxious to avoid the predicament described in *On the Beach* and ominously prefigured by the Cuban Missile Crisis.[28]

Framing its anti-nuclear arguments within a nationalist discourse that defined New Zealand as a Pacific nation, the NZCND campaigned for a nuclear-free zone in the southern hemisphere under the slogan 'No Bombs South of the Line'. French nuclear testing in the Pacific aided the campaign. Unconstrained by a special relationship to France, the National government protested the tests, but this official opposition raised the question why British or American tests should be considered more acceptable. Seeking to silence the NZCND clamour, Prime Minister Holyoake declared that he wanted the entire world to become nuclear-free instead of creating a local zone in the South Pacific. Norman Kirk, the leader of the Labour opposition, called Holyoake's bluff by agreeing on the ultimate goal but stressing the need to take a 'useful first step' through a 'nuclear-free zone by international agreement' in the South Pacific. Like Kirk, other Labour MPs brought the arguments of the anti-nuclear movement into Parliament's debating chamber.[29]

The ANZUS Council and New Zealand diplomats moved to counter this growing anti-nuclear movement. The Council described a nuclear-free zone as dangerous, destabilizing the strategic balance and thus likely to increase the possibility of aggression. Corner, testifying to a UN committee in 1963, referred to the nuclear issue 'that has been much in the public mind in my own country'. He endorsed nuclear-free zones, but insisted that this required the cooperation of all nuclear powers. He urged the UN to consider the criteria for the establishment of such zones. This response, in combination with the Partial Test-Ban Treaty, also enacted in 1963, may explain why the anti-nuclear movement began to subside just as an international crisis in Vietnam diverted the energies of peace activists concerned that New Zealand's membership in SEATO would drag it more deeply into the conflict.[30]

Determined to put an international face on its deployment of American troops in Vietnam in 1965, President Lyndon Johnson requested New Zealand's military support. Holyoake pointed to the 'confused state of opinion' in New Zealand and instability in Vietnam as a reason for delaying his response. In Washington, administration officials impressed upon George Laking, the New Zealand ambassador, that New Zealand must cooperate. McIntosh concluded that New Zealand might confront 'a strategic task of frightening dimensions' if US forces withdrew from Vietnam due to lack of support from its allies. Convinced that 'being frozen out of inner circles in Washington' was the 'ultimate disaster', New Zealand officials persuaded Holyoake to send an artillery unit in the name of 'collective security'. For the first time, New Zealand forces embarked on a combat mission without British involvement, a development that created 'disquiet' and a sense of 'moral uneasiness'.[31]

Committees on Vietnam, often led by peace movement veterans, began to take shape in 1965 while the Holyoake government still pondered the appropriate response to US requests. The opposition to Holyoake's decision to send troops to Vietnam showed the influence of the American anti-war movement in strategy, language and actions as television and air travel brought New Zealand and American anti-war activists closer together. Student newspapers reported 'teach-ins'. Chapman, the veteran anti-nuclear activist and political scholar, was one of the featured speakers at the University of Auckland's teach-in. By 1970, the anti-war movement included a young Helen Clark who studied politics with Chapman. The *New Zealand Listener* praised the widespread debate about Vietnam as 'the most encouraging reaction to foreign policy since the end of World War II'. The editor described a 'wider interest in Asia, a more sensitive appraisal of New Zealand's place in the South Pacific, and a new feeling of obligation towards Asian neighbours' as contributing to a growing disenchantment with ANZUS and SEATO. The debate grew more vociferous as the anti-war protesters underwent the same radicalization occurring in the United States. Indeed, Holyoake pointed to just such similarities to 'demonstrations overseas' to depict them as lacking in 'originality' and thus as unworthy of being considered a valid expression of public opinion. Despite Holyoake's carefully calibrated military commitment, the involvement in Vietnam served as a crucible for a new generation of political leaders and challenged official control of foreign policy.[32]

New Zealand's other special relationship grew increasingly attenuated at the same time. The British announcement in July 1967 of its decision to withdraw its forces 'east of Suez' weakened the still existing military and diplomatic ties with New Zealand. Britain's entrance into the European Economic Community (EEC) eroded trade relations, the strongest remaining element of the relationship. As a symbolic response to this change, the Department of External Affairs became the Ministry of Foreign Affairs, which now included the United Kingdom within its scope. The late 1960s thus represented an important change in New Zealand's triangulated pattern of special relationships as one came closer to dissolution and the 'political headaches' caused by the other grew more painful.[33]

In the early 1970s, Labour intensified its attack on the National government policy in Vietnam while enunciating a more independent foreign policy vision. As Norman Kirk, the Labour leader, put it in April 1970, 'The whole basis on which we built our defence thinking is being dissolved' because of the 'decisions of our friends rather than the actions of our enemies'. He predicted the 'reduction to a mere shadow of the present American military presence and the almost total elimination of the British military presence' when the Vietnam War ended. At the same time, he refused to be associated with those antiwar organizations that voiced enthusiastic support for the National Liberation Front and the Democratic Republic of Vietnam.[34] Kirk thus continued the anti-communist stance of Fraser and his predecessors even as he sought to challenge the foreign policy assumptions that had brought New Zealand into Vietnam.

Anti-nuclear activism began to flare up once again in 1972. The yacht *Greenpeace III* took New Zealanders to protest French nuclear testing. A few months later, Kirk pledged that Labour, if it won the forthcoming election, would send a frigate to the nuclear test site as a 'silent accusing witness'. When Labour defeated National in December 1972, Prime Minister Kirk quickly announced the withdrawal of New Zealand forces from Vietnam. When peace negotiations in Paris stalled, leading to the 'Christmas bombing' of 1972, Kirk criticized the reversion to 'the bloody business of war'. Tempering his criticisms, he reaffirmed New Zealand's commitment to ANZUS in the same letter to President Nixon. Despite receiving an aggrieved response from Nixon, Kirk reiterated his determination to 'express New Zealand's opinions as a nation' rather than 'opinions put into New Zealand's mouth by international ventriloquism'.

New Zealand, according to Kirk, had 'emerged from the phase in its national development where it allowed its policies to be determined by the views and interests of its most influential ally'. True to his promise, he dispatched the frigate *Otago* to the French test site, taking credit for drawing worldwide attention to the issue of nuclear testing in the Pacific as a result of television coverage of the ship's presence. Kirk expressed his desire for ANZUS to be renegotiated on more equal terms in keeping with a 'moral' foreign policy based upon 'self-reliance' and 'independence of judgment and action' in a communication to the Australian Prime Minister, but the other ANZUS partners remained satisfied with the status quo.[35]

Turning its attention to the other special relationship, the Labour government legislated for a new Royal Titles Act. This version gave Queen Elizabeth the title of the Queen of New Zealand and omitted her position as Queen of the United Kingdom. The Queen herself opened Parliament under her new title to read the New Zealand version of the 'address from the throne' that included the pledge that 'New Zealand will continue to speak out for what it believes to be right and will act on the basis of its independent judgment'. After 2 days, she attended the first New Zealand Day, another nationalist gesture that combined tradition and innovation. Choosing to rename the day set aside to commemorate the signing of the Treaty of Waitangi between Queen Victoria and Maori, the name change marked a more self-conscious construction of nationhood that removed the British presence from the national story.[36] This vision of an independent New Zealand included a nationalized British monarch as it tacitly recognized the disappearance of the special relationship with her government.

The Labour government's desire to place a nuclear-free South Pacific on the international agenda faced opposition from officials in the Defence Department and the Ministry of Foreign Affairs. Committed to the principle of nuclear deterrence and to ANZUS, they feared 'the damage that might result' to relations with the United States, Australia and France. When Kirk died in August 1974, his successor Bill Rowling took up the campaign for a nuclear-free zone by proposing a resolution to the United Nations. Despite a warning from British officials that this would be unacceptable, and clear indications of American and Australian opposition, the resolution went to the General Assembly. Having secured the endorsement, the Labour government sought to develop greater regional cooperation in Southeast Asia while seeking the abolition of SEATO.[37] Taking the policy of détente beyond the American conception, the policy direction increasingly defined New Zealand as a Pacific nation with a stronger focus on its ties to Asia.

When National defeated Labour in late 1975, the newly elected government expressed its determination to improve its relationships with 'friends such as Britain and the United States'. Its spokesmen declared the South Pacific Nuclear-Free Zone 'dead' and turned New Zealand Day back into Waitangi Day. As a gesture of goodwill to his ANZUS partners, Prime Minister Robert Muldoon announced that New Zealand would allow visits by nuclear-powered ships. The anti-nuclear movement had gained the ideal bogeyman. It also found a new focus on the safety of nuclear-powered ships that might be carrying nuclear weapons.

The arrival of US ships ensured a recurrent focus of public attention on the nuclear issue and attracted new recruits while these provocations placed pressure on the Labour Party to take a firmer stand on ANZUS.[38]

The revival of Cold War tensions in the early 1980s aided the growth of this activist anti-nuclear movement, domestically and internationally. Reagan's military build-up heightened fears about nuclear war and raised insistent questions about the costs of alliances during an escalating arms race. The Labour Party responded to these tensions by drafting a foreign policy programme proclaiming New Zealand's right to promote a nuclear-free South Pacific, its status as an equal partner in ANZUS and respect for New Zealand sovereignty. As expressed by Lange, who replaced Rowling in 1983 as Labour leader, this policy was not conceived as an 'unfriendly gesture' towards any country. Although Lange believed in the possibility of developing a non-nuclear defence relationship within the ANZUS framework, the policy challenged a crucial element of the special relationship with the United States and, to a lesser extent, the remaining military ties with the United Kingdom.[39]

Public agitation over the nuclear issue soon caused Muldoon to call a 'snap election' in July 1984 after two National MPs voted for an anti-nuclear private member's bill sponsored by a Labour MP. Although the bill did not pass, the election put Labour into power. As observed by Gerald Hensley, a long-serving diplomat and then the head of the Prime Minister's Department, the election had 'overflown a whole age group', shifting power from the World War II generation to the 'baby boomers' with the slightly older Lange at their head. Described by this archetypal realist as coming from the 'antiwar generation', the peace activists in the Labour Caucus shared a passionate commitment to the party's anti-nuclear platform and to national sovereignty. In the words of Helen Clark, the members of this group saw New Zealanders as being transformed into the 'Pacific people which we must become' in opposition to an older generation who had defined New Zealand as a 'small nation' dependent on the United States and the United Kingdom for protection.[40] Seeking to kick aside the security blanket of special relationships, they wanted New Zealand to mature into an independent Pacific nation. Their anti-nuclear commitments clearly threatened the special relationships that two generations of officials had dedicated themselves to preserving.

The United States' policy of 'neither confirm nor deny' about whether its ships carried nuclear weapons set up an inevitable collision between the new government's anti-nuclear goals and cooperation among the ANZUS partners. Miscommunications added to the tensions as Secretary of State George Shultz and Paul Wolfowitz, meeting Lange shortly after the election victory, believed that he had promised them to allow American ships to visit New Zealand ports. Merwyn Norrish, secretary of foreign affairs, who attended the meeting, did not hear a commitment from Lange to change the policy. In Norrish's view, 'Shultz heard what he wanted to hear', but he also believed that the Labour government 'implemented this policy in a muddled rather than a coherent way' leading to charges of 'deviousness or a deliberate intention to mislead' on the part of aggrieved US officials.[41]

After 6 months of delicate negotiations, the United States sent a ship to New Zealand ports. Anti-nuclear activists mobilized to take a tough line against the visit. The Labour Party executive argued that there was 'no need to attempt to accommodate the American point of view'. Lange and Deputy Prime Minister Geoffrey Palmer found themselves in the middle between 'domestic uproar and American fury'. Cautious officials advised Lange that 'implementing the policy would do great damage to our relationship with our allies', but he decided to disregard that advice. Forced to choose between acquiescing to the Australian and United States interpretation of ANZUS and Labour's nuclear-free policy, the New Zealand government refused permission for the *USS Buchanan* to dock in February 1985.[42]

Believing that Lange had deceived Shultz and Wolfowitz, Reagan administration officials developed a series of retaliatory actions to prevent other nations from adopting the New Zealand position. Shultz told a press conference that New Zealand and the United States 'part as friends but we part on security matters'. Having worked for 6 months to prevent this crisis, New Zealand officials wondered whether they 'had been deceived' by a prime minister who had failed to accept a face-saving compromise – or had they 'simply deceived' themselves in their desire to maintain ANZUS? The officials tried to 'limit the fallout on our national interests' but they could not preserve New Zealand's participation in ANZUS once the Labour government announced plans for legislation to ensure that New Zealand would remain 'nuclear-free'. They mourned the loss of 'a priceless advantage, a close and beneficial relationship with the only world power in a position' to 'guarantee its security'. These diplomats blamed the curse of 'politics' and naivety for having triumphed over 'statesmanship', suggesting that dramatic gestures had replaced 'careful negotiation' and the 'willingness to compromise'. Only slightly veiled, their recollections expressed a disdain for a prime minister who had failed to heed their advice. In their view, the precious 'talisman' that had formed the basis for New Zealand's foreign policy since 1951 had been recklessly discarded due to the idealistic foolishness of peace zealots and grandstanding politicians.[43]

Lange and Clark responded to such criticisms. Lange made his most important public statement shortly after the decision to deny entrance to the *USS Buchanan*. He debated Jerry Falwell at the Oxford Union to the displeasure of his officials and Prime Minister Margaret Thatcher. Lange argued that 'to compel an ally to accept nuclear weapons against the wishes of that ally is to take the moral position of totalitarianism which allows for no self-determination' in a speech that called nuclear weapons 'morally indefensible'. Lange scored a victory that many New Zealanders relished over the leader of the Moral Majority, but also over the Reagan Administration, which he had implicitly accused of totalitarian tendencies.[44]

Clark, a decade away from becoming prime minister, described New Zealand's actions as a 'mould-breaking' decision that would determine its future foreign policy. A 'small' nation had disengaged from the 'nuclear weapons strategies of the superpowers'. As chair of a Special Parliamentary Select Committee,

Clark introduced the nuclear-free legislation in 1987. She cuttingly dismissed Muldoon's contribution to the debate on the bill as a 'voice from the past'. Gary Knapp of the Democrats endorsed the legislation, declaring that 'smaller nations' could no longer 'stand by dumb victims, sitting in servile silence'. At the third reading, Lange described the bill as a 'turning point' that represented a 'fundamental reassessment of what constitutes security' for the first time in 40 years. When the debate concluded, the legislation passed into law with a majority of 10. Despite the partisan rancour displayed in the debate, the law would not be repealed even when National won three successive electoral victories in the 1990s.[45]

Although some New Zealanders complained about 'peaceniks' having 'managed to achieve a public relations victory for the Soviets' by 'upsetting our ANZUS treaty', their views did not attract majority support. Despite criticisms of 'our professional anti-Americans', Lange, Knapp and Clark saw their position vindicated. A 1986 report discovered that 90 per cent of New Zealanders did not want nuclear weapons in their country, even though 77 per cent wanted to maintain an alliance with the United States. In Lange's assessment, backed up by public opinion polls, the more the Americans 'protested, the more the New Zealand public backed the policy and, in doing so, came to question the value of the military connection'. Letters in the *New Zealand Listener* praised 'Our David' for 'his courageous stand before the superpower giants' and described him as speaking on behalf of the 'ordinary people of the world'. Another letter referred to ANZUS as 'a dangerous anachronism'. An exuberant peace movement celebrated the legislation in a rally outside Parliament. A veteran activist admitted that it was 'disorienting' to see 'demonstrators praising the government of the day'. 'It's not normal, is it?', he asked a reporter.[46] Protestors had moved not only from the streets to the parliamentary lawn but into Parliament to pass the legislation. While the 'Z' that Lange had suggested be dropped from ANZUS in a humorous quip did not disappear, nor did the 'N'; New Zealand had, in fact, departed from the military alliance and ended its special relationship with the United States.

As conceded by one senior official, a national consensus formed in opposition to nuclear weapons. New Zealanders prided themselves that 'little New Zealand sent an influential message to the world', a conviction that became 'unshakeable' and embedded in the national identity. In an era in which superpowers suffered defeat at the hands of smaller nations like Vietnam, Iran and Afghanistan, New Zealand had flexed its own version of the 'powers of the weak'. The peace movement, anti-nuclear politicians and the New Zealand public had wrested control from the diplomats and the Reagan administration. Kirk's prophecy, uttered 13 years earlier, had come to pass. The special relationships had 'dissolved' because of the decisions of New Zealand's 'friends'. New Zealand and the United States became 'just friends'.[47] When the special relationships dissolved, the smaller partner turned to the remaining elements in its foreign policy repertoire: global citizenship, Asia-Pacific location, free trade, morality and independence.

When New Zealand scholars analysed this development, they identified with a 'small state' which had learned 'to stand on its own feet'. True to Kirk's vision, New Zealand's foreign policy now rested on 'independent action, moral example and South Pacific identity', rather than special relationships with powerful states. New Zealanders no longer imagined their island nation, in Lange's words, as a 'small country in peril' with the United States playing the role of 'its inevitable rescuer' or Britain the protective mother. Using that same language of familial romance, the end of New Zealand's role in ANZUS resembled the initial court-ship and consummation in that New Zealand took the initiative at both the beginning and the end. New Zealand officials had yearned for a protector and achieved their goals. After 30 years, the Labour government spurned the offer of protection because it relied upon the 'threatened use of nuclear weapons'. Having rejected the terms of the special relationship as it was understood by the other partners, New Zealand, in turn, was spurned.[48] In both consummation and dissolution of these two special relationships, the larger states had dictated the terms. While the relationships lasted, the smaller partner needed to demonstrate its commitment repeatedly with only the promise of reciprocity from the larger powers in case of peril.

Sending troops and accepting nuclear testing were two of the costs of these relationships. As the peril grew less and the costs of protection accelerated, a moment of reckoning resulted in a decision to alter the terms of the relationship. The smaller partner made the first move towards a new post-Cold War era where neither nuclear weapons nor special relationships offered the same benefits as before. From a realist view only, New Zealand's isolation enabled it to avoid paying the price for the rash actions of its politicians and peace activists. From a romantic view, it was a remarkable achievement for a once marginalized group of dissenters to contribute to New Zealanders' sense of national identity. Given the economic crisis engulfing New Zealand in the mid-1980s, the decision to withdraw from a nuclear alliance may be described as yet another exercise in cost-cutting. The ambiguous dissolution of New Zealand's special relationships could thus be read as a nationalist triumph, a political misadventure or economic rationality. In the context of a waning Cold War, small states and nationalities gained greater freedom to manoeuvre. Like Eastern Europe, New Zealand responded to a collapsing Cold War system and helped to speed up the collapse by becoming detached from one of the constituent elements of that international order – the special relationships that provided security but at a significant cost that New Zealand no longer wished to pay.

Notes

1 F. L. W. Wood, *New Zealand in the World*, Wellington: New Zealand Department of International Affairs, 1940, pp. 132–33.
2 Prime Minister M. Joseph Savage, Radio Address, 5 September 1939, reprinted as 'Loyal Support: Dominion and Britain: Prime Minister's Address', *The Evening Post*, 6 September 1939; 'Pledge to Britain: New Zealand's Part: Fullest Co-operation', *The Evening Post*, 2 September 1939; 'Faith in Our Case: New Zealand's Support:

Broadcast by Mr. Fraser', *Evening Post*, 4 September 1939; P. Fraser (Acting Leader), 5 September 1939, Legislative Council and House of Representatives, 1st Session, 26th Parliament, 1 September to 7 October 1939, *New Zealand Parliamentary Debates*, vol. 256, Wellington: R. E. Owen, Government Printer, 1940, p. 20.

3 D. Lange, *Nuclear Free: The New Zealand Way*, Auckland: Penguin, 1990, p. 8.

4 J. Henderson, 'The Foreign Policy of a Small State', in J. Henderson, K. Jackson and R. Kennaway (eds) *Beyond New Zealand: The Foreign Policy of a Small State* Auckland: Methuen, 1980, pp. 2–8; P. Landais-Stamp and P. Rogers, *Rocking the Boat: New Zealand, the United States and the Nuclear-Free Zone Controversy in the 1980s*, New York: Berg, 1989, p. 158; New Zealand Institute of International Affairs (hereafter NZIIA), *New Zealand in World Affairs*, vol. 1, Wellington: Price Milburn, 1977; M. McKinnon, *New Zealand in World Affairs, 1957—1972*, vol. 2, Wellington: NZIAA, 1991; R. G. Patman, *New Zealand & Britain: A Special Relationship in Transition* Palmerston North: Dunmore Press, 1997; M. Templeton, *Standing Upright Here: New Zealand in the Nuclear Age, 1945–1990*, Wellington: Victoria University Press, 2006; A. Trotter (ed.) *Fifty Years of New Zealand Foreign Policy Making: Anniversary Volume*, Dunedin: University of Otago Press, 1993; R. Kennaway and J. Henderson (eds) *Beyond New Zealand II: Foreign Policy into the 1990s*, Auckland: Longman Paul, 1991; M. McKinnon, *Independence and Foreign Policy: New Zealand in the World Since 1935*, Auckland: Auckland University Press, 1993; M. Clark (ed.) *For the Record: Lange and the Fourth Labour Government*, Palmerston North: Dunmore Press, 2005; *Background to the ANZUS Pact: Policy-making, Strategy, and Diplomacy, 1945–55*, Christchurch: Canterbury University Press, 1995; S. Hoadley, *New Zealand United States Relations: Friends, No Longer Allies*, Wellington: New Zealand Institute of International Affairs, 2000; K. Clements, *Back from the Brink: The Creation of a Nuclear-Free New Zealand*, Wellington: Allen and Unwin, 1988; E. Locke, *Peace People: A History of Peace Activities in New Zealand*, Christchurch: Hazard Press, 1992; and R. Rabel, *New Zealand and the Vietnam War: Politics and Diplomacy*, Auckland: Auckland University Press, 2005.

5 A. McIntosh, 'Origins of the Department of External Affairs and the Formulation of an Independent Foreign Policy', NZIIA, *New Zealand in World Affairs*, pp. 9–36, 17, 21; 'American Ostriches', *The Evening Post*, 5 January 1940; 'Willing to Stand', *New York Times*, 6 July 1940; 'United States and New Zealand To Exchange Envoys', *New York Times*, 8 February 1941; 'Fraser Reaches London', *New York Times*, 21 June 1941; 'J. G. Coates, NZ Envoy Here', *Washington Post*, 22 June 1941; 'Fraser Here to Confer with Roosevelt', *New York Times*, 26 August 1941; 'Fraser Sees Unity in Pacific Defense', *New York Times*, 27 August 1941.

6 McKinnon, *Independence and Foreign Policy*, pp. 45, 50; H. R. Miller, 'NZ Sets up Legation', *Washington Post*, 11 November 1941; 'NZ Names Nash First Minister to US', *New York Times*, 29 December 1941; 'New Zealand Leader Hits Strategy Critics', *New York Times*, 27 January 1942; E. T. Folliard, 'Nash Urges Single Command for Entire Pacific War Area', *Washington Post*, 1 February 1942; 'Thousands Cheer US Troops in Auckland', *Washington Post*, 18 March 1941; McKinnon, *Independence and Foreign Policy*, pp. 46–50; W. D. McIntyre, 'The Future of the New Zealand System of Alliances', *Landfall*, December 1967, vol. 84, pp. 329–45.

7 'Riot in Auckland over Protests', *New York Times*, 29 January 1940; 'N. Z. Stiffening War Laws', *New York Times*, 29 February 1940; 'Our Internal Enemies' *The Dominion*, 9 February 1942; 'New Zealand Faces Its Responsibilities', *The Evening Post*, 2 September 1939; 'Emergency Powers: More Authority Taken', *The Evening Post*, 4 September 1939; 'Citizens to Help To the Common End: Public Meeting soon: Mayor's Statement', *The Evening Post*, 5 September 1939; 'On the March', *The Evening Post*, 4 January 1940; Locke, *Peace People*, pp. 97–120; Christian Pacifist Society and Peace Pledge Union, 'Why Not Peace Now', Wellington: 1940, A-Peace-1930s and 1940s, Ephemera-A-Peace and Pacifism, Ephemera Collection, Alexander

Turnbull Library, Wellington, New Zealand (hereafter cited as EPH/ATL); E. Crane, *I Can do No Other: A Biography of the Reverend Ormond Burton*, Auckland: Hodder and Stoughton, 1986.

8 A. O'Grady, *Alan Brash: Voice for Unity*, Auckland: Pace Publishing, 1991, p. 45; D. McEldowney (ed.), *Presbyterians in Aotearoa 1840–1940*, Auckland: Presbyterian Church, 1990; 'Vote for Efford, The Peace Candidate', Pamphlet No. 4; L. A. W. Efford, 'A Final Letter', Christchurch: 5 February 1943, Christchurch: H.W. Bullivant Company, 1943, EPH/ATL; Lincoln Efford, 'Victory for Humanity: Mr. Lincoln Efford States His Case', Christchurch: 1943, B-Peace-1930s and 1940s, EPH-B-EPH/ATL; 'Efford, Lincoln Arthur Winstone, 1907–62: Pacifists, Social Reformer, Adult Educationalist', *Dictionary of New Zealand Biography* <www.dnzb.govt.nz> (accessed 19 July 2008).

9 Lincoln Efford, 'You, the Atomic Bomb and World Peace', Christchurch: Peace Union, n.d., as quoted in Locke, *Peace People*, p. 126; See also, Locke, *Peace People*, pp. 102–15, 124–25.

10 C. Berendsen to A. McIntosh, 1 October 1945, in I. McGibbon (ed.) *Undiplomatic Dialogue: Letters between Carl Berendsen & Alister McIntosh, 1943–1952*, Auckland: Auckland University Press, 1993, p. 100l; F. L. W. Wood, 'New Zealand Foreign Policy 1945—1951', NZIIA, *New Zealand in World Affairs*, vol. 1, pp. 89–113, 103;

11 W. D. McIntyre, 'Peter Fraser's Commonwealth: New Zealand and the Origins of the New Commonwealth in the 1940s', in *New Zealand in World Affairs*, pp. 39–88, 60–71; C. Berendsen to A. McIntosh, 9 June 1947; A. McIntosh to C. Berendsen, 14 July 1947; C. Berendsen to A. McIntosh, 28 July 1947; A. McIntosh to C. Berendsen, 19 August 1947; C. Berendsen to A. McIntosh 25 August 1947; C. Berendsen to A. McIntosh, 4 September 1947; C. Berendsen to A. McIntosh, 25 October 1947; C. Berendsen to A. McIntosh 18 December 1947, all in McGibbon (ed.) *Undiplomatic Dialogue*, pp. 127–54; A. C. Wilson, *New Zealand and the Soviet Union, 1950–1991*, Wellington: Victoria University Press, 2004, pp. 20–23.

12 W. D. McIntyre, 'Peter Fraser's Commonwealth', in *New Zealand in World Affairs*, pp. 39–88, 86–87; New Zealand Peace Council, 'The Council's Policy', EPH-A-Peace, 1949, PR05–0222; Christian Pacifist Society of N.Z., 'Christ and Conscription' Wellington: 1949, EPH-A-Peace, Pr 05–0023, Religious Society of Friends in NZ, 'Youth and Conscription', EPH-A-Peace, 1949, EPH/ATL; C. Bollinger, 'The Referendum Exposed', Wellington: 1950; D. Davin, 'Mood Subjective (Oxford)', *Here and Now*, 1 October 1949; A. R. D. Fairburn, 'Mr. Fraser's Way of Doing Things', *Here & Now*, 1 October 1949.

13 C. Berendsen to A. McIntosh, 25 June, McGibbon (ed.) *Undiplomatic Dialogue*, p. 265; Doidge quoted in McKinnon, *Independence and Foreign Policy*, p. 117; D. P. Costello to A. McIntosh, 9 August 1947; C. Berendsen to the Minister of External Affairs, 30 January 1951; C. Berendsen to the Minister of External Affairs, 8 February 1951; Department of External Affairs, Memorandum by the Department of External Affairs on the General Attitude to the Japanese Settlement, Wellington, 11 August 1947; 'Report on the British Commonwealth Conference', Canberra, 26 August–2 September 1947, and 'Comments and Proposals Regarding New Zealand Policy Towards Certain Issues of the Japanese Peace Settlement'; A. McIntosh, Note by the Secretary of External Affairs on a Conversation with [P. Shaw] the Head of the Australian Mission in Tokyo, 17 November 1949; Extract from Minutes of the Commonwealth Meeting on Foreign Affairs, Colombo, 11 January 1950; 'The Secretary of State for Commonwealth Relations to the Minister of External Affairs', 18 April, 1950; A. McIntosh, 'Note on Discussion Held in the Department of External Affairs, 19 March 1951, all in R. Kay (ed.) *The ANZUS Pact and the Treaty of Peace with Japan, Documents on New Zealand External Relations*, vol. III Wellington: Historical Publications Branch, Department of Internal Affairs, 1985, pp. 90, 95, 179, 288–90, 291–97, 297–310, 339–47, 445, 583, 663; C. Berendsen to A. McIntosh,

2 April 1951; C. Berendsen to A. McIntosh, 25 June 1951, in McGibbon (ed.) *Undiplomatic Dialogue*, pp. 256, 265.

14 P. Fraser to the New Zealand Ambassador [C. Berendsen], Washington, 20 July 1949; F. Doidge, Record of Conversation with Mr J. Foster Dulles, 19 October 1950; Notes on Discussions Held in the Department on External Affairs, 19 March 1951, all in Kay (ed.) *The ANZUS Pact and the Treaty of Peace with Japan*, pp. 486–87, 409, 662–64; C. Berendsen to A. McIntosh, 25 November 1950, in McGibbon (ed.) *Undiplomatic Dialogue*, p. 248; British Foreign Office official C. H. Johnson quoted in McIntyre, *Background to the ANZUS Pact*, p. 329.

15 R. L. Hutchens to Foss Shanahan, 9 February 1951; Notes on the Australian-New Zealand-United States Talks in Canberra, 15–17 February 1951; Joint Australian-New Zealand Consultations with Mr. Dulles, Canberra 7 March 1951; G. Walker to Sidney Holland, 15 March 1951; Notes on Discussions Held in the Department of External Affairs, 19 March 1951; The Minister for External Affairs [Australia] to the Minister of External Affairs [New Zealand], 16 April 1961, all in Kay (ed.) *The ANZUS Pact and the Treaty of Peace with Japan*, pp. 585, 598–600, 640–41, 658–65, 664, 695.

16 C. Berendsen to A. McIntosh, 10 September 1951, in McGibbon (ed.) *Undiplomatic Dialogue*, pp. 276–82; C. Berendsen to F. Doidge, 25 September 1951; Statement by the delegate of New Zealand, Sir C. Berendsen; Statement by the delegate of Australia, Ambassador Spender; Statement by the leader of the delegation of the United States of America, Mr Dean Acheson; J. Foster Dulles, all in Kay (ed.) *The ANZUS Pact and the Treaty of Peace with Japan*, pp. 764–71; D. McLean, 'A Serious Non-Meeting of Minds', in Clark (ed.) *For the Record*, pp. 144–48, 144, 145.

17 Statement by Dulles on Behalf of the United States as Co-Sponsor of the Draft Treaty of Peace with Japan, San Francisco, 5 September 1951; C. Berendsen, Statement by the New Zealand Delegate at the San Francisco Conference, 6 September 1951, all in Kay (ed.) *The ANZUS Pact and the Treaty of Peace with Japan*, pp. 1136, 1143, 1163; C. Berendsen to Alistair McIntosh, 10 September 1951, in McGibbon (ed.) *Undiplomatic Dialogue*, 279. Privately diplomats like McIntosh tried to get Britain into ANZUS but faced too much resistance from Australia and the United States. See A. McIntosh to F. Corner, 3 October 1952; F. Corner to A. McIntosh 10 October 1952; F. Corner to A. McIntosh, 11 December 1952, all in McGibbon (ed.) *Unofficial Channels: Letters between Alister McIntosh and Foss Shanahan, George Laking and Frank Corner 1946–1966*, Wellington: Victoria University Press, 1999, pp. 106, 107, 108.

18 J. Rae, 27 September 1951, House of Representatives, lst Session, 30th Parliament, 25 September to 14 November 1951, *New Zealand Parliamentary Debates*, Vol. 295, Wellington: R. E. Owen, Government Printer, 1952, p. 11; New Zealand Student Labour Federation, 'While We Go Marching', EPH-A-Peace, 1951, EPH/ATL; W F Monk 'New Zealand from the North', *Pacific Affairs*, September 1953, vol. 16, p. 227.

19 Interview with F. Corner, in Rabel, *New Zealand and the Vietnam War*, p. 371, fn 87; E. Halstead, 29 June 1954, House of Representatives, 5th Session, 30th Parliament 22 June to 5 August 1954, *New Zealand Parliamentary Debates*, vol. 303, Wellington: R. E. Owen, Government Printer, 1954, pp. 65–66; I. McGibbon, *New Zealand and the Korean War, Volume I: Politics and Diplomacy*, Auckland: Oxford University Press, 1992, p. 17.

20 A. McIntosh to C. Berendsen, 14 June 1951, in McGibbon (ed.) *Undiplomatic Dialogue*, p. 264; R. Goodman, *'Unseemly Ally': An Examination of American Life & Policy*, Auckland: Progressive Books, 1951; Editorial, 'Twelve Months of Sound Government', *Here and Now*, November 1950; G. H. O. Wilson, 'Korea—An Interim Assessment', *Here and Now*, March 1951; R. Goodman, 'Minority Report: Where's the Enemy?' *Here and Now*, January–February 1951; 'Notes', *Here and*

Now, January–February 1951; R. Goodman 'The Death of American Liberalism', *Here and Now*, March 1951; L. F. Rudd, 'A Pact for the Pacific: Yes', *Here and Now*, January–February 1951; M. Finlay, 'A Pact for the Pacific; No', *Here and Now*, January–February 1951; W. T. G. Airey 'Treaty with Japan'? *Here and Now*, 8 May 1951; O. Wilson, 'After Formosa', *Here and Now*, March 1953. *Here and Now* sometimes appeared monthly; sometimes weekly; and sometimes bimonthly and occasionally suspended publication.

21 'About Ourselves', *Here and Now*, October 1952; 'Comment from the Capital', *Here and Now*, October 1952; R. Goodman, 'Does the Peace Movement want Peace?' *Here and Now*, August 1951.

22 O. Wilson, 'ANZUS and US', *Here and Now*, December 1952; O. Wilson, 'After Formosa', *Here and Now*, March 1953.

23 P. Matthews, 'The Choice before Us in Asia', *Here and Now*, February 1954; 'Another Regional Defence Treaty', *Here and Now*, October 1954; Scrutineer, 'What Are We Up to in Asia?' *Here and Now*, February–March 1955; K. Sinclair, 'Independence and Morality', *Here and Now*, October 1957.

24 Memorandum on 'Indo-China and the United Nations', Department of External Affairs, Prime Minister's Office, 8 April 1954, quoted in Rabel, *New Zealand and the Vietnam War*, p. 19; D. E. McHenry and R. N. Rosecrance, 'Exclusion of the United Kingdom from the ANZUS Pact', Boston: One World Peace Foundation, 1958; Clifton Webb, Minister of External Affairs, quoted in Chalmers M. Roberts, 'New Zealand Gives U.S. Setback on Asia Block: Envoy Declares Anti-Red Planning without Britain is Inconceivable', *New York Times*, 2 May 1954; Willis Airey, 'What SEATO Means', 27 May 1955, Auckland: The Pilgrim Press, 1955 p. 9; M. Ladd Thomas, 'A Critical Appraisal of SEATO', *The Western Political Quarterly*, December 1957, vol. 10, pp. 926–36;

25 Airey, 'What SEATO Means', pp. 19, 23; F. Corner, London to A. McIntosh, 13 July 1953, McGibbon (ed.) *Unofficial Channels*, pp. 138, 141; Keith Holyoake, House of Representatives, 3rd Session, 31st Parliament, 19 September to 25 October [1957] *New Zealand Parliamentary Debates*, vol. 314, Wellington: Government Printing Office, 1957, pp. 2916, 2923; M. Templeton, *Ties of Blood & Empire: New Zealand's Involvement in Middle East Defence and the Suez Crisis, 1947–57*, Auckland: Auckland University Press, 1994, pp. 1, 210–15.

26 Landais-Stamp and Rogers, *Rocking the Boat*, pp. 158–59; *Timaru Herald* quoted in Locke, *Peace People*, p. 162; R. Chapman, 'A Movement against Nuclear Weapons', *Here and Now*, November 1957; B. Edwards, *Helen: Portrait of a Prime Minister*, Auckland: Exisle Publishing, 2001, pp. 93–101.

27 M. Woodward, *SEATO: No Place for New Zealand*, Christchurch: The New Zealand Campaign for Nuclear Disarmament, 1962, p. 1; The New Zealand Campaign for Nuclear Disarmament, 'This is Our Purpose' [adopted 1961], quoted in Locke, *Peace People*, pp. 165–66.

28 D. Lange, *Nuclear Free – The New Zealand Way*, Auckland: Penguin, 1990, pp. 10–11; D. Lange, *My Life*, Auckland: Penguin, 2005, p. 157; M. Woodward, 'The Bomb, a New Zealand View', Christchurch: New Zealand Campaign for Nuclear Disarmament, 1963; Locke, *Peace People*, pp. 158–79.

29 M. Thorn, *Stick Out, Keep Left, An Autobiography*, Auckland: Auckland University Press, 1997; Holyoake quoted in Locke, *Peace People*, p. 182; N. Kirk, Leader of the Opposition, 10 July 1963, House of Representatives, 4th Session, 33rd Parliament, 20 June to 2 August 1963, *New Zealand Parliamentary Debates*, vol. 335, Wellington; Government Printer, 1963, p. 478; *Locke, Peace People*, pp. 180–87.

30 ANZUS Council meeting in Wellington, as reported in 'ANZUS Block Views Reds as Threat', *Christian Science Monitor*, 7 June 1963; F. Corner, *New Zealand External Affairs Review*, November 1963, quoted in Locke, *Peace People*, pp. 184–85; see also, Locke, *Peace People*, p. 186.

31 Alistair McIntosh, Keith Holyoake and unnamed official, quoted in Rabel, *New Zealand and the Vietnam War*, pp. 85, 86, 93, 80, 101; K. Holyoake, 27 May 1965, House of Representatives, 2nd Session, 34th Parliament, 27 May–8 July 1965, *New Zealand Parliamentary Debates*, vol. 342, Wellington: R. E. Owen, Government Printer, 1965, p. 7; NZIIA, 'New Zealand Foreign Policy with Special Reference to Southeast Asia', Wellington: NZIIA, 1965, p. 23.

32 Rabel, *New Zealand and the Vietnam War*, pp. 161–65, 123; B. Mitcalfe, 'Committee on Vietnam: An Interim History'; *Salient*, 8 August 1965; M. Bassett and R. Nola (eds) *New Zealand and South-East Asia: Lectures Given at a 'Teach-in' on South East Asia, 12 September 1965*, Auckland: Committee on South-East Asia, 1966; M. Holcroft, 'Editorial', *New Zealand Listener*, 6 August 1965; K. P. Clements, 'The New Zealand Peace Movement and Political Action', in Kennaway and Henderson (eds) *Beyond New Zealand II*, pp. 226–35; 'Peace, Power & Politics in Asia: An international conference on Vietnam, SEATO and Political Stability in Asia', 30–March 2–April 1968, Wellington, EPH-A-Peace and Pacifism, 1968, EPH/ATL; A. Taylor (ed.) *Peace, Power and Politics in Asia*, Wellington: Organising Committee of the PPA Conference, 1969; Clements, *Back from the Brink*, p. 105; Committee on Vietnam [Wellington], 'Failure of a Mission '69', EPH-A-Peace and Pacifism, 1969; EPH/AT.

33 P. Edmonds to Minister of External Affairs, 3 January 1968, in Rabel, *New Zealand and the Vietnam War*, p. 219; McKinnon, *Independence and Foreign Policy*, pp. 167–68; F. Corner to G. Laking, 15 July 1969; G. Laking to K. Holyoake, 17 July 1969; F. Corner to Ministry of External Affairs, 16 October 1969, all quoted in Rabel, *New Zealand and the Vietnam War*, pp. 266–67, 269.

34 N. Kirk, 16 April 1970, House of Representatives, 1st Session, 36th Parliament, 12 March to 24 April 1970, *New Zealand Parliamentary Debates*, vol. 365, Wellington: A. R. Shearer, Government Printer, 1970, pp. 504–5; Rabel, *New Zealand and the Vietnam War*, pp. 293–316.

35 N. Kirk to R. Nixon, 22 December 1972; F. Corner to Ambassador, Washington; R. Nixon to N. Kirk enclosed in Chalmers Wood to N. Kirk, 27 December 1972, Prime Minister's Office records, all quoted in Rabel, *New Zealand and the Vietnam War*, pp. 330–31; N. Kirk, quoted in D. McCraw, 'From Kirk to Muldoon: Change and Continuity in New Zealand's Foreign-Policy Priorities', *Pacific Affairs*, 1982–1983, vol. 55, pp. 640–59, 644; N. Kirk, 24 July 1973, House of Representatives, 1st Session, 37th Parliament 3 July to 31 July 1973, *New Zealand Parliamentary Debates*, vol. 384 Wellington: A. R. Shearer, Government Printer, 1973, pp. 2593–95; N. Kirk, 14 July 1973, quoted in C. P. Eyley, *Protest at Moruroa: First-Hand Accounts from the New Zealand-Based Flotilla*, Auckland: Tandem Press, 1996, p. 11; N. Kirk to Gough Whitlam, 23 July 1973, quoted in Templeton, *Standing Upright Here*, p. 195; McGraw, 'From Kirk to Muldoon', p. 644.

36 Royal Titles Act (1974), House of Representatives 2nd Session, 37th Parliament, 4 February to 14 March 1974, *New Zealand Parliamentary Debates*, vol. 389, Wellington: A. R. Shearer, Government Printer, 1974, pp. 1–3; p. 4.

37 I. Cross, 'Editorial', *New Zealand Listener*, 24 May 1975; R. Mann, R. Northey, B. Kirkwood, M. Stenson and O. Wilkes, 'A Nuclear NZ? A Public Report on the US Government's Proposal to Use NZ Ports for its Nuclear-Powered Warships', Christchurch: NZ Campaign for Nuclear Disarmament NZCND, 1975; McCraw, 'From Kirk to Muldoon', pp. 645–46.

38 B. Talboys, 21 January 1976, quoted in Templeton, *Standing Upright Here*, p. 302; M. C. Pugh, *The ANZUS Crisis, Nuclear Visiting and Deterrence*, Cambridge: Cambridge University Press, 1989, pp. 101–11; Clements, *Back from the Brink*, pp. 97–122.

39 W. E. Rowling, 'New Zealand Foreign Policy: Time for a Change?', *New Zealand International Review*, 1984, vol. 9; Lange, *My Life*, p. 137; Clements, *Back from the Brink*, p. 129.

40 G. Hensley, *Final Approaches: A Memoir* Auckland: Auckland University Press, 2006, p. 266; H. Clark, 'Reviewing New Zealand's Defence and Security Policies during IYP [International Year of Peace]', *Peacelink*, March 1986, vol. 39.

41 M. Norrish, 'The Lange Government's Foreign Policy', in Clark (ed.) *For the Record*, pp. 150–57, 151, 154; McLean, 'A Serious Non-Meeting of Minds', in Clark (ed.) *For the Record*, pp. 148, 149.

42 M. Pugh, 'Wellington against Washington: Steps to Unilateral Arms Control', *Arms Control*, 1986, vol. 7, 65, quoted in Clements, *Back from the Brink*, p. 134; M. Wilson, *Labour in Government 1984–87*, Wellington: Allen and Unwin, 1989, pp. 64–65; McLean, 'A Serious Non-Meeting of Minds', p. 148, 149; Lange, *My Life*, p. 205; D. Beatson 'All at Sea over Anzus', *New Zealand Listener*, 16 February 1985; J. A. Moller, J. Loughnan, D. P. Barron, A. MacFarlane, 'ANZUS Debate', *New Zealand Listener*, 23 February 1985; see also Templeton, *Standing Upright Here*, pp. 385–427; Clements, *Back from the Brink*, pp. 128–45.

43 G. Shultz, press conference 11 August 1986, quoted in Templeton, *Standing Upright Here*, p. 481; see also, Templeton, pp. 450–81; McLean, 'A Serious Non-Meeting of Minds', pp. 148–49; Hensley, *Final Approaches*, p. 279, see also pp. 280–83.; Norrish, 'The Lange Government's Foreign Policy', pp. 155, 157.

44 D. Lange, 'Nuclear Weapons are Morally Indefensible', 1 March 1985, Oxford Union, Public Address: http://www.publicaddress.net/default,1578.sm#post;

45 H. Clark, quoted in Clements, *Back from the Brink*, p. 141; H. Clark, 12 February 1987, House of Representatives, 2nd Session, 41st Parliament, 16 December 1986–12 February 1987, *New Zealand Parliamentary Debates*, vol. 477, Wellington: V. R. Ward, Government Printer, 1987, p. 6990; Gary Knapp, 12 February 1987, House of Representatives, 2nd Session, 41st Parliament, 16 December 1986–12 February 1987, *New Zealand Parliamentary Debates*, vol. 477, Wellington: V. R. Ward, Government Printer, 1987, p. 6994; David Lange, 4 June 1987, House of Representatives, 2nd Session, 41st Parliament, 28 April to 4 June [1987], *New Zealand Parliamentary Debates*, vol. 480, Wellington, 1987, pp. 9276–77.

46 D. Welch, 'Bowled Over by It All' *New Zealand Listener*, 9 March 1985; Defence Committee, 'Defend & Security: What New Zealanders Want: Report of the Defence Committee Enquiry', Wellington: 1986, pp. 40, 41, 38; 'ANZUS Debate' *New Zealand Listener*, 23 February 1985; B. Jason, P. Haig, 'The ANZUS Debate' *New Zealand Listener*, 23 March 1985; D. Pratt, 'The ANZUS Debate' *New Zealand Listener*, March 1985, vol. 30.

47 Norrish, 'The Lange Government's Foreign Policy', Clark, *For the Record*, p. 155; N. Kirk, 16 April 1970, *New Zealand Parliamentary Debates*, vol. 365, pp. 576–77.

48 J. Henderson, 'New Zealand and the Foreign Policy of Small States', in Kennaway and Henderson (eds) *Beyond New Zealand II*, pp. 3–13, 7; R. Kennaway, 'The ANZUS Dispute', in Kennaway and Henderson (eds) *Beyond New Zealand II*, pp. 7, 67–81, 78; D. Lange, 'Facing a New Reality', *New Zealand International Review*, November–December 1987, vol. 12; D. Lange, 'Address to the United Nations Conference on Disarmament', Geneva, 5 March 1985, quoted in Kennaway, 'The ANZUS Dispute', p. 75.

7   Testing the limits of a special relationship
US unilateralism and Dutch multilateralism in the twenty-first century

Giles Scott-Smith

Since World War II, the Netherlands has built a solid reputation as a 'loyal ally' of the United States. There have been serious disagreements between the two countries on specific policy issues, but there has remained an underlying recognition among the Dutch that these should not disrupt a relationship considered fundamental. Within the context of US global power, the Netherlands have fulfilled several important functions. The country has been a close ally within international organizations such as NATO and the UN. It has acted as an ideal middle-power operating as a 'bridge' between Americans and Europeans (arguably far more suited to and more successful in this role than the United Kingdom). It has a long tradition as a nation defending the moral-legal order in international relations. And it has long been a proponent of free trade.[1] Yet, in the early twenty-first century all these issues were put to the test due to the rise of US unilateralism under President George W. Bush. After surveying the importance of NATO for Dutch foreign relations since World War II, the chapter continues by outlining the issues of the last few years that have caused Dutch–American relations to become unsettled through the clash of security interests and international law. How has this close bilateral relationship been affected, and what are the prospects for the future?

The Cold War, NATO and the end of neutrality

After World War II, the Netherlands abandoned its policy of neutrality, held since 1839, by first signing the Brussels Treaty in 1948 and then joining NATO as a founding member in 1949. This move was backed by all the major political parties, not so much with enthusiasm, but as a logical necessity to bind the United States to the security system of Europe. The religious input (both Protestant and Catholic) into Dutch political and social life, combined with the standpoint of the strong Labour party, resulted in solid anti-communist sentiments.[2] Foreign Minister Dirk Stikker, who signed the treaty, did attempt to withhold Dutch support in return for concessions from the United States, but this was not taken seriously in Washington.[3] There was certainly discontent with the failure of the United States to wholeheartedly support the attempt to regain control of the

East Indies, but the loss of this major colony in 1949 also proved pivotal in redirecting Dutch security concerns to the Atlantic region.[4] NATO immediately became and has remained the bedrock of Dutch security policy, leading to the much-used epithet of the Netherlands as a 'loyal ally'.[5] There have been three Dutch NATO secretary-generals (Dirk Stikker, Joseph Luns, and Jaap de Hoop Scheffer), a record only matched by the British, a sure sign of American support for the binding role that the Dutch play so well in the Alliance.

There are many examples of the positive Dutch attitude towards NATO. The country supported the entry of the Federal Republic of Germany into the organization, and the integration of German forces into a US-led Atlantic alliance was considered far more preferable than the option of a European defence community. Although the Dutch disagreed with how President Dwight D. Eisenhower dealt with Suez, believing that the United States undermined the unity of the alliance, in the same month (November 1956) the parliament accepted the stationing of US nuclear weapons on Dutch soil to upgrade NATO defences. In 1958, the Netherlands was the first NATO ally whose jet fighters were equipped with these weapons, which remained under the control of the US military.[6] In the 1960s, the Netherlands again proved to be steadfast in its backing for US leadership by rejecting the opportunity to develop a European nuclear force (the Multilateral Force plan). The Dutch also reacted quickly when de Gaulle withdrew from NATO's central military command structure in 1966, swiftly agreeing to host US forces and the Allied Forces Central Europe (AFCENT) command centre in Brunssum (*sic*).[7] In the late 1960s the US embassy in The Hague confirmed that 'US–Netherlands relationships in NATO can be characterized as "special"', and that it was essential to recognize 'the value of a continued "special relationship"'.[8]

However, from the late 1960s onwards NATO did start to become the focus for criticism within Dutch politics and society. The rise of the New Left within the Labour party led to votes being held at its party congresses on whether the Netherlands should leave NATO. Despite being heavily defeated, these motions were a clear sign that the instinctively pro-NATO Cold War politics of the Dutch social democratic left was now over.[9] Under the Labour-led coalition of 1973–77 policy was dominated by pro-atlanticist ministers for both foreign affairs and defence, but the increasing dominance of the left in the party led to it opposing NATO's 1979 Twin Track decision, involving the upgrading of NATO's nuclear forces, throughout the following decade.[10]

The period from 1980 to 1985 was the most tense for Dutch–American relations. The combination of a powerful peace movement with anti-nuclear sentiments within the large Labour and Christian Democratic parties created a vulnerable situation for a series of governments to accept the deployment of Cruise missiles on Dutch soil.[11] Walter Laqueur's typology of the Dutch idealist penchant for neutralism as 'Hollanditis' exemplified the perceived transformation of the Netherlands from loyal ally to the weak link in the NATO chain. Yet, the political and policy-making elite held firm, manoeuvring their way through both domestic opposition and foreign pressure to sustain the Dutch contribution to the Alliance.[12]

The end of the Cold War brought with it a re-evaluation of Dutch foreign policy. Under Foreign Minister Hans van Mierlo (1994–98) a deliberate attempt was made to shift attention to European developments in the wake of the Maastricht Treaty and the effort to build a common foreign and security policy. However, these deliberations only resulted in a major policy paper in 1995 that referred as much to the need to maintain traditional interests (transatlantic relations) as it did to new factors in world politics, such as the EU and the rise of East Asia.[13] The choice for the transatlantic option, as Robert Russell pointed out almost 40 years ago, was a choice for freedom of action separate from the interests and demands of the Netherlands' larger European neighbours, and this factor remained pivotal throughout the 1990s.[14]

US unilateralism v. Dutch multilateralism: Security Policy

Nevertheless, after 2000 the unilateralism of the Bush administrations put Dutch atlanticism to the test. Three examples are given here to illustrate the consequences for the Netherlands of loyalty to the Western alliance under American leadership: Iraq, Afghanistan and the Joint Strike Fighter.

Iraq

Two days before the invasion of Iraq, on 18 March 2003, the Dutch government under Jan Peter Balkenende announced that they would adopt a position of political but not military support for the imminent war. This was despite the fact that there was considerable public opposition to the war, divisions in the government over its legitimacy and a widespread belief that the path through the UN should be followed. In late May 2003, with President George W. Bush having declared the war to be over, Balkenende announced the placement of 1,350 Dutch military in Muthanna province in southern Iraq as part of the international stabilization force. In June 2004, following a visit of Balkenende to Bush and heavy pressure from the United Kingdom, the government proposed and parliament agreed to extend the troops' stay in Iraq until March 2005, but insisted that they would stay no longer. The troops were then withdrawn without much incident, having sustained two fatalities.

However, since then the Iraq issue has continued to rumble in Dutch politics. Firstly, in November 2006 the *Volkskrant* presented its readers with a Dutch Abu Ghraib. The newspaper released information that Military Intelligence and Security Service (MIVD) personnel had carried out violent interrogations in November 2003 in buildings of the Coalition Provisional Authority in the town of Samawah, about 230 miles southeast of Baghdad. Prisoners were forced to wear darkened goggles, which were sometimes removed and bright lights were shone at them. They were also kept awake for long periods by being soaked with water, and were exposed to high-pitched sounds.[15] Coming 5 days before the national elections, these revelations seemed to be deliberately timed to have an impact on the results, and Defence Minister Henk Kamp demanded a full enquiry into how and why the information was released at that time.[16]

Secondly, there has been the question of why the Dutch government joined the 'Coalition of the Willing', in stark contrast to the Belgians, Germans and French. In September 2002 Balkenende had received a 'for your eyes only' report from Tony Blair that held the intelligence information on the military threat posed by Saddam Hussein's Iraq, including the background to the '45 minute' claim. This was revealed in August 2003 by Balkenende during a parliamentary debate, and it became apparent that he had not discussed the issue with any of his ministers. The opposition parties, which included Labour, accused Balkenende of leading the Netherlands into support for the war based on false information from the British, although the then foreign minister and later NATO secretary-general, Jaap de Hoop Scheffer, insisted that the decision had been based not upon Iraq's threat to the Netherlands but upon its endless refusal to comply with previous UN resolutions.[17] Scheffer had even stated publicly in September 2002 that new UN resolutions were not necessary to justify a war against Iraq, a position which went further than any other US ally at that time.[18] What is more, Kamp refused to allow a public examination of the views of the MIVD on the report from Blair and on the Iraqi threat.[19] The official line was clear: It was the violation of UN resolutions, and not the presence of weapons of mass destruction (WMD), that led the Dutch government to support the war. It was therefore based on principle, not pre-emption.

However, as the full extent of the misinformation surrounding the Iraq war has gradually been revealed in both the United States and the United Kingdom, increasing scrutiny has been directed towards Balkenende's original decision to support Operation Iraqi Freedom. The first critical examination of the Dutch decision-making process on Iraq appeared in the *NRC Handelsblad* on 12 June 2004, which exposed the MIVD's heavy scepticism over Iraqi possession of WMD in the run-up to the war.[20] The MIVD did not encourage the same politicized conclusions from the intelligence on Iraq as the British and American governments did – but this did not prevent the Dutch government from ignoring the nuances and backing the war option. What is more, there was serious disquiet within the ministries of foreign affairs and defence over the lack of legitimacy for a war with Iraq if the Security Council did not sanction such a move. 'These civil servants saw it coming that the Netherlands would face a principled choice between its clear atlanticist tradition and its reputation as champion of international law', *NRC Handelsblad* noted, 'Could The Hague support the United States if, without a specific mandate from the Security Council, it began a war on its own?'[21]

Balkenende's choice for 'political, not military support' seemed to be the way out in the short term, with the determination that Iraq had ignored twelve previous UN resolutions and had not cooperated with the UN weapons inspectors being enough to justify Dutch troops being sent to Iraq after the official end to hostilities had been declared. However, was it only 'political support'? On 22 March, 2 days after the invasion began, Air Force Lt. Col. Jan Blom, stationed with a Patriot missile NATO unit in Turkey but present in the Persian Gulf on a training mission, appeared at a major press conference behind US Army General

Tommy Franks. Franks was then able to include the Netherlands, alongside the British, the Australians and the Danes, as part of the 'Coalition of the Willing' that made up the invasion force. An embarrassed Dutch government rushed to claim that it was all a mistake, Blom having been asked to join a meeting without any knowledge of what it was supposed to represent. Since then the suspicion has grown that it was no accident Blom was present that day. It has emerged that Dutch F-16s were conducting reconnaissance flights over Iraq already in late 2002.[22] Dutch Special Forces were active in northern Iraq in early 2003, and the submarine *Walrus*, under US operational command from June 2002, had been stationed in the Persian Gulf to observe Iranian naval units.[23] It now appears that in late November 2002 the United States delivered a list of requests for military support to the Dutch government, including use of Rotterdam and Schiphol as transit points and an array of land, sea and air force units.[24] It remains unclear what the precise reaction was from The Hague, but the signs are clear that some deals were made to ensure Dutch participation. The fact that de Hoop Scheffer, who clearly committed the Netherlands to the US–UK camp in late 2002, was named the next NATO secretary-general during that same period is also a clear sign of close cooperation between the two governments.[25]

At first a parliamentary enquiry into this affair seemed a definite possibility. Balkenende and his then coalition allies in the Liberal party steadfastly refused to accept this, but from 2003 until 2006 the Labour party, which possessed a major lead in the opinion polls during much of this period, held fast to its demand for such an enquiry. However, Labour failed to become the largest party in the November 2006 elections, and the most likely option for a new stable governing cabinet was through a Labour-Christian Democrat coalition. This put Labour's demand for an enquiry up against the fact that its main target, Jan Peter Balkenende, was now the party's most likely coalition partner. Compromise prevailed, and the subsequent coalition policy agenda announced in February 2007 contained no mention of this issue, allowing the Socialist Party (SP) to outflank Labour on the left and pursue a public campaign to mobilize support for an enquiry. In July 2007 the SP, together with several other parties, secured a debate in the upper house of the Dutch parliament, but the resulting vote went 39–36 against their enquiry proposal. However, by late 2008, even some Christian Democrats were pressuring Balkenende on this issue, and in March 2009 the government set up an independent commission, with a limited mandate, to investigate.

Afghanistan

Afghanistan became a political issue soon after the withdrawal of Dutch troops from Iraq. Although there were already around 600 Dutch military personnel in Kabul, in December 2005 the Dutch government under Balkenende sent 1,750 extra troops to Uruzgan province as part of the International Security and Assistance Force (ISAF) being run by NATO, with the intention that they would remain there until August 2008. An attempt by the smallest coalition party (D66) to question the mission in particular, and the relationship with the United States in general, failed to split the government. Parliamentary opposition faded once the Labour party were accommodated with promises that the main aim of the mission was to be reconstruction and not counterterrorism. Guarantees from the United States, the United Kingdom and the Afghani government over the treatment of any suspects that the Dutch might hand over to other authorities also swung opinion in favour. Above all, the need to maintain unity within NATO played a particular role in the positive Dutch decision.[26]

Nevertheless, problems remained. The then minister of defence, Henk Kamp, refused to clarify what exactly the Dutch attitude was towards the opium trade.[27] The *UN Office on Drugs and Crime* (UNODC) reckoned that 87 per cent of the world's opium production was from Afghanistan, where it was calculated that about 52 per cent of the GDP ($2.7 billion) came from this industry.[28] The 2006 harvest rose 47 per cent, to around 6,700 tons, enough to produce 670 tons of heroin. Kamp did not deny that Dutch ISAF troops may become involved in the destruction of poppy fields if it fell under their task of supporting the regional Afghani government, even though this was not an official task of ISAF. Kamp's problem was that the United States, under the guise of Enduring Freedom, wanted to act unilaterally to destroy the poppy harvest, in direct opposition to the official standpoints of both the ISAF and the Afghani government. With no alternative source of income, this policy threatened to increase support among the farmers for resistance against the military forces in Afghanistan – including the Dutch. In January 2007 the Afghan president Hamid Karzai finally stated that there would be no spraying of opium fields with pesticide from the air, thus rejecting US demands.[29] However, Afghan forces have undertaken ground operations against the opium farmers, with potentially dangerous consequences for the ISAF mission.

Meanwhile, throughout 2007 the decision on whether the Dutch forces would remain longer than the August 2008 deadline gradually increased in significance.[30] Early signs indicated that there was a determination to push through an extension of the Dutch commitment. Defence Minister Eimert van Middelkoop stated openly in June 2007 that the cabinet had the 'political intention' to prolong, an honest announcement that got him into trouble for apparently ignoring the need to get parliamentary support. In August the chief of staff, Dick Berlijn, went a step further by declaring that it would be 'a moral failure' for a prosperous nation like the Dutch to turn its back on the mission. Meanwhile, NATO was a constant factor in the political deliberations, something that van Middelkoop had admitted back in March when he said that pressures from abroad for a prolonging of the mission were growing. This pressure went public in September when the secretary-general of NATO, de Hoop Scheffer, with a complete lack of respect for diplomatic protocol, trumpeted that 'no one can leave. No one is going to leave. I can honestly not believe that the Netherlands will be the only one to leave'. It was clear early on that the Dutch government was working hard to find other NATO partners to join it in the Afghan endeavour, a condition for its continued commitment. By the time of the NATO summit in Noordwijk in October sufficient, if limited, agreements had been reached with Hungary, the

Czech Republic, Slovakia, France (training units only) and possibly aspirant NATO member Georgia. Therefore, when on 30 November the Dutch cabinet finally announced that Dutch troops would be staying in Uruzgan until December 2010, everyone had been expecting it for several months.[31]

Yet, the apparent straightforwardness of the decision hides some major complications. Despite previous agreements the Dutch forces have been coopted into Enduring Freedom operations over the past years, and hardline US tactics have not helped the confidence-building measures of the Dutch forces one bit. Some commentators, notably Ko Colijn, have pointed out that the Netherlands has effectively been drawn into the 'Global War on Terror' despite denying any connection with it. By associating the Netherlands's security policy so closely with NATO, the Dutch government effectively had nowhere to go except to continue in Afghanistan. Since late 2007 de Hoop Scheffer and others have repeatedly stated that the future of NATO as a credible organization lies in how it deals with the Afghanistan mission. Under these circumstances any other decision by The Hague was impossible. Ever since the beginning of the Afghan mission the association with counterterrorism had been placed within the broader, more palatable cause of reconstruction and development, thereby preventing a cabinet split and abiding by the expected norms of Dutch foreign policy interests.[32] However, despite the Dutch commitment, tensions remain with the United States, its main ally.[33]

The Joint Strike Fighter (JSF)

The JSF story gives a perfect indication of the strength of atlanticist opinion within the world of Dutch politics, the military and big business. In 2002, the government agreed to join in the development of the JSF, the intended successor to the F-16. The deal involved an investment of $800 million in the project, with the proviso that parts of the development and production would be channelled to Dutch companies. However, problems with the prototype meant that already in 2003 there were serious doubts over whether the final model would meet the expected requirements. Cooperation with partners, particularly the United Kingdom, ran into trouble when the United States refused to share the necessary technological specifications. Delays have moved full-scale production back to 2013. Other higher-tech options, such as Unmanned Combat Aerial Vehicles, and the changing nature of warfare itself, have thrown other questionmarks at the JSF.[34]

However, the Dutch, in comparison with just about every other major contributor (British, Danish, Norwegian, Turkish, and – as observers – the Israelis) have kept a low profile during these difficulties and have not shown any interest in changing course. Potential competitors, such as the Eurofighter and the French Rafale, have not been considered as serious options, a clear reflection of the solid transatlantic perspective of Dutch industry, the Ministry of Defence, and the Air Force. In terms of outlook and material the Dutch military is fully 'embedded' in logistical compatibility with US forces. When the General Auditor's Office produced a critical report in October 2006, claiming that the total costs would eventually reach €14.6 billion for 85 aircraft, it was ignored by the government.[35] In November 2006, less than two weeks before the elections, the Ministry of Defence signed a Memorandum of Understanding to further commit the Netherlands to the JSF development process. Up to that point Dutch companies had earned a total of €720 million, even though it was budgeted in 2002 that a total of €6.2 billion would return to the Netherlands via business contracts. The signing just before the elections was deliberate. 'The Labour party must now realize that the point of no return has been reached', said Rob de Wit, manager of Philips affiliate Dutch Aero.[36] Once again, as with the parliamentary enquiry into the Iraq war, the post-election coalition-building compromises forced the Labour party to retreat. A definite decision on whether or not to buy the JSF will now only be taken in 2010, at which point the Dutch will be so far involved it is hard to imagine any other outcome. In May 2009 it was announced that the development phase would now run to 2016, absorbing an extra $2.4 billion in costs.

Dutch multilateralism: The importance of international organizations

The JSF episode has exposed the Dutch commitment to atlanticism. With its economic landscape dominated by several influential multinationals, such as Shell, Unilever, KLM, Akzo Nobel and Philips, the Dutch were long committed to a free trade policy, and their reliance on foreign raw materials and markets ensured an internationalist outlook. Products and services delivered to the European Union, America, Asia and Africa generate close to 60 per cent of Dutch GDP. Commercial services dominate the national economy, with Rotterdam the largest sea port in Europe and Schiphol the third largest airport for freight traffic. The necessity of a stable international economic order has therefore always been paramount for the Dutch, and they have contributed a great deal of expertise and commitment within international organizations during the twentieth century to ensure this. This reflects their belief both in the necessity of achieving international order through negotiation and the need to secure Dutch interests by arranging compromises between the larger powers. As Voorhoeve noted, 'An important means of indirectly exercising economic influence is by participation in international conferences and organizations. Dutch delegations to international economic conferences and such bodies as the EEC, IMF, GATT, Benelux, OECD, World Bank and UN agencies have usually been large and active'.[37]

It was also not just a question of quantity, but also of quality. The Americans had great respect for the abilities of their Dutch counterparts in the foreign policy field. Alongside the three Dutch NATO secretary-generals, several other top officials played a key role in developing the post-war international landscape, such as Emile van Lennep (secretary-general of the OECD 1969–84) and Finance Minister Dr. Piet Lieftinck (executive director of the IMF 1956–76, director of the World Bank 1956–71). Within the EEC, prior to the entry of the United Kingdom in 1973 the Dutch fulfilled a crucial role in defending not only the principle of free trade against French protectionism, but also in opposing de Gaulle's attempt at political hegemony via the Fouchet plan. The Dutch always managed to maintain a positive approach to European integration within a consistent atlanticist context.[38]

Several US ambassadors have spoken openly about the importance of the Netherlands as both an international political hub and as an essential bilateral trade and investment partner. William Tyler (1965–69), who went to The Hague after serving as assistant secretary of state for European affairs, spoke of the country as an ideal 'listening post' for what was going on around Europe.[39] His successor William Middendorf (1969–72) had this to say:

> First off, in the Netherlands you have to understand, it's all business, and they're very practical . . . Charlie Tanguy here, who was then the Netherlands desk officer was able to arrange for a number of meetings in New York with major corporations like IBM and others, at Chase, and Citibank who had huge international departments doing business with the Netherlands, and Chemical Bank. We had a number of meetings there, and businessmen were giving us the benefit of where they thought the Netherlands fitted into the European scene, and how important the Netherlands was in the business sense, plus their role in NATO, OECD, and all the other functions where the Netherlands was a key leader in international organizations. It made my job very easy because at one point the Netherlands had the Secretary General of the OECD, the head of the Bank of International Settlements, Joseph Luns at NATO, and the [UN's] Foreign Agricultural Organization chief.[40]

William Dyess (ambassador from 1981 until 1983) also referred to how

> the Dutch were into everything. At that time they were the largest investors in this country. Now the British are, but they were the largest investors. They are into everything. They were in the Sinai and various peace-keeping forces. They were in the U.N. They were on the Security Council, the Common Market. You name it, the Dutch were in it.[41]

The bilateral economic relationship is considerable. In 2003 the Netherlands was the fourth largest investor in the United States, behind the United Kingdom but in terms of per capita investment way ahead. In 2001, it stood at $9,754 per capita, compared to $3,629 for the United Kingdom and $1,252 for Japan. In the other direction, the United States has used the Netherlands as an ideal platform for Foreign Direct Investment (FDI) within the Euro-zone. In 2003, the United States invested far more in the Netherlands than in any other EU state, around 10 per cent of all US FDI.[42] As the JSF story shows, the two economies, or better said the two economic mentalities, are closely interwoven.

US unilateralism v. Dutch multilateralism: International law, norms, and values

In November 2006, the then foreign minister Bernard Bot outlined his vision on Dutch foreign policy in the Netherlands' version of *Foreign Affairs*, the *Internationale Spectator*. Bot saw a necessary shift from the explicit 'pure multi-lateralism' of the post-World War II era towards a 'realistic multilateralism' that would reflect the changing circumstances in international politics. Pure multilat-eralism was characterized by commonly accepted rules and an equality before the (international) law that reduced the differences in power between nations. In this scenario the interests of the Netherlands coincided wholly with the interests of the most important international organizations, such as the EU, NATO and the UN. Looking at it from the perspective of Dutch tradition, the 'norms and values' of the pastor combined perfectly with the trading interests of the businessman. For Bot it was necessary to adjust to the fact that this post-war international order was now changing, due in part to the rise of new powers (China, India, Brazil) and the stagnation in the EU surrounding both internal and external policy. As a result, the Netherlands would continue to strive for its place in the world market and the maintenance of the international legal order, but it would do so out of its own national interest and no longer with the conviction that this could be blended perfectly into the common good.[43]

In contrast to his measured opinion in this article, Bot gave a speech at the Roosevelt Academy in Middelburg in January 2007 in which his analysis of the world situation went several critical steps further. Claiming that 'the exist-ing legal order is losing legitimacy', Bot pointed to four cases where this was being demonstrated: The struggle over nuclear power with Iran; Serbia's refusal to hand over war criminals as part of its passage towards EU membership; the 2006 US–India nuclear deal, which violated the Non-Proliferation Treaty; and the arrest and detention of illegal combatants by the United States outside any accepted conventions of international law. It was remarkable to hear from a Dutch foreign minister that two of the four examples illustrating the breakdown in legal conventions directly involved the United States. For Bot, the position of the Netherlands, and specifically The Hague as the 'legal capital of the world', remains an essential aspect of Dutch national identity, and right should continue to prevail over might as much as possible. It has been precisely in this field that the main clashes between the Netherlands and the United States have taken place over the past few years, when the Bush administration began pursuing a unilat-eralism deliberately unshackled from the need for international consensus. Two specific examples of this crumbling trust will be given here.

The 'Hague Invasion Act'

On 1 July 2002 the Rome Statutes of the International Criminal Court (ICC) came into effect, enabling the actual establishment of the ICC in The Hague. There had been much controversy surrounding this court, particularly concerning the refusal of the United States to allow its nationals to come under its jurisdiction. On 3 August 2002 President Bush signed the American Servicemembers Protection Act, a body of measures designed to deny the ICC any legitimacy. It soon became known as The Hague Invasion Act, since it included the authorization of the use of military force to liberate any American citizen, or citizen of a US ally, being held by the ICC.[44] However much this may have been an act of clumsy intimidation, the gratuitous rejection of Dutch identity and sovereignty in this legislation caused an understandably angry response from the Netherlands. In April 2009 the Dutch Foreign Minister called once again for its removal from the statute book.

Extraordinary rendition

In 2005, the issue of 'extraordinary rendition' became a major issue in Dutch–American relations. During the 1990s there developed a practice of abducting criminal suspects in a third country in order to bring them to justice elsewhere. So long as there existed an official arrest warrant, there was cooperation between the abductors and the third country itself, and the aim was to bring the suspect before a court of law, then rendition could be defensible. Thus, President Clinton authorized Presidential Decision Directive 39 in the wake of the 1993 World Trade Center bombing, which stated that, if normal extradition procedures were unavailable or inapplicable, the support of local authorities could be requested to bring a suspect to the United States for trial. However, already during Clinton's time there was discussion over the option of taking suspects to another country to avoid intelligence information leaking through the openness of the US court system. Therefore, even before 9/11 the procedure had altered from one of due process to one of information-gathering by any means necessary, including abducting and transporting suspects to countries whose security services had a proven record of torture, such as Morocco, Egypt and Syria.[45] As 'unlawful combatants' in the War on Terror they were effectively removed from the established norms of legal procedure.

When news of the secret prisons and clandestine CIA flights became known in late 2005, Foreign Minister Bot reacted strongly, stating that such illegal US activity could have consequences for Dutch participation in military missions together with the Americans, as in Afghanistan. Bot raised the issue in the NATO Council and received assurances from Secretary of State Condoleeza Rice that the United States did not torture and that the Netherlands had not been implicated in either the transport or detention of suspects. For the Dutch, it was essential that their identity as upholders of international law not be damaged by being implicated in these activities. It is clear that several European countries have cooperated in this process, with their security service personnel being able to question suspects abducted by the Americans and held at Guantánamo Bay, the Bagram base in Afghanistan, or other secret locations. As far as is known, the Dutch security service (AIVD) has cooperated in information-sharing but has not been present at any of the interrogation centres. Whether this would have been different had there been Dutch suspects involved remains an open question. However, independent investigators have established that, between 2002 and 2006, at least six CIA flights had passed through Rotterdam airport and one through Schiphol.[46]

The announcement of President Bush on 6 September 2006, which confirmed the existence of the rendition programme and the secret prisons, came as a special blow to Bot, who admitted that his criticism of rendition had already led to 'a small ice age' between the Netherlands and the United States during that year.[47] Looking for a way out, Bot offered the services of Dutch legal expertise to try and find a way forward on the status of illegal combatants and where they fit within international law. At the end of 2006 an informal, independent international commission was convened to study the problem in order to resolve the difference of opinion between the two countries. Bot himself, when asked in Middelburg in January 2007, did not give a clear picture on what the timetable for the commission was, or what influence it would have on Dutch or US policy, but he did mention that 'the Americans are favourable about the group' and its goals. The danger was that the Dutch would be drawn into compromises with the Americans which would ultimately weaken their standpoint on international law. It was highly unlikely that the Americans would abandon extraordinary rendition, their use of military tribunals, lack of legal process and use of torture simply because of Dutch moral concern. However, the moves by President Obama in 2009 to close the prison in Guantanamo and to abandon torture successfully defused the issue.[48]

Conclusion: Plus ça Change, Plus ça Meme Chose?

Despite Iraq, despite Afghanistan and despite the anti-Bush public mood, foreign policy did not feature prominently in the November 2006 Dutch parliamentary elections. The document that outlined the winning coalition's policy agenda, adopted in February 2007 by the Christian Democrats, Labour, and the smaller Christian Union, referred to foreign policy in only two of its fifty-three pages.[49] Perhaps this apparent lack of interest was precisely *because of* the general anti-Bush (and anti-EU) mood. There remains at this time no desire among the political class to confront the realities of Dutch atlanticism even in an era of strong US unilateralism, because this would mean accepting that a re-evaluation of principles was necessary. Minister Bot, the one member of the previous government who did raise serious concerns over US policies, was publicly rebuked by Minister-President Balkenende and was not asked to retain his post in the new coalition. His successor, Maxime Verhagen, soon showed that he was not going to push any issue that might disrupt a smooth transatlantic relationship. Although there have been rumblings within the Labour party, the leadership successfully sidelined them and the coalition agreement has effectively killed them off. The Socialist Party, the one party that did present a broad election campaign agenda for foreign affairs, focused on transatlantic relations only in the sense of rejecting the limitless expansion of NATO's mission, epitomized by ISAF in Afghanistan.

There are significant voices, notably Labour's State Secretary for European Affairs Frans Timmerman, who have been calling for a general move away from an automatic atlanticism towards a more flexible understanding of Dutch interests in a global political and economic environment. However, the question remains as to whether the opportunity will arise for such figures to demonstrate what this might mean in practice. Other signs of serious discontent have also been evident. In 2005, Karel van Wolferen, professor at the University of Amsterdam, published, together with journalist Jan Sampiemon, a book titled *A Turning Point in the Nation's History* in which they called for a realistic understanding of how the first Bush administration had negated all accepted norms and values that provided the basis for the Atlantic community. The divide that was opening up between US national interests and the interests of a stable world order, they argued, was raising serious questions for the Netherlands. Emphasizing that he was not anti-American, van Wolferen at least wanted Dutch policymakers to deal with the fact that US policies were already breaking up the transatlantic alliance. No step forward could be made, in the direction of the EU, the UN, or wherever, without first addressing what was going on with the United States.

Why has this re-evaluation, *pace* Bot, not occurred? Van Wolferen listed four reactions to the current state of affairs. There are the 'knee-jerk Atlanticists' who would do anything to prevent a disruption to the 'special relationship'. There are also those on the Right who express sympathy for the values of the neoconservative agenda and its call to bring democracy to the Middle East. On the Left there has been a too-easy tendency to categorize recent events as age-old US imperialism, without recognizing how novel the current situation actually is. Finally, there are many 'pragmatists' who simply see no alternative to accepting US hyper-power, and who, in doing so, pass the initiative to Washington to continue benefiting from its divide-and-rule approach to European affairs.[50] A year after their book's publication, van Wolferen and Sampiemon commented bitterly on the inability to generate any meaningful interest or debate within the Dutch media on the how and why of the 'Global War on Terror'. Official statements were accepted at face value, opinion pieces supporting US policy were regularly selected from American sources, and those who questioned these developments were marginalized. For these authors, the Netherlands, from a lack of courage to face up to reality, had become little more than a 'vassal state' unable to appreciate how its leader was bringing it into greater danger:

> Above all it is clear how strong the psychological blockage is in the Netherlands to accept that our protector from the past half century no longer provides protection. . . . The Netherlands had nothing to gain from the illegal occupation of Iraq. The NATO operation in Afghanistan is doomed. Meanwhile the inhabitants there have every reason to see the Netherlands as an accomplice of an aggressive power that is taking it out on their lives.[51]

For critics such as van Wolferen, Sampiemon and fellow journalist Henk Hofland, there is a desperate lack of reflection on how to turn justifiable concern about US policies into constructive politics at the national level. The Dutch leadership instead prefers to ignore, or at best downplay, the criticism, assuming that there has been no 'turning point', only an awkward but temporary phase. The one moment when a serious reflection on Dutch commitments abroad could have occurred free of dogma was during 2002 when Pim Fortuyn led a remarkable upsurge of popular discontent against the established parties in the direction of the May 2002 elections. Fortuyn was unencumbered by tradition and voiced at various moments his disbelief in the worth of NATO and, in particular, his opposition to the JSF. Not long before the elections the then US ambassador Clifford Sobel visited Fortuyn and was able to convince him to accept the JSF. However, the extent of Fortuyn's views on NATO in general were not to be known. On 6 May 2002 Fortuyn was murdered outside a radio studio in Hilversum by a radical environmental activist, his death throwing his party into disarray and removing any chance of a wide-ranging re-assessment of Dutch foreign policy.

Since then there has been a return to normalcy. As the author of the 'loyal ally' thesis, Alfred van Staden, remarked in a think-piece in late 2006, any workable international order requires American cooperation, and attempting to achieve anything without the United States would only encourage its unilateralist tendencies. In his view the EU offers no opportunity for alternatives since the malaise surrounding the constitution took hold (a malaise which the Netherlands played a central role in with the negative result of its referendum in June 2005). Only those nations that remain allies can expect to function as 'correcting-mechanisms' to reconcile US power with the demands of international law and legitimacy.[52] This continues to be the dominant line in the Netherlands today. The special relationship, despite accumulating criticism, remains intact.

Notes

1 Joris Voorhoeve, later Foreign Minister, has characterized Dutch foreign policy as having been driven since the seventeenth century by three predominant themes: Neutralist abstentionism, maritime commercialism and internationalist idealism. See J. Voorhoeve, *Peace, Profits and Principles: A Study of Dutch Foreign Policy*, The Hague: Nijhoff, 1979, pp. 42–53.

2 A. Lijphart, *The Politics of Accommodation: Pluralism and Democracy in the Netherlands*, Berkeley: University of California Press, 1968. Although the Communist Partij Nederland (CPN) did poll 10.6 per cent in the 1946 elections, a sustained anti-communist campaign by successive Dutch governments, combined with a decline in the CPN's popularity due to events such as the Soviet invasion of Hungary, meant the party never again gained a similar level of success.

3 B. Zeeman, 'Belgium, the Netherlands, and Alliances 1945–49', PhD dissertation, Leiden University, 1993.

4 H. A. Schaper, 'Het Nederlandse veiligheidsbeleid, 1945–50', in N. C. F. van Sas (ed.) *De Kracht van Nederland*, Haarlem: Becht, 1991, pp. 150–70; W. Klinkert and G. Teitler, 'Nederland van neutraliteit naar bondgenootschap. Het veiligheids-en defensiebeleid in de twintigste eeuw', in B. de Graaf, D. Hellema, and B. van der Zwan (eds) *De Nederlandse buitenlandse politiek in de twintigste eeuw*, Amsterdam: Boom, 2003, pp. 9–36.

5 A. van Staden, *Een Trouwe Bondgenoot: Nederland en het Atlantisch Bondgenootschap 1960–1971*, Baarn: In den Toren, 1974; A. van Staden, 'De rol van Nederland in het Atlantisch Bondgenootschap: Wat veranderd en wat uiteindelijk blijf', in van Sas (ed.) *De Kracht van Nederland*, pp. 219–31; the issue of whether the Netherlands has an

identifiable tradition in foreign policy (Voorhoeve), including its loyalty to the transatlantic alliance (van Staden), has been a contested issue in Dutch historiography since the early 1980s. See for instance the different points of view in B. Bot et al., *Lijn in de Buitenlandse Politiek van Nederland*, The Hague: Sdu, 1984.

6   J. W. Honig, *Defence Policy in the North Atlantic Alliance: The Case of the Netherlands*, Westport CT: Praeger, 2003.

7   A. Kersten, 'Neutralising Political Poker Play with a Cardboard Pistol: Dutch Reactions to France's Withdrawal from NATO's Integrated Defence (1966)', in M. Vaisse, P. Mélandri and F. Bozo (eds) *La France et l'OTAN 1949–1996*, Armées: Interventions, 1996, pp. 451–67.

8   '1968 – State of US–Netherlands Relations', 16 January 1968, and 'Annual Policy Assessment', 27 September 1968, Box 2363, POL 1 NETH-US, Subject-Numeric Files, RG 59, National Archives, College Park, Md.

9   See F. Zuijdam, *Tussen Wens en Werkelijkheid: Het Debat over Vrede en Veiligheid binnen de PvdA in de Periode 1958–1977*, Amsterdam: Aksant, 2002, pp. 133–216. New Left opposition to NATO was an outgrowth of several factors: Criticism of the Vietnam war; rejection of NATO membership for rightist regimes such as Greece, Portugal, and Spain; and the aim to re-configure East–West relations through recognizing the GDR in particular and Detente in general.

10 M. Kuitenbrouwer, 'Een Realistische Idealist: Max van der Stoel (1973–77 en 1981–82)', in D. Hellema, B. Zeeman, and B. van der Zwan (eds) *De Nederlandse Ministers van Buitenlandse Zaken in de Twintigste Eeuw*, The Hague: Sdu, 1999, pp. 243–56.

11 See B. J. van Eenennaam, *48 Kruisraketten*, The Hague: Sdu, 1988.

12 W. Laqueur, 'Hollanditis: A New Stage in European Neutralism', *Commentary*, 71, August 1981, pp. 19–26; R. van Diepen, *Hollanditis: Nederland en het Kernwapendebat 1977–1987*, Amsterdam: Bert Bakker, 2004.

13 D. Hellema, 'Een Charmant Bewindsman: H.A.F.M.O. van Mierlo (1994–98)', in D. Hellema, B. Zeeman and B. van der Zwan (eds) *De Nederlandse Ministers*, pp. 295–307.

14 R. Russell, 'The Atlantic Alliance in Dutch Foreign Policy', *Internationale Spectator*, 1969, vol. 23, pp. 1189–1208.

15 'Nederlanders martelden Irakezen' [The Dutch tortured Iraqis], *De Volkskrant*, 17 November 2006.

16 Under pressure to explain itself, the *Volkskrant* published the background to the case. The paper had been put onto the story by a retired General who wanted the facts to come out. 'De Missie van Generaal X', *De Volkskrant*, 10 February 2007, p. 28.

17 A full summing-up of the Iraq issue in Dutch politics is J. Boom, 'Explosief Materiaal', *De Groene Amsterdammer*, 13 April 2007, pp. 10–12.

18 K. van Wolferen and J. Sampiemon, *Een Keerpunt in de Vaderlandse Geschiedenis*, Amsterdam: Meulenhoff, 2005, p. 117.

19 <http://www.novatv.nl/index.cfm?ln=nlandfuseaction=artikelen. detailsandachtergrond_id = 5168> (accessed 27 March 2007).

20 J. Oranje, 'Hollandse Oorlogslogica', *NRC Handelsblad*, 12 June 2004, <http://www. nrc.nl/binnenland/article380237.ece/Hollandse_oorlogslogica> (accessed 6 April 2007).

21 Ibid., 'Daar zag men aankomen dat Nederland, dat weliswaar een Atlantische traditie heeft, maar ook een reputatie als voorvechter van het internationaal recht, voor een principiële keuze kwam te staan. Kon Den Haag de VS steunen als die, zonder specifiek mandaat van de Veiligheidsraad, op eigen houtje een oorlog zouden beginnen?'

22 H. Jaspers, 'Geheime Nederlandse steun aan de oorlog van Bush'.<http://www.open-heidoverirak.nu/databank/Geheime%20Nederlandse%20steun%20aan%20de%20 oorlog%20van%20Bush.html> (accessed 6 April 2007).

23 K. Colijn, 'Kwestie-Irak blijft kabinet plagen', *Vrij Nederland*, 31 March 2007, pp. 15–16.

24 'Nederland en de oorlog tegen Irak', KRO Reporter (text based on a television documentary aired on Sunday 25 March 2007), <http://reporter.kro.nl/uitzendingen/2007/irakoorlog/LeesVerder.aspx> (accessed 6 April 2007).
25 Colijn, 'Kwestie-Irak', pp. 16–17.
26 H. Hofland, 'Uruzgan als Nederlands Moeras', and Aukje van Roessel, 'Rekken en erbij Blijven', *De Groene Amsterdammer*, 20 January 2006, p. 7.
27 J. Boom, 'De Oorlog tegen het Rode Goud', *De Groene Amsterdammer*, 10 February 2006, pp. 16–17; 'Maar we laten ons niet afslachten', interview with Minister Henk Kamp, *De Groene Amsterdammer*, 9 February 2007, pp. 10–13.
28 <http://www.nato.int/docu/review/2006/issue1/dutch/analysis.html> (accessed 27 March 2007).
29 'Bucking US, Afghanistan won't Spray Heroin', Associated Press, 25 January 2007, <http://www.msnbc.msn.com/id/16807707/> (accessed 10 April 2007).
30 The former Defence Minister Joris Voorhoeve has himself entered the debate, calling for no extension beyond August 2008: 'Nederland moet niet in Uruzgan blijven', *Vrij Nederland*, 12 May 2007, pp. 22–23.
31 'Nederland moet blijven in Uruzgan', *NRC Handelsblad*, 23 November 2007, <http://oruzgan.web-log.nl/uruzgan_weblog/2007/11/nederland_moet_.html> (accessed 28 August 2008); A. van Roessel, 'Nederland heeft al ja gezegd', *De Groene Amsterdammer*, 2 November 2007, p. 11.
32 On the development of a post-Cold War and especially post-9/11 peacekeeping role for Dutch forces and the determination of the Dutch military to work closely with the United States, see C. Klep, 'Peacekeeping and the War on Terror 1989–2007', in H. Krabbendam, C. A. van Minnen, and G. Scott-Smith (eds) *Four Centuries of Dutch–American Relations*, Amsterdam: Boom & New York: State University of New York Press, forthcoming 2009.
33 On 17 January 2008 Defense Secretary Robert Gates claimed that some NATO partners were inadequately prepared for the kind of counter-insurgency tactics that Afghanistan demanded. By comparing the successful approach of US forces with other forces, it appeared that he was criticizing the Dutch, British, and Canadians operating in the southern provinces. Such an accusation was not appreciated in the Netherlands, which over the last decade has deliberately adapted its military for this kind of challenge, and Gates rescinded his comments with an apology. See 'Ongelukkige kritiek op een ongelukkige moment', *De Volkskrant*, 18 January 2008.
34 F. Slijper, 'JSF: Hoogvlieger of Zinkend Schip?', *Kleintje Muurkrant* 405, 26 August 2005, <http://www.stelling.nl/kleintje/405/JSF.htm> (accessed 10 April 2007).
35 F. Slijper, 'Vervolgbesluit JSF', *Kleintje Muurkrant* 418, 10 November 2006, <http://www.stelling.nl/kleintje/418/JMYM1163165649.html> (accessed 10 April 2007).
36 'Amerikaanse Gevechtsvliegtuig als Banenmotor', *NRC Handelsblad*, 10 November 2007, p. 13.
37 Voorhoeve, *Peace, Profits and Principles*, p. 15.
38 This has changed in recent years, the 'no' vote in the referendum on the EU constitution in June 2005 indicating that Dutch support for further integration was seriously waning. J. A. Schoneveld, *Tussen Atlantica en Europa: Over Opkomst en Ondergang van de Spagaat in de Nederlandse Buitenlandse Politiek*, PhD dissertation, Leiden University, 2000, pp. 30–39.
39 William R. Tyler, interview with Charles Stuart Kennedy, 17 November 1987, Foreign Affairs Oral History Collection of the Association for Diplomatic Studies and Training (hereafter cited as ADST), <http://memory.loc.gov/cgi-bin/query/r?ammem/mfdip:@field(DOCID+mfdip2004tyl02> (accessed 6 April 2007).
40 J. William Middendorf II, interview with Charles Stuart Kennedy, 28 July 1993, ADST, <http://memory.loc.gov/cgi-bin/query/r?ammem/mfdip:@field(DOCID+mfdip2004mid01> (accessed 6 April 2007).

41 William J. Dyess, interview with Charles Taber, 29 March 1989, ADST, <http://memory.loc.gov/cgi-bin/query/r?ammem/mfdip:@field(DOCID+mfdip2004dye01> (accessed 6 April 2007).

42 For further details of the financial and economic relationship see the website of the Royal Netherlands Embassy, Washington D.C., <http://www.netherlands-embassy.org/article.asp?articleref= AR00000237EN> and <http://www.netherlands-embassy.org/article.asp?articleref=AR00000718EN> (accessed 6 April 2007).

43 B. Bot, 'Met Overtuiging en Berekening: Van Zuiver naar Realistisch Multilateralisme', *Internationale Spectator*, 2006, vol. 60, pp. 547–51.

44 'US Hague Invasion Act becomes Law', Human Rights Watch, <http://www.hrw.org/press/2002/08/aspa080302.htm> (accessed 6 April 2007).

45 J. van Buuren, 'Amerikaanse Bluf', *De Groene Amsterdammer*, 6 January 2006, pp. 10–11.

46 J. Boom, 'Een Nieuwe Ijstijd', *De Groene Amsterdammer*, 22 September 2006, p. 14.

47 Ibid.

48 Ibid., 'Bot biedt VS juridische hulp aan inzake Guantanamo Bay', *NRC Handelsblad*, 12 October 2007.

49 'Coalitieakkord tussen de Tweede Kamerfracties van de CDA, PvdA, en ChristenUnie', 7 February 2007, pp. 13–15, <www.regering.nl/dsc?c=getobjectands=objandobjectid=74638> (accessed 7 February 2008).

50 Van Wolferen and Sampiemon, *Keerpunt*, pp. 98–103.

51 K. van Wolferen and J. Sampiemon, 'De Ondoordringbare Opiniemist', *De Groene Amsterdammer*, 6 October 2006, p. 28.

52 A. van Staden, 'Nederland en de Transatlantische Samenwerking: Apologie zonder Nostalgie', *Internationale Spectator*, 2006, vol. 60, pp. 568–72.

8 An aborted special relationship
US–Russia relations in the post-Cold War world: 1989–2007

Alex Marshall and J. Simon Rofe

When the Berlin Wall fell in November 1989 it signified the end of an epoch in US–Russia relations. Within 2 years, the Soviet Union would cease to be, and the United States would have led a UN coalition on a policing mission in the Middle East that gave hope for a New World Order. In light of such change the prospect for a harmonizing of relations between Washington and Moscow seemed not only possible, but probable. Yet, it has been impossible to provide a consistent narrative to the subsequent relationship. The aim of this paper is to examine bilateral relations between Moscow and Washington in the post-Cold War era, and particularly in the twenty-first century, in light of a special relationship discourse.

The paper is governed by this overarching effort to assess the extent to which the relationship between Moscow and Washington can be considered within the special relationship paradigm. The paper argues that US–Russian relations can be seen in light of a special relationship hypothesis, if that acknowledges that special relationships have less to do with wholly harmonious relations, and considerably more to do with an ongoing mutual distrust accompanied by moments of close concord. The Russia–US relationship is one characterized by long periods of mutual hostility and suspicion, underwritten by each having a unilateral global view, temporarily assuaged by episodes of considerable mutual support. These incidents typically occur when both regimes are represented by characters who can work together in a personable manner; thus alluding to the importance of individual relations in a Russia–US special relationship. The issues which bring each party together can be of a very far-reaching nature for either's national security: the sale of Alaska in the 1860s and the mutual threat of German Fascism during World War II, to the more contemporary issue of the control of nuclear weapons within the borders of the former Soviet Union in the 1990s. In brief here, the experience of the Cooperative Threat Reduction Programme (CTRP) showed that cooperation in even the most sensitive areas was possible. With the nuclear issue often being cited as a key determinant of special relationships (with the United Kingdom post-1945, and in recent times US–India relations), this suggested a degree of 'specialness', albeit one with a lead nation and a patron; a client if you will. Such measures were indicative of the positive hue that the relationship had in the immediate post-Cold War era: one lending itself to 'special' status, and the expectation that relations would continue in such a fashion.

This aligns with Alex Danchev's analysis of 'specialness' as a 'process of interaction, laced with expectation'.[1] It is the failure of each party consistently to deliver on such expectations in US–Russian relations that prevents a special relationship of the variety that typifies the Anglo-American relationship (amongst others). Instead a Russia–US special relationship must acknowledge that it is unique to relations between Moscow and Washington, and determined by differing conceptions of national interest.

The substance of the paper focuses on the period following the demise of the Soviet Union between 1991 and the end of 2007. It argues that four phases can be identified; the first constitutes a honeymoon period, in the aftermath of the collapse of the Soviet Union, which would see Russia become an integral part of the Western world; the second period sees a souring of Russia–US relations, epitomized by disagreement over NATO involvement in Kosovo; the third phase concerns the impact of 9/11 in providing a harmonizing opportunity in the Global War on Terror; while the fourth stage encompasses the increasing difficulties that characterized the relationship in 2005–7, as Putin's Russia followed a distinctly nationalist outlook which has meant 'Washington and Moscow increasingly look at each other through the old Cold War prism'.[2] Structurally the chapter will begin by outlining the historical trends of Russia–US relations, before it examines the factors that gave hope for a special relationship in the early to mid-1990s. Prominent amongst these will be the case of the CTRP as an indicator of closeness during the 1990s on an issue reflecting the national security interest of both nations. The chapter will then go on to explore the differing interpretation of state sovereignty brought about by NATO involvement in Kosovo in 1999, justified as humanitarian intervention in the West, as the beginning of a re-appraisal from both parties. We then look to the aftermath of 9/11 in Russia–US relations and the declaration by the Bush administration of the Global War on Terror, before providing an assessment of the relationship since the March 2003 US-led coalition invasion of Iraq. The chapter concludes that the defence of individual national interests ultimately determines the nature of Russia–US relations, even when, on the Russian side at least, the explicit ideological element of foreign policy formation has been much diminished. Russia's attempt to rebuild its foreign policy around its business interests – what Russia sees as part of its becoming a 'normal Western nation' – has in fact more often antagonized rather than smoothed relations with Washington, where the business lobby/foreign policy nexus is, arguably, already deeply entrenched. Russia's new business-orientated view of foreign affairs led the 2003 American invasion of Iraq, for example, to be widely interpreted in Russia not so much as an ill-conceived democratizing crusade, but as the most primitive kind of 'hostile takeover' of the Iraqi oil industry, where Russian and French companies had already made considerable investments.

As such this assessment contributes to the special relationship discourse by suggesting that Russia–US relations can be considered special. Most of the time the relationship has been framed in terms of suspicion, as during the Cold War, but at other times open support has been indicative of the importance with which each nation has viewed the other. When either nation, though most typically the United States, attempts to treat the other as just *another* nation in the international system, the relationship's specialness is lessened. Thus, the terming of the relationship as 'special' between Moscow and Washington is not indicative of relations being *good* or *bad*, but acknowledges a duality comprising cooperation *and* distrust. The implication for viewing relations between Moscow and Washington in light of a special relationship discourse, is therefore to emphasize that the label 'special' is appropriate both during episodes of close cooperation *and* simultaneously during typically longer periods of mutual distrust. As there is next to no nascent cultural understanding, none of what Dean Acheson termed a 'common fate' with regard to transatlantic relations, when moments of cooperation have passed, Russia–US relations have the appearance of returning to normalcy. Crucially, these episodes are connected, and so it is entirely likely that even when Russia–US relations appear at their bleakest, as they did so often in the Cold War, moments of harmony will again arise.

Historical context

The diplomatic history of relations between Russia and the United States of America has long been an ambiguous one, characterized by extensive periods of outward hostility. Perhaps surprisingly however, these same periods were periodically punctuated by extraordinary moments of cooperation and mutual support. During the nineteenth century, the Tsarist regime, as an absolute autocracy, occupied the opposite end of the political spectrum from the United States, and was a frequent subject of public criticism in Washington due to its apparent toleration of anti-Semitic pogroms. Nonetheless, the sale of Alaska to the United States at a discount price during the 1860s by Tsar Alexander II in retrospect appears a generous gift, whilst the Tsarist government's strong support of the North during the American Civil War served as an important continental counterweight to Britain, which covertly supported the Southern secessionist states throughout that conflict. (In the war's aftermath, Washington tried unsuccessfully to sue Britain for artificially prolonging the struggle by her covert re-supplying of the South, demanding recompense from London for the 'indirect' damages incurred to the tune of £8 billion in contemporary money).[3] During the 1870s and 1880s, American precision machine tool and manufacturing firms gained lucrative contracts for re-equipping the Tsarist army with the latest in modern military technology. Even into the later Soviet period the enormous mechanization and industrialization initiated by Stalin after 1928 could scarcely have occurred, at least initially, without the provision of tractor plant, machine tools and technical assistance in massive amounts from the United States. Consequently, it is a massive irony of history that one of the best contemporary eye-witness English-language accounts of the Soviet Union in the 1930s remains that of John Scott, an American engineer who worked in the vast Siberian steel production mills of Magnitogorsk (the initial design of which were themselves inspired by Pittsburgh).[4] In the broader sense the Soviet government was also inestimably assisted during its early and most critical years of existence by the famine relief program instituted under the leadership of US Secretary of Commerce (and future President) Herbert Hoover's American Relief Association (ARA) in 1921–23.[5] Nonetheless, the emergence of the Soviet government to full power in both Russia and the broader Soviet Union after 1922 is traditionally interpreted by most scholars to have inaugurated a long period of growing tension and hostility between the United States government and the successors to the Tsars. This ultimately became full-blown after 1948 with the onset of the global Cold War. As the historian Odd Arne Westad has recently and insightfully documented, this conflict may have been entirely inevitable due to the conflicting ideologies of the two states. The United States had conceived of itself since its very creation as being a central bastion in an 'empire of liberty', whilst the Bolshevik's fundamental aims was to create what they saw as an 'empire of justice' on Earth. Given the fundamental compromise within every human society between attaining absolute liberty and absolute social justice, two such states which aimed to bring about either extreme were therefore almost inevitably bound to view each other as adversaries.[6]

This notion was given its rhetorical apogee by Ronald Reagan when speaking to the National Association of Evangelicals in 1983:

> [L]et us pray for the salvation of all of those who live in that totalitarian darkness – pray they will discover the joy of knowing God. However, until they do, let us be aware that while they preach the supremacy of the state, declare its omnipotence over individual man, and predict its eventual domination of all peoples on the earth, they are the focus of evil in the modern world.[7]

In light of such views it is somewhat remarkable that the Cold War ended at the end of the decade with such accord, and in doing so signalled a period of close association and, crucially, hope in Russia–US relations.

The carriers of hope in the early and mid-1990s

Following the demise of the Soviet Union hopes initially ran high on both sides of the Atlantic for a new era to dawn in American–Russian relations. Relations between Presidents Gorbachev and George H. W. Bush had already become strong. This facilitated Gorbachev's own determination to abandon the Soviet Union's East European satellites entirely and let democratization take its course, no matter what the immediate consequences.[8] Judging by the caustic assessment of Vladimir Kriuchkov, Gorbachev's own KGB chief (and one of the key players behind the botched 1991 August coup against Gorbachev), the Soviet president was seen by some to have placed extreme, perhaps even excessive, faith in President Bush as an honest strategic partner and ally. Having received the verbal promise from Secretary of State Baker that, in return for a reunited Germany, NATO would not expand even 'one inch' to the east, Gorbachev, in Kriuchkov's account, was strategically 'completely oriented on Bush. Attempts to caution him were met with grins and objections. "Bush won't let me down. Anyway, you can't trick me"'.[9] In the wake of the Soviet Union's final demise, and the emergence of the Russian Federation as a new and independent actor (simultaneously invalidating, in *American* eyes, any earlier verbal promises), relations between Presidents Bill Clinton and Boris Yeltsin were initially, if anything, even sunnier.

In conjunction with such hope, it is important to acknowledge the personable relationship between Clinton and Yeltsin in light of the discourse on special relationships that stresses the importance of individual personal relations. Strobe Talbott, Clinton's principal Russia adviser, and later deputy secretary of state, suggests in his 2002 memoir, *The Russia Hand: A Memoir of Presidential Diplomacy*, that it was the personal relationship between Clinton and Yeltsin which was the nexus of Russia–US relations, arguing 'government-to-government relations often succeeded or failed on the basis of personal relations'.[10] He went on to state that Clinton had seen in Yeltsin 'both a very big man and a very bad boy, a natural leader and an incurable screw-up. All this Clinton recognized, found easy to forgive and wanted others to join him in forgiving'.[11] For all Yeltsin's known proclivities to alcohol, depression, and anarchic decision making, the mutually-needy Yeltsin and Clinton, in the words of Talbott, 'bonded. Big time'.[12] Harold P. Smith Jr., Clinton's assistant secretary of defence for nuclear, chemical and biological defense programmes, stated of his role in the CTRP (that will be discussed presently) that it 'is amazing that it comes down to just a few individuals. I can't say more than that'.[13] Talbott later boasted that American discovery of the fact that they could manipulate Yeltsin and exploit his weaknesses meant that they were often 'able to bring Yeltsin around to a position more consonant with US interests than the Russian political and military establishment favored'.[14] In return, Yeltsin's own erratic behaviour, most notably such constitutionally illegal acts as his initial destruction of the Soviet Union, and his subsequent bombardment of the Russian White House (home to the State Duma, the Russian parliament) in October 1993, went essentially unreprimanded. This was largely because Yeltsin himself, with his relentlessly pro-market policies, was perceived on the American side as being, whatever his other personal and political failings, the one force that could effectively prevent communism ever returning to Russia. It is important to acknowledge here the legacy that previous Russia–US distrust exerted, particularly in Washington, in terms of providing a governing mindset, but equally that such discussions took place within an atmosphere that saw Russia–US dialogue as somewhat inevitable in the future. As Clinton himself is alleged to have expressed it, 'Yeltsin drunk is better than most of the alternatives sober', and when Yeltsin trailed his communist rival by registering at only six per cent in the polls in January 1996, prior to his bid for a second term that same July, Western public relations specialists were rushed in to reinvigorate his campaign, in much the same manner that Western economic specialists from the Harvard Business School had earlier been rushed in to 'fix' the Russian economy after 1991.[15]

Thus, America actually participated in, and presided over, the early establishment of a media-manipulated 'managed democracy' in Russia today which, under Putin, became an object of such violent criticism amongst some circles in the West. As others have pointed out, Putin in many ways merely inherited and built upon a system first established by Yeltsin.[16] His tremendous and genuine public popularity, however, also arose at least in part by his masterful rhetorical celebration of Russia's 'liberation' from foreign tutelage, and from his firm actions against the most unpopular components of Yeltsin's own legacy, namely the Putinite campaign to eliminate the Russian oligarchs as a *political* class.

The importance of the Yeltsin-Clinton personal relationship aside, mutual cooperation during the 1990s through the Cooperative Threat Reduction Act of 1993 (CTR) gave further cause for hope. This agreement evolved out of the Soviet Nuclear Threat Reduction Act of 1991 sponsored by Senators Sam Nunn and Richard Lugar. Their original aim was to enhance US national security by assisting the states of the former Soviet Union in controlling and protecting their nuclear weapons, weapons-usable materials, and delivery systems.[17] Senator Nunn stated then that 'I know of no more urgent national security challenge confronting our nation, nor do I know of any greater opportunity . . . to reduce the dangers confronting us'.[18] This ethos survived the end of the George H. W. Bush administration, and allowed Clinton's secretary of defence William J. Perry to state in 1995 that the programme was 'vital to our defense' because it sought to 'reduce the nuclear threat to the United States'.[19] Within a matter of years, under the CTR Program, nuclear weapons were entirely removed from Kazakhstan, Belarus and Ukraine and transported safely to Russia itself.[20] Sarah Mendelson, in reviewing Talbott's book for *Foreign Affairs*, convincingly argued that the removal of nuclear weapons from Ukraine was 'one of the most underappreciated events of the 1990s'.[21]

What this meant for US–Russian relations was wrapped in the language of hope of continued warming in the Moscow–Washington relationship. Yeltsin's first foreign minister was the unremittingly pro-Western Andrei Kozyrev, who saw the 'the goal of nuclear disarmament' as meaning 'the establishment of a "special kind of relationship" with the United States'.[22] For the Russian Foreign Minister to utilize such language is indicative of the view that this was the probable future for US–Russian relations. At least part of the success of the programme can be attributed to the close association between Harold P. Smith Jr. and General Yevgenii Maslin, who, as head of the 12th Main Directorate, was responsible for the transportation and storage of all nuclear weapons in the former Soviet Union. The latter became, in the words of the former, a '*sine qua non* for success' in understanding the 'unique, possibly fleeting' moment that the CTR program offered.[23]

Yet, a number of impediments meant progress stalled in the wider acceptance of the programme. These impediments – fear of intelligence gathering, NATO's nuclear deployments, bureaucratic inertia, legal restrictions and simple pride – bear a striking resemblance to the factors that one could point to in 2007 as suggesting a deterioration of Russia–US relations.[24] Crucially, these factors persist, and are only temporarily trumped by the close cooperation exhibited in this field: thus validating the case presented here that mutual distrust is a continuum, and that moments of harmony are transient but recurrent features of relations between Moscow and Washington. As such the critics of the whole CTR programme – particularly during what might now be considered the heyday of neoconservatism in the aftermath of 9/11, and with the abrogation of the Anti-Ballistic Missile (ABM) treaty – may have won the 'headline' battle in denigrating the programme, but the fact that almost $400 million has been approved for the programme for FY 2007 means that $5.5 billion dollars will have been spent on the programme since its inception.[25] Equally, the decision in April 2002 by the then Russian prime minister, Mikhail Kasyanov, to allow CTR specialists into four additional sites without fanfare or wide publicity illustrates that the programme retains its legs away from the spotlight and despite what some see as its inherent problems.[26] Crucially, the risk of 'rogue' Russian nukes has reduced considerably, though it will never disappear entirely. In this light, Harold Smith Jr. has suggested that a further opportunity exists for Russia–US cooperation in the post-9/11 world, namely in identifying the nuclear signature of any future nuclear explosion, and thereby providing a level of deterrence towards those regimes who might seek to disseminate fissile material to terrorists groups. Overall cooperation on the issue of controlling and disarming nuclear weapons is illustrative of the degree to which Russian–American relations *can* obtain a remarkable degree of closeness, underwritten and eventually surpassed by mutual suspicions and reassessments of each country's national interest.

Russian compliance to the Conventional Forces in Europe (CFE) treaty was also striking in the mid-1990s, even though it imposed severe asymmetric disadvantages upon Russia itself. Under the terms of the treaty, Russia was now permitted to maintain levels of conventional equipment that were only about a third of NATO's and barely twice those permitted to the Ukraine. Foreign minister Andrei Kozyrev was nonetheless adamant that 'the CFE treaty should enter into force without renegotiation and be fully implemented as soon as possible'.[27] That such faith was placed in the likes of this treaty was a key component of the Yeltsin–Clinton years and augured well for Russia–US relations 5 years short of the new millennium.

'Cloud cover over Kosovo'

The Kosovo crisis of 1999, when Russian and NATO forces almost came to blows at Pristina airport , is widely and correctly, seen as a major cloud darkening the horizon over a potential new Russian–American special relationship. The storm cloud came into view over differing perceptions of what constituted legitimate action within the new international system that had emerged after 1991, and were to be felt far beyond the Balkans. The Russian position was shaped by Yevgenii Primakov (foreign minister 1996–98, Russian prime minister September 1998–May 1999), who replaced the relentlessly pro-Western Kozyrev in January 1996. Primakov had extensive experience from the Soviet period and had begun his career as a Middle Eastern correspondent for *Pravda*, before moving on into both Soviet academe and the foreign intelligence service (SVR) of the Soviet KGB. Primakov's views on foreign affairs were orientated around the need as he saw it to establish a 'strategic triangle' of Russia, India and China in order to re-impose a new balance and create a truly multipolar world order; a 'realist' balance-of-power perspective firmly in the tradition of Henry Kissinger. On his own desk, however, sat a bust of Chancellor Gorchakov, a nineteenth-century Russian foreign minister who had helped restore Russia to the role of an important actor in European affairs following the debacle of the Crimean War of 1853–56. In a characteristic misreading of overarching strategic trends, Strobe Talbott for his own part felt that Primakov's essentially pragmatic *Realpolitik* views on foreign affairs meant that the Americans 'might actually get more business done with Primakov'.[28] Instead, Primakov's views, as representing an emerging Russian approach, were rather conditioned by two governing issues: perceptions on the Russian side over a serious lack of 'positive baggage' emerging out of the Russia–US bilateral relationship, and a corresponding and (after Primakov's departure) growing drive within Russian foreign policy circles for Russia to become increasingly active rather than reactive in world affairs.[29]

At the same time within important states of the Western block, the creation of a new 'strategic agenda' in foreign policy was acquiring a momentum of its own. On 22 April 1999, Prime Minister Tony Blair famously articulated in his speech to the Economic Club of Chicago, regarding the Kosovo crisis, that the 'global interdependence', brought about by ever-accelerating economic globalization (the latter also a favourite theme with the Clinton administration) carried implications not just for trade but for traditional definitions of national sovereignty: that human rights violations within nation state boundaries now 'must not stand'. In the same speech he expressed the need, again characteristically mirroring and sympathetic but also manipulative to Clinton's own views, that 'Russia's past has been as a world power that we felt confronted by. We must work with her to make her future as a world power with whom we co-operate in trust and to mutual benefit'.[30] Neither Blair nor Clinton appeared conscious of the fact that the new foreign policy agenda being created over Kosovo ran directly contrary to Russia's own views on a proper international order, making the aforementioned partnership more difficult to achieve. Primakov's immediate successor as foreign minister, Igor Ivanov, identified the same growing sense of global interdependence that Blair did, but held starkly different views over a proper international order within such a context. For Ivanov, such an international order had to be centred not on intangible moral principles, but on the hard institutional fact of the United Nations, and particularly the Security Council, whilst Russia's own role within such an order would also be shaped by its own national interests, not by the desires, values or moral crusading of others.[31] Ivanov's views, embodied in the 2000 Russian Foreign Policy Concept (part of a series of new initiatives, including a new Military Doctrine, that institutionally captured for the first time Russia's mature view on the post-Cold War world) reflected a natural evolution of Primakov's views. They also illustrated that, whilst Yeltsin still possessed the power erratically to switch his ministers upon a whim, more conservative views on the international order within Russia's policymaking elites were steadily coalescing and acquiring real strength, thus allowing former State Department and Pentagon official Wayne Merry to opine in early 2008 that 'Russia's concept [of sovereignty in international relations] is that of a nineteenth century great power, one of a small number of rule-making states exercising true sovereignty'.[32] At the time, however, Yeltsin's own accelerating physical and mental incapacity, increasingly visible to all around him, rendered him an ever-weaker 'alternate pole' of decision making for Western leaders to depend on in order to bypass this nascent new establishment. Blair's blunt statement in Chicago regarding the Balkans that 'Bismarck was wrong' was therefore destined to be directly interpreted as a dangerous and radical shift within Russia's increasingly *Realpolitik*-orientated foreign policy cadres. Above all, from the Russian perspective, what Blair and Clinton were now proposing looked less and less like dialogue, and more like a communicative one-way street; namely the creation of a new interventionist agenda, pushed through with the use of force (NATO), to the total and deliberate neglect of the accepted and established multilateral management institutions (notably the United Nations), institutions that represented both the norms of an international system of great powers and also their role in balancing each other.

The 1999 Kosovo Crisis was a crystallizing moment in post-Cold War US–Russian relations. The immediate military crisis of the symbolic Russian 'dash' for Pristina airfield, met by the laconic response of General Sir Michael Jackson to the American General Wesley Clark's request to pre-emptively occupy the airfield – that he (Jackson) would 'not be responsible for starting World War III' – came as a starkly sobering moment within the bilateral special relationship.[33] Whilst the immediate rift was papered over by the incorporation of Russian forces into the general peacekeeping taskforce KFOR (though not under NATO command), the aforementioned Russian Foreign Policy Concept of 2000 reflected the perceived 'lessons' of Kosovo from the Russian perspective. These included the perception that 'integration processes, in particular in the Euro-Atlantic region, often assume a selective and restrictive character. Attempts to belittle the role of the sovereign state as a fundamental element of international relations create the threat of arbitrary interference in internal affairs'.[34] Russia's role in response was 'to achieve a multipolar system of international relations that would genuinely reflect the diversity of the contemporary world. . . . Such a world order can be guaranteed to be effective and durable if interests are taken into account on a reciprocal basis. [It should be] a system based on the principles of equality, mutual respect, and mutually beneficial cooperation. The United Nations should remain the principal center for managing international relations in the twenty-first century'.[35]

For the Russian mind, the prospect of changes to the concept of national sovereignty in international relations posed severe problems. In the latter half of 1999, Chechen rebel forces both carried out a series of bombings in Russia itself and invaded neighbouring Dagestan. The Second Chechen War which then began saw a long-running Russian conflict against militant radical Islam again flare up on Russian soil, with international extremists playing a role there just as they had in

Afghanistan during the 1980s.[36] Russia's consciousness of the vulnerability of its southern frontiers also led it, in the first half of 2001, to bolster the Ahmed Shah Massoud-led Northern Alliance/United Front forces in Afghanistan with new helicopters and what amounted to a regiment of T-55 tanks and BMP-1 armoured personnel vehicles, thereby facilitating its own war against the local Taliban prior to 9/11. In stark contrast to the United States, the Russian government had viewed the rise of the Taliban in Afghanistan as an extremely dangerous regional threat from the very beginning.[37] Russia's 'war on terror' under the newly elected president Vladimir Putin was therefore already full blown when, on 11 September 2001, the Pentagon and New York World Trade Centre were attacked by Al Qaeda, creating a sudden and dramatic convergence of mutual security interests. After 9/11, relations therefore initially appeared destined to again take a turn for the better, with the new American president, George W. Bush, declaring of Putin that he had looked into his eyes and seen his soul: 'This is the kind of fellow who when he says yes, he means yes, and when he says no, he means no'.[38]

The global war on terror as an opportunity?

Just over a year after the tragic events of 9/11 had unfolded on millions of television screens across the globe, in October 2002, Andrew Kuchins of the Carnegie Endowment for International Peace stated that 'the improvement in US–Russian relations stands as one of the major positive developments from the shock to the international system brought on by the terrorist attacks on the WTC and the Pentagon last September'.[39] Kuchins had good grounds to make this case. However, the opportunity, so far as there ever was one, was fleeting, and typical of the Russia–US special relationship. At least at first, Putin appeared an individual prepared to make considerable concessions, even against the initial reservations of some of his own military and foreign policy elite, to the point that when he met Bush in Slovakia at the beginning of 2005, he remarked that 'it is true that over the past few years, through joint efforts, we have been able to accumulate a unique cooperation': a special relationship in all but name.[40]

The opportunity to become more intimate with Washington, 'Putin's gamble' in the words of Oksana Antonenko writing in 2001, was to allow the Americans military access to Central Asia and to provide substantial logistical and intelligence support. This, again, reflected the significant role that a powerful individual could have within the Russian–American special relationship in terms of bypassing intransigent bureaucracies on both sides; however the reasoning behind the gambit was always an explicit longer-term promotion of Russian national interests in a 'partnership of equals' with the United States.[41] Another commentator eruditely suggested that 'US–Russian cooperation on counterterrorism came into existence because of shared fundamental interests, not a common ideology or mutual sympathy'.[42] Whatever the motivation, US and Russian efforts therefore suddenly synergized in a manner that made the military campaign against the Taliban both rapid and stunningly effective. The 2001–2 campaign in Afghanistan could not have occurred in the manner that it did without the devastating asymmetric advantages provided by American airpower, precision guided munitions, satellite technology and special forces; however, without the presence of Northern Alliance forces, which the Russian government had patiently backed for years against the Taliban, there would have been virtually no conventional forces on the ground itself to profit by America's spectacular application of firepower. Though it unfolded only in a very indirect manner therefore, the campaign itself was the product of a truly joint national effort. However, Russian elites soon felt that their contribution was being undervalued by their American partners. Russia had decades worth of intelligence and personal contact and familiarity with Afghanistan, but the rush to embed and foster divergent local clients became apparent as quickly as 2002, when the soon-to-be removed Afghan Defence Minister Marshal Fahim visited Moscow, whilst President Hamid Karzai visited the United States and Japan.[43] Growing doubts over the sincerity of America's intentions in Central Asia, and in particular over the status of American bases there as a purely temporary rather than permanent phenomenon, led rapidly to a classic geopolitical conflict for influence that would have been familiar to any student of the nineteenth-century 'Great Game'. In April 2005, Stephen Blank, an associate of RAND as well as a lecturer at the US Army War College, stated of Central Asia that 'it does not suffice to be able to deploy and sustain long-range strike forces in the theatre; the theatre itself must be cooperatively reordered by the United States, its other partners, and host governments, working together to stabilize it and legitimize US presence and a political order that has a genuine chance to evolve in a liberal, democratic direction enjoying popular support. America must also develop an appropriate long-term and multi-dimensional strategy for retaining permanent access to the area'.[44] In the light of such rhetoric in this and in previous years, Russia began taking corresponding countermeasures, both through the forum of the Shanghai Cooperation Organisation, and via strengthening bilateral military, economic and political ties with the Central Asian states, a process typified by the acquisition of a new airbase in Kyrgyzstan, the signing of a major 25-year gas contract with Turkmenistan, and the acquisition of a sophisticated space observation complex in Tadjikistan. This pattern of competition for influence has most recently culminated in the ejection of American forces from Uzbekistan, Uzbekistan's re-entry into the Russian-led Collective Security Treaty Organization (CSTO), and the CSTO's own subsequent visit in March 2007 to Afghanistan to explore bilateral contacts with President Karzai.[45] This illustrates the affirmation of renewed Russian interest in its near abroad: the satellite states that made up the Soviet Union which have in the form of the Commonwealth of Independent States been 'the dominant priority in Russian foreign policy since the early 1990s'.[46]

The factors undermining the ability of the War on Terror to serve as a suitable and sustainable glue holding together in a more positive direction the Russian–American special relationship came about through a conglomeration of both old and new factors. The Georgian 'Rose Revolution' of 2003, supplanting the ex-Soviet foreign minister and president of Georgia, Edward Shevardnadze, with the American-educated Mikhail Saakashvilli, coming as it did immediately in the wake of promising business discussions that would have allowed Russia greater access to the Georgian energy market, was interpreted extremely cynically both by the Kremlin and by most of the Russian media as an American-backed *coup*.[47] The role of American NGOs and Civil Society organizations across the whole of the former Soviet space, including in the subsequent Ukrainian and Kyrgyz 'Colour Revolutions', was rapidly interpreted to be a new form of 'covert action' carried out by proxies of the American government.

Yet, amongst other new factors, Russia's steadily growing economy, supplemented by sky-high oil and gas prices after 2003, also meant that the more active foreign policy agenda first developed by Primakov and Ivanov now had real and growing weight behind it. Under Putin, foreign debts were paid off, GDP maintained a steady six to seven per cent per year growth rate, and the Russian budget came into surplus, with a stabilization fund of some $80 billion established for any possible future downturn in world oil prices. Russian economic decisions could therefore now occur without prior consultation with the American embassy in Moscow or the IMF, a state of affairs best summed up by the Kremlin's own current favourite epithet for the Russian political system: 'sovereign democracy'. Though still not entirely able to compete on an equal footing with American largesse, Russia's reorientation of its foreign policy priorities away from 'the West' to the states of the 'near abroad' reflected a pragmatic and hard-nosed utilization of growing economic and political resources. Within this new 'energy game', Eastern Europe again became a 'grand chessboard', with an accompanying race by both sides to gather 'allies and clients'. The American-backed Baku-Tbilisi-Ceyhan (BTC) pipeline through the Trans-Caucasus was countered by Russian development of warmer bilateral political relations with Turkey and by the strategic new 'Blue Stream' gas pipeline across the Black Sea. American efforts to create a new energy conduit from the Caspian basin that would very substantially bypass the Russian pipeline grid meanwhile – the long proposed but long-delayed Nabucco Project via Turkey, Bulgaria, Romania, Hungary and Austria – was blocked by Hungary's backing of an alternative Russian project to further develop the 'Blue Stream' line.[48] The Kremlin has therefore now come to assume not only that, 'as a big country, Russia is essentially friendless', but also that the era of continually retreating before the interests of other powers must now fundamentally come to an end.[49]

Putin and George W. Bush: 2006–7

The St. Petersburg gathering of the G8 in July 2006 was a clear indication that Russia under Putin had placed a narrower interpretation of Russian national interest at the centre of its strategic goals. In other words, it had given up on the concept so prevalent just a dozen years before that Russia would integrate into a Western-orientated international system; it was prepared to go it alone and by no longer seeking to buy into the West it had shed any pretence of being dependent. The reasons for this were clear from the theme that Putin made central to the conference: energy.[50] Of the states gathered in St. Petersburg, Russia was the one with the greatest energy exports and, given the presence of key European consumers of this energy, Russian importance to the forum was reinforced. The centrality of energy should have been of little surprise, given that it was only 6 months previously that Gazprom, Russia's state-run gas monopoly, cut supplies to the Ukraine as a means of making a wider political point of Russian importance. This move drew stinging criticism from US Vice President Dick Cheney, who stated in a speech in Vilnuis, Lithuania's capital, in May 2006: 'No legitimate interest is served when oil and gas become tools of intimidation or blackmail, either by supply manipulation, or attempts to monopolize transportation'.[51] Yet, even with such a categorical statement Cheney went on to say that 'none of us believes that Russia is fated to become an enemy', and that a 'Russia that increasingly shares the values of this community can be a strategic partner and a trusted friend as we work toward common goals'. This mixed picture in the spring of 2006 revealed what might be seen as recognition in Washington of the importance Putin had placed on the economic line of development. This line had, however, been predominant in Putin's thinking since at least early 2003, allowing one observer of Russia to remark that the policy of 'real *ekonomi*' was allowing Putin to look 'westward not for political advantage but for foreign investment and access to foreign markets'. This was succinctly expressed as 'the Russian economy determines Russian foreign policy and not vice versa'.[52] This helps, in a marginal way at least, to explain Russian acquiescence to the US-led invasion of Iraq, alongside an acceptance that there was little Russia or the international community could have done to stop the Bush administration. However, that was 2003, and by the time Putin spoke on 2 March 2007 in Munich, this economic emphasis was balanced by a realization of the political capital it could purchase. He stated clearly that 'there is no reason to doubt that the economic potential of the new centres of global economic growth will inevitably be converted into political influence'.[53] If this did not comprise a clear warning to the 'old' centres of economic power, then what accompanied it certainly did. In explicit language Putin looked to Washington as the key threat to global security:

> We are seeing a greater and greater disdain for the basic principles of international law. And independent legal norms are, as a matter of fact, coming increasingly closer to one state's legal system. One state and, of course, first and foremost the United States, has overstepped its national borders in every way. This is visible in the economic, political, cultural and educational policies it imposes on other nations. Well, who likes this? Who is happy about this?

Putin's unambiguous message here was that Russian consideration of international politics, and of the United States role in it, had evolved to a point where Russia was itself strong enough to offer, in public, a critique of Washington's policy. In doing this it is worth pondering whether Russia has gone beyond Andrew Monaghan's assessment of being 'calmly critical' of Washington, and ask: Where does this leave our assessment of the Russia–US special relationship?

It is evident in Putin's comments that the United States mattered to the Russian premier and, in simple terms, this was itself indicative of the special relationship between Moscow and Washington. If we consider the importance of status – of being treated as important in the Russian mind – and return to the St. Petersburg conference, we can see that Putin's policy aimed at ensuring Russia had a voice whenever the world's weighty issues were discussed. In doing this, Putin confirmed the importance to the Russia–US relationship of each nation's view of the other. While the state of the relationship may contain more prickly rhetoric, that Russia is important to the United States and the United States is important to Russia is clear. As such, assessment of Yevgenii Volk, the head of the Heritage Foundation in Moscow, on the eve of the St. Petersburg conference in July 2006 is worth considering. He stated that 'prestige is the most important issue for Putin at [the] summit, the confirmation that Russia is a full-fledged G8 member', and crucially, 'the acknowledgement that Russia has restored its position in the world'.[54] This view was confirmed in the aftermath of Putin's speech in Moscow the following February, firstly in the *Financial Times* leader ('It is about Russia wanting to be seen as a player once more on a wider stage'), and then in James Davis's colourful comments that 'Russia has returned – in her own right – claiming a seat as a major international power in pursuit of her own interests, no longer interested in seeking admission as a "country cousin" to the club of the Euro-Atlantic democracies or willing to defer to US guidance or interests'.[55]

How did Russia appear to Washington in the final stages of the George W. Bush administration? When reading any of the key administration proclamations of strategy in the new security environs of the post 9/11 world (the National Security Strategy of 2006, National Strategy for Combating Terrorism 2006, War on Terror Five Years On), Russia appeared to be significant in American thinking. In the first of these documents Russia was given its own heading, a privilege denied to other nations which one might think would warrant such an honour, including China, Iraq and North Korea. The second and third documents gave prominence to the 'Global Initiative to Combat Nuclear Terrorism' signed by Putin and Bush in July 2006 (and perhaps hinting at a close understanding of a particular issue in the future akin to the CTRP). Yet, even in acknowledging Russia as a separate entity worthy of America's attention, the message still had a preaching tone in respect to the promotion of democracy. The National Security Strategy stated that the United States would encourage 'Russia to respect the values of freedom and democracy at home and not to impede the cause of freedom and democracy' elsewhere in the world.[56] It is worth noting here that this illustrates a consistent strand to the American attitude towards Moscow since the end of the Cold War. What is key here is the reception that American calls for more open democracy receive in Moscow. In other words, in understanding the Russia–US relationship one needs to consider the balance between the Russian perception of American words, and the American intent behind them. In responding to Putin's speech in February 2007, Bush chose to acknowledge the areas of common understanding and not to dwell on the differences in approach. The American president personalized his response, saying of Putin that 'he is a person with whom I have had agreements and disagreements throughout the course of my presidency and his'.[57] Further acknowledgement of the role Russia played in the agreement with North Korea in mid-February 2007, and could have played in resolving the outstanding disagreements with Iran, was testament to a wider appreciation that considering Russia could help the United States to achieve its own goals. This extended as far as former US Ambassador to the United Nations John Bolton hoping that Putin's words in Munich were a 'misimpression about the United States, and not a change in Russian policy'.[58] In this assessment they could be the same thing at the same time, which reveals much about a special relationship between Moscow and Washington.

Reports of harmony in Russia–US relations, like Mark Twain's wry remark of his death, may have been exaggerated during the early 1990s and again in the aftermath of 9/11, but that perpetual suspicion again came to the forefront illustrates the transitory nature of these moments. Importantly for the discourse on special relationships, and acknowledging the uniqueness of this relationship, this is implicit to Russia–US relations.

Conclusions

Since the end of the Cold War in 1989–91, Russian–American relations, despite initial hopes for a far warmer and closer mutual understanding, have in fact settled back into a traditional pattern of underlying mutual hostility and annoyance, interspersed with short-lived attempts at closer cooperation and mutual assistance. That events should have taken this classical turn was, initially at least, unexpected, since the Cold War was traditionally viewed almost entirely as a conflict of political ideologies. With the demise of communism as a ruling ideology in Russia and the eager adoption of free-market principles instead by the westward-leaning Yeltsin administration after 1991, taken together with truly unprecedented levels of mutual military cooperation in overseeing and neutralizing the threat of Soviet nuclear capabilities falling into the wrong hands, hopes ran high in both Washington and Moscow that a new era was truly dawning in an Russian–American special relationship. Indeed, it was argued in 1997 that 'denuclearising three of the Newly Independent States (NIS) and a legacy of increased Russian control over "loose nukes" throughout the former Soviet Union will arguably be the most important foreign-policy achievements of the first Clinton administration'.[59] The comradeship of Clinton and Yeltsin augured hope – that crucial ingredient in a special relationship. 'Although the recipe has not always produced success', Sarah Mendelson writes, 'personalities clearly help drive the US–Russian relationship'. While this did facilitate success in the CTRP, and at the highest level, it also allowed for the souring as personnel changed during the course of the late 1990s. Beginning in 1994, the relationship on both sides slowly curdled, to the point where some individuals began to warn of a 'new Cold War' again on the immediate political horizon.[60] Many in Russia consider the responsibility for the economic instability of the 1990s to lie firmly with Washington. They consider that Russia's subsequent economic success, achieved in spite of outside assistance, allowed Putin to advance a Russian strategy which sought meaningful partnerships with states across the Middle East, Russia's near abroad, and the Far East – most notably with China, as well as the United States. Thus, Putin claimed in 2005 that he could 'see no alternative to the consistent strengthening of the Russia–US relationship', while criticizing Washington in Munich some 2 years later.[61]

In Washington, there appeared a somewhat begrudging realization that Russia had an important role to play in the international system. The Bush administration's unremarkable response to Putin's Munich speech revealed a greater sophistication in addressing Russian participation in American decision making. The key aspect in relations between Moscow and Washington by 2007 was an absence of expectation: a loss of faith if you will. Of course other special relationships have apparent barriers but they do not wholly influence the mainstream discourse. The dearth of expectation in Russia–US relations was seen in Moscow's perception that American rhetoric, especially under the Bush administration, embodied a perpetual 'double standard', and that Russia would never be treated as a respected partner. At the same time, Putin's articulation of a Russian-centred world view was perceived in Washington to be a case of the Russian bear coming out of hibernation, and preparing for a Spring feeding season. The latest 'Grand Strategy' produced for NATO, the premiere American security alliance, was nonetheless marked by an attempt at striking a paradoxical balance. Noting that continuing structural and demographic weaknesses in Russia probably hindered it from becoming in reality the type of imminent threat that some commentators feared, the report then went on to strike what appeared a conciliatory note: 'Cooperation with Russia must be based on strict reciprocity'. However, here policy became blurred, since whilst it was mildly suggested that 'Western nations should take into account legitimate Russian interests in their security arrangements', a line was also drawn that 'Russia should never be given a unilateral veto over Western decisions'. This suggested that accurate assessment of the prevailing power balance was still very much a work in progress, and that mutual disagreement would continue to ensue over what constituted legitimate levels of 'reciprocity'. That the report went on to stress the importance of Russia maintaining existing arms treaties such as the Conventional Forces in Europe (CFE) and Intermediate-Range Nuclear Forces (INF) treaties, even given American abandonment of the ABM treaty, highlighted the perception problem in microcosm.[62]

This chapter has analysed the key factors behind this turn of events, which reflects the reiteration of a classic pattern in Russian–American relations, and has suggested that this pattern is somewhat inevitable in relations between Moscow and Washington. If the reader can excuse the alliteration, the Russia–US relationship, because of its moments of closeness against a backdrop of distrust based on differing conceptions of the role each other should play, has an *indistinct dichotomy*. This allows for simultaneous harmony in certain areas and discord in the round. Nonetheless, the use of the adjective 'special' can apply to two such large and resource rich nations, because their global views inescapably take into consideration each other. As such the specialness carries little qualitative value; in the case of relations between Moscow and Washington, 'special' does not mean 'good'. What it does mean is that the relationship is not – at the present time at least – one of 'client' or of 'allies', but one where 'there are disagreements, but there's also a relationship in which . . . [one] can find common ground to solve problems'. It is, to use Bush's word, 'complicated'.[63]

Notes

1 Alex Danchev, *On Specialness: Essays in Anglo-American Relations*, Basingstoke: Macmillan, 1998, p. 12.
2 Dmitri Simes, 'Losing Russia', *Foreign Affairs*, 2007, vol. 86, pp. 36–52.
3 On this episode in Anglo-American relations, see Eric J. Graham, *Clyde Built: Blockade Runners, Cruisers and Armoured Rams of the American Civil War*, Edinburgh: Birlinn Ltd. 2006, pp. 6–8. On Russian–American relations in general during this period, see the first two volumes in the now-classic trilogy of Norman E. Saul, *Distant Friends. The United States and Russia, 1763–1867*, Kansas: University of Kansas Press, 1991, and *Concord and Conflict: The United States and Russia, 1867–1914*, Kansas: University of Kansas Press, 1996.
4 On the nineteenth century arms trade see Joseph Bradley, *Guns for the Tsar: American Technology and the Small Arms Industry in Nineteenth-Century Russia*, DeKalb: Northern Illinois University Press, 1990. See also John Scott, *Behind the Urals: An American Worker in Russia's City of Steel*, Indiana: Indiana University Press, 1989.
5 On Hoover's program, see Benjamin M. Weissman, *Herbert Hoover and Famine Relief to Soviet Russia: 1921–1923*, Stanford, California: Hoover Institution Press, 1974.
6 Odd Arne Westad, *The Global Cold War: Third World Interventions and the Making of Our Times*, Cambridge: Cambridge University Press 2005, particularly chapters one and two.
7 <http://www.ronaldreagan.com/sp_6.html> (accessed 21 January 2007).
8 In March 1988 Gorbachev had formally repudiated the Brezhnev doctrine by reaffirming the 'impermissibility of interference in internal affairs under any pretext whatsoever'. The Polish crisis during the early 1980s had formed a key turning point in movement towards this new position, as is chronicled by Matthew J. Ouimet, *The Rise and Fall of the Brezhnev Doctrine in Soviet Foreign Policy*, Chapel Hill & London: The University of North Carolina Press, 2003.
9 Vladimir Kriuchkov, *Lichnoe Delo* ii, Moscow: 'Olimp', AST, 1996, p. 45.
10 Talbott's analysis seemingly underplays his own relationship with his Russian counterpart, Yuri Mamedov, with whom he would slip away from negotiations to enjoy a film at the cinema in Washington. Strobe Talbott, *The Russia Hand: A Memoir of Presidential Diplomacy*, New York: Random House, 2003.
11 Talbott, *The Russia Hand*, pp. 185–86.
12 Perry Anderson, 'Russia's Managed Democracy', *London Review of Books*, 25 January 2007, vol. 29, p. 3, <http://www.lrb.co.uk/v29/n02/ande01_.html> (accessed 12 February 2007).
13 Harold P. Smith Jr. in conversation Harry Kriesler on University of California Television, 26 January 2006, <http://globetrotter.berkeley.edu/people6/HSmith/hsmith-con3.html> (accessed 10 March 2007).
14 <http://www.powells.com/review/2002_06_06.html> (accessed 9 April 2007).
15 Talbott, *The Russia Hand*, p. 185.
16 Anderson, 'Russia's Managed Democracy'.

17 The original act received bipartisan support with Republicans and Democrats in the Senate voting 86 to 8 in favour of the legislation.

18 US Senate Committee on Armed Services, 'Assisting the Build-Down of the Former Soviet Military Establishment: Hearings before the Committee on Armed Services', 101st Cong., 1st session, 5–6 February 1992, Washington: Government Printing Office, 1992, pp. 1–2.

19 Department of Defense, Annual Budget briefing by Secretary of Defense William J. Perry, delivered 7 February 1995, <http://www.defenselink.mil/transcripts/transcript. aspx?transcriptid=99> (accessed 3 March 2007). Perry's counter that the programme was 'defense by other means' addressed the fact that it was jointly administered by the Department of Defense (DOD), Department of Energy (DOE), Department of Commerce and the Department of State. Criticism of the Nunn-Lugar CTR programme has been vociferous since the mid-1990s. As an example see Rich Kelly, *The Nunn-Lugar Act: A Wasteful and Dangerous Illusion*, Cato Foreign Policy Briefing No. 39, 18 March 1996.

20 Although cooperation on reductions in chemical weapons stockpiles was considerably slower, and eventually ground to a halt, the primary purpose of the program was to address the nuclear issue in an era before chemical weapons were routinely lumped together with nuclear ones in the dialogue of 'Weapons of Mass Destruction'.

21 Sarah E. Mendelson, 'The View From Above: An Insider's Take on Clinton's Russia Policy', *Foreign Affairs*, July/August 2002, pp. 150–56, <http://search.ebscohost. com/login.aspx?direct=true&db=buh&AN=6836491&site=ehost-live> (accessed 3 March 2007).

22 Alfred Rieber, 'How Persistent are Persistent Factors?', in Robert Legvold (ed.) *Russian Foreign Policy in the 21st Century & The Shadow of the Past*, New York: Columbia University Press, 2007, p. 259.

23 Harold P. Smith Jr., 'Implementation of President Clinton's Cooperative Threat Reduction Program 1993–97', Conference on the Clinton Presidency, Hofstra University 12 February 2006. Smith puts great emphasis on the mutual individual support: 'The key to success in implementing cooperative threat reduction was, purely and simply, cooperation. Where cooperation existed, the programs moved quickly and were highly effective; where cooperative was begrudging, the pace of threat reduction was glacial'.

24 Harold P. Smith Jr., 'Consolidating Threat Reduction', *Arms Control Today*, November 2003.

25 Cooperative Threat Reduction Annual Report to Congress Fiscal Year 2007, <http:// www.dtra.mil/documents/oe/ctr/FY07%20CTR%20Annual%20Report%20to%20 Congress.pdf> (accessed 3 March 2007).

26 Harold P. Smith Jr., 'Consolidating Threat Reduction', *Arms Control Today*, November 2003.

27 Thomas Ambrosio, *Challenging America's Global Preeminence: Russia's Quest for Multipolarity*, Aldershot: Ashgate Publishing, 2005, pp. 40–41.

28 Talbott, *The Russia Hand*, p. 194.

29 Andrew Monaghan, '"Calmly Critical": Evolving Russian Views of US Hegemony', *The Journal of Strategic Studies*, 2006, vol. 29, pp. 971–91, 989.

30 <http://www.pbs.org/newshour/bb/international/jan-june99/blair_doctrine4–23.html> (accessed 21 January 2007).

31 Igor Ivanov, *The New Russian Diplomacy*, Washington D.C.: The Nixon Center, 2002, pp. 13–37. Stressing the importance of indigenous historical tradition and continuity in the shaping of present-day Russian foreign policy.

32 Wayne Merry, 'Russia's Pyrrhic Victory', *The National Interest*, 18 January 2008, <http://www.nationalinterest.org/Article.aspx?id=16662> (accessed 17 February 2008).

33 BBC News, 'Confrontation over Pristina airport', <http://news.bbc.co.uk/1/hi/world/europe/671495.stm accessed> (accessed 21 January 2007). The danger of any conflict was minimalized as it quickly emerged that the Russian forces involved were not equipped to fight, instead they were soon running short of clean drinking water.
34 Ivanov, *The New Russian Diplomacy*, p. 169.
35 Ibid., pp. 168–71.
36 Shamil Basaev's main military lieutenant, Khattab, was of Jordanian origin. Yet another Chechen extremist, Zelimkhan Yandarbaev, was eventually killed in Qatar by a car bomb widely assumed to have been planted by the Russian intelligence services.
37 Anthony Davis, 'How the Afghan War was Won', *Jane's Intelligence Review*, February 2002, p. 7.
38 Quoted in 'President Bush and President Putin Discuss Strong U.S.–Russian Partnership', Constitution Hall, Bratislava Castle, Bratislava, Slovakia, 24 February 2005, <http://www.whitehouse.gov/news/releases/2005/02/20050224-29.html> (accessed 21 January 2007).
39 Andrew C. Kuchins, 'Explaining Mr Putin: Russia's New Nuclear Diplomacy'. *Arms Control Today*, October 2002.
40 'President Bush and President Putin Discuss Strong U.S.–Russian Partnership', 24 February 2005.
41 Oksana Antonenko, 'Putin's Gamble', *Survival*, 2001–2, vol. 43, pp. 49–60.
42 Simes, 'Losing Russia', p. 42.
43 Yuri V Bossin, 'U.S. and Russian interests in Afghanistan: will partnership crack?', <http://www.cacianalyst.org/view_article.php?articleid = 37> (accessed 21 March 2007).
44 Stephen Blank, 'After Two Wars: Reflections on the American Strategic Revolution in Central Asia'. *Conflict Studies Research Centre*, April 2005, Central Asian Series 05/14, frontispiece.
45 Roy Allison, 'Strategic reassertion in Russia's Central Asian policy'. *International Affairs*, 2004, vol. 80, pp. 277–93, and <http://www.eurasianet.org/departments/insight/articles/eav031507a.shtml> (accessed 21 March 2007).
46 Monaghan, 'Evolving Russian Views', pp. 987–1013, 989.
47 '. . . it is clear that Washington has adopted Georgia as its main client in the region. The United States has provided equipment and training to the Georgian military enabling Saakashvili to take a harder line toward Russia'. (Simes, 'Losing Russia', pp. 41–42).
48 <http://www.eurasianet.org/departments/insight/articles/eav032707a.shtml> (accessed 8 April 2007).
49 Dmitri Trenin, 'Russia Leaves the West', *Foreign Affairs*, 2006, vol. 85, pp. 87–96.
50 The importance of Energy security in the current international climate is clear to many and what is becoming equally clear is that Russia is prepared to play this game. Daniel Yergin, 'Ensuring Energy Security', *Foreign Affairs*, March/April 2006, pp. 69–82 http://search.ebscohost.com/login.aspx?direct=true&db=buh&AN=19895478&site=e host-live accessed 3 March 2007.
51 Vice President Dick Cheney's remarks at the 2006 Vilnius Conference, Reval Hotel Lietuva, Vilnius, Lithuania 4 May 2006, <http://www.whitehouse.gov/news/releases/2006/05/20060504-1.html> (accessed 21 January 2007).
52 Harold P. Smith Jr., 'Consolidating Threat Reduction', *Arms Control Today*, November 2003.
53 Vladimir Putin's Speech at the 43rd Munich Conference on Security Policy 10 February 2007, <http://www.securityconference.de/konferenzen/rede.php?menu_2007 = &menu_konferenzen = &sprache = en&id = 179&> (accessed 21 March 2007).

54 Yevgeny Volk quoted in Clair Bigg, 'Russia: Energy Security, Nuclear Proliferation Top G8 Agenda', 14 July 2006, <http://www.rferl.org/featuresarticle/2006/07/9c39023c-27e2–4db3–9e3c-10987a8907a8.html> (accessed 21 March 2007).

55 *Financial Times*, 14 February 2007. James Davis, 'Munich Revisited', *The National Interest Online*, 13 February 2007, <http://www.nationalinterest.org/Article.aspx?id=13586> (accessed 14 March 2008).

56 National Security Strategy of the United States, March 2006, <http://www.whitehouse.gov/nsc/nss/2006/> (accessed 21 November 2007).

57 White House Press Conference, 14 February 2007, <http://www.whitehouse.gov/news/releases/2007/02/20070214–2.html> (accessed 4 January 2008).

58 Peter Fedynsky, Voice of America, Washington, 22 February 2007, <http://www.voanews.com/english/archive/2007–02/2007-02-22- voa23.cfm?CFID = 119020131&CFTOKEN = 59370670> (accessed 4 January 2008).

59 Jason Ellis, 'Nunn-Lugar's mid-life crisis', *Survival*, 1997, vol. 39, pp. 84–110.

60 Senator Joseph I. Lieberman (I-Conn.) said after hearing Putin's address that it was full of dangerous 'Cold War Rhetoric'. See <http://lieberman.senate.gov/newsroom/release.cfm?id=269163&&> (accessed 21 January 2007). An alternative view is provided by Konstantin Kosachev, 'America and Russia: from Cold War to Cold Shoulder', *Financial Times*, 23 March 2007.

61 'President Bush and President Putin Discuss Strong U.S.–Russian Partnership', 24 February 2005.

62 General K. Naumann, General J. Shalikashvili, Field Marshal The Lord Inge, Admiral J Lanxade and General H. van der Breenan, 'Toward a Grand Strategy for an Uncertain World: Renewing Transatlantic Partnership', Lunteren, the Netherlands: Noaber Foundation, 2007, p. 65.

63 White House Press Conference, 14 February 2007.

9 The ecstasy and the agony
The rise and fall of US–Iran relations

Donette Murray

> You thought you understood Iran because the Shah spoke English and because his cabinet had read Shakespeare. You thought he was good because you could see a reflection of yourself in him. But he understood Iran as little as you, and that's why you both failed.[1]

James Bill, perhaps the most insightful of a generation of analysts who watched the ecstasy of US–Iran relations turn into a paralysing agony, commented that 'few international relationships have had a more positive beginning than that which characterized Iranian–American contacts for more than a century'.[2] America's policy, described by one observer as 'pinball rather than chess', is replete with grave political errors and miscalculation, fraught diplomacy, military failures, confusion, frustration and sustained high drama.[3] Indeed, what makes it irresistible is the fact that its legacy is still with us today. History, it is often said, is doomed to be repeated by those who forget it. Remembering is important, but irrelevant, arguably, if one's memory is flawed or incomplete. Understanding is much more critical. It may not prevent further strife, for it is often more of a case of the past being recognizable in the present rather than the events (and mistakes) of earlier times being repeated. The value, however, lies in illuminating contemporary relationships and informing debate. It may not provide answers but, at the very least, it makes the questions intelligible.

This chapter explores the highs and lows of an intimate and complex relationship that substantially advantaged the United States before hurting it most deeply. It comprises three sections: Section one assesses the rationale underpinning this relationship – what the United States wanted and why – and explores the inability or unwillingness of successive administrations (particularly in the 1970s) to contemplate alternative policies. Section two examines the collapse of relations during the 1978–79 Revolution, again analysing what the United States sought from a new relationship with the Islamic Republic of Iran and the implications of Carter's attempts to craft a new, viable policy. Section three concludes with a 'lessons to be learned' examination of the strengths and weaknesses of US policy towards Iran and asks what insights this most critical period provides for future relations.

The ecstasy

America's relationship with Iran must be seen in the context of the convergence of a series of wider foreign policy goals that included confounding the Soviet threat, augmenting the United States' intelligence capacity, securing energy supplies, enhancing regional stability and benefiting from arms sales. 'The Shah', explained one US Undersecretary for Security Assistance, 'is sitting on an area of the world we consider necessary for our own national security'.[4] Indeed, at the height of this relationship, Carter's Assistant Secretary of State, Alfred Atherton, ventured:

> I do not think it can be disputed that a strong and secure Iran, sharing our objectives of global peace, stability and economic well-being, is essential to the peace and continued progress of the states in the Persian Gulf region and to our own interests there.[5]

Moreover, this applied not only to the United States but was a sentiment shared across the Atlantic in Britain where Iran, according to the *Guardian* newspaper, was seen as 'an unwavering obstacle to the Soviet drive for supremacy in Asia, a barrier of stability between zones of turmoil in the Arab world and the Indian subcontinent'.[6] By the late 1970s, Iran had become, in the words of the British ambassador, Sir Anthony Parsons, 'a weighty regional buttress to overall Western, not simply American, geopolitical interests'.[7] Three considerations in particular influenced this thinking: firstly, America needed allies and the Shah was a force multiplier, allowing the United States to maintain power albeit at the necessary and acceptable cost of subletting US foreign policy. Furthermore, Nixon's embrace of *Realpolitik* dictated that the Shah be positively celebrated. To do less would undermine his and, therefore, America's goals in the region. Secondly, underpinning the actions of successive administrations was the belief that socio-economic development was the key to mitigating instability in Iran. As far as many in Washington were concerned, the faster change happened the more likely it was that Iran would not succumb to internal disputes. Finally, and perhaps most significantly, the obvious gains accrued from this relationship were seductive and tangible, as a 1974 Embassy assessment conveys:

> [The] US for its part has [a] great stake in Iran's survival and welfare because (A) it has ability and willingness to play responsible role in region; (B) it has history of cose [sic] and friendly ties with US; (C) it is reliable and important source of oil and other resources; (D) it is growing market for our good and services ($7 billion in US civilian and military contracts in past 2 years) and a hospitable location for US investment;(E) it provides essential air corridor between Europe and Orient; and (F) it allows us to use its territory for special communications and intelligence facilities.[8]

America's investment – seen most visibly in Nixon's 1972 'blank cheque' offer of anything short of nuclear weapons – bought an attractive package: a regional ally or surrogate willing to oppose the Soviets and advance US interests in the region, intelligence (much needed after 80 per cent disappeared as a result of Britain's withdrawal from the region in the late 1960s), a secure supply of oil and a means of recycling petrodollars via arms sales. In short, one could argue, as Ledeen does, that 'the American special relationship with Iran has been much criticized, but in context it must be considered an excellent decision by both parties'.[9] A stark and increasingly uncomfortable truth, however, lay not far below: The United States could not afford to lose the Shah but had no attractive policy alternatives in gestation should his grip start to weaken. The risks and disadvantages were not inconsiderable.

To begin with, America had become too closely tied to a two-faced ally who was not averse to fomenting trouble through his very public denunciations of the United States. 'Like Br'er Rabbit stuck to the Tar Baby', *The New York Times* pointed out, 'Washington is thus to some extent hostage to the Shah for years to come, no matter who is President'.[10] This was reflected in British analysis from the period. 'I am struck', one official wrote,

> by the way the whole inverted pyramid rests on one fallible point – the Shah himself. Although plans for a smooth succession have been laid down, should the Shah die, but one cannot help wondering if the whole design would not collapse without his personal drive. It is a point we should never lose sight of . . .[11]

As early as the beginning of the 1970s, a series of special reports in *The Guardian* concluded that the Shah's regime was built on precarious foundations.[12] Indeed, the fragility of the Shah's dream prompted the British Ambassador to Iran to conclude in June 1972 that 'the time may have come for us and the Americans to consider advising the Shah of the possible consequences of continuing the present system of government'.[13] On both sides of the Atlantic, however, officials noted that this was rather easier said than done. One significant difficulty was that the Shah, as UK ambassador Sir Peter Ramsbotham noted in his valedictory message, was not amenable to such advice: 'There is a mounting self-confidence, a displeasing arrogance (he now talks about "my oil"), a *hubris* which, I fear, may sooner or later invite a matching *nemesis*' (original underlining).[14]

A second negative development was a rise in anti-Americanism engendered by the perception that the United States was responsible for the Shah's excesses. This was reinforced by the growth in number of American personnel in Iran and evident in a pervasive resentment at the notion that Iran was being manipulated and controlled by a foreign power. Witness the response of one local newspaper when *Newsweek* suggested that the United States was in danger of losing control over Iran: 'Frankenstein monster or angel, we certainly are no one's creature'.[15] What is more, the United States had little useful intelligence about Iran, hampered as it was by an inability to develop contacts with opposition figures for fear of risking the Shah's wrath.[16] Finally, one major downside of the white hot arms trade (besides accusations of interference and corruption and the worry that sophisticated United States matériel might end up in the hands of a revolutionary government) was a rise in the price of oil, which was fuelling and being fuelled by the huge arms industry.[17] Individually, these were all concerns of note and should have caused enough alarm to trigger a re-examination of US policy and the provision of a 'plan B'. To understand why this did not happen requires a closer look at administration dynamics and strategic outlook.

No alternative policies?

In the pre-Carter period, the gains, as discussed above, were tangible. Moreover, critically, the disadvantages would only kick in if the Shah were to fall. This reinforced Washington's desire to ignore warning signs and downplay potential problems. It was hoped that the economic progress, largely fuelled by Iran's prodigious oil revenues and the Shah's US-equipped and trained army would keep a lid on things.[18] Policymakers, however, failed to adequately grasp what a British Embassy staffer noted was the regime's main failure – which lay 'not in its economic policies – people are materially better off – but in its failure to provide effective education and cultural underpinning to the present dizzying process of physical change'.[19] Such calculations were themselves compounded by several other factors. Firstly, Washington's support of Iran was a centrepiece of its policy of bolstering allies and utilizing proxies; to reverse this would be admitting wider conceptual problems at a time when America's international options appeared to be diminishing. Secondly, friendships are hard to walk away from. As Ali Ansari points out, 'under Nixon, US–Iran relations became US–Shah relations. The relationship was based on personalities rather than states, and as a consequence became all the more intimate, if demographically limited'.[20] At the same time, the Shah was becoming increasingly independent and not shy about throwing this weight around, telling press conferences in August 1976: 'If you try to take an unfriendly attitude toward my country, we can hurt you as badly, if not more so, than you can hurt us . . .'.[21] US officials knew that states were queuing up to do business with the oil-wealthy Iran and, for good reason, feared that America could lose out if the Shah took his business elsewhere.[22] Indeed, the Persian monarch, it was reported, personally threatened Secretary of State Henry Kissinger that he would shut down the US intelligence operation in Iran if any action was taken to check SAVAK's (Organisation for State Security and Information) activities in the United States.[23] The State Department was uncomfortably aware that its influence was limited, a fact not lost on Britain's Foreign and Commonwealth Office (FCO) which noted: 'The last time, to our knowledge, the Americans interfered in internal matters in this way (the appointment of Amini as Prime Minister), the Shah certainly held it against them and they were in the dog-house for four years'.[24] A third factor was that, although officials were aware of the implications of growing instability, the news was often very mixed. One CIA profile of the Shah described him as a 'brilliant but dangerous megalomaniac who is likely to pursue his own aims in disregard of US interests'.[25] As early as 1972, the British were discussing the fact that what was happening in Iran 'was not a situation which can go on forever'.[26] Indeed, in discussions between the CIA and their British counterparts about the question of succession, it was the British who were more sanguine about a peaceful transition.[27] This negativity, however, was balanced by equally positive assessments, such as Ambassador Parson's expression of confidence in 1975 that, in 3 years' time, Iran would be looking back on 6 years of development remarkable by most other countries' standards.[28] Not surprisingly, compared with the distinctly unpalatable alternative, such assessments ensured *shahophile* policymakers were pushing against an open door. Finally, there was a tendency, as far as Iran was concerned, to see threats as being external. The Shah's state, after all, was regarded as 'a rock-like bastion surrounded by turbulent water full of malevolent creatures'.[29] This was convenient and comforting because, more often than not, the United States had higher priorities and more tangible threats to confront.

More of the same?

After he assumed the presidency in 1977, Jimmy Carter declined to depart from the Iran legacy bequeathed to him. Oil, stability, and a friendship underpinned by longevity had made the Shah an enduring ally.[30] As Carter noted in his memoirs:

> I continued, as other Presidents had done before me, to consider the Shah a strong ally. I appreciated his ability to maintain good relations with Egypt and Saudi Arabia, and his willingness to provide Israel with oil in spite of the Arab boycott. At the time of his visit to Washington in November 1977, I was especially eager to secure his influence in support of Sadat's dramatic visit to Jerusalem.[31]

Several other factors further reduced the likelihood of the new administration dramatically shifting course. In a post-Vietnam, post-Watergate era, America's options were perceived by many as being more limited than at any time in its recent past. A reluctance to get involved in regional issues, coupled with a resignation about the reduced capacity of American power, meant that there was little will to contemplate a significant new role involving greater involvement abroad for the wounded superpower. At the same time, Carter owed a debt to (and had enormous personal sympathy for) the powerful urge emanating from the left wing of the Democratic party which fixated on the promotion of human rights and zero tolerance of culpable (particularly rightist) regimes. Iran, while a natural target of this *Moralpolitik*, was also considered a key bulwark by the *Realpolitikers* in the administration, thus ensuring that an ideological tug-of-war hampered policymaking.[32] The debate about arms sales was a prominent example. What's more, the administration not only had several higher, time-consuming priorities such as the Camp David talks, China and the SALT negotiations, but also considered the Shah's threats credible.[33] Domestically, the White House was concerned about the legacy issue of arms sales. By the late 1970s, half of these – some

700,000 jobs – was tied up in Iran.[34] (According to one estimate, the United States received $2 from Iran from arms and technology purchases for every $1 it spent on Iranian oil.[35]) The advantage accrued from this lucrative arrangement was sweetened further by the belief that withholding these weapons was unlikely to promote human rights or power sharing. Such analysis dovetailed nicely with Carter's view that his position on such issues was and indeed had to be more nuanced than many of his critics accepted.[36] This, in turn, also reinforced another Carter truism – that the United States wasn't really a deciding factor and should have a more realistic appreciation of the extent to which it could influence or coerce other states.[37] Combined, these assessments exerted a strong tendency towards inertia. In short, Iran, as one diplomat baldly stated, was 'too important for us to risk'.[38] And with the addition of one final constraint, any chance of an effective re-evaluation was demolished: the Carter administration was attempting to do a jigsaw with an incomplete picture.

In August 1977, the CIA ruled out radical change in Iran and confidently predicted that the Shah would be an active participant in Iranian life well into the 1980s.[39] With equal confidence, however, Policy Planning staffer Theodore Moran warned that the Shah's allocation of 25 per cent of government spending to the military was likely to leave 'insufficient resources to head off mounting political dissatisfaction, including discontent among the groups that have traditionally been the bedrock of support for the monarchy'.[40] Non-American sources added similar warnings. In 1976, the US embassy in Tehran was told by the Israelis that the greatest threat to the Shah came from the Islamic clergy. Later, a French diplomat warned that the Shah would not survive.[41] These reports had little discernable impact in Washington. Two specific problems made this the case. Intelligence gaps of various kinds meant that important information, such as Khomeini's treatise on Islamic government, was overlooked; analysts were for example unaware that the Shah had been critically ill with cancer since the early 1970s.[42] This was compounded by the fact that it was almost impossible to independently verify (particularly alarming reports), given America's operational reliance on SAVAK.[43] This mixed bag led to the reluctance to contemplate a Shah-less Iran, evident in the administration's early analyses, including the Department of Near Eastern Affairs' refusal to sign off on an assessment that included an option that the government might collapse.[44] State Department Iran specialist Henry Precht, the instigator of this heel dragging (but subsequent convert to the unpopular notion that the Shah was finished), reportedly claimed later that 'analysis was filtered to eliminate any consideration of the issue of whether there was internal instability in Iran and whether the United States should be selling arms to the Shah'.[45] Secretary of State Cyrus Vance's worthy but ill-used 'dissent channel', put in place to catch unpopular or unsolicited and alternative policies, failed to make an impact.[46] The State Department's explanation that it was 'unprepared for the collapse of the Pahlavi regime because we did not want to know the truth' was, in reality, only partially true.[47] There were certainly those who recognized that there were no good options for dealing with a dictator like the Shah, the best of a bad bunch having come and gone in the 1950s and 1960s.[48] It is also easy to see how 'clientitis' affected many of those who had invested considerable time and energy on the high maintenance monarch.[49] Yet, many of the administration's foreign service personnel (particularly in the Human Rights Bureau) were not only delighted to see the end of autocratic rule in Iran, but had been actively working for this from the earliest days of Carter's presidency.[50] In truth, as former Policy Planning Director Anthony Lake observed, the administration's Iran analysis was possessed of a 'Rashomon-esque' quality.[51] It was also infused with a palpable helplessness. Brzezinski's demand 'tell me how to make it work' of Iran analyst Henry Precht was also a plea. By the late 1970s, the United States was simply in too deep.

The agony

When the end finally came it took Washington's breath away. 'The roar of the collapsing Pahlevi pillar', Bill wrote, was 'heard around the world'.[52] The Carter administration may have understood that a tangled web had brought the Shah down. Indeed, the president commented less than a month after Khomeini's triumphant return to Iran: 'I don't know of anything we could have done to prevent the very complicated social and religious and political interrelationships from occurring in Iran in the change of government . . . we'll just have to make the best of the change'.[53] Nevertheless, recognizing the multifaceted nature of the Iranian revolution offered little comfort to those now tasked, for the first time in several decades, with redesigning America's policy. In essence, Carter wanted to preserve the Shah if possible and, if this was beyond his gift, the next best option, as he saw it, was to preserve a pro-American regime. At the same time, however, the president didn't want to be seen to be interfering. 'We have no inclination to try to decide the internal affairs of Iran', he told a press conference as the revolution gathered pace in the autumn of 1978.[54] Ultimately, despite considerable prevarication, much handwringing and near intervention, Carter found that he could not save the monarch who was unable to save himself. After the Shah's departure and the return of Khomeini in early 1979, the administration chose to shift its focus to the development of relations with the new government, the maintenance of some kind of strategic asset and the re-establishment of America's face in the region. 'I can't stress how badly we've been hurt by what's happening in Iran' one diplomat lamented, 'And I don't know how we're going to recuperate what we've lost'.[55]

Coming to terms with a revolution

The administration found itself in this position for several reasons. As the revolution gathered momentum throughout 1978, officials struggled to correctly identify what was going on. This predictive and analytical failure did not transform 'inchoate unrest' into a revolution, as Henry Kissinger alleged, but did complicate the formulation of a coherent response to the crisis.[56] Several factors are salient. As Ansari notes, the Shah's own smoke and mirrors were partly to blame: 'Having cultivated the image of a dictator in full control of his country's destiny, the Shah's inability to fulfil his autocratic promise was perplexing domestic opponents and foreign allies alike'.[57] It may also have been due, as Parsons later argued, to 'a failure to interpret correctly the information available to us. We were looking down the right telescope but were focused on the wrong target'.[58] 'We should have seen it coming and been prepared', one official in Washington noted, 'but the threat of an internal revolt was seen as the least likely contingency'.[59] Even among the academic community, few commentators had predicted the trajectory and fallout of the revolution. This 'historical myopia', as Brzezinski's point man on Iran, Gary Sick, describes it, was fuelled by fears that premature precautionary moves would only make things worse. And yet, despite the fact that, by the autumn of 1978, only a small minority of the administration's Iran experts believed the Shah would still be on his throne a year later, the higher echelons had still to meet to discuss the situation described by the media as 'out of control'.[60]

Quite simply, no one in Washington wanted to make 'the call'.[61] Eventually, although a considerable range of negative assessments slowly accumulated, at least in the case of the State Department, this effectively got stuck behind a preoccupied Vance, who only came to realize in mid-December that Mohammad Reza Shah was finished. A later Congressional investigation concluded that this had produced a 'broad failure involving the entire policymaking system'.[62] Certainly, even as the penny was dropping, Washington's room for manoeuvring had dissipated; analysts' late-forming conclusion that the Shah was mortally wounded did not easily or quickly stretch to providing a strategy for picking up the pieces. The Pahlavi regime in Iran was not the only one in disarray. As one official lamented, 'He [the Shah] doesn't know what to do next, and neither do we'.[63] Amidst the melee, signs that the clerics may themselves be undone, encouraged by pro-Shah activists and friends, fed this fantasy.[64] Confronted with only unsatisfactory options, policymakers clung doggedly to the 'abiding hope' that the situation would somehow right itself.[65]

Doing the jigsaw

Much of the administration's confusion was down to the persistence of the confusing intelligence picture highlighted above. From Iran, alongside positive reports (of which there were many) came warnings of doom and gloom from officials like John Limbert and Michael Metrinko, who argued that the opposition to the Shah comprised more than a small group of 'red and black' malcontents. In Metrinko's view, an ingrained hatred of the Shah was spreading throughout society. His analysis, however, was generally given low priority.[66] Indeed, even after 9 November 1978, when Ambassador Sullivan sent his 'thinking the unthinkable' telegram, effectively overturning nearly 2 years worth of positive assessments, he chose not to contradict the positive messages still reaching Washington from his staff. Back in Washington, things were no clearer. The 1978 National Intelligence Estimate (NIE) on Iran had been dropped because the three

main agencies could not agree.[67] (The intelligence community also had considerable reservations about SAVAK's information, which it viewed of the 'Chicken
Little' variety but, as already noted, had no other options, given the Shah's refusal
to allow anything else.[68]) Equally debilitating was the failure of analysts pouring
over material, such as Khomeini's October 1979 interview with Italian journalist
Oriana Fallaci cited below, to catch and convey the Supreme Leader's attitude
towards the United States:

> When we have been bitten by a snake, we are even afraid of a piece of rope
> which from afar looks like a snake. And you have bitten us too much, and
> too long . . . we are afraid of your ideas and of your customs. Which means
> that we fear you politically and socially.[69]

As a result, according to a report into the intelligence failure, 'long-standing US
attitudes toward the Shah inhibited intelligence collection, dampened policymakers' appetite for analysis of the Shah's position and deafened policymakers to the
warning implicit in current intelligence'.[70] This embarrassment forced the director of Central Intelligence, Stansfield Turner, to admit that 'we let him [Carter]
down badly with respect to our coverage of the Iranian scene . . . we were just
plain asleep'.[71] The embassy had become the focus and conduit for intelligence
from Iran, yet prior to the hostage crisis, a changeover of staff saw the insertion of
a small and inexperienced intelligence team. Thus, when this asset was knocked
out in November 1979, the United States lost its eyes and ears in Iran.[72] It had
absolutely nothing to fall back on.

Distractions and divisions

Preoccupation with other affairs was partly to blame. It was also true, however,
that even when full attention was finally given, this had the curious effect of
reducing the degree of expertise involved. As one former foreign service officer
observed, 'the more serious the international crisis, the less expertise that is
brought to bear on it. This is because these crises are handled at the very highest level'.[73] Where Iran was concerned, this had particularly unfortunate results.
Reports of periodic disputes among senior officials – which made administration
policy appear confused and indecisive – may have been somewhat exaggerated
by the media. Nevertheless, there is little doubt that the way Carter chose to
organize his national security apparatus – greater transparency and a high tolerance of dissent – and the potency of the much discussed Vance-Brzezinski clash
(i.e., *Moral-/Realpolitik* clash) – morphed into something more substantial and
damaging than simply a disagreement over methods rather than goals (certainly
for the higher level officials, if not for the ideologues in their respective camps).[74]
This became more acute after the seizure of the hostages in November 1979 as
the perceived options – none of which were considered attractive – declined.[75]
These bureaucratic battles and constraints, piled on top of the intelligence failures, produced an environment in which officials struggled to determine how

their actions would play out in Tehran and resorted to setting up study groups to ascertain whether positive US statements would help or hinder the Shah. The ramifications of a revolutionary Iran certainly elicited different assessments, ranging from Brzezinski's stress on the importance of Iran as a geopolitical asset whose loss 'shattered the strategic pivot of a protected tier shielding the crucial oil rich region of the Persian gulf from possible Soviet intrusion' to the view espoused by some in the State Department that the Shah's reluctant departure might contain a silver lining in the shape of a 'soft landing' that would allow Iran to realize its democratic potential.[76] Reconciling these perspectives was difficult indeed. This was evident, for example, in the disagreements over embassy security only days before the takeover, in which the State Department rejected the immediate emergency planning proposed by the White House and the Pentagon because officials judged the political situation sufficiently benign.[77]

Becoming the Great Satan

Gaps in Washington's institutional memory meant that no one, for example, took much notice of the fact that 4 November (the day the embassy was stormed) was the anniversary of Khomeini's exile and, a year earlier, the date of bloody clashes between the Shah's US-trained army and revolutionary forces. As former hostage Mike Metrinko observed:

> There was a failure to understand the vast degree of suppressed hatred that had been caused by our bringing about the collapse of the Mossadeq government. That was Iran's chance to become democratic. We screwed it up, and we bragged about it.[78]

A pervasive lack of empathy exacerbated this still further. As one journalist remarked a short time after the end of the hostage crisis: 'We simply could never understand that 52 Iranians were as important to other Iranians as 52 Americans were to other Americans, and that a lot more than 52 Iranians had been killed by our own client, the Shah'.[79]

Combined, these limitations ensured that the administration was poorly placed not only to grasp the strength of latent negative feeling towards the United States but also to conceive of what a post-Shah Iran would look like. As the National Security Council (NSC) staffer Howard Teicher noted, no one 'really knew what they [Iranians] were trying to achieve. Was it a Sunni *versus* Shia struggle playing out on a modern stage?'[80] The media was similarly perplexed. In November 1978, *The New York Times* columnist Flora Lewis wrote:

> There is no ideology, no promising creed to dull the pain of drastic upheaval and transformation, only the promise of material benefit, higher living standards – all this calculated on the basis of per capita income, high-rise housing, cars, TV sets, foreign holidays and foreign fashions. That means a vacuum of spirit and of ennobling hope.[81]

Lewis was not alone in failing to appreciate the extent to which Khomeini would fill this vacuum. Also overlooked was the fact that the clerics did not amount to a homogenous force – at the time of the revolution, four out of the five Grand Ayatollahs privately denounced Khomeini's view of an Islamic government. This was not because the administration was incapable of a more nuanced approach. On several occasions Carter spoke of the need to see what was happening 'not in terms of simplistic colors of black and white, but in more subtle shades'. The United States, he urged, 'must devise intelligent and thoughtful responses'.[82] Such a pragmatic, rational assessment was reinforced by requests for food supplies and spare parts and the fact that, as Menashri noted, the new government 'vacillated between resentment at former American policies and a desire to maintain reasonably normal ties'.[83] Collectively, these signs gave succour to the belief that America could, as Carter hoped, make the best out of a difficult situation. Yet, despite having transcended some of the more simplistic assessments of what was going on in Iran, policymakers were unable to translate this into meaningful policy.

In one area, in particular – attempts to reactivate CIA networks, including attempts to recruit Bani-Sadr, one of Khomeini's most senior lieutenants (and the man who would become Iran's president) – proved especially dangerous.[84] As a result, much weight was placed on the new government to shore up tentative ties at a fragile time. As Sick later acknowledged, meetings such as that which took place in Algiers between Brzezinski and members of the provisional government shortly before the hostage crisis almost certainly hastened the day when the thread finally snapped.[85] Doubtless, much of this rationale grew from a preoccupation with searching for reflections of what officials recognized from their own political system and political practices. This, Rubin suggests, created the expectation 'that Teheran must act pragmatically to attain objective national interests'.[86] Unfortunately, what was considered pragmatic from Tehran's perspective was regarded very differently in Washington. It was also complicated by the fact that many of Iran's new leaders were not conversant in the forms of communication used in international diplomacy (or had chosen to disregard these norms). Try as he might, therefore, Carter found that subtlety went out the window. The vitriol emanating from Tehran evoked an emotional reaction that resulted in Washington missing a rather substantial point, as Beeman shows:

> Drawing upon the imagery of the United States as the Great Satan should have somehow alerted the American analysts that the epithet was not being directed at the United States or its citizenry, but rather at Iran and its citizens. It was an attempt to show Iranians that the United States and all it supported, principally Shah Mohammad Reza Pahlavi, was a force alien to Iran and its civilization – a force attempting to corrupt the Iranian people.[87]

Not surprisingly, it took some time for officials to internalize the fact that this emotional hostility to the United States was, as one commentator put it, 'a crucial element of Iranian revolutionary politics, not merely an act of defiance or retribution and not at all the mindless, crazy gesture it seemed'.[88] Furthermore, the febrile, chaotic nature and pace of politics in Iran engendered confusion about who was in control and presented a problem for policymakers confronted with editorials penned by a disbelieving and critical press:

> The administration [admonished *The Washington Post*] obviously should not act in a way likely to endanger the lives of the Americans being held hostage at the US embassy in Tehran. But to say that is not to counsel pussycat acquiescence in the reckless way the Iranian authorities-cum-mob are behaving. It is fraudulent to suggest that the poor officials are helpless to control the mob's behaviour. They are not.[89]

The Iranian politicians Washington had thought were able to control the unsettling excesses of the most radical clerics were, if anything, unwittingly undermined by America's overtures. This was a critical miscalculation. The opposition, in its broadest incarnation, had two goals: removal of the Shah and the end of foreign domination of Iran. As Scott Armstrong wrote in his exposé of the crisis, however, 'It was perhaps the failure of American analysts to recognize the extent . . . [of the latter] that led to so great a misunderstanding of what Iran would be like after the Shah was toppled'.[90] For those who would come to dominate the revolution, a resumption of ties of any sort was ideologically inconceivable. More than this, it provided a heaven-sent excuse for neutralizing those judged incompatible with the new Islamic Republic.

An unforgivable sin

The seizure of the US embassy in November 1979 brought into sharper focus the realization that Washington was dealing with a regime not only of uncertain composition, but one that was playing by different rules and shaped by an opaque domestic agenda. The administration's response to this unprecedented breech of international law was the final factor to shape America's embryonic Iran policy.

Conservative commentator William Safire may have been at the extreme end of the spectrum in calling Khomeini's 'provocation' 'heaven-sent', but his argument that the president's job was 'neither to turn the other cheek nor to retaliate in fury, but to use this incident with audacity to assert American power in the mid-East and to reverse the strategic decline over which he has presided' resonated around the country. It certainly made Carter's job more difficult.[91] In response, the administration debated the 'virtues and vices' of maintaining a highly focused emergency atmosphere *versus* adopting 'a settled-in, long-term, unexcited effort' to secure their release. In the end, the argument was clinched by the president's response to the affair.[92] Here Carter made something of a rod for his own back. The hostages became personal to him for two reasons: first, he calculated that making it so would reduce the likelihood that they would be harmed. Second, such a policy allowed him to advance and defend a policy of military restraint.[93] Predictably, as a result, it became personal to the US public too.

In this light, Carter's commitment not to let the crisis drag on rang increasingly hollow and his perceived impotence grew.[94] This was not within his gift. Instead, he was compelled to preside over a precarious balancing act, as *The New York Times* reported:

> By not fully defining the threat and not setting the deadlines, Mr. Carter leaves time for Iran to react to the pressure without appearing to succumb to it . . . further pressure could be truly crippling [and could mean] taking the blame for all the revolution's chaos – and making an aroused people more likely to bear the pain.[95]

To his critics, Carter's actions were not only unsuccessful, but dangerous. In Safire's view, 'we fairly preened in patience, gloried in impotence, and accepted gratefully the unanimous sympathy of other nations. By reveling in our victimization, we have heartened terrorists around the world'.[96] In hindsight, Vance more or less concurred:

> It was a mistake for us not to have played down the crisis as much as possible . . . The more we declared our fear for their safety and our determination to leave no stone unturned to gain their freedom, the greater their value became to Khomeini and the Islamic extremists.[97]

What the administration had less control over were the constraints used so effectively as sticks with which to attack the president. These were plentiful. In addition to concerns about the collapse of Iran following Iraq's September 1980 invasion and the instability caused by the Soviet Union's December 1979 invasion of Iran's neighbour, Afghanistan, the administration worried that a freezing of Iranian assets might upset international banking and provoke states like Saudi Arabia to withdraw their huge deposits, thus causing a run on and perhaps the collapse of the dollar.[98] The administration also worried that any US moves that aided Iran, such as removing the sanctions in response to the release of hostages (promised before the Iraq invasion), would provoke a negative reaction from Jordan, Iraq and Saudi Arabia, potentially, among other things, threatening the delicate Camp David negotiations.[99] These considerations, *The New York Times* reported, 'Would make it very difficult for Mr. Carter to take any overt steps to aid Iran, such as sending spare parts, in order to end the hostage crisis'.[100]

The context, of course, was also infused with self doubt, typified by remarks such as Joseph Sisco's musing that 'there was a time when we could overwhelm these global issues by our preponderant strength. We can no longer do so . . . We are in the midst of developing a policy of selective engagement in a more unpredictable world'.[101] This was matched by a wariness that even talking to Iran about the hostages was tantamount to negotiating with terrorists and therefore a dangerous precedent that should be avoided.[102]

Domestically, the impact and role of the media often complicated diplomacy by putting 'into concrete what could have been dismissed as a muttering behind closed walls'. This was problematic, officials pointed out, because, whereas diplomats were interested in keeping Iran's positions ambiguous or fluid, journalists tended to ask questions with the aim of eliminating ambiguities.[103] Despite the periodic appearance of more supportive pieces, pressure from media around the country to act was substantial.[104] As one senior official remarked in a newspaper interview, 'Critics failed to understand how little the Administration could do to affect the course of the Iranian crisis. There was just no major action that we could have taken that would have yielded positive results'.[105]

In short, as Teicher affirmed, the fabric of decision-making was very complex, but in the end, decisions were not. The United States had limited choices.[106] Ultimately, Carter's realization that the crisis would end at a time of Tehran's choosing, and the most that Washington could usefully do was apply diplomatic and financial pressure (excepting, of course, the failed rescue attempt), was vindicated. Nevertheless, the safe return of the hostages did little to assuage or mitigate the profoundly negative perceptions that came to surround his actions. In the end, although Carter did not have to choose between US national honour and the lives of 52 American citizens, the perception lingered that he put the hostages' lives first. While this was tolerable, indeed praiseworthy, during their captivity, once they had been freed, it looked like a character failing that had compounded the emasculating hostage crisis. For many, it summed up America's failure to find a way of dealing with a former friend turned foe.

Lessons to be learned

Five aspects of America's Iran policies in this period, though not easily remedied, were clearly problematic. First, in the Carter era, America was seen as weak and impotent and, as such, invited challenges. Carving out a new position for the United States in the post-Vietnam, post-Watergate period was never going to be easy. Indeed, America's 44th President, Barack Obama, faces a similar challenge in the wake of George W Bush's neo-imperial presidency. For Carter, an acceptance of the limitations confronting the United States, in light of a new geopolitical reality, proved hard to come to terms with. Second, the United States failed to sufficiently understand Iran – its leaders and problems – during the growth of the cliency relationship and in the revolutionary period. Third, Carter's personalizing of the hostage affair and the way he allowed Iran, the revolution and the crisis to be simplified, succeeded in exacerbating the crisis and ensured that its legacy would be more bitter and malignant than it might otherwise have been. Fourth, successive administrations failed to produce a coherent policy and a realistic appreciation of what could be done. As Rubin says, '*All* sides have tended to exaggerate the importance of American actions and decisions on events in Iran. In studying the history of the two nations' relations one is most impressed with Washington's difficulties in influencing Iranian affairs'.[107] Progress was never impossible, but so often was complicated, even negated, because of timing. As former *charge d'affairs* Bruce Laingen observed, if there was a lesson to be drawn from the foreign policies that led to the hostage crisis, it was 'to recognise that there is a time for an idea whose time has come. In Iran in 1979, this was Islam, the will of the people, and belief that the Shah had to go'.[108] More often than not, it proved to be external developments, such as the Iraqi invasion of Iran that provided a small amount of lubrication for what had quickly become a paralysed relationship. Until this point, it was hostages that facilitated the consolidation of the revolution. Their purpose, after Saddam Hussein's attack, quickly diminished. Fifth, a lack of long-term institutional memory made it very difficult for policymakers to comprehend the nature of the relationships their predecessors had carved out with Iran. This had particular relevance for those critical junctures regarded by many in Iran as evidence of American duplicity and nefarious intent. As Sick points out, 'The US government has a short memory . . . in Washington, by 1978 the events of 1953 had all the relevance of a pressed flower'.[109] Policymakers missed many signs because these were simply not relevant to them.

Yet, despite all this, one positive element is worthy of note. Quiet, pragmatic diplomacy, coupled with financial pressures, produced results. After the hostages were released, *The New York Times* wrote, 'America's patience in the hostage crisis was not a mark of weakness but of exemplary strength'.[110] This was reiterated in the note passed by the Spanish Ambassador to Tehran to the captive Laingen, which read 'patience is a bitter cup that only the strong can drink'.[111] Sanctions did play a part because, as White House Counsel Lloyd Cutler observed:

> Contrary to most of the complaints and disappointments that were publically [sic] expressed about the allies not supporting us; it was their sanctions added on top of ours that I think finally made the difference when Iraq invaded Iran and the Iranians had no place to turn for money or spare parts or new weapons or anything.[112]

Indeed, the reported cost to Iran of the hostage affair ($10 billion by March of 1981 and lawsuits costing the government some $500,000 per month in lawyer fees) was hardly mitigated by the final deal which left Tehran considerably worse off than before the crisis. Although America's military might did not deter the hostage takers, this blunt and largely irrelevant tool, limited as it was as a means of coercing a change in behaviour, did play a role, according to hostage negotiator Warren Christopher, after the hostages were taken. Its value lay in its use as a deterrent against further harm.[113] Moreover, as *The New York Times* acknowledged, 'by largely resisting knee-jerk reactions Carter avoided both the disastrous extremes into which it would have been so easy to slip: risking or starting a war the consequences of which were and are incalculable, or ignominiously yielding to blackmailers and kidnappers passing themselves off as a civilized Government'.[114] In the final analysis, however, the president's success in this respect was and remains overshadowed by the failures of policy, intelligence and bureaucracy; his administration's assessment of the revolution – first ordered and then mothballed – would surely have included some if not all of the following lessons learned:

> When dealing with Iran, although rhetoric has often outpaced reality, pragmatism is also possible.
>
> History is today and memories are long. Perceptions are hugely important, perhaps more so than reality.
>
> The United States struggles to understand its former ally. Reducing relationships and states to 'Good' and 'Evil' is unhelpful and counterproductive; Iran's internal politics and domestic imperatives have always been hugely important.
>
> Interference or involvement in the affairs of another state comes at a price; the law of unintended consequences has a nasty habit of sneaking in.
>
> Intelligence is critical and knowing who you are dealing with and how to reach out in a positive way is imperative.
>
> Timing is everything and cannot be separated from good intelligence.
>
> Assumptions must be challenged.
>
> Making policy up on the hoof is problematic.
>
> Hypocrisy and double standards – condoning the abuses of the Shah in one era then criticizing the excesses of the revolutionary government in another – has left the United States open to charges which are always difficult to refute and recover from.

Ignoring Iran has not worked. It has an uncanny knack of insinuating itself into United States affairs. After decades of ecstasy and the painful experience of the hostage crisis-dominated revolution, the United States can ill afford to let the stalemate continue or deteriorate further. In 2009, as in 1979, the United States has much at stake in the region, too much arguably to allow the legacy of what has gone before to continue to poison relations. Moving forward, however, is only possible with an understanding of what went wrong before.

Notes

1 Iranian journalist quoted in Robin Wright, *In the Name of God*, London: Bloomsbury, 1991, p. 22.
2 James A. Bill, *The Shah, The Ayatollah and the US*, New York: The Foreign Policy Association, 1988, p. 5. For a more recent account, see Kenneth Pollack, *The Persian Puzzle: The Conflict between Iran and America*, New York: Random House, 2004.
3 Mansour Farhang, 'US Foreign Policy toward the Islamic Republic of Iran: A Case of Misperception and Reactive Behavior', in H. Amirahmadi (ed.) *The United States and the Middle East: A Search for New Perspectives*, Albany: State University of New York Press, 1993, p. 172.
4 Y. Alexander and A. Names, *The United States and Iran: A Documentary History*, Lanham: Aletheia Books, 1980, p. 435.
5 Alfred L. Atherton Jr., Assistant Secretary of State Bureau of Near Eastern and South Asia Affairs, 29 July 1977, quoted in Alexander and Names, *The United States and Iran*, p. 446.

6 David Hirst, 'Shadows on the throne', *The Guardian*, 10 August 1972.
7 Anthony Parsons, 'Iran and Western Europe', in R. K. Ramazani (ed.) *Iran's Revolution: The Search for Consensus*, Bloomington: Indiana University Press, 1990, p. 69.
8 Telegram from Ambassador Richard Helms, US Embassy in Tehran to State Department in Washington, 'Iran's current foreign relations: an analysis', 26 June 1974, Electronic Telegrams, 1/1/1974 – 12/31/1974, Central Foreign Policy Files, Record Group 59, US National Archives.
9 M. Ledeen and W. Lewis, *Debacle: The American Failure in Iran*, New York: Vintage Books, 1982, p. 52.
10 Tom Wicker, 'President and Shah', *The New York Times*, 6 August 1976. For the Shah's view of the relationship see Mohammad Reza Pahlavi, *Answer the History*, New York: Stein & Day, 1980.
11 P. K. Williams to Clark and Wright, 22 October 1974, FCO8/2262, UK National Archives.
12 David Hirst, 'Iranians' Great Leap forward', *The Guardian*, 11 August 1972.
13 Sir Peter Ramsbotham to Foreign Secretary, 17 June 1972, FCO8/1882, UK National Archives.
14 Sir Peter Ramsbotham, Valedictory Despatch, 1974, FCO 8/2262, UK National Archives.
15 'Begrudging Iran its new power', *Kayhan International*, 16 October 1974, FCO 8/2262, UK National Archives.
16 The United States was reduced in the mid-1960s to establishing a listening post in the US embassy compound to monitor radio transmissions by Iranian intelligence.
17 In hearings into Grumman arms sales, Senator Church noted that 'the appetite for sophisticated weapons feeds the need for revenues to pay for the arms; this leads to more pressure for oil price increase'. The result was that sellers were inflating the cost of the weapons to pay for the oil, which in turn led to pressure for new oil price rises. As far as Church was concerned, the case 'illustrates that the matter is entirely out of our [Congress's] hands, and may be beyond the effective control of the government' and 'we depend heavily on the sale of arms to buy the oil, even though we know we're selling a big war out there'. Seymour M Hersh, 'Jets for Iran: Did Grumman Influence U.S.?', *The New York Times*, 18 September 1976.
18 These sentiments were echoed by the British who commented that 'we can only continue to hope that a combination of increasing material well-being and the all pervading scrutiny of the security forces, will be sufficient to keep the situation under control until the time comes for the Shah peacefully to yield up power to his successors (monarchical or otherwise)'. P. R. H. Wright to Sir Peter Ramsbotham, 9 November, 1974, FCO8/1882, UK National Archives.
19 Memorandum from R. J. Alston to FCO, 4 November 1975, FCO8/2496, UK National Archives.
20 Ali M Ansari, *Confronting Iran*, London: Hurst, 2006, p. 57.
21 Shah's response to question posed by US journalist about ceasing to provide Iran with arms. Eric Page, 'US Influence on Iran: Gigantic and Diverse', *The New York Times*, 30 August 1976.
22 The Shah told reporters in 1979 that 'there are many more sources available in the world just waiting for the moment for us to go and shop in their shops'. Bernard Gwertzman, 'Shah Cautions US against arms cut', *The New York Times*, 7 August 1976.
23 'Shah's Threats to Kissinger Revealed', *The Washington Post*, 31 July 1979.
24 Sir Peter Ramsbotham to Patrick Wright, 2 November 1972, FCO8/1882, UK National Archives. Britain certainly had evidence to support this from experience. The Shah took great offence at the fourth (out of five) articles on Iran published by the Guardian in 1972, to such a degree that the UK ambassador, who noted that this has 'affected

his attitude to Britain and the British government' and was 'so bitter and intemperate that I am not reporting them', was compelled to smooth things over by writing to the editor. Sir Peter Ramsbotham to Anthony Parsons, 17 August 1972, FCO8/1882, UK National Archives.

25 Eric Pace, 'Troubled Iran Celebrates Reign of Shah's Father', *The New York Times*, 3 March 1976.

26 Sir Peter Ramsbotham to Patrick Wright, 2 November 1972, FCO8/1882, UK National Archives.

27 Memorandum on Iran's Internal Situation by P. K. Williams, 28 October 1975, FCO8/2496, UK National Archives.

28 Anthony Parsons 'Iran: Annual Review for 1975', 15 December 1975, FCO8/2494, UK National Archives.

29 *The Financial Times*, 20 August, 1973.

30 William H Sullivan, *Mission to Iran*, New York: W. W. Norton, 1981, p. 20. The Shah helped counter an insurgency in Oman, actively supported US goals in the Horn of Africa, and was seen as a strategic asset providing a buffer against the Soviet Union and a pro-Soviet Iraq. Thus, while the arms sales were heavily criticized during the early part of the revolution, this was predictably more muted after the Soviets invaded Afghanistan and Iraq invaded Iran. James Schlesinger, 'Now Who's Saying the Shah was Arms-Happy?', *The Washington Post*, 9 October 1980.

31 Jimmy Carter, *Keeping Faith: Memoirs of a President*, London: Collins, 1982, p. 435.

32 For more on this see Ofira Seliktar, *Failing the Crystal Ball Test: The Carter Administration and the Fundamentalist Revolution in Iran*, New York: Praeger, 2000; Coral Bell, *President Carter and Foreign Policy: The Costs of Virtue?* Canberra: The Australian National University Press, 1980.

33 Cyrus Vance, *Hard Choices: Critical Years in America's Foreign Policy*, New York: Simon & Schuster, 1983, p. 326.

34 Bernard Weinraub, 'The US Policy on Arms has a life of its own', *The New York Times*, 18 September 1977.

35 Nicholas Gage, 'U.S.–Iran Links Still Strong', *The New York Times*, 9 July 1978.

36 'Tears and Sympathy for the Shah', *The New York Times*, 17 November 1977.

37 The US, according to Sick, was ill equipped and unaccustomed to give the kind of advice that might have made a difference to his handling of the revolution. Interview with Gary Sick, 16 May 2007; Carter, *Keeping Faith*, p. 435.

38 Nicholas Gage, 'U.S.–Iran Ties Strong but Controversial', *The New York Times*, 9 July 1979.

39 David Menashri, *Iran: A Decade of War and Revolution*, New York: Holmes and Meier, 1990, p. 47.

40 Scott Armstrong, 'Carter Held Hope Even After Shah Had Lost His', *The Washington Post*, 25 October 1980.

41 Gregory F. Treverton and James Klocke, *The Fall of the Shah*, Georgetown University: Institute for the Study of Diplomacy, Washington D.C., 1994, p. 3. The warnings were confirmed by Ambassador Sullivan himself. Sullivan, *Mission to Iran*, p. 144.

42 'Shah's Admission To U.S. Linked To Misinformation On His Sickness', *The New York Times*, 13 May 1981. Officials claimed in 1981 that had they known about this they would have begun to consider his policy towards his regime.

43 Henry Precht quoted in G. Treverton and J. Klocke, *The Fall of the Shah of Iran*, p. 2.

44 Howard Teicher and Gayle Radley Teicher, *Twin Pillars to Desert Storm: America's Flawed Vision in the Middle East from Nixon to Bush*, New York: William Morrow, 1993, p. 33.

45 Ibid., p. 34.

46 Anthony Lake, who was put in charge of the mechanism, thought it very sad but was at a loss to explain why it wasn't used. Interview with Anthony Lake, 29 March 2007.

47   Charles Kurzman, *The Unthinkable Revolution in Iran*, Cambridge, Mass.: Harvard University Press, 2004, pp. 1–4.

48   Interview with Anthony Lake, 29 March 2007.

49   This term was used by Howard Teicher and Policy Planning Department staffer Theodore Moran. Interviews with Teicher, 30 October 2007, and Moran, 23 May 2007.

50   Interview with Ted Moran, 23 May 2007.

51   Like the four conflicting perspectives of the participants of a rape in the Japanese film *Rashomon*, US officials experienced the same events yet perceived them very differently, extrapolating different conclusions, strategies and lessons. Interview with Anthony Lake, 29 March 2007.

52   James A. Bill, *The Eagle and the Lion: The Tragedy of American–Iranian Relations*, New Haven: Yale University Press, 1988, p. 243.

53   President Carter, Press Conference, 27 February 1979, quoted in Alexander and Names, *The United States and Iran*, p. 479.

54   Carter continued, 'He [the Shah] may not be moving fast enough for some; he may be moving too fast for others . . . I don't want to get involved in the specifics'. Carter Press Conference, 10 October 1978, quoted in Alexander and Names, *The United States and Iran*, p. 460. To some extent, it was the specifics that now eluded the President and his most senior advisers. 'We knew little about the forces contending against him', the president noted in his memoirs, 'but their anti-American slogans and statements were enough in themselves to strengthen our resolve to support the Shah as he struggled for survival'. Jimmy Carter, *Keeping Faith*, p. 440.

55   James M Markham, 'Iran Crisis Undermining U.S. in Gulf Area', *The New York Times*, 8 February 1979.

56   Kissinger quoted in Barry Rubin, *Paved with Good Intentions: The American Experience and Iran*, London: Penguin Books, 1981, p. 255.

57   Ansari, *Confronting Iran*, p. 77.

58   Anthony Parsons, *The Pride and the Fall: Iran 1974–1979*, London: Jonathan Cape, 1984, p. 134.

59   'U.S., Short on Intelligence and Tied to the Shah, Decided it had to Support Him', *The New York Times*, 15 November 1978.

60   Scott Armstrong, 'As Turmoil Turns to Crisis, the U.S. Urges a "Crackdown"', *The Washington Post*, 27 October 1980; Jonathan C. Randal, 'Iran: "Situation is Out of Control"', *The Washington Post*, 29 October 1978.

61   Gary Sick, *All Fall Down: America's Tragic Encounter with Iran*, New York: Random House, 1985, pp. 41–42. Sick attributes the lack of such a meeting to the fact that senior officials believed that they Shah could and would 'pull it out'. Interview with Sick, 16 May 2007.

62   Jim Hoagland, 'Reactions to Shah's Crisis Called a Broad Failure', *The Washington Post*, 25 January 1979.

63   Jim Hoagland, 'Shah's Turning to Military Rule Wins White House Support', *The Washington Post*, 7 November 1978.

64   Youssef M. Ibrahim, 'Unrest Said to Show Rising Opposition to Khomeini', *The New York Times*, 17 August 1979.

65   Interview with Sick, 16 May 2007. Even officials who felt the Shah was on his way out were not seriously arguing that the administration could do anything to separate itself from a ruler the United States had supported for 25 years. Hoagland, 'Shah's Turning to Military Rule Wins White House Support'.

66   Scott Armstrong, 'Failing to Heed the Warnings of Revolution in Iran', *The Washington Post*, 26 October 1980. Sick confirms this noting that some dispatches were sent as airgrams. Interview with Sick, 16 May 2007. Brzezinski later argued that 'a policy of conciliation and concessions might have worked, had it been adopted two or three years earlier, before the crisis reached a politically acute phase'.

Zbigniew Brzezinski, *Power and Principle: Memoirs of the National Security Adviser 1977–1981*, New York: Farrar, Straus, Giroux, 1983, p. 355.

67 The DIA and CIA were optimistic, whereas the State Department's Bureau of Intelligence was less so. *The New York Times* reported that a 'full-dress update' was not done because the CIA decided that it would be a 'pointless waste of relatively limited analytical assets'. Tad Szulc, 'Shaking up the CIA', *The New York Times*, 29 July 1979; Rubin, *Paved with Good Intentions*, p. 208.

68 SAVAK reportedly often overlooked things that may have been useful, for example, a warning about the Soviet coup in Afghanistan in 1978. Scott Armstrong, 'Failing to Heed the Warnings of Revolution in Iran', *The Washington Post*, 26 October 1980. An Inter-Agency memo produced in lieu of the document hedged its bets saying that there was limited immediate danger but considerable problems ahead. Seliktar, *Failing the Crystal Ball Test*, p. 92.

69 Oriana Fallaci, 'An Interview with Khomeini', *The New York Times*, 7 October 1979.

70 Jim Hoagland, 'Reactions to Shah's Crisis Called a Broad Failure', *The Washington Post*, 25 January 1979.

71 Stansfield Turner, *Burn Before Reading: Presidents, CIA Directors, and Secret Intelligence*, New York: Hyperion, 2005, p. 180.

72 Stansfield Turner, *Terrorism and Democracy, Boston*, Boston: Houghton Mifflin, 1991, pp. 25, 29. An alleged exchange between Turner and Mondale about what an Ayatollah was, apparently witnessed by Gary Sick, concluded without either having been able to explain it to the other!

73 Bill, *The Eagle and the Lion*, p. 10. For example, at the time of the Jaleh Square massacre, the administration's top Middle East staff was tied up in Camp David and unavailable to lower level analysts like Henry Precht. Interview with Harold Saunders, quoted in Treverton and Klocke, *The Fall of the Shah of Iran*, p. 4.

74 Richard Burt, 'U.S. Strategy on Iran Stirs a Fierce Debate', *The New York Times*, 12 January 1979; Teicher and Teicher, *Twin Pillars*, p. 78. Distrustful of covert operations, significant human intelligence reductions were implemented.

75 David Houghton, *US Foreign Policy and the Iran Hostage Crisis*, Cambridge, Cambridge University Press, 2001, p. 80.

76 Brzezinski, *Power and Principle*, p. 356.

77 Editorial, *The Washington Post*, 9 November 1979.

78 Houghton, *US Foreign Policy and the Iran Hostage Crisis*, p. 65.

79 A. M. Rosenthal, 'America in Captivity', *The New York Times*, 17 May 1981.

80 Interview with Howard Teicher, 30 October 2007.

81 Flora Lewis, 'Iran: Future Shock', *The New York Times*, 12 November 1978.

82 Terence Smith, 'President Cautions Foreign Policy Foes', *The New York Times*, 23 February 1979.

83 David Menashri, *Iran, A Decade of War and Revolution*, New York: Holmes and Meier, 1990, p. 97.

84 Scott Armstrong, 'Iran Documents Give Rare Glimpse of a CIA Enterprise', *The Washington Post*, 31 January 1982.

85 Sick, *All Fall Down*, p. 190.

86 Barry Rubin, 'Iran is Running A Risk', *The New York Times*, 12 December 1980.

87 William O. Beeman, *The 'Great Satan' vs the 'Mad Mullahs': How the United States and Iran Demonize Each Other*, Westport, Conn.: Greenwood, 2005, p. 49.

88 Flora Lewis, 'Hostage Crisis Cracked U.S. Mirror–And the World's', *The New York Times*, 18 January 1981.

89 'Recklessness in Iran', *The Washington Post*, 6 November 1979.

90 Scott Armstrong, 'As Turmoil Turns to Crisis, the U.S. Urges a Crackdown', *The Washington Post*, 27 October 1980.

91 William Safire, 'A Time for Daring', *The New York Times*, 26 November 1979.

92   'After the Ayatollah', *The Washington Post*, 12 December 1979.

93   Carter was also in receipt of 'real-time', KH-11 satellite imagery of the US embassy in Tehran – the first time this had been available to a president – and could literally see the compound, if not the hostages themselves. Christopher Andrew, *For the President's Eyes Only: Secret Intelligence and the American Presidency from Washington to Bush*, London: Harper Collins, 1996, p. 449; 'For America, A Painful Reawakening', *The New York Times*, 17 May 1981.

94   'Carter Vows Crisis Won't Drag on', *The Washington Post*, 15 December 1979.

95   'How Tight the Screw?' *The New York Times*, 13 December 1979.

96   William Safire, 'Patience Is Not Fortitude', *The New York Times*, 17 December 1979.

97   Vance, *Hard Choices*, p. 380. According to Vance's deputy, Warren Christopher, as many as ten top officials spent 1–2 hours each day on the crisis. Warren Christopher, *American Hostages in Iran: The Conduct of a Crisis*, New Haven: Yale University Press, 1985, pp. 4–5.

98   'Putting The Hostages' Lives First', *The New York Times*, 17 May 1981.

99   Scott Armstrong, 'Vance, For a Moment, Turns the President Around on Iran', *The Washington Post*, 29 October 1980. As part of the Camp David agreement, Israel was being asked to give up the oil fields in the Sinai, so the loss of Iranian oil (50 per cent of Israel's supply) would hit them hard and, it was feared, could derail the talks.

100 Richard Burt, 'Hostages and War Combine to Shape U.S. Policy in Gulf', *The New York Times*, 25 October 1980.

101 Joseph J. Sisco, 'Our Uncertain Image', *The New York Times*, 8 July 1979.

102 Daniel Pipes, 'Beware, A Hostage Deal Might Hurt the U.S.', *The New York Times*, 29 October 1980.

103 Steven R. Weisman, 'U.S. Aides, Shunned in Iran, Complain of TV Diplomacy', *The New York Times*, 11 December 1979.

104 David Bird, 'Editorials Around Country Apply Pressure on Carter to Act in Crisis', *The New York Times*, 13 November 1979.

105 Richard Burt, 'U.S. Strategy on Iran Stirs a Fierce Debate', *The New York Times*, 12 January 1979.

106 Interview with Howard Teicher, 30 October 2007.

107 Rubin, *Paved with Good Intentions*, p. 254.

108 'Diplomat Recalls Long Months Without An Embassy', *The New York Times*, 5 February 1981.

109 Sick, *All Fall Down*, p. 7.

110 'Strength, Weakness and Patience', *The New York Times*, 28 January 1981.

111 Ibid.

112 Lloyd Cutler, Oral History Interview, 2 March 1981, Jimmy Carter Presidential Library.

113 Christopher, *American Hostages*, p. 23.

114 Tom Wicker, 'In the Nation: The Root of the Crisis', *The New York Times*, 28 December 1980.

10 America's Israel/ Israel's America

Ian J. Bickerton

To explore the US–Israel relationship is to enter a world of illusions and misperceptions. For most Americans, misperceptions have not just overtaken, they have replaced the reality of the relationship. Discourse in which evidence is presented and assessed has been replaced by repeated assertions of strong convictions. It is impossible to briefly summarize the multifaceted and rapidly evolving US–Israeli relationship, but certain themes and threads run through the ways Americans and Israelis perceive themselves. The phrase 'America's Israel, Israel's America' neatly encapsulates the dichotomies and dilemmas surrounding the visions Americans and Israelis have of each other. The element of possession, control, or at the very least influence, of one over the other is integral to the characterizations of the relationship by both Americans and Israelis – whether they are supporters or critics of the relationship.

I

How do Americans view Israel? In the United States, two contrary propositions compete to describe Israel and its relationship with the United States. The majority of Americans see Israel as a stable, democratic and militarily strong Jewish state that acts as America's proxy (in some scenarios 'client') in the Middle East. Israel is seen as a key strategic partner in America's hegemonic drive for control of the region's vital oil resources. In this portrayal, the United States has exhibited an unqualified support for Israel because Israel represents a Western model of modernity in the Middle East and in doing so has sought to break down opposition to US capital and Americanization in the region.[1]

These views are supported by a belief in the moral justification for a Jewish state, a shared US and Israeli anti-Arab racism, and a fascination with Israel because of the belief that the Jewish state has imitated or mirrored the United States since its origins. The United States has, accordingly, benefited from its support of Israel because Israel assisted the United States in checking Soviet expansionism and helped align Arab elites into the American sphere of influence. Israel's role in assisting Jordan's King Hussein resist the PLO, Syrian and Iraqi attempts to overthrow him in September 1970, and its invasion and occupation of Lebanon from 1982 until 2000, allegedly to support Christian governments against radical insurgents, are given in evidence of this argument.[2]

The second thesis, held by a minority, is that the US exhibits, in the words of former Undersecretary of State George Ball and his son Douglas, 'a passionate attachment' to Israel which damages American interests in the region and increases risks to American security.[3] According to critics of the US–Israel relationship the reasons for this destructive situation are to be found predominantly in the actions of an Israel lobby whose influence has permeated all areas of American government and leadership.[4] There is often a rider to this argument which asserts that, despite its dependency status and the inordinate amount of aid that it receives from the United States, Israel dictates US policy in the region, almost always against America's own best interests.

Proponents of both views start with the unshakable conviction that the relationship between the United States and Israel is special, even unique. The first reference I have found to the term 'special' to describe the relationship was in the Israeli State Archives in Jerusalem in the report of a meeting on 8 October 1953 between Secretary of State John Foster Dulles and the Israeli ambassador to the United States, Abba Eban. Dulles told Eban that the people and government of the United States 'ascribed to their friendship with Israel a special importance going beyond that which normally attaches to their friendship with many other countries'. Dulles gave two reasons. In addition to the Jewish population in the United States, Dulles singled out the profound contribution to fundamental American culture and morality of what he defined as America's Judeo-Christian heritage. He told Eban that he had delivered a sermon on that very topic a few days ago in a church founded by his father in upstate New York. He said he had based his sermon on the Epistle of St. Paul to the Hebrews.[5]

Clearly, advocates of both propositions outlined above agree that there is a symbiotic relationship between the United States and Israel, although they disagree on the domestic basis or foundations of the close ties. Both scenarios, while containing elements of truth, gravely – even dangerously – misrepresent the historic evolution and nature of the relationship. The information presented to buttress these contrary claims is frequently self-serving and is rarely subjected to critical or contextual assessment. At times it seems that academic discussion of the US–Israel relationship is merely an extension of domestic US political discourse.

There are several reasons for this unsatisfactory situation. The first is that for the most part we are talking about current events, and the documents needed to form an accurate and complete assessment of the policymaking process are simply unavailable or incomplete. US archival, presidential library and other executive agency and private documents are far from complete beyond the 1970s. My examination of the records of correspondence and meetings between Jewish organizations and individuals and the White House in the Truman, Eisenhower, Kennedy, Johnson, Ford and Reagan presidential libraries, exploring the relationship between American Jewry and the presidents, reveals gaps in the holdings that make any meaningful judgements speculative rather than conclusive.

These restrictions apply even more to Israeli records and those of the Palestinians and Arab states. Thus, we are reliant upon public records, memoirs and/or oral testimony of (self-interested) participants, and the writings of investigative journalists. However voluminous and interesting these materials may be, they are no substitute for the detailed official records of policy deliberations made at the time.

Secondly, few scholars and commentators seem able to discuss the relationship without distortions borne of passion and/or bigotry. Thirdly, much of the dialogue (if that is the correct term for the heated exchanges between advocates of both positions) is not about the bilateral relationship as such, but about the wisdom of American policy towards the Middle East. Fourthly, a considerable amount of the discourse reflects animosity towards Israel and its conduct. Finally, people read the present relationship back into the past and few writers appear to remember the years prior to 1967. Before the Arab–Israeli war of 1967, in which Israel demonstrated its superior military capabilities over its adversaries, Israel had sought arms and an alliance with the United States, with little success. The path of the US–Israel relationship had been, and remained for several years to come, far from smooth or untroubled. The current stage of the relationship, in which the United States allegedly demonstrates 'undeviating support for Israel' (Jimmy Carter), could be said to date only from 11 September 2001.[6] Following the al-Quaeda attacks on the US mainland, Israel immediately promoted itself as a key partner in the struggle against terrorism and thereby gained strong American endorsement for its relentless campaign against Palestinian leader Yasser Arafat and his people.

I should clearly state the basic premises on which I base my own position. The first is the unremarkable recognition that the United States follows policies designed to serve its own interests, and the state of Israel does the same. Sometimes the policies and interests of these two nations are congruent, sometimes – more often than acknowledged – they are not. My second underlying premise is that since 1945 the executive branch has been increasingly more important in formulating and executing foreign relations than the legislative branch of the US government. Obviously the two branches of the government are involved, as are any number of third parties we might want to identify. The public record indicates that the Israel lobby focuses its activities primarily on influencing members of Congress and congressional elections. My view is that when it comes to comparing power (the executive) and influence (the lobby and Congress), power wins every time. In the years since World War II, the influence of Congress in determining foreign policy has declined, notwithstanding the power Congress exercises over appropriations bills. The Israel lobby has grown in size at least, if not in power. However, the power of the executive has expanded exponentially.

Increasingly, the National Security Council, the secretary of state and a few trusted advisors, together with the president, make up a small elite who determines US foreign policy. This elite group is largely immune from the political considerations lobby groups depend upon for their effectiveness. Executive decisions are made away from the full light of public exposure. The records of such decisions made in the past thirty or more years are inaccessible – despite the revelations of investigative journalists and self-serving memoirs. Most of my evidence comes from White House files. These files reveal the inescapable truth that once the president and his advisors identify an interest group that is seeking to challenge or alter the course of executive branch policies – especially in the vital area of foreign policy and national security – the president acts to counter its influence, more often than not successfully.[7]

I should mention two further caveats before proceeding. The first is to remind ourselves that the executive branch does not speak, and has not spoken, with one voice on the question of relations with Israel. Deep internal divisions have always made the formulation of a consistent Middle East policy difficult. Presidents, national security advisors and departmental heads have rarely agreed on the extent to which the United States should support Israel. Attempts to measure the influence of particular individuals or groups on the decision-making process that do not explore the multitude of factors at work within the executive branch are simply inadequate.

Next, we assume that Israelis and diaspora Jews share identical views about Israel, and the relationship between Israelis and the diaspora. They do not and never have. There was considerable disagreement between Israelis and Jews in the United States – especially in the early years of the state – over the meaning of Israel and who was to speak for Israelis and who was to speak for Jewish nationals of other countries. Israel's first prime minister, David Ben Gurion, did not want competitors among the Zionist leaders of the United States telling him how to run the foreign or domestic policies of Israel, nor did he want them telling him how to define modern Jewish identity. He wanted American Jewry to do what it was told, which was essentially to support Israel in everything it did. There was a conscious policy of 'negation of the diaspora'.[8]

In the United States, Israel initially acted as a catalyst, becoming part of the ethnic identity of American Jews. The 'inner reinforcement' of Jewish values in Israel was an important stimulant to American Jews.[9] Over time, however, a majority found they had less need for Israel and distanced themselves from the Zionist solution to the issue of living a Jewish life. Israel's survival was important for their sense of Jewish identity, and its destruction would constitute one of their greatest personal tragedies, but American Jews began to believe that Israel was more dependent upon them for survival than they were dependent upon Israel. American Jews dramatically increased their direct financial contributions and political lobbying for US support for Israel following the 1967 war. This led them to believe they could, or should, dictate to Israelis how to behave. Israelis, meanwhile, bitterly resented what they saw as gratuitous intrusion into Israeli political and security matters.[10]

In fact, while American Jews remain staunchly pro-Israel, ideologically they have felt free to criticize the Israeli occupation of the West Bank and other policies relating to the Palestinians. In 1991, the American Jewish Committee survey of Jewish attitudes towards Israel indicated that 68 per cent agreed that 'caring about Israel is a very important part of my being a Jew'. 72 per cent said they felt 'close to Israel'. At the same time 55 per cent had no objection to American Jews publicly criticizing Israeli government policies. For their part, Israelis remained reluctant to recognize that the American Jewry had its own identity, voice or power. They still wanted Jews in the United States to do what they were told by Israel and for them to support the Jewish state without question. American leaders were described and dismissed as 'self appointed'.[11] The paradox is that, while so dismissing them, Israeli leaders overestimated the influence of the Israel lobby in Washington politics.

It is also a mistake to think that rabbis and communal leaders speak for diaspora Jews or for Israelis. To rabbis and communal leaders in diaspora communities, encouraging support for Israel, and discouraging dissent, is a means of consolidating Jewish ethnic/cultural identity. In recent years, support for Israel has diminished among the younger generation of American Jews. This is why there is such concern among the leaders of establishment Jewish groups about recent expressions of criticism by Jews of Israeli policies towards the West Bank settlements, Jerusalem and the treatment of Palestinians. In Israel public debate over security and political issues is far more lively and 'robust' than that taking place within diaspora communities.[12]

How do Israelis view America? Most regard the United States as Israel's closest friend, obligingly acting as its protector, banker and champion in the United Nations. The United States carries out the wishes of Israel and supports its policies. Yossi Melman and Dan Raviv describe the relationship between the United States and Israel as one of the strongest, if strangest, in history. They note that it cannot be explained by one single event, personality or motive, but rather is the product of unexpected occurrences and dramatic coincidences and add that the whole of the relationship is larger than its parts. They believe the United States acts this way because of a sense of guilt over the Holocaust, a sense of a shared Judeo-Christian culture, a political identification with a democratic Israel, and shared ideals and goals in the international arena. In addition, Israel sees America as the location of the largest Jewish community in the world, well educated, wealthy, highly motivated and organized, and electorally strategically located to exercise significant influence over the county's political processes.[13]

Israel allegedly benefits by receiving US support for what it regards as its ongoing war of survival. Israeli revisionist historian Tom Segev attributes the 1978 Camp David agreements, the peace agreements with Egypt and Jordan, the 1993 Oslo Accords with the PLO, and Israel's withdrawal from Lebanon in 2000 to the sponsorship of the United States and the willingness of the American people to finance them.[14]

However, critics of Israeli policy like Segev and American commentator Noam Chomsky complain that the United States has assisted Israel to function as a colonial settler and nationalist occupying state, at the very least since 1967. Since that year, Israel has been an occupier rather than victim. To its critics, Israel has been able to sustain this policy because of capital inflow from the United States, 70 per cent of which, they argue, was not intended for economic gain but was provided to enable Israel to maintain a strong military force.[15]

As in all such situations, there is sufficient truth in the misperceptions constructed about US–Israel relations to sustain and satisfy most people. The positive images of Israel extolled by successive presidents as well as the majority of Americans, and the negative, denigrating portrayals of Arab states and Muslims, especially since 11 September 2001, have significantly influenced the formulation of US attitudes towards Israel. However, we must keep in mind that the world of perception is a world of smoke and mirrors. It should not replace the empirical world in which we live and act.

II

The relationship between the United States and Israel is not as straightforward as the scenarios outlined above suggest. The United States had less to do with the parties reaching the agreements singled out by Segev than he asserts. Washington went along with them because they promised lessened conflict. What we describe as a dependency relationship is a failure to recognize the nation of Israel acting independently of US direction. While the United States and Israel may see eye-to-eye on many issues relating to the Middle East, it is doubtful that the Americans are capable of controlling Israeli actions – especially when it comes to questions relating to Israeli security. Israel has framed its conflict with the Palestinians (and other Arab states) in existential terms; Israelis believe they are engaged in a struggle in which the survival of the state is at stake. Haunted by memories of the Holocaust, there is no way Israel's leaders will allow their policies to be dictated to – or shaped – by any outside party, including the United States.

In reality, the United States has never agreed with Israel's expansionist policies in relation to the territories it occupied in the 1967 war, or Israel's refusal to accept a viable independent Palestinian state. Little noticed in the heated exchanges about the nature of the US–Israel relationship is that the United States has not formally recognized Israel's annexation of East Jerusalem or the Golan Heights, and has not recognized the legality of the West Bank settlements. What successive administrations have done since 1967 is to make the best of a bad situation. There is little the United States could do, or could have done, that would have made any substantive difference to Israeli policy or behaviour, short of military intervention, to enforce a solution backed by the US/UN. That was the situation in 1947–48, and has remained the situation since. There is little evidence to suggest that a reduction in US financial or military assistance would significantly alter Israel's policies. It is inconceivable that Israel's leaders, who have lived in the shadow of the Holocaust, would allow the state's security policies to be dictated or shaped by an outside power, however strong the relationship. Israel's leaders have made that plain enough over the years. Indeed, US economice 'assistance' programmes to Israel were scheduled to cease at the end of 2008. The term 'assistance' in this context is something of a misnomer, but that is another story. If the United States refused to provide or sell weapons or make loans available to Israel, it would simply further develop its own already strong arms industry, and look elsewhere to countries such as the United Kingdom and France to supplement its ground and air equipment elsewhere.

For the first 30 years after 1948, there seemed little pressing need for the United States to intervene militarily. The neighbouring Arab states acquiesced in the *status quo*. Jordan benefited, annexing most of what was to have been the Palestinian state. Arab states would not have welcomed the presence of American troops in Palestine, even to assist in the formation of a Palestinian state, any more than they welcomed them in Lebanon in the 1980s or Iraq today. Corrosive tensions between the Arab states kept them from providing any unified support for a Palestinian state – something the Palestinians and Israelis understood very well. The Palestinians appeared in disarray and unable to form or govern a state of their own. In addition, US military intervention would almost certainly have invited an unwelcome military response from the USSR, something Washington wanted to avoid. Following 1967, even given Israel's close call in the 1973 Arab–Israeli war, there was no way, short of all out war against a very militarily powerful and triumphant Israel, that Israeli ambitions and policies could have been curtailed.

Let us be clear at the outset what military intervention in this context would have involved. Secretary of State George Marshall told President Harry S. Truman in March 1947 that 100,000 US troops would have been needed to stop the fighting between Jews and Arabs in Palestine.[16] The United Kingdom had been unable to do so with as many as 80,000 troops. Since 1967 the number needed would have been considerably higher. About 6,000–7,000 United Nations Interim Force in Lebanon (UNIFIL) troops did not prevent Israel's invasion of Lebanon in 1982, nor three times since, and it is unclear how many more troops would have been required to discourage the Israeli assaults. Nor has hostile world opinion deterred Israel from pursuing its goals. The ongoing targeted assassinations against those it regards as Palestinian terrorists, its continued settlement building in the West Bank, and its invasions of Lebanon and the recently evacuated Gaza Strip are just the most obvious examples of unilateral Israeli actions.

The US–Israel relationship is not static; it has undergone dramatic shifts. For the first decade of Israel's existence, the United States was hesitant to embrace and support the Jewish state. Its future was uncertain, the population – certainly its leadership – was drawn from the Eastern Bloc in Europe and suspiciously left-ist in political orientation, and US oil interests appeared far from secure in face of Arab hostility to the new state. The Arab–Israeli wars of 1967 and 1973 brought about a major shift in American thinking towards Israel, and by the end of the Nixon administration Israel was regarded as an important regional strategic ally. Since then, strengthening ties with Israel has become a central element of US foreign policy. This transformation has been mirrored by the rise in activity and visibility of what is known as the Israel lobby in American domestic politics.

An enormous amount has been written on the Israel lobby and its role in controlling, shaping or determining the US–Israel relationship. Well known critical commentators include Noam Chomsky, George W. and Douglas B. Ball,

Cheryl Rubenberg, and Paul Findley. Most recently, John Mearsheimer and Stephen Walt have reignited the debate with their book *The Israel Lobby and US Foreign Policy*. Mearsheimer and Walt do not add much that is new in terms of the overall arguments, but they do bring the debate up to the War in Iraq, and their critique is the most measured in tone. They restate and reinforce the arguments of previous critics of the lobby, particularly those of Janice J. Terry.[17]

Who is the Israel lobby and what do (people say) they do? I am happy to use the definition provided by Mearsheimer and Walt: 'We use the Lobby as a convenient short-hand term for the loose coalition of individuals and organizations who actively work to shape US foreign policy in a pro-Israel direction'.[18] The lobby, they emphasize, is not a unified movement with a central leadership, and individuals within it disagree on certain issues. Its core comprises American Jews who make a significant effort in their daily lives to bend US foreign policy so that it advances Israel's interests. They also acknowledge that not all Jewish-Americans are part of the lobby, because Israel is not a salient issue for many of them. In a 2004 survey, for example, roughly 36 per cent of Jewish-Americans said they were either 'not very' or 'not at all' emotionally attached to Israel.[19] The lobby also includes prominent Christian evangelicals (Christian Zionists) who believe Israel's rebirth is part of Biblical prophecy, support its expansionist agenda, and think pressuring Israel is contrary to God's will. In addition, the lobby's membership includes neoconservative gentiles.

Mearsheimer and Walt detail how the lobby musters votes for congressional candidates who are pro-Israel, instigates letter-writing campaigns, raises financial contributions and supports pro-Israel organizations. Key organizations in the lobby also directly target the administration in power. The lobby tries to prevent critics of the Jewish state from getting important foreign policy appointments which, Mearsheimer and Walt claim, forces aspiring policymakers to become overt supporters of Israel. This is why public critics of Israeli policy have become an endangered species in the US foreign policy establishment. The two authors argue that the situation is especially pronounced in the Bush administration, whose ranks include fervently pro-Israel individuals like Elliot Abrams, John Bolton, Douglas Feith, I. Lewis ('Scooter') Libby, Richard Perle, Paul Wolfowitz and David Wurmser. These officials consistently pushed for policies favoured by Israel and backed by organizations in the lobby.[20]

Mearsheimer and Walt contend that, in addition to trying to influence government policy directly, the lobby strives also to shape public perceptions about Israel and the Middle East. Accordingly, pro-Israel organizations work hard to influence the media, think tanks and academia, because these institutions are critical in shaping popular opinion. In Washington and around the world, the American Israel Public Affairs Committee (AIPAC) is seen as the voice of the American Jewish community. AIPAC is a private corporation and its executive committee includes representatives from each of the 50 organizations that make up the Conference of Presidents of Major American Jewish Organizations, from B'nai B'rith and Hadassah to major synagogues. AIPAC is their voice in Washington. It cultivates influence and it has become bi-partisan in approach. Former Illinois Congressman Paul Findley claims that presidents fear it and that

Congress does its bidding. Prestigious universities shun academic programmes and grants which it opposes. Giants of the media and military leaders buckle under its pressure.[21]

AIPAC's critics believe all this is the result of the active efforts of around 250,000 Jews representing a total of between five and six million people who make up between two-and-a-half and three per cent of the population. In reality, in 1967 AIPAC had been broke; in 1974, under its second head Morris Amity, it had less than 10 staff members, and Amity had to explain even to Jewish audiences that AIPAC was not OPEC. When Thomas Dine took over as executive officer in 1980, it had less than 10,000 members with an operating budget of less than $1.5 million.[22]

Mearsheimer and Walt argue that what sets the Israel lobby apart is 'its extraordinary effectiveness'.[23] They hasten to add, before proceeding to lament the activities of the lobby, that:

> There is nothing improper about American Jews and their Christian allies attempting to sway US policy toward Israel. The lobby's activities are not the sort of conspiracy depicted in anti-Semitic tracts like the *Protocols of the Elders of Zion*. For the most part, the individuals and groups that comprise the lobby are doing what other special interest groups do, just much better.

They also assert that the pressure of the lobby to support Israel distorts American Middle East policy decisions. US support for Israel is, according to Mearsheimer and Walt, 'a liability' in the war on terror and the broader effort to deal with rogue states.[24]

III

The Jewish/Israel lobby was small and marginal to policymaking in the Middle East until the late 1960s. Lobbyists had to be careful of the charge of dual loyalty. During the 1950s they favoured supporting US policies, rather than those of Israel, whenever a conflict of interest appeared imminent. The Israel lobby was never a shaper of policy; it was rather more an augmentation and adjustment, a fine-tuning, rather than a determinant of policy. It worked more efficiently when what it was proposing coincided with policies of administrations; when it supported US policies.[25]

What is missing from Mearsheimer and Walt and their predecessors is any detailed evidence of just how the activities of the lobby were or are translated into policy. In their chapters purporting to show how the lobby 'guides' the policy process and how it 'shapes' recent American Middle East policy, there is little more than assertions that Israel, through the lobby, has been effective in achieving its goal of a supportive policy from Washington. It is a terrific exploration of the US political landscape, but it does not reveal the deliberations of policymakers. Mearsheimer and Walt argue, for example, that the Israel lobby was behind the 2003 US invasion of Iraq, citing several statements by prominent public figures to that effect. Prominent Israeli leaders and several US Jewish neoconservative spokesmen argued hard for the invasion of Iraq; but the United States would almost certainly be in Iraq today even if there had been no Israel lobby. The origins of the tragic Iraq quagmire go back in US history at least to the administration of George H. W. Bush. Many Israeli leaders opposed the attack on Iraq, favouring an attack on Iran. The case could be made that they went along with the Iraq invasion knowing that Iran was still on Washington's agenda.

The public actions of the lobby do not, and indeed cannot, demonstrate the causal link between those actions and policy outcomes. Often policy emanating from Washington coincides with the wishes of lobby members, but that is not proof of causation. And therein lies the problem. My research in the presidential libraries suggests that long-standing personal and informal friendships and associations were far more important to presidents, secretaries of state, other executive heads and their advisors than the actions of lobbyists. The relationship between Arthur Dean and Secretary of State John Foster Dulles during the Eisenhower administration might be seen as one example of this kind of connection. Dean worked with Dulles in the Wall Street offices of Oliver and Cromwell prior to Dulles being appointed secretary of state, succeeding him as chairman of the firm. Dulles used him as an important channel of communication between himself and the Israeli ambassador. Jewish and non-Jewish friends of Dulles urged a whole raft of policies, sometimes favouring Israel, often not.[26]

Virtually everyone involved in the debate about the US–Israel relationship has something to gain by distorting the power of what was for many years called the Jewish lobby, and is now known as the Israel lobby. Israel benefits from the notion that it is backed by the diplomatic voice and force of the United States. The Arab states, including the Palestinians, can argue that their plight is the result of an all-powerful US–Israel combination that perpetuates their tragic situation, and thereby deflect criticism from their own shortcomings and failures. American Jews, especially religious and lay leaders, can take credit for playing a prominent role in maintaining the security of Israel, enhancing their own importance in their respective communities in the process. And members of Congress can also point to their voting record of support for Israel in the expectation of ensuring Jewish voter and financial backing.[27]

The question is to what extent the activities of the Israel lobby influence, shape, direct or determine US foreign policy towards Israel and the Middle East more broadly. Put another way, the question is would US policy toward Israel and the Middle East be significantly different if there were no Israel lobby? It is hard to see how. The Middle East remains strategically important to the United States, and its oil resources are central to the well-being of the US economy. The United States and the Arab states of the region are co-dependent, and their interests and relationships are independent of the existence (or non-existence) of Israel, and America's relationship with the Jewish state. The Arab states (and the Muslim world as well) did not translate their anger at US support for Israel into anti-American policies. During the Cold War most of the Arab states in the Middle East were highly conservative. They saw the Soviet Union and communism as a far greater threat to their regimes than any US pro-Israeli posture.[28]

IV

An objective assessment of the public record suggests that the Israel lobby has been nowhere near as effective as its critics maintain. In no particular order of importance let me list a number of occasions between 1947 and 2001 where US and Israeli interests have not coincided, and where the United States has not shown Israel the unwavering support the Israel lobby allegedly sought. Rather than being 'extraordinarily effective', the record suggests that the Israel lobby has had relatively modest success in its efforts to produce a pro-Israel policy.

It is repeatedly asserted that the United States played a key role in the establishment of the Jewish state, and that prompt US recognition assured Israel's future. To this is often added the notion that the United States was motivated by guilt or remorse over the Holocaust. Moreover, some argue that President Truman, in response to Jewish/Zionist lobbying, recognized the new state in order to secure the 'Jewish vote' in the 1948 presidential election.[29] Much of this is propaganda and exaggeration. Most of the senior figures in the administration in the years 1945–48 opposed the establishment of a Jewish state in Palestine, felt little or no guilt over US policy in relation to the Holocaust – in fact, quite the opposite, they felt that they had been the saviours of European Jewry – and were motivated more by the need to reduce the cost of occupying and stabilizing Europe by agreeing to allow Jewish displaced persons to migrate to Palestine.

The United States initially supported the partition of Palestine because the Soviet Union supported it, and Truman was not going to allow the Soviet Union to gain a foothold in the region at the expense of the United Kingdom and the West if he could prevent it by supporting partition.[30] If Truman's motivation was to attract Jewish voters, and I do not believe it was, it was very ineptly handled by the president and the Democratic party. Truman did not carry the states he might well have expected to if he had had the support of the Jewish vote.

When fighting began between the Jewish Agency and Palestinians in the period from January through May 1948, the United States refused to sell or provide arms to the Jewish side and the Jewish Agency purchased arms with Soviet approval from Czechoslovakia. Once it became clear that the British were withdrawing and the future seemed uncertain, the United States advocated trusteeship of the area in dispute. There was considerable concern in Washington that the socialist Jews of the new state might align themselves with communist Russia and it was, in fact, the Soviet Union that was the first to offer *de jure* recognition.[31] The United States held back until early 1949. In 1950, following Israel's independence, the United States slapped an arms embargo on the area including Israel (the Tripartite Declaration of the United States, United Kingdom and France). None of these actions reflect strong support for Israel.

Washington did agree to Negev being part of Israel, largely because it was thought it would make the Israelis more amenable to negotiate and less insecure. Given that it was unthinkable in the West that, once established, Israel would be dismantled, the choice for the United States was to defend Israel with US troops or to sell it its arms. The second course was far cheaper and easier, with less economic or military involvement. Comparing US actions in relation to Jordan and Lebanon to those in relation to Israel, we see that in 1958 the United States landed marines in Lebanon (and again in the early 1980s) to defend the government, and in 1957 and 1963 dispatched the Sixth Fleet in the Eastern Mediterranean to defend Jordan's King Hussein against Palestinian coups. During this period, Saudi Arabia was armed, Egypt was armed, Iraq was armed and Israel was armed. Up until the mid 1960s France, Germany and the United Kingdom were the principal suppliers of arms to Israel.

There were other examples of US opposition to Israeli policies against the wishes of the Israel lobby. In 1953, the United States opposed Israel's scheme to divert water from the Jordan River north of Lake Kinneret, and Israel later (in 1959) developed its National Water Carrier from the lake itself. Israel did not inform Washington of its participation in the UK, French and Israeli allied attack on Egypt in October 1956, and Eisenhower's decisive action resulted in Israel's withdrawal from the Sinai following the assault. Egyptian president Gamal Abdul Nasser's decision to turn to the Soviet Union in the mid-1950s had little to do with US support for Israel. Nasser had sought Soviet economic assistance because of the US-sponsored Baghdad Pact, Washington's reversal of its promise to provide economic assistance for the building of the Aswan Dam, and Dulles's hostility to neutralism. Nasser was understandably more hostile to Israel after 1956, but not because of Israel's relationship with Washington.

In the Eisenhower Doctrine promulgated in early 1957, the United States pledged economic and military aid to any nation in the Middle East threatened by international communism. However, it was not invoked when Israel felt threatened by a Syrian-Soviet arms deal in the Summer of 1957 or the formation of the Syrian-Egyptian United Arab Republic (UAR) in February 1958. The United States also rejected Israel's efforts to join NATO in late 1957. In the Summer of 1958 Washington refused Israel's offer of help to contain Nasser when it was thought he was planning a coup against King Hussein. In August 1958, Dulles called Israel 'this millstone around our necks'.[32] During these years, Israel and the Israel lobby had sought, without much success, to play upon American's sense of guilt over the Holocaust to evoke US sympathy for Israel.[33]

US military assistance to Israel has attracted considerable attention, but it should be remembered that in the mid-1960s the United States became the principal arms supplier to pro-Western Jordan, deepening the American commitment to King Hussein despite initial Israeli objections. Jordan, not Israel, was seen as the key to precarious stability in the Middle East. In 1963, President John F. Kennedy ordered the Sixth Fleet and a battalion of US Marines into the eastern Mediterranean to ensure the continuity of the Jordanian monarchy against a potential coup by Palestinian-led rebels. In August 1964, the United States agreed to supply Jordan with tanks, and 18 months later (February 1966) with combat aircraft. In 1968–70, after the June 1967 war, 100 tanks and 36 F-104 Jets were shipped to Jordan. Israel's attack on Samu in Jordan in November 1966 upset Washington. The assault damaged US interests and permanently shattered an Israel-Jordan unwritten agreement not to cross each other's borders. The United

States encouraged the sale of German tanks to Israel in 1964 as a way to compensate and restrain Israeli leaders who were alarmed by Soviet arms sales to Iraq, Syria and Egypt. Throughout this period, Washington provided Israel with arms and economic aid in order to compensate it for not taking more aggressive action, such as waging pre-emptive war on Syria and Egypt. Frustrated Israeli leaders responded by threatening to seek arms from the USSR.[34]

The United States would not enter any agreement guaranteeing Israel security in the 1950s and 1960s despite Israel's claims about a communist threat, and did not provide arms until Kennedy agreed to sell 'defensive' Hawk anti-aircraft missiles in August 1962. Although Kennedy agreed to supply the missiles because Israel promised it would not go ahead with the development of nuclear weapons, it did so anyway. Nor could Washington persuade Israel to move on the issue of Palestinian refugees. During these years, the United States remained cool and distant according to Israeli revisionist historian Avi Shlaim. Johnson refused to add offensive weapons to arms sales to Israel as Washington regarded the Jewish state as stronger than its neighbours. The United States wanted Arab support for the containment of communism, and Washington always put Cold War considerations ahead of Israel's interests.[35]

The United States was powerless to stop Israel in 1967. Nor, despite the Eisenhower Doctrine and a former verbal assurance given by Dulles to Golda Meir concerning the Straits of Tiran, would Washington provide Israel with a NATO-type guarantee that an attack on Israel would elicit an armed US response in support of the Jewish state, which may have acted as some restraint upon Israel. US intelligence revealed that Nasser's troop formations were defensive. A majority of Americans would not have supported US military intervention to support Israel. Israel's cabinet decision to go to war in early June 1967 was made despite an explicit warning from President Lyndon B. Johnson that if it did launch a pre-emptive attack it would be on its own.[36]

Furthermore, until recently most commentators argued that in the case of the 1973 war, Israel was caught unawares, or that Egypt's was a surprise attack. We now know that Israeli leaders chose a course that they knew left Egypt few choices but to attack, and that they did not inform the United States, or their own population for that matter, of their knowledge or their decision. In April 1973 the Israeli cabinet decided not to inform Washington of its decision to refuse to negotiate with Egypt when presented with a proposal from President Anwar Sadat in February 1973 that included ending the conflict between Israel and Egypt within a framework of an overall comprehensive settlement of the Arab–Israeli conflict. Israel's cabinet knew that its refusal would most likely lead to war with Egypt in the near future. Sadat had expelled Soviet forces in the middle of 1972, and he believed if Israel accepted the settlement he proposed war could be avoided. Faced with Tel Aviv's intransigence and arrogance, Washington could not influence Israel to negotiate with Sadat. At the end of the 1973 war, the United States rescued units of the Egyptian army by pressing Israel to stop advancing and by insisting on a cease-fire. The United States became Egypt's patron in the 1980s, after the Camp David peace agreement, providing large-scale arms supplies and other military and financial assistance while asking for little in return.[37]

From the 1970s through to the 1990s, the United States tried to avoid antagonizing Arabs by not being seen to support Israel. Washington believed that if it supported Israel, conservative Arab nations, would turn to the USSR for arms and support, fuelling an arms race and instability in the region. Accordingly, the United States projected itself as the honest broker of disengagement and peace agreements between Israel and the Arab states. However, in the peace treaties signed between Israel and Egypt in 1979, and Israel and Jordan in 1994, the initiatives did not come from the United States but from the parties themselves. Also, the 1993 Israel-PLO Oslo Accords came through private negotiations of the parties, rather than through any US initiative.[38]

Washington nevertheless maintained some semblance of balance during the 1980s and 1990s. The United States arranged safe passage out of Lebanon for Palestinian leader Yasser Arafat in 1982 when he was under siege in Beirut by the Israeli army. Despite the opposition of the Israel lobby, Washington initiated a dialogue with the Palestine Liberation Organization (PLO) in 1988 and often ignored the terrorism of PLO member groups. It became the patron of the Palestinians between 1993 and 2000. The United States worked hard to mobilize financial aid to the Palestinian Authority. Arafat was frequently invited to the White House and the United States refrained from criticism of the Palestinian Authority. President Bill Clinton went to Gaza and made a very sympathetic speech to an audience of Palestinian leaders. Finally, the United States tried to broker a peace agreement that would produce an independent Palestinian state with its capital in East Jerusalem. After Arafat rejected the US peace attempts and did not implement the ceasefires he promised, criticism from American leaders was restrained. The United States did not express an 'anti-Palestinian' policy except in the sense that it opposed Palestinian efforts to destroy Israel's existence, while supporting efforts to find a compromise solution to the conflict that would help satisfy moderate Palestinian goals.[39]

The main shift in US–Israel relations occurred following the tragic events of 11 September 2001. The Bush administration dispensed with previous policies in which, however implausible it may have appeared to some, the United States sought to strike a delicate balance in their dealings with Israel and the Arab states in order to be seen as a credible mediator in the Arab–Israeli conflict, and decided to regard Israel as a valuable ally in the war against terrorism. In the past the United States had urged an end to violent clashes between Israelis and Palestinians and others. Bush abandoned this role, some would say pretence, of the United States as honest broker in the Arab–Israeli conflict in favour of a pro-Israeli policy. Bush's decision to give Israel the green light to destroy Hezbollah in Lebanon in 2006 was seen as clear and dramatic evidence of this shift. However, like President Ronald Reagan before him, who had approved the 1982 Israeli assault on the PLO, Bush did not want the Israeli invasion of Lebanon to weaken the Lebanese government. Some argue that this was the work of the Israel lobby. Given the chaos in Iraq, I find it hard to see how the United States could have done much to influence the actions of Iran, Syria, Lebanon, Hezbollah, the Palestinian Authority or Israel, the major actors in the catastrophic events of 2006 leading to Israel's invasion, short of the dispatch of armed force – an untenable alternative.

V

At the heart of the attack on the influence of the Israel lobby is the assumption that a pro-Israel policy is damaging to US interests in the Middle East. The elephant in the room is, obviously, American oil interests. However, oil is not a major factor in influencing the US relationship with Israel, and has not been one since 1950 when the Truman administration approved the financial arrangement known as the 50/50 split with Saudi Arabia. Under this imaginative scheme the Arabian American Oil Company (ARAMCO), which held the largest oil concession in Saudi Arabia, agreed to pay 50 per cent of its oil revenues to the Kingdom, and in return the US treasury agreed that it would regard such payments as income tax paid to the foreign state – although at the time Saudi Arabia had no income tax.[40]

In effect this meant a direct treasury-to-treasury transfer. It was a form of foreign economic (and soon military) assistance. Congress was not involved in the negotiations or decision. It was made by the executive in order to secure the close strategic cooperation of Saudi Arabia in the establishment of air and sea bases to protect the southeastern flank of Europe from communist encroachment. By 1951 Saudi Arabia was receiving $100 million of US taxpayers money, a sum far in excess of aid provided to Israel. Furthermore, the oil industry informed Washington in the early 1950s that although the Arab oil-producing states did not like the fact of Israel, they would not allow US policy towards the Jewish state to interfere with cooperation on oil production. They have kept their word.[41]

US oil policy in the past 50 years has been much misunderstood. Price has not been governed by supply shortage – there has in fact been an oversupply of oil. The primary goal of Washington and the major oil cartels has been to keep the price of oil low enough to ensure prosperity and enable capitalist growth in the United States, but high enough to ensure corporate profits. The key to the importance of oil is it interconnectedness with the arms, financial, engineering and construction industries, and their relationship with Washington. Between the 1950s and 2000 the world's arms trade underwent privatization. In the period 1963–1974, arms sales to the Middle East went from 10 per cent of global arms imports to 36 per cent, half of which was supplied by the United States. Israel is a small player in this context. Saudi Arabia spent $52.4 billion between 1985 and 1992 on arms imports. The four major defence contractors in the United States, namely, Boeing, Northrop Grumman, Lockheed Martin and Raytheon, sold over $150 billion worth of arms in the 1990s. From 1994 to 2002, the Pentagon concluded over 3,000 contracts valued at $300 billion with 12 military/service/ construction companies. 2,700 of the contracts went to Bechtel and Kellogg Brown & Root, many to Middle East projects. What Washington is seeking was to increase or decrease tensions in the Middle East in such a way as to create the conditions to maximise the profitability of these interconnected interests.[42]

To argue that the Israel lobby has anything like the influence and role of oil and its related interests – especially during both the Bush administrations – is to grossly overstate the case. The sums transferred to the Arab oil producing nations – in fact informal and unacknowledged economic assistance – make the amounts provided to Israel seem paltry by comparison. What is more, the United States has not just invested cash in these countries, it has built huge military installations, provided military assistance, overthrown governments and protected others by military force and warfare on a scale never dreamed of in relation to Israel and its security.

The country in the Middle East with which the United States had the closest special relationship was, and remains, Saudi Arabia. In 1945, President Franklin Delano Roosevelt told the King of Saudi Arabia, Ibn Saud, that his country was more important to US diplomacy than virtually any other country.[43] The other country of equal importance at the time was, of course, the United Kingdom. Saudi, Iranian, Iraqi, Kuwaiti and Gulf oil flows were essential to the economic reconstruction of Europe and US forces in Japan and Korea. In the early 1950s the CIA assisted in the overthrow of Iranian Prime Minister Mohammed Mossadeq. The United States built a military base in Dhahran, and in the early 1970s Secretary of State Henry Kissinger prevented USSR-backed Iraq from gaining hegemony over the Persian Gulf by strengthening with military force the monarchical governments of Iran and Saudi Arabia. Successive US administrations and the Saudis have insulated that relationship from the US relationship with Israel.[44] No amount of special pleading will alter the fact that Israel – and/or the Israeli-Palestinian conflict – has hardly been centre stage in the formulation of US military or foreign policy in the Gulf region over the past two decades.

In the end, however misguided and mistaken, the misperceptions of the US–Israel relationship have become the reality, and there appears no way of altering that. The truth that lies beneath the surface events and emotional currents surrounding them has not yet been revealed. The US–Israel relationship is now enshrined in the public and official mind as the perceptions would have it; it is shrouded in myth and legend.

Notes

1 See, for example, Steven L. Spiegel, *The Other Arab Israeli Conflict*: *Making America's Middle East Policy from Truman to Reagan, Chicago*: Chicago University Press, 1985.
2 Yossi Melman and Dan Raviv, *Friends in Deed*: *Inside the US–Israel Alliance*, New York: Hyperion, 1994, pp. 216–22.
3 George W. Ball and Douglas B. Ball, *The Passionate Attachment*: *America's Involvement with Israel, 1947 to the Present*, New York: Norton, 1992, p. 11. In 1986, American scholar Cheryl Rubenberg argued that after the establishment of Israel in 1948 in the face of Arab opposition, the United States assumed what was termed a 'moral commitment' to assure the security and survival of the Jewish state. The definition of US national interest in the Middle East was expanded to include the 'security and survival of Israel'. According to Rubenberg, 'such a moral commitment to another state, especially one founded on psychological imperatives, is unique in the annals

of international relations and foreign policy. . . . Nothing in the core values (as this concept is understood in international relations theory) of American political culture accounts for a definition of the national interest that includes a commitment to the security and survival of Israel'. Cheryl A. Rubenberg, *Israel and the American National Interest: A Critical Examination,* Urbana: University of Chicago Press, 1986, p. 10.

4 The most recent attack on the relationship and the role of the Israel lobby is that of John J. Mearsheimer and Stephen M. Walt, *The Israel Lobby and US Foreign Policy*, London: Allen Lane, 2007.

5 Abba Eban to Israel Foreign Ministry, memorandum of conversation, 8 October 1953, FOF, 2455/10, Israel State Archives.

6 Jimmy Carter, *Palestine: Peace Not Apartheid*, New York: Simon and Schuster, 2006, p. 17.

7 President Dwight D. Eisenhower was especially adept at misleading reporters at press conferences.

8 Melvin Urofsky, *We Are One! American Jewry and Israel*, New York: Anchor, 1978, pp. 34–44, details the dispute between the American Jewish Committee and David Ben Gurion about the relationship linking American Jews and Israel.

9 Gershon Shaked, 'Can Israeli Culture Survive the American Challenge?', *Moment*, 1989, vol. 14, pp. 57–59.

10 Jerold S. Auerbach, *Are We One? Jewish Identity in the United States and Israel*, New Brunswick: Rutgers University Press, 2001, explores the troubled relationship between American Jews and Israel in the years following 1967. See especially Chapter 3.

11 J. J. Goldberg, 'Separated by a Common Cause', *The Jerusalem Report*, 27 February 1992, pp. 18–22.

12 Contrast, for example, the difference in the tone of reviews of Meirsheimer and Walt, The Israel Lobby published in Israel to those written by Jewish reviewers in the United States. See Daniel Levy, 'Deal With It', *Ha'aretz*, 9 October 2007. Levy describes the response of some American reviewers as 'pavlovian' in their vilification of the book. He states that the book is 'not a hateful screed. Painful, yes. Prejudiced, no'.

13 Melman and Raviv, *Friends in Deed*, p. xiv. See also Michael B. Oren, *Power, Faith and Fantasy: America in the Middle East, 1776 to the Present*, New York: Norton, 2006.

14 Tom Segev, *Elvis in Jerusalem: Post-Zionism and the Americanization of Israel*, New York: Holt, 2002, p. 64. See also Bashir Abu-Manneh, 'Israel in US Empire', *New Formations*, 2006, vol. 59, pp. 34–51.

15 Baruch Kimmerling has described the militarization of Israel, commenting that the notion of a civilian military has been a dominant factor in Israeli society. Religious Zionism has amplified the desire to control all of the conquered area to make it irreversible. Kimmerling laments that this has corrupted Israeli society to the point that it has become what he describes as a Herrenvolk democracy in the image of South Africa rather than a liberal democracy. Kimmerling, *Politicide: Ariel Sharon's War Against the Palestinians*, London: Verso, 2003, pp. 35–42.

16 Senate Memorandum, State of Israel Folder, McGrath Papers, Harry S Truman Presidential Library, Independence, Mo., cited in Ian J. Bickerton, 'President Truman's Recognition of Israel', *American Jewish Historical Quarterly*, 1968, vol. 58, p. 221.

17 Janice J. Terry, *US Foreign Policy in the Middle East: The Role of Lobbies and Special Interest Groups*, London: Pluto Press, 2005.

18 Mearsheimer and Walt, *The Israel Lobby*, p. 112.

19 Ibid., p. 115.

20 Ibid., p. 239. One trouble with this list is that Feith and Perle, for example, are also members of the Center for Security Policy, the major think tank of the weapons lobby representing the interests of such companies as Lockheed Martin, Northrop Grumman and Boeing.

21 Paul Findley argues that although AIPAC is only a part of the Jewish lobby, in terms of direct effect on public policy it is clearly the most important. 'It is no overstatement to say', he asserts, 'that AIPAC has effectively gained control of virtually all of Capitol Hill's action in Middle East policy. Almost without exception, House and Senate members do its bidding because most of them consider AIPAC to be the direct Capitol Hill representative of a political force that can make or break their chances at election time'. Findley, *They Dare to Speak Out: People and Institutions Confront Israel's Lobby*, Chicago: Lawrence Hill Books, 1989, p. 25.

22 Melvin and Raviv, *Friends in Deed*, pp. 307–9.

23 Mearsheimer and Walt, *The Israel Lobby*, p. 150.

24 Ibid., p. 13.

25 See the correspondence of Joseph Proskauer, President of the American Jewish Committee, in the Dwight D. Eisenhower Presidential Library, Abilene, KS. (hereafter cited as DDEL).

26 Dean was particularly useful in providing Dulles with advice on Israel-Egyptian relations in the months December 1955–March 1956. See Correspondence and Telephone Calls, John Foster Dulles Papers, DDEL.

27 Virtually all presidential candidates since 1948, as well as members of the House and Senate, have made their voting record on matters relating to Israel known during election campaigns.

28 Arthur Goldschmidt Jr., *A Concise History of the Middle East*, 4th ed., Boulder: Westfield Press, 1991, pp. 283–91. See also Adeed Dawisha, *Arab Nationalism in the Twentieth Century: From Triumph to Despair*, Princeton: Princeton University Press, 2003, pp. 160–66.

29 Michael J. Cohen, *Palestine to Israel: From Mandate to Independence*, London: Frank Cass, 1988, pp. 198–220 examines the literature on Truman's recognition of Israel.

30 Bickerton, 'Truman's Recognition of Israel', pp. 226–29.

31 Ibid., pp. 224–25.

32 Avi Shlaim, *The Iron Wall: Israel and the Arab World*, London: Allen Lane, 2000, p. 204.

33 See Files of the American Zionist Organization, DDEL.

34 Zach Levey, 'United States Arms Policy Toward Jordan, 1963–68', *Journal of Contemporary History*, 2006, vol. 41, pp. 527–43.

35 Shlaim, *Iron Wall*, p. 189.

36 Ahron Bregman, *Israel's Wars: A History Since 1947*, London: Routledge, 2000, pp. 82–83.

37 Ibid., pp. 102–23.

38 Shlaim, *Iron Wall*, pp. 512–16.

39 Barry M. Rubin, *The Tragedy of the Middle East*, Cambridge: Cambridge University Press, 2002, pp. 229–34.

40 George C. McGhee, *Envoy to the Middle World: Adventures in Diplomacy*, New York: Harper, 1983, pp. 323–26.

41 'Diminishing Security of Western Interests in the Middle East', memorandum to John Foster Dulles, April 1953, John Foster Dulles Papers, DDEL.

42 Retort et al, *Afflicted Powers: Capital and Spectacle in a New Age of War*, London: Verso, 2005, pp. 67–72.

43 Daniel Yergin, *The Prize: The Epic Quest for Oil, Money and Power*, New York: Simon & Schuster, 1991, pp. 403–5.

44 In more recent times, for example, associates of Secretary of State James Baker and Vice President Richard Cheney, powerful figures in both Bush administrations, had millions of dollars at stake in Middle East oil ventures. It was highly unlikely that these two would favour Israel at the behest of an Israel lobby if they thought doing so would jeopardize American financial interests in region. Retort, *Afflicted Powers*, p. 41.

11 US–Israel relations

A special friendship

Lee Marsden

> We will speak up for our principles and we will stand up for our friends in the world. And one of our most important friends is the State of Israel.
>
> George W. Bush

The United States relationship with Israel has been one of the closest and most controversial relationships the country has experienced since the end of World War II. Ever since President Harry Truman became one of the first world leaders to recognize the existence of the Jewish state in 1948 the relationship has developed and grown over time to become arguably America's most intimate bilateral relationship. Apart from rocky periods under Dwight Eisenhower[1] and the first George Bush, where American national interests in securing oil supplies and Arab support in the Cold and Gulf Wars took precedence, Israel has been supported and sustained by successive administrations. This support has often come at great cost to the United States in terms of economic, military and political support as they have sought to protect and promote the interests of Israel in the face of widespread opposition throughout the Middle East. And yet, after 60 years, that supportive relationship is taken as a given in world politics. Indeed the relationship has deepened significantly under the younger Bush administrations and it is unthinkable for any future prospective presidential candidate to contemplate running for office without declaring unconditional support for the State of Israel.

In the 2008 presidential race, both main party candidates stressed their pro-Israel credentials at the American Israel Public Action Committee (AIPAC) annual policy conference. Barack Obama declared that his commitment to Israel was to 'make sure that the bond between the United States and Israel is unbreakable today, unbreakable tomorrow – and unbreakable forever'.[2] In similar vein John McCain sought to explain what he claimed critics of the alliance are unable to understand:

> They do not fully understand the love of liberty and the pursuit of justice. But they should know those ties cannot be broken. We were brought together by shared ideals and by shared adversity; we have been comrades in struggle and trusted partners in the quest for peace. We are the most natural of allies and like Israel itself – that alliance is forever.[3]

The shared ideals of freedom, liberty, democracy and ultimately prevailing through adversity to a peaceful future is a narrative that has become a mantra for US and Israeli leaders as they stand together against 'autocratic' and 'despotic' forces in the Middle East. In this narrative the United States is able to identify and become as one with a pioneer nation, making the desert blossom and bringing civilization or democracy at least to a lawless region. According to opinion polls this is a discourse that many Americans accept. Throughout the Bush presidency sympathy in the Middle East situation has been overwhelmingly with the Israelis over the Arab nations. At the outset of the Bush administration Gallup polls indicated that support for Israel at 51 per cent was much higher than support for the Arab nations at 16 per cent. By 2007 that support had grown to 58 per cent against 20 per cent for the Arabs.[4] Such high levels of support require further explanation beyond this simple narrative.

In this chapter we consider the US–Israel relationship during the Bush administration seeking to understand the nature and practice of this special relationship. International relations scholars John Mearsheimer and Stephen Walt have suggested that an Israel Lobby exists which has significantly influenced US policy in the Middle East. The chapter goes on to examine the influence of the constituent parts of such a lobby during the Bush years, exploring the Jewish pro-Israel lobby, neoconservatives and Christian Zionist influence on US policy towards Israel and its neighbours in the region, arguing that the Bush presidency was responsive to such influence resulting in policy decisions that strengthened the bilateral relationship while negating prospects for a peaceful resolution of the Israel–Palestinian conflict.

Domestic sources of US policy towards Israel

In March 2006 leading realist scholars John Mearsheimer and Stephen Walt produced one of the most devastating critiques of the US–Israel relationship to have been written. Writing in the *London Review of Books*, the authors castigated a policy they claimed was driven by special interests rather than the national interests of the United States.[5] They identified these special interests as a combination of Jewish supporters of Israel, neoconservatives and Christian evangelicals, who together make up what they describe as an 'Israel Lobby', a loose grouping of organizations which seek to turn US foreign policy in a pro-Israel direction. Simultaneously the authors published their more detailed working papers online and in 2007 produced their seminal work *The Israel Lobby and US Foreign Policy*.[6]

The central thrust of Mearsheimer and Walt's argument that US support for Israel increases anti-Americanism and runs counter to its interests is summarized by the authors:

> Steadfast support for Israel can no longer be justified by the argument that it helps us defeat a great power rival; instead, backing Israel unconditionally helps make the United States a target for radical extremists and makes

America look callous and hypocritical in the eyes of any third parties, including European and Arab allies.[7]

Certainly there are many groups within the United States actively engaged in
attempting to persuade the executive and legislature to support Israel uncon-
ditionally. This chapter seeks to identify these groupings and assess the actual
impact they have on US policy towards Israel. The 'Israel Lobby' thesis has
been subject to considerable academic scrutiny and vilification from members of
the 'lobby'.[8] It is the contention of this chapter that an understanding of domestic support for Israel is crucial to understanding how the US–Israel has grown
stronger during the Bush administration.

American Jewish supporters of Israel

Foremost in Mearsheimer and Walt's account are a large number of Jewish
organizations which have been formed to support Israel through informing
and educating the American public and politicians about the benefits of a
close relationship with a state portrayed by them as being the only democracy in the region. Core organizations within this grouping include the Zionist
Organization of America (ZOA), Conference of Presidents of Major America
Jewish Organizations, Anti Defamation League (ADL), and American Israel
Public Affairs Committee (AIPAC), America Jewish Committee and American
Jewish Congress. These organizations are actively engaged in political lobbying
on behalf of Israel. In 2007, four of these organizations spent over $1.5 million
on lobbying politicians. AIPAC, one of the most effective lobbying organiza-
tions in America, spent $980,000, while ZOA spent $252,120, the American
Jewish Committee $165,299, and American Jewish Congress $130,000.[9] The
Conference of Major American Jewish Organizations consists of the leaders of
55 different organizations with the intention of speaking on their community and
Israel's behalf with one voice specifically to the executive. AIPAC largely lobby
the legislature but, as we shall see, the executive also maintains a close relationship with the organization.

Other significant Jewish organizations include Americans for a Safe Israel,
American Friends of Likud, Religious Action Center for Reform Judaism and
Israel Policy Forum. These groupings seek to advocate on behalf of Israel and
focus politicians' and supporters' attention on Israel. The Israel Policy Forum,
for example, describes itself as an advocacy organization seeking to encourage
'active and sustained American diplomatic efforts' to secure a peaceful resolution
of the Arab–Israeli conflict. In order to achieve this goal, with a clear subtext that
any settlement must be on Israel's terms, they mobilize philanthropic, academic,
political and Jewish organizations to lobby legislators and the executive around
this issue.[10] Other groups, including B'nai B'rith and Hadassah, although not
involved in lobbying directly themselves, nonetheless encourage their members
to do so. These organizations are complemented by think tanks which add
academic credibility and support to their agenda, such as the Jewish Institute for

National Security Affairs (JINSA), Middle East Forum (MEF) and Washington Institute for Near East Policy (WINEP). JINSA links the US military with Jewish community leaders and arranges educational trips for the military to Israel, seeking to link US defence policy with Israel's security.[11]

The Jewish population of the United States numbers over five million people, slightly over 40 per cent of world Jewry, almost as many as in Israel. This corresponds to just under 2 per cent of the population but is significant because numbers are concentrated in key electoral states including California (2.9 per cent), Florida (3.9 per cent), New York (5.7 per cent) and New Jersey (8.7 per cent).[12] Pro-Israel organizations and individuals make significant contributions to the campaign expenses of politicians sympathetic to their cause. In the 2008 elections pro-Israel groups and individuals contributed $8.7 million to favoured candidates ($6.4 million from individuals and $2.3 million from 31 political action committees). 95 per cent of all monies went to incumbents, dividing about 60–40 Democrats to Republicans.[13] These are not inconsiderable sums, but they are still relatively insignificant when compared with a presidential race where campaign expenditure exceeded $1 billion, and with the average expenditure for each candidate for the House of half a million dollars and for the Senate of $1.7 million.[14]

So if financial inducements are insufficient to command support for Israel, other factors must also be at work. The effectiveness of AIPAC, one of the principal lobbying organizations, enables supporters of Israel to get their message across to decision makers in the legislature and executive. AIPAC as a nonpartisan organization has lobbied candidates and elected officials on Israel's behalf for over 50 years. Over this time the organization has grown to include over 100,000 activists and staff across America. The message at all levels to these officials is that support for the US–Israel relationship is in America's interest. AIPAC emphasizes that this relationship is based on shared values and threats as democracies and targets of Islamic radicalism and terrorism. Foreign military and economic assistance to Israel is regarded as essential to help 'convince Arab states that there is no alternative to peace negotiations with Israel'.[15] AIPAC seeks to maintain funding for Israel, ensures that the United States prevents third parties from attempting to impose a peace settlement, and to have the resources to fight terrorism. The organization also lobbies to move the US embassy from Tel Aviv to Jerusalem and in support of the security fence effectively annexing land in the Occupied Territories.[16]

Over the years AIPAC has effectively secured the support of the overwhelming majority of both houses of Congress behind a pro-Israel agenda. An examination of the voting records of congressmen and senators throughout the Bush years reveals that scarcely 20–30 members have been willing to vote against measures supported by AIPAC in relation to Israel. In order to secure support, AIPAC has developed a close working relationship with candidates and incumbents. All candidates are screened by the organization for their views on Israel. Supportive candidates are endorsed, told what policy line to talk on issues pertaining to Israel, and introduced to other donors and funding sources. Those candidates and incumbents not considered reliable in supporting Israel are likely to find their opponents supported by the organization instead.

AIPAC members are provided with congressional voting records noting how every representative has voted, with the implied threat that unsatisfactory voting records will result in losing office with funding potentially withdrawn or transferred to an opponent. AIPAC provides each member of both houses and their staffs with their biweekly *Near East Report* reporting events in the Middle East from a pro-Israeli perspective. They are also on hand to assist and advise on drafting legislation, speeches, talking points and tactics to promote activities and legislation beneficial to Israel. The closely related American Israel Education Foundation funds trips to Israel for legislators, rewarding and encouraging ongoing support for the state.[17]

AIPAC is one of the most efficient lobbying organizations within the American polity, and its power of patronage is reflected in the ability to attract leading political actors from both parties to the annual AIPAC Policy Conference, securing commitments to further assist and stand by Israel. In June 2008, the conference attracted the two presidential candidates Barack Obama and John McCain, Secretary of State Condoleezza Rice, Senator Hillary Clinton, Speaker of the House Nancy Pelosi, Senate Majority Leader Harry Reid and Minority Leader Mitch McConnell, and House Minority Leader John Boehner among many others, including Israel's prime minister, Ehud Olmert. Both presidential candidates and the secretary of state declared themselves to be among friends, with Obama promising that 'Jerusalem will remain the capital of Israel and it must remain undivided', and McCain insisting that America and Israel are 'the most natural of allies and like Israel itself – that alliance is forever'.[18]

Neoconservatives and Israel

Neoconservatives have long been among the groups most supportive of Israel, and this became increasingly significant following the events of 11 September 2001, when their foreign policy prescriptions were eagerly adopted by the Bush administration. Three of the key actors in shaping a more aggressive US foreign policy – Paul Wolfowitz, Douglas Feith and Richard Perle – had worked together in previous administrations, consistently linking US national security interests with those of Israel.[19] In 1996, neoconservatives Perle, Feith, David and Meyrav Wurmser, Charles Fairbanks, James Colbert, Robert Loewenberg and Jonathon Torop, working on an Institute of Advanced Strategic and Political Studies project *A New Israeli Strategy Toward* 2000, wrote a policy document *A Clean Break: A New Strategy for Securing the Realm* for Likud leader Benjamin Netanyahu in the 1996 Israel elections. The document called for a clean break with the Oslo peace accords, the undermining of Palestinian leader Yasser Arafat, military strikes against Syria and its positions in Lebanon, the overthrow of Saddam Hussein in Iraq and the abandonment of Israel's socialist foundations. *A Clean Break* was designed to enable a Likud government not simply to 'contain its foes' but to 'transcend them'.[20]

While leading neoconservatives encouraged a more aggressive Israeli policy towards its neighbours abroad, so at home they called for the Clinton administration to be more robust in using US power to advance America values internationally by supporting allies and confronting enemies. The Project for the New American Century's (PNAC) statement of principles in 1997, signed by leading neoconservatives and fellow travellers, including Dick Cheney and Donald Rumsfeld, called for the energetic projection of US power around the world.[21] The following year, in an open letter to President Clinton on Iraq, support for Israel was linked clearly to this strategic recommendation.[22] Upon assuming office in January 2001, President Bush appointed many of the PNAC signatories to significant positions responsible for national security and foreign affairs, including Dick Cheney, Elliot Abrams, Richard Armitage, John Bolton, Paula Dobriansky, Zalmay Khalilzad, Richard Perle, Donald Rumsfeld and Paul Wolfowitz.

Stefan Halper and Jonathon Clarke argue that neoconservatives during the Bush administration united around three themes: A dichotomous world view which differentiates between good and evil, whereby it behoves the good to confront the evil; that international relations rest on military power and the willingness of states to use it; and that the United States should focus its attention on threats in the Middle East and from global Islam.[23] Among those seeking to advance such a policy position were the vice president's chief of staff Lewis 'Scooter' Libby, the president's special advisor Elliott Abrams, and Deputy Secretary of Defence Paul Wolfowitz; John Bolton, David Wurmser, Richard Armitage, Paula Dobriansky and Zalmay Khalilzad served at the State Department; and Richard Perle and Eliot Cohen were appointed advisors on the Defense Policy Board.

Neoconservatives represent an East Coast intellectual elite with small outposts at Stanford's Hoover Institute and the University of Chicago.[24] They include academics such as Aaron Friedberg and Bernard Lewis at Princeton University, and Yale professor Donald Kagan. Think tank members Max Boot, Robert Kagan, Daniel Pipes, Meyrav Wurmser, David Frum and Norman Podhoretz, among others, can be found at think tanks favourably disposed towards neoconservative outlooks, including the American Enterprise Institute, Hudson Institute, Foundation for the Defense of Democracies, Center for Security Policy, MEF, JINSA and WINEP. Many leading neoconservatives have worked for one or more of these organizations at some stage. Neoconservatives are also particularly well represented in the media, particularly on foreign policy op-ed pages of the *Wall Street Journal*, *Commentary*, *Weekly Standard*, edited by William Kristol, and the *New York Sun*. Neoconservative Charles Krauthammer is a columnist for the *Washington Post* and Fox News.[25]

Although many American Jewish supporters are antithetical to neoconservatives' social conservatism, they are nonetheless able to make common ground with them over the issue of Israel. The closeness of leading conservatives to policy positions adopted by Netanyahu, Likud and AIPAC during the Bush presidency served to join the movements in common cause. While AIPAC has numerous supporters within Congress, neoconservatives were able to bring the interests of Israel into the heart of the administration through key appointments in the Defence and State departments and National Security Council. The linkage of Israel's and America's national security needs and their alliance in the face of terrorism over the course of the Bush years has become largely accepted by politicians in the legislature. Neoconservative think tank members have been regular expert witnesses before committees on all matters pertaining to the Middle East and prolific policy paper and briefing writers to inform politicians and the public about their position on Israel.

American Jewish supporters of Israel and neoconservatives have adopted similar strategies in attempting to control the debate around issues concerning Israel. AIPAC intimidates political opponents through the use of incentives and punishments to procure support for its policy positions through the use of campaign finance, resources and voting records. Meanwhile, neoconservatives have sought to close academic opposition to uncritical support for Israel. Daniel Pipes, Director of MEF, launched Campus Watch in 2002, a website encouraging students to report any university activities, including lectures and seminars, that depart from unequivocal support for Israel's actions.[26] Academic staff, particularly in Middle East studies, are targeted by Campus Watch and left with a clear message that deviation from a pro-Israel line could have career consequences for the noncompliant professor, while supporters of Israel are introduced to a whole network of career opportunities.

Christian Zionism

The third actor in the pro-Israel triumvirate to seek to influence administration policy towards Israel and the Middle East is the Christian Right and, more specifically, the Christian Zionist movement within this group. I have argued elsewhere that under a Republican administration and President George Bush, in particular, this group constitutes the most important of the three.[27] Christian Zionism has long antecedents dating back, in its more recent manifestations, to the nineteenth century and the teachings of John Nelson Darby (1800–81). Darby's teachings were taken up in America by revivalist preachers Dwight L. Moody and Billy Sunday and made accessible to all through the Scofield Reference Bible. Initially confined to Protestant fundamentalists, Darby's teaching on premillennial dispensationalism revolves around the idea that human existence consists of seven ages or dispensations, beginning in the literal Garden of Eden and ending with the return of Christ with his church to reign for a thousand years. Premillennial dispensationalists consider that we are in the sixth dispensation and interpret the political and natural events occurring today as a sign that the return of Christ is imminent and could even occur in this generation.

An integral part of dispensationalist thinking is that the future of the church is intimately bound up with those of the Jewish people. Darby and subsequent followers argued that the covenant between God and Israel is eternal and exclusive and cannot be abrogated (Genesis 12:1–7; 15:4–7; 17:1–8; Leviticus 26:44–45; Deuteronomy 7:7–8). As part of this covenant the land of Canaan, the Promised Land of the Old Testament, is seen as an everlasting possession to the Jewish people.[28] One of the key signs of the imminent return of Christ will be that Jews from around the world will 'return' to Israel (Jeremiah 23:7–8). Christian Zionists see their role as hastening or preparing for the Second Coming of Christ by facilitating that return and recognizing God's special relationship with the Jewish people. Indeed, they emphasize that the blessings and cursing/ judgement of God are based on how individuals and nations deal with the Jewish people, and in particular with the state of Israel (Genesis 12:3).[29] According to Christian Zionists, Israel must occupy all the Promised Land, including the West Bank and East Jerusalem. It must rebuild the Third Temple either on or adjacent to the Al-Aqsa mosque, the second most holy Muslim site. Another sign of the end times will come when the armies of Russia and the Arabs join forces to attack Israel (Ezekiel: 37, 38; Revelation 9:16).[30]

Such views were relatively insignificant throughout most of the nineteenth and twentieth centuries. American evangelicals, along with the majority of Christendom, accepted replacement theology, that is the idea that God's old covenant with the Jews had been replaced by a new covenant with the Christian church. All the promises in the bible pertaining to the Jewish people were now transferred to the church, and Jews could only inherit these promises by converting to Christianity. Darby's and his successor's teaching ran counter to the prevailing trend until the creation of the state of Israel in 1948, and more especially the Israeli victory in the Six-Day war and the capture of East Jerusalem and biblical Judea and Samaria. Since the 1980s the dispensationalist belief in a separate covenant, rather than replacement theology, has become dominant in Christian circles.[31] This time period coincides with the emergence of organized and politicized socially conservative Christianity in the late 1970s with the formation of the Moral Majority under Jerry Falwell.[32] The four organizing principles of the movement were opposition to abortion, support for traditional marriage, a strong US defence and support for Israel.[33]

Such views are popularized in a plethora of end times, prophetic and apocalyptic literature widely read among the conservative evangelicals who form a substantial core of Republican Party supporters. Hal Lindsey's *Late Great Planet Earth*, Tim LaHaye's and Jerry Jenkins's series of twelve books in the *Left Behind* series and John Hagee's *Jerusalem Countdown* have sold many millions of copies across America and throughout the world.[34] Such views are now widely held by as many as 25 million evangelicals in America who are passionately concerned about the fate of Israel.[35] As traditional Christian denominations declined throughout the second half of the twentieth century, those adopting Christian Zionist positions, including pentecostal, charismatic, independent, renewal and Southern Baptist churches, have grow exponentially.

Since the 1970s there has been a rapid growth in the number of Christian Zionist organizations formed to support Israel and influence US policy in a similar direction. The successor to the Moral Majority, the Christian Coalition founded by Pat Robertson, campaigned vigorously on Israel's behalf. Other groups include Richard Hellman's Christians' Israel Public Action Campaign,

Christians Friend of Israel Communities, which twins evangelical churches with settlements in the occupied territories, the Jerusalem Prayer Team and Bridges for Israel, whose mission is to enable Jews to immigrate to Israel. The National Christian Leadership Council, Unity Coalition for Israel and the International Christian Embassy Jerusalem, as well as many mega churches, including Pastor John Hagee's Cornerstone Church in San Antonio, Texas, also have active links with Israel. Hagee has effectively become the leader of the Christian Zionist movement in America, forming Christians United for Israel (CUFI) in 2006, bringing together four hundred pastors from around the country to create a Christian Zionist equivalent of AIPAC.

Christian Zionists have forged links with Jewish American supporters of Israel and neoconservatives, cooperating and competing at times to influence legislators and the executive. CUFI organizes 'Nights to Honour Israel' events across America and encourages the support and involvement of local rabbis and Jewish leaders. Since 2006, an annual summit in Washington D.C., held in July, has been organized and combined with a mass lobby of Congress in support of Israel. The summits have been addressed by Benjamin Netanyahu, Israeli ambassadors and Senator Joseph Lieberman, while Hagee has spoken at the AIPAC Policy Conference, forging closer links with what is seen as a complementary organization. David Brog, nephew of former Israeli prime minister Ehud Barak and ex-chief of staff for Senator Arlen Specter, serves as CUFI's executive director and has led efforts to convince Jewish supporters of Israel that Christian Zionists should be viewed as righteous gentiles involved in a common struggle to maximize support for Israel.[36] This viewpoint was adopted by Abraham Foxman and the ADL, even though Hagee's comments that the Holocaust was part of God's plan to return Jews to Israel strained the burgeoning relationship.[37]

Relationships have also been developed with neoconservatives, principally through the agency of neoconservative Gary Bauer, former presidential candidate and signatory to the PNAC statement of principles. Bauer, a member of the Council for National Policy, Board member of CUFI and president of American Values, was co-founder in 2002 of the American Alliance of Jews and Christians. Bauer was a key advisor to John McCain's presidential campaign in 2008, convincing the Christian Right that a McCain/Palin ticket would represent their interests in a McCain presidency. At the 2008 CUFI Washington Summit Daniel Pipes and William Kristol were among the speakers. Ralph Reed, former leader of the Christian Coalition and campaign aide for George W. Bush in 2000, joined with Rabbi Yechiel Eckstein's International Fellowship of Christians and Jews to form a Stand for Israel in 2002. Neoconservatives including Frank Gaffney, president of the Center for Security Policy, and Robert Satloff, executive director of WINEP, are regular contributors to CUFI summits and celebrations.

Although close relationships exist between Jewish supporters of Israel, neoconservatives and Christian Zionists, strategy is not coordinated but complements and supplements the efforts of each to ensure that Israel is never far from the attention of legislators, the executive, the media and the public. Christian Zionists during the Bush administration have also been prominent members of Congress, including former leaders of the House Richard Armey and Tom DeLay, and Senators James Inhoffe and Sam Brownback. Christian Zionist leaders have been regular visitors to the White House as a reward for Christian Right support in the 2000 and 2004 elections, and take part in weekly conference calls with the White House.

Adopting similar strategies to AIPAC, Christian Zionist organizations and churches are able to mobilize their supporters through e-newsletters and action alerts to lobby Congress and the White House for action supporting Israel and against perceived opponents of Israel. Politicians are nurtured and either supported or opposed by Christian Zionists depending on their position on Israel. A carrot-and-stick approach is adopted with the use of punitive measures such as scorecard voting records being made available to constituents, supporting opponents, vilification in the secular and religious media, and mass lobbying of Capitol Hill and the White House if support for preferred policy positions on Israel is not forthcoming. Politicians supportive of Israel are rewarded by positive feedback to constituents, campaign finance and workers, internships from Christian College and university students, speaking engagements, and access to the comprehensive network of Christian broadcasters on radio, television and the Internet.

Christian Zionists, in addition to their general support for Israel, have made clear their opposition to any suggestion that Israel trades land for peace as running counter to their eschatological position. Gary Bauer and the late Ed McAteer (Religious Roundtable) have spoken in favour of a greater Israel and removing Palestinians from the West Bank.[38] Christian Zionists' hatred of Islam also determines their attitude to Israel's neighbours. Pat Robertson uses his *700 Club* daily news/current affairs programme broadcast around the world to release a stream of invective against Islam, in both its moderate and radical form, describing it on 28 April 2006 as a 'bloody, bloody, brutal type of religion . . . not a religion of peace'. Franklin Graham, son of Billy Graham, does not consider Islam to be 'a wonderful, peaceful religion' and reminded NBC viewers that 'it wasn't Methodists flying into those buildings . . . It was an attack on this country by people of the Islamic faith'.[39] John McCain's Christian Zionist supporter John Hagee coined the phrase 'Islamofascism' to describe radical Islam, and CUFI regional director and patriot pastor Rod Parsley has called upon Christians to wage war to destroy Islam, which he considers a false religion.[40]

US–Israel relations under George W. Bush

Over the course of Bush's 8 years in office, the relationship between Israel and the United States has grown stronger than at any other time in the history of the two countries. Writing in 2003, David Frum, Bush speechwriter and the inventor of the phrase 'Axis of Evil', described Bush as 'one of the staunchest friends of Israel ever to occupy the Oval Office'.[41] Since the foundation of the state in 1948 the United States has diverted about one-fifth of its foreign assistance to Israel, approximately $3 billion per annum. In July 2007 the State Department announced a further military aid package of $30 billion over 10 years.[42] Over the course of the first 7 years, US grant assistance to Israel has totalled nearly $20 billion.

US Grant Assistance to Israel
FY2001–FY2006 (in $ millions)

Year	Military	Economic	Jewish refugee resettlement	American schools and hospitals	Other grants	Total
2001	1975.6	838.2	60.0	2.25	–	2876.05
2002	2040.0	720.0	60.0	2.65	28.0	2850.65
2003	3086.4	596.1	59.6	3.05	–	3745.15
2004	2147.3	477.2	49.7	3.15	9.9	2687.25
2005	2202.2	357.1	50.0	2.95	–	2612.15
2006	2257.0	237.0	40.0	–	0.5	2534.5
2007	2340.0	120.0	40.0	–	0.2	2500.2
TOTAL	**16048.5**	**3345.5**	**359.3**	**14.05**	**37.9**	**19805.95**

Table adapted from US Grant assistance to Israel in Clyde R. Mark, 'Israel US Foreign Assistance', Congressional Research Service (July 12, 2004), and US State Department, USAID, Congressional Budget Justification for FY2007, Foreign Operations, March 2007.

Table adapted from US Grant assistance to Israel in Clyde R. Mark, 'Israel U.S. Foreign Assistance', Congressional Research Service (July 12, 2004), and US State Department, USAID, Congressional Budget Justification for FY2007, Foreign Operations, March 2007.

Israeli Prime Minister Ehud Olmert, commenting after President Bush's first visit to Israel in the final year of his presidency, said that he had proved 'a great friend of Israel in the White House'. Olmert confirmed that Bush had neither put pressure on Israel nor required any commitments from them.[43] Indeed, Bush's policy towards Israel during his tenure has been unfailingly supportive based upon his identification of Israel as being on the right side of the line he drew metaphorically after 9/11 between those for America, freedom and liberty, and those against. In many ways Bush has sought to deliver what Christian Zionists, neoconservatives and Jewish supporters of Israel have wanted, and to a large extent they pushed at an open door. Early difficulties in the relationship between the executive and the pro-Israel triumvirate were resolved with greater consultation of Christian Zionists on decisions about Israel.

Under the Oslo Accords, Israel was to withdraw from areas of the West Bank, which were to be controlled by the Palestinian Authority. In April 2002, however, Israel launched a military offensive in the West Bank, which was immediately denounced by the Bush administration with demands for an Israeli withdrawal. Bush was subject to the full might of the Christian Zionist lobby as Jerry Falwell organized supporters to overwhelm the White House with over 100,000 emails complaining about his withdrawal demands and calling for Israel to be allowed to carry to whatever security measures it considered appropriate. Tom DeLay, Richard Armey and Trent Lott admonished Bush in person, and Congress overwhelmingly adopted a resolution supporting Israeli actions and condemning the Palestinians. The White House ceased further objections to Israeli military actions.

In the build-up to the Iraq war Bush announced a Roadmap for Peace in the Middle East in order to shore up support for an alliance to topple Saddam Hussein. The Roadmap was to be a time-delineated process for achieving peace in the Middle East based on trading land for security. Bush became the first US president to commit his administration to seeking a two-state solution. Christian Zionists baulked at the idea of Israel conceding any land, but the removal of Yasser Arafat, the bête noir of the lobby, as interlocutor largely assuaged their concerns. Nonetheless, 50,000 postcards sent to the White House noted their objections. After this no attempts were made to stick to deadlines and no pressure applied to Israel to keep to the Roadmap. When Israel pursued a series of targeted assassinations against Palestinian leaders in 2003 the initial objections of the administration were muted following the rapid response emails, telegrams, letters, postcards and phone calls sent to the White House. Thereafter such assassinations were overlooked by Bush and the State Department.

The administration learnt from these experiences and thereafter consulted Christian Zionists on strategy in the Middle East. Ariel Sharon's unilateral decision to withdraw from Gaza while consolidating and increasing settlements in the West Bank in contravention of the Roadmap was discussed before the announcement at a special meeting with Christian Zionist leaders convened by Elliott Abrams and Tim Goeglein. The meeting was designed to reassure them that Gaza was not part of biblical Israel and that the move would strengthen Israeli security.[44] Neoconservatives, Jewish supporters of Israel and Christian Zionists supported the administration's replacement of Yasser Arafat with Mahmoud Abbas as chief Palestinian negotiator, as he was rightly perceived as a weaker negotiator and more amenable to agreeing to a peace settlement on Israeli terms. Although the latter was easily elected as Palestinian president following the death of Arafat, the Palestinian Liberation Organisation failed to win parliamentary elections, losing to Hamas in January 2006. The Bush administration, despite pressure from Christian Zionists, AIPAC and Congressional resolutions, neglected to insist on the exclusion of Hamas from the elections. However, Bush subsequently succeeded in building an international coalition to place sanctions on the Hamas government and secure its removal from power until the movement established de facto control of Gaza in 2007.

The refusal to negotiate with Hamas met with approval across the triumvirate as did the disproportionate use of pressure on the Palestinians to abide by the Roadmap while allowing Israel to change facts on the ground by continuing to build and increase the size of settlements in the West Bank and East Jerusalem. UN special envoy to the Middle East peace process Alvaro de Soto revealed US manipulation of the quartet[45] involved in the peace process, which prevented improvements on access and movement in the Palestinian Territories.[46] Former British prime minister Tony Blair's appointment as special envoy ensured continuity in a policy that excluded Hamas and failed to make demands of Israel to achieve peace.

The Bush administration's policy of reminding Israel of its obligation under international law not to build more settlements in occupied territory while not penalizing such actions struck the right chord with Christian Zionists, neoconservatives and Jewish pro-Israeli supporters. Similarly, the administration's veto of nine UN Security Council resolutions critical of Israel's actions in the Occupied Territories met with widespread approval. Equally well received was the administration's abstention on a Security Council resolution calling on Israel and Hamas to implement an immediate ceasefire, enabling Israel the time it wanted in its attempt to crush Hamas, in the dying weeks of the Bush presidency. However, the refusal of the administration to relocate the US embassy in Israel from Tel Aviv to Jerusalem, which was passed by Congress and yet was vetoed every 6 months by President Bush, has been less popular. Despite the last-minute attempts to revive the peace process at Annapolis, and subsequent visits to Israel by President Bush, a peace settlement was further away by the end of the Bush years than it was at the end of the previous administration.

When it comes to dealing with Israel's neighbours the administration has carried out measures that have coincided with Israel's and the pro-Israel supporters strategic interests. The naming of an Axis of Evil in the aftermath of September 11th targeted two opponents of Israel in Iraq and Iran, whilst simultaneously sending a warning message to Syria. The decision to attack Afghanistan and announce a War on Terror was taken in direct response to the New York and Washington attacks, rather than because of Israel. However, Al Qaeda are one of Israel's enemies, and the War on Terror automatically placed Israel on America's side in any conflict against Islamic extremism, including Hamas and Hezbollah. The war against Iraq, inspired by neoconservatives and given 'just war' legitimacy by the Christian Right,[47] was not primarily for Israel's defence, yet the removal of a Saddam Hussein, who had launched attacks on it during the first Gulf War, benefited Israel.

In 2005, after international pressure orchestrated by the United States, the Syrian army and security services withdrew from Israel's northern neighbour Lebanon. This provided Israel with the opportunity to launch a retaliatory attack against Hezbollah in July 2006 following the abduction of three of its soldiers. Israel launched a ferocious attack destroying much of southern Lebanon and killing over 1000 Lebanese, but was unable to defeat Hezbollah who continued to fire rockets into northern Israel. At the time there was international pressure on Israel to cease its disproportionate offensive. CUFI and AIPAC lobbied the administration and Congress calling for the Israelis to be allowed more time to destroy Hezbollah. CUFI claims success for the administration's delay in calling on Israel to end the conflict even though Hezbollah emerged politically much stronger.[48]

The triumvirate has been particularly active in calling for tough measures to be taken against Iran for its support of Hezbollah, Hamas and Iraqi insurgents, and against President Ahmadinejad's call for Israel to be 'wiped off the map'. Iran's nuclear programme was viewed by the triumvirate and the Bush administration as a major security threat to Israel's and America's security. The administration coordinated international sanctions against Iran, but despite bellicose rhetoric adopted diplomatic measures rather than military confrontation to combat the perceived threat. Indeed, *The Guardian* newspaper reported that Bush had expressly forbidden an Israeli strike against Iran's nuclear installations.[49] While Bush's approach reflected the chastening experience of protracted conflicts in Afghanistan and Iraq, it has resisted the more bellicose remonstrations of Christian Zionists to carry out a pre-emptive attack on Iran.[50]

Overview and summary

During the course of the Bush administration, US–Israel relations have grown closer as Israel has become identified as an important ally in war against Islamic extremism, rather than being seen as a contributing factor to that extremism. The alliance between the two countries has become stronger, reinforced by a domestic constituency led by Christian Zionists, neoconservatives and American Jewish pro-Israel supporters. At the end of the Bush presidency there is no pressure on Israel to cede land for peace on anything other than its own terms. The Palestinian Authority has been considerably weakened and divided, Syrian troops removed from Lebanon, Saddam Hussein removed from power, and Iran constrained by international sanctions. The West Bank security wall has almost been completed, annexing Palestinian land, and settlement building continues apace in East Jerusalem and the West Bank without US censure. Although the triumvirate did not manage to persuade Bush to attack Iran or move the US embassy to Jerusalem, the administration met most of its demands and continued to support Israel in all international fora.

George Bush has, in some ways, held the ground against those in the triumvirate that would seek to advance a more bellicose support for Israel and preclude Israel ceding land in any peace settlement. In advocating a two-state solution to the Arab–Israeli problem, Bush was influenced more by the Israeli government than domestic supporters of Israel seeking to determine Israel's response to its own security. Bush's lack of commitment to the project until the end of his presidency, and a refusal to engage with Hamas, ensured that the two-state solution was doomed to failure to the delight of Christian Zionists and neoconservatives. The US–Israel relationship despite this, or maybe because of it, remains stronger than ever. President Bush's closing remarks to the Knesset on 15 May 2008 reflected this unshakeable reality: 'You have raised a modern society in the Promised Land, a light unto the nations that preserves the legacy of Abraham and Isaac and Jacob. And you have built a mighty democracy that will endure forever and can always count on the United States of America to be at your side. God bless'.

Notes

1 D. Allin and S. Simon, 'The moral psychology of US support for Israel', *Survival*, 2008, vol. 45, pp. 123–44.
2 Barack Obama speech to AIPAC Policy Conference, 4 June 2008, <http://www.aipac. org> (accessed 5 October 2008).
3 John McCain speech to AIPAC Policy Conference, 2 June 2008, <http://www.aipac. org> (accessed 4 October 2008).
4 Gallup opinion polls in each February from 2001 to 2007 asked the public 'in the Middle East situation; are your sympathies more with Israel or with the Arab nations?', Jewish Virtual Library, <http://www.jewishvirtaullibrary.org/jsource/ US-Israel/gallup.html> (accessed 5 October 2008).
5 John Mearsheimer and Stephen Walt, 'The Israel Lobby', *London Review of Books*, 23 March 2006.
6 John Mearsheimer and Stephen Walt, 'The Israel Lobby and US Foreign Policy', *Harvard Working Papers*, <http://ksgNo.tes1.harvard.edu/Research/wpaper.nsf/rwp/ RWP06–011> (accessed 3 June 2006). John Mearsheimer and Stephen Walt, *The Israel Lobby and US Foreign Policy*, London: Allen Lane, 2007.
7 Mearsheimer and Walt, *Israel Lobby*, p. 75.
8 See Aaron Friedberg, 'An Uncivilized Argument', *Foreign Policy*, July–August, 2006; Dennis Ross, 'The Mind-Set Matters', *Foreign Policy*, July–August, 2006; Ben Fishman '"The Israel Lobby": A Realistic Assessment', *Orbis*, 2008, vol. 52, pp. 159–80; George Shultz, 'The "Israel Lobby" Myth', *U.S. News and World Report*, 9 September 2007; David Gergen, 'An Unfair Attack', *U.S. News and World Report*, 26 March 2006. Attacks claiming the authors are motivated by anti-Semitism have come from among others Michael Gerson, 'The Seeds of Anti-Semitism', *Washington Post*, 21 September 2007; Eliot Cohen, 'Yes, It's Anti-Semitic', *Washington Post*, 5 April 2006; and Jeffrey Goldberg, 'The Usual Suspects', *The New Republic*, 10 October 2007. Walter Russell Mead just stops short of calling the authors anti-Semitic but places their contribution in the same stream in 'Jerusalem Syndrome: Decoding the "Israel Lobby"', *Foreign Affairs*, November/December 2007.
9 Information provided by the Center for Responsive Politics website, <http:// www.opensecrets.org/pacs/industry.php?txt=Q05&cycle=208> (accessed 4 October 2008).
10 See Israel Policy Forum website, <http://www.israelpolicyforum.org/display. cfm?id=1> (accessed 8 October 2008).
11 Information available no JINSA website, <http://www.jinsa.org> (accessed 11 October 2008).
12 Jewish Virtual Library, American–Israeli Cooperation Enterprise website, <http:// www.jewishvirtuallibrary.org/jsource/Judaism/jewpop.html> (accessed 9 October 2008).
13 Center for Responsive Politics, <http://www.opensecrets.org/pacs/industry. php?txt=Q05&cycle=2008> (accessed 9 October 2008). These figures cover the period up until 17 September 2008.
14 Center for Responsive Politics, figures based on data released by FEC on 6 October 2008, <http://www.opensecrets.org/overview/index.php?cycle=2008&Type= A&Display=A> (accessed 9 October 2008).
15 AIPAC, *AIPAC Briefing Book 2007–2008*, Washington, D.C.: AIPAC, 2007, p. 9.
16 Ibid.
17 Mearsheimer and Walt, *The Israel Lobby*, pp. 154–62, and AIPAC website, <www. aipac.org> (accessed 10 October 2008).
18 Barack Obama speech to AIPAC Policy Conference 2008, Washington, D.C., 4 June 2008, and John McCain speech at the conference on 2 June 2008, <www.aipac.org> (accessed 20 August 2008).

19 Stephen Green, 'Serving Two Flags: The Bush Neo-Conservatives and Israel', *Counterpunch*, 3 September 2004, <http://www.counterpunch.org/green09032004. html> (accessed 11 October 2008).

20 Institute for Advanced Strategic and Political Studies, 'A Clean Break: A New Strategy for Securing the Realm', <http://www.iasps.org/strat1.htm> (accessed 11 October 2008).

21 Project for the New American Century, 'Statement of Principles', 1997, <http://www. newamericancentury.org/statementofprinciples.htm> (accessed 23 January 2008).

22 Project for the New American Century, 'Letter to President Clinton on Iraq', 1998, <http://www.newamericancentury.org/iraqclintonletter.htm> (accessed 11 October 2008).

23 Stefan Halper and Jonathon Clarke, *America Alone: The Neo-Conservatives and the Global Order*, Cambridge: Cambridge University Press, 2004, p. 11.

24 Halper and Clarke, *America Alone*, p. 15. This view was confirmed by former ambassador to the United Nations John Bolton when interviewed by the author in Washington D.C., 19 July 2007. Bolton denied being a neoconservative.

25 Mearsheimer and Walt, *The Israel Lobby*, pp. 129–31, and Halper and Clarke, *America Alone*, pp. 13–15.

26 Campus Watch, <http://www.campuswatch.org> (accessed 11 October 2008).

27 Lee Marsden, *For God's Sake: The Christian Right and US Foreign Policy*, London: Zed Books, 2008.

28 International Christian Embassy Jerusalem, 'A Defence of Christian Zionism', <www. icej.org/article.php?id=3464> (accessed 21 October 2006).

29 John Hagee, *Jerusalem Countdown*, Lake Mary, Florida: Front Line, 2007, p. 118.

30 Michael Northcott, *An Angel Directs the Storm: Apocalyptic Religion and American Empire*, London: I.B. Tauris, 2004, p. 61.

31 David Brog, *Standing with Israel*, Lake Mary, Florida: Front Line, 2006, p. 52.

32 For more detailed information, see Steve Bruce, *The Rise and Fall of the New Christian Right: Conservative Protestant Politics in America 1978–88*, London: Clarendon Press, 1990; Clyde Wilcox and Karin Larson, *Onward Christian Soldiers?* Boulder CO: Westview Press, 2006; and Lee Marsden, *For God's Sake: The Christian Right and US Foreign Policy*.

33 David Brog, 'Jews and Evangelicals Together', Interview with National Review, 22 May 2006, <http://article.nationalreview.com/?q=ZDFiODgxY2ZkZjNhY2JmMm FjN2RkNDg4MTE0NGVlYzA> (accessed 12 October 2008).

34 Hal Lindsey, *The Greatest Works of Hal Lindsey: The Late Great Planet Earth/Satan is Alive and Well on Planet Earth*, New York: Inspiration Books, 2006; Tim LaHaye and Jerry Jenkins, *Left Behind*, Carol Stream Ill.: Tyndale House, 1995; John Hagee, *Jerusalem Countdown*.

35 Donald Wagner, 'Christian Zionists, Israel and the "Second Coming"', <www. informationclearinghouse.info/article4930.htm> (accessed 21 October 2006).

36 Brog, *Standing with Israel*; J. Glazov, 'Standing with Israel', *Frontpage Magaine. com*, <www.frontpagemag.com/Articles/ID=22701> (accessed 19 April 2007); T. Zahavy, '"Christians are Hearing the Message" interview with David Brog', *New Jersey Jewish Standard*, 31 August 2006.

37 B. Broadway, 'The Evangelical–Israeli Connection', *Washington Post*, 27 March 2004; Stephen Zunes, 'US Christian Right's Grip on Middle East Policy', *Asian Times*, 14 July 2004.

38 Martin Durham, 'Evangelical Protestantism and Foreign Policy in the United States after September 11', *Patterns of Prejudice*, 2004, vol. 38, pp. 141–62, 153.

39 Stephen Mansfield, *The Faith of George W. Bush*, New York: Penguin/Strang Communications, 2004, p. 140.

40 David Corn, 'McCain's Spiritual Guide: Destroy Islam', *Mother Jones*, 12 March 2008, <http://www.motherjones.com/washington_dispatch/2008/03/john-mccain-rod-parsley-spiritual-guide.html> (accessed 13 October 2008).

41 David Frum, *The Right Man: An Inside Account of the Surprise Presidency of George W. Bush*, London: Weidenfeld & Nicolson, p. 248.

42 BBC News, 'US Military Aid for Middle East', 30 July 2007, <http://news.bbc.co.uk/1/hi/middle_east/6922664.stm> (accessed 14 October 2007).

43 Prime Minister Ehud Olmert, 'Remarks to the Cabinet Following President Bush's Visit', 13 January 2008, <http://www.jewishvirtuallibrary.org/jsource/Peace/OlmertCabinet.html> (accessed 13 October 2008).

44 R. Perlstein, 'The Jesus Landing Pad', *The Village Voice*, 2004, <http://www.villagevoice.com/news/0420perlstein,53582,1html> (accessed 17 October 2007).

45 The quartet of special envoys involved in the peace process includes the United States, Russia, the European Union and the United Nations.

46 Alvaro de Soto, 'End of Mission Report', confidential report leaked to *The Guardian*, 13 May 2007.

47 See *For God's Sake*, pp. 278–79.

48 David Brog, 'Christians are Hearing the Message', *New Jersey Standard*, 31 August 2006.

49 Jonathon Steele, 'Israel asked US for green light to bomb nuclear sites in Iran', *The Guardian*, 25 September 2008.

50 See John Hagee's *Jerusalem Countdown*.

12 The death of a peculiar special relationship

Myron Taylor and the religious roots of America's Cold War

Andrew Preston

The study of history is littered with artificial divisions of chronology. Eras are said to have begun or ended in a specific year – often on a specific date – lending historical explanation and analysis a precision that is far too narrow to be possibly accurate. Precise beginnings and endings are often misleading, for they conceal other factors independent of particular dates that played as important a role in shaping events. In the history of American foreign relations, for example, the notion that US involvement with World War II began with the Japanese bombardment of Pearl Harbor on 7 December 1941 ignores the escalation of tensions between the United States and the fascist powers, and the changes in the political economy and ideology of all countries, that long predated the attack.

Although historians of American diplomacy have not given such precise chronological definition to the origins of the Cold War, a perception nonetheless persists that it was something radically different from World War II. To be sure, some intra-alliance tensions existed, but these have been viewed as somehow separate and detached from the larger, epochal struggle that followed and consumed the energies of much of the world for the next four decades. Even scholars who do not subscribe to the idea that there was a 'lost chance' for permanent peace between the United States and the Soviet Union assume that World War II and the Cold War were closely related but fundamentally different, like relatives who may share a bloodline but otherwise have little in common. However, a significant share of American opinion – particularly religious opinion – about the Soviet Union did not change, either with Soviet entry into the war in June 1941, American entry in December, or with the end of the war in 1945. These Americans, informed by their religious faith and suspicious of official communist atheism, never accepted the Soviet Union as a partner for world peace or stability. For many American Christians, the Cold War had already been underway for quite some time by 1941. Yet were this is not to say that World War II and the Cold War were fundamentally the same conflict; nor is it to say that World War II was simply a prelude to the Cold War.[1] Important distinctions between them exist, and on those distinctions hang the origins of the Cold War. The historian's task, then, is to highlight continuity while respecting difference.

President Franklin D. Roosevelt certainly envisioned continuity between wartime collaboration and the post-war settlement. During the war, when Americans and

Soviets cooperated to defeat Nazi Germany, he spoke of the two systems, capitalist and communist, becoming increasingly similar, with the United States becoming increasingly statist by entrenching and enhancing the New Deal, and the Soviet Union becoming increasingly democratic by permitting ever greater levels of political and religious freedom. FDR acknowledged, of course, that the United States would never become a communist state, just as he recognized that it was unlikely that the Soviet Union would ever become a true liberal democracy. However, Roosevelt believed their differences were becoming less pronounced, and when combined with the fact that Washington and Moscow would be the two most powerful states following the war, he believed it was critical to establish some sort of working relationship with the Kremlin. It would be a peculiar special relationship, but a special relationship nonetheless – and, most importantly, a necessary one if the world hoped to avoid another world war in the future.[2]

Reflecting these hopes, and in recognition of its tremendous wartime suffering and sacrifice, the Soviet Union's image in the United States underwent something of a rehabilitation during the war.[3] However, if Roosevelt believed in the necessity of American–Soviet cooperation, and if many Americans were willing to support this policy, many others were not. The Soviets, of course, bore the brunt of fighting with the Nazis, and without them victory over Germany would be impossible; yet the nagging suspicion that the Soviets were also despotic – perhaps just as despotic as Nazi Germany – refused to go away. In gauging American perceptions of the Soviet Union – and especially of the influence of communism upon Soviet ideology, capabilities and intentions – few groups better reflected this ambivalence than America's Christians. In the ongoing debate over whether to accept the Soviet Union as a full-fledged partner in the defeat of fascism and the construction of a new world order, many Christians, whether liberal or conservative, Protestant or Catholic, were less willing to excuse the Soviets' internal politics and less sympathetic to Soviet national interests than FDR. They had been noticeably reticent on wartime collaboration, and were even more noticeably reluctant about post-war cooperation.

If World War II marked the zenith of Soviet–American cooperation, it also triggered the explosive growth in American religion in two ways: both the sheer number of the faithful and, perhaps more importantly, their intensity increased dramatically.[4] American Christianity, in turn, was not only growing during the war years, it was also reasserting its traditionally dominant political influence. With an integral role in domestic politics, American Christians effectively held a popular veto over any American–Soviet plans for collaboration. As W. Averell Harriman, Roosevelt's politically astute ambassador to Moscow, noted, the 'religious question . . . was regarded by Roosevelt as a matter of the highest domestic priority'.[5] And if officials in Washington and Moscow were ever going to form a peculiar special relationship between capitalist democracy and communist autocracy, they would first have to convert America's churches. Rather than accept an unholy alliance with Soviet communism, however, many American Christians called attention to the fundamental incompatibility of the Soviet and American systems. Following the death of Roosevelt in April 1945 and the end of the war 4 months later, and especially with the increasingly erratic and apparently expansionist nature of Moscow's post-war behaviour, religious sceptics found their voice moving swiftly from the margins to the mainstream. Vindicated, they helped ensure the early death of what would have been a peculiar special relationship indeed.

In the summer of 1941, when Americans began debating whether to fund the Soviets' defence against the German offensive – a policy the Roosevelt administration was on the verge of adopting and was in the midst of promoting – anti-communists used religion as a way to discredit the Soviet Union. Playing on the president's own ideological formulations of freedom, Father John LaFarge, a Jesuit priest, insisted that any American aid be conditional upon Stalin's acceptance of four religious freedoms.[6] Other anti-communists saw value in the tactic and stressed, perhaps disingenuously, the need for the Soviet Union to liberalize its official stance on freedom of worship. Louis Waldman, a socialist and labour leader, declared before a conference of progressives that if 'Russia is to be saved, it must be saved as a democracy', a condition that Americans had 'the right to demand of the Government of Russia' because of the military and economic aid America was proposing to send to the Soviets. Waldman's prerequisites for democracy were limited to 'freedom of speech, freedom of religion, freedom of the press and freedom of political organization'.[7]

A few months later, Roosevelt discovered for himself just how passionately anti-communist – and, more importantly, just how deeply suspicious of the Soviet Union – American Christians could be. He had already encountered difficulty privately convincing the Pope – and eventually, through the Vatican, millions of American Catholics – that aiding the Soviets was both necessary and wise.[8] Anticipating religious opposition to the extension of Lend-Lease aid to the Soviet Union, Roosevelt told reporters at a press conference in October 1941 that the Soviet constitution of 1936 protected religious freedom because it guaranteed both freedom of religion and freedom 'equally to use propaganda against religion, which is essentially what is the rule in this country; only we don't put it quite the same way'.[9] Roosevelt's rather clumsy invocation of the doctrine of the separation of church and state in the Soviet Union provoked a furious reaction. Roman Catholics, who had a long history of anti-communism and had recently witnessed Soviet persecution of Catholics in Poland and the Baltic states, were particularly upset. Religious freedom in the USSR was a 'hollow mockery', declared Reverend Edmund A. Walsh, Georgetown University's vice president. The Soviets demanded American money, ships and weapons, Walsh charged, and even American 'blood if that be necessary'. But they would 'not permit [Americans] to have a word to say respecting the freedoms for which you shall make these sacrifices'.[10] The president's statement would be 'humorous', the Knights of Columbus similarly intoned, 'if the facts were not so tragic'.[11]

However, protest came not only from Catholics. Protestant leaders, including religious liberals, also strongly criticized Roosevelt's formulation of religious freedom. Raymond J. Wade, a Methodist bishop from Detroit, cut to the heart of the distrust: 'Undisputed imprisonment and slaying of tens of thousands of priests . . . together with thousands of closed churches, speak louder than printed words'. And Luther A. Weigle, president of the liberal, ecumenical Federal Council of Churches (FCC), said the American and Soviet traditions of a disestablished church were fundamentally different because Moscow 'accepts atheism as the accepted philosophy of the State'.[12]

Although these fears softened, they did not disappear in 1941 when Americans and Soviets found themselves fighting the war on the same side. To be sure, Stalin's decision to allow more actual religious freedom removed much of the sting from the Christian anti-communist critique, and many religious Americans, including some in government, shared Roosevelt's belief in the eventual symmetry of the American and Soviet ways of life.[13] Nonetheless, suspicions about communist atheism and the official persecution of Christian churches in the Soviet Union continued to persist. A 1942 State Department study of religious attitudes in the United States noted that while many of the most liberal denominations, such as the Unitarian Church, were enthusiastically optimistic about religious freedom in the Soviet Union, most others, including mainline religious liberals, were not.[14] America had intervened not only to defeat fascism but to help rebuild the world upon values and ideals that the communist, atheist and undemocratic Soviet Union simply did not share. As the Reverend Fulton J. Sheen, a prominent Catholic priest, explained over his nationally syndicated radio programme, *The Catholic Hour*, 'Russia . . . is on our side of the war but Russia is not yet on our side of the revolution; please God some day it may be'.[15] At the other end of the political and theological spectrum, the Protestant theologian and renowned liberal Reinhold Niebuhr warned that 'the lack of democracy in Russia is more dangerous' than the Soviet Union's defenders assumed.[16] To many American Christians, then, the wartime alliance with the Soviets was a marriage of convenience rather than a case of true love. At the most, American Christians were willing only to suspend their anti-communism temporarily.

Few people were as active, or as instrumental, in framing these issues and the surrounding debate as Myron C. Taylor, who served for a decade as a special envoy to Pope Pius XII for Presidents Franklin D. Roosevelt and Harry Truman. As a prominent figure in American religious, business and political circles, Taylor is an ideal prism through which to examine American religious attitudes towards the Soviet Union. A wealthy entrepreneur who capped a successful business career as the CEO of US Steel, Taylor was also a prominent layman in the Episcopal Church. He had endeared himself to Roosevelt when he chose compromise over conflict and avoided labour strife at US Steel's Illinois plant by coming to terms with the Steel Workers' Organizing Committee (SWOC) in 1937. As a successful industrialist, Taylor's natural sympathies did not lie with labour; in settling with SWOC, he had been motivated more by the prospective loss of revenue than by adherence to the New Deal's protection of organized labour. Nor, similarly, did they lie with communism, either at home or abroad. While he was willing to respect the different religious views of Jews, Muslims and Buddhists, he declared to a wartime audience when cooperation with the Soviets was official policy: 'I cannot respect the man who has no religious belief'.[17]

However, despite being conservative in matters political, financial and religious, Taylor was ideally suited to represent two liberal Democratic presidents in the Vatican. Indeed, it was precisely his combination of conservatism and personal loyalty that made Taylor so useful to Roosevelt and Truman, because it entrusted him to a reflexively conservative Vatican and much of the religious community in the United States.[18]

Upon his original appointment in 1940, Taylor's objective was to smooth relations between Washington and the Vatican as they both searched for an early end to the war. With American intervention in December 1941, Taylor's task shifted to securing the Vatican's cooperation with the Allied war effort, but in essence his role continued to be a facilitator of harmonious relations between Roosevelt and the Pope. To this end, Taylor helped burnish the Soviet Union's image on religious freedom and tolerance, as his attempt in the summer of 1944 to ease tensions between the Vatican and Moscow over the treatment of Polish Catholics on the Eastern Front exemplified.[19] These efforts, however, were pursued for the sake of defeating Nazi Germany, not in the name of working harmoniously with Soviet communism. Taylor's anti-communism was as consistent as it was passionate, even if the war compelled him to work with the Soviet Union for the time being. He therefore agreed with Roosevelt that Germany must be prevented, at almost any cost, from defeating the Soviet Union. As Taylor later put it, although Soviet communism habitually violated 'the most treasured values and aspirations of human society', so too did German Nazism, which was, at present, the far greater threat. In this context, aid to the Soviet Union, and 'not to Communism, alien alike to America's and Britain's faith and way of life', was in the interests of American national security.[20] Thus an important part of Taylor's duties at the Vatican was the tactical softening of the Pope's own official anti-communism – tactical because Taylor recognized that it would be a temporary exigency for victory in the war.

Although he had already formed strong opinions about the nature of communism, Taylor sought advice on the subject from religious leaders and government officials. What he discovered only reinforced his original hostile instincts. Leopold Braun, the chaplain to American Catholics in Moscow, confessed to Taylor he had at first been 'completely bewildered and literally stupefied' by Roosevelt's comparison of Soviet and American constitutional guarantees of religious liberty. It was true, Braun conceded, that the 1936 constitution did provide for religious freedom, but he also charged that it was essential to separate words from deeds. Seen from this perspective, Russian Catholics lived under religious oppression, not liberty. For emphasis, Braun pointed out that 'every single Catholic member of clergy in the USSR has been arrested, imprisoned or exiled!!!', while others had been summarily executed. Such was the totality of the communists' religious persecution that Protestants, Orthodox Christians and Muslims suffered, too. 'Against the will of believers and after exorbitant taxes had been paid', Braun pleaded, 'churches were forcibly closed and transformed into garages, store-houses, sewing shops, cinemas, restaurants, etc.'[21] 'Freedom of worship, even in its most restricted sense', Edward Mooney, the Catholic archbishop of Detroit, bluntly told Taylor in late 1942, 'does not actually exist in Russia today'.[22]

Most intriguingly, in 1942 Taylor also sought advice from the very person who, four years later, would first formulate the strategy of containment, namely, diplomat George F. Kennan. A Soviet specialist and fellow sceptic of communism, who at the time was posted to the US Embassy in Lisbon, Kennan told Taylor that Soviet leaders 'see in the Church . . . a spiritual rival' that posed a direct challenge to their political authority. Although there were signs of increased religious freedom in the wartime Soviet Union, Kennan stressed that this was a temporary tactic designed to help win the war rather than a genuine conversion to the benefits of religious liberty. Hostility to religion was simply too firmly embedded in communist doctrine. The Kremlin, he noted,

> did all in its power to build Communist ideology into something like a competing religious life in its own right, with similar requirements of spiritual devotion and even of public profession in ceremony and symbol. That this latter effort could not be successful – that Christian faith could not be adequately replaced by a materialistic economic doctrine which had no answers to the problems of suffering and death – is obvious to all of us who have been brought up in a Christian atmosphere.

It was even in Moscow's interest to tolerate greater levels of religious freedom once the war was over. After all, the Nazis were able to win the allegiance of many non-Jewish people they had conquered in Soviet lands by allowing them freedom of worship. However, would Stalin actually loosen his grip on religion in the USSR once the pressure of the war had eased? Kennan doubted it.[23] The implications of Kennan's analysis were clear: Soviet communists could not share power or authority with any others; theirs was an absolutist vision of politics and society. The prospects for post-war cooperation were correspondingly bleak.

Yet Taylor did not press these concerns until the end of the war, when Soviet cooperation would be neither essential nor expected. For now, the Soviets' contributions on the Eastern Front were simply too vital to the war effort. While the Soviet Union presented a potential long-term challenge, Germany was an actual and immediate threat. This was certainly Roosevelt's view, and so it was also the view Taylor promoted at the Vatican. For the time being, Taylor told the Pope in the Fall of 1944, cooperation with Stalin was critical, if distasteful. Only once the war was over, he believed, could opponents of communism turn their full attention to the Soviet problem.[24]

Once victory over Germany and Japan was indeed secured, Taylor intensified his suspicions regarding Soviet communism. It was at this moment, early in the Cold War and with American foreign policy somewhat directionless, that he sought to clarify the nature of the Soviet threat for President Truman. For Taylor, the issue was not exactly cloudy. 'The cause of Communism *versus* Christianity and Democracy', he told Truman in 1946, 'transcends minor differences in the Christian creeds. It is the *Great Issue* of the future and thus of today'.[25]

Yet, initially, Truman was not interested. Instead, he attempted to fulfil what he believed had been Roosevelt's policy – that is, trying to work with the Soviet Union.[26] Accordingly, after the war Truman kept Taylor in Washington, away from the fiercely anti-communist Vatican; the president even contemplated terminating the Taylor mission altogether.[27]

With the rapid deterioration in relations between Washington and Moscow, Truman soon changed his mind and Taylor returned to Rome. With neither the Americans nor the Soviets willing to enforce their mutually exclusive visions for post-war order through military force, ideology itself became a central battleground. The conflict with fascism, of course, had been defined largely as a clash of values and morals, but what made the Cold War different was the primacy of ideology. The struggle with communism would define the future because American democracy had a vision for a just and lasting post-war peace, and only communism blocked its path. After the war, American leaders sought, albeit gradually at first, an anti-Soviet policy that would augment traditional military and diplomatic policy. Containing communism would not simply further American interests, it would significantly advance the welfare of people everywhere by bringing them the same blessings of liberty and prosperity that Americans enjoyed. Indeed, the security of people everywhere, not just in America, depended upon the protection and promotion of freedom. This universalistic principle, of course, formed the basis of American war aims even before America itself had entered the war; the Four Freedoms speech and the Atlantic Charter of 1941 were the most famous expressions of this worldview.[28] However, peace would require religious as well as political and economic foundations – hence the freedom of worship was the second of Roosevelt's Four Freedoms. Already in December 1939, before these ringing public declarations, Roosevelt said as much privately to the Pope: 'When the time shall come for the re-establishment of world peace on a surer foundation, it is of the utmost importance to humanity and to religion that common ideals shall have united expression'.[29] And only Americans could act as this unifying force. This, and not simply the narrow pursuit of self-defence, was America's true calling in the war. 'Because we know we are in the right', Taylor wrote to Pius XII in 1942,

> and because we have supreme confidence in our strength, we are determined to carry through until we shall have won complete victory. The only thing that would make us lay down the arms taken up in defense of national security and world decency would be the complete and forthright acceptance of the Atlantic Charter and the Manifesto of the United Nations. . . . Our cause is just. We fight, with conscience clear, for the moral rights of our nation, and for the liberties of our people; our victory will ensure these rights and liberties to the world. Even our enemies know that we seek no aggrandizement. Precisely for the reason that our moral position is impregnable, we are not open to the compromises usual to those who look for merely material gains, and who will bargain for half a loaf if they cannot have the whole.

The American people, he concluded, fight in 'the conviction that anything less than complete victory would endanger the principles we fight for and our very existence as a nation'.[30] Taylor left unsaid exactly how this vision would be evaluated in Moscow.

Taylor was not alone in viewing the war in such stark, moralistic terms; nor was he alone in carrying this essentially anti-communist vision through to the post-war world. Despite notable exceptions, a similar attitude prevailed among many religious leaders in America. Within a few years, it would prevail in the Truman administration, too: America fought not just for itself, but for all humanity; compromise was tantamount to surrender. It is not surprising, given the stridency of Taylor's declaration of American war aims that equated morality with security, and given Truman's subsequent acceptance of this formulation, that problems would arise between Soviet and American post-war visions of world order. In the 'deepening uncertainties which surround us', he wrote to Taylor in 1947, it was imperative that America pursue 'the advancement of moral world order and lasting peace'. Truman urged his envoy to impress upon the Pope that 'the people of the United States strive towards the same goal, that our faith is firm, our will is determined, and our spirit is undaunted'. The stakes were simply too high for Americans to behave otherwise. 'In keeping with the traditions of our national life', he urged, 'the truth must be the basis of our thought, as the needs of humanity above mere selfish national interest must be the goal of our action'.[31] Once the war was won, Americans no longer needed to tolerate Soviet abuses of political and religious liberty. Indeed, following victory in the war over fascism Taylor simply continued his efforts, this time to forge an anti-communist holy alliance.

Taylor's post-war efforts would at most warrant a footnote were it not for his close working relationship with Truman. Kept in the dark by Roosevelt during his brief term as vice president, surrounded by powerful decision-makers who had shaped American strategy during the war, unsure but untrusting about the Soviet Union's motives and ultimate objectives, yet certain that a post-war international system had to be built along American lines, from the Spring of 1945 to the Winter of 1947 an impressionable Truman was in need of guidance, direction and assurance. With little doubt about the nature of the Soviet threat, Taylor could provide all three. And once Truman had decided upon a strategy of containment, Taylor was still useful for his eagerness to build transatlantic, anti-Soviet alliances of American and European religious leaders. Taylor's key contribution, then, was to provide the essential ideological glue for an increasingly robust ideological approach to the Soviet Union.

Thanks to Truman's own religiosity, it was a powerfully strong glue. Although he had a rather simple religious outlook and attended church infrequently, Truman, as one of his biographers puts it, was 'deeply religious in a larger sense'.[32] As a Baptist, he was instinctively attuned to the principle that religion must be separate from government – otherwise, government would trample on people's rights by favouring one religion over others, or even persecuting adherents to the unofficial faith. As one of America's traditional outsider and therefore vulnerable religious groups, Baptists placed a higher value on the separation of church and state than most other religious faiths. America, Truman wrote in his posthumously published history of the United States, had been founded by people motivated primarily by flight from religious persecution in Europe, where 'it was believed that royalty . . . were placed in their position by God's direction, and that people who differed from them in religious beliefs – or any other kind of beliefs, for that matter – were going against the will of God. Well, I felt that was nonsense the moment I was old enough to read about it and start thinking about things of that sort'. The religious migration of these first Americans, Truman concluded, illustrated that they 'did a lot of thinking about what really constituted human liberty, and about freedom and their own welfare and the welfare of the people around them'. Thomas Jefferson built Americans' political liberty upon the principle that church and state should be completely separate, leaving people to choose their form of worship for themselves.[33]

This is not to argue that Truman based US foreign policy on the lessons of the Bible or the dictates of the Southern Baptist Convention. However, it does suggest that he was susceptible to viewing the world in the dichotomous terms of right and wrong. The Truman Doctrine, for example, with its moral clarity between the good of democracy and the evil of communism, fits neatly into this moralistic view of the world.[34] It also suggests that he viewed threats to religious liberty, especially violations of the church-state divide, as particularly serious. In a time of geopolitical uncertainty, Truman's religiosity provided a clear sense of what was right and what was wrong, which in turn guided his approach to emergent threats such as those posed by the Soviet Union.

Truman believed in America's mission to enlighten the world and protect its own security within the world by spreading American values. As a universalistic faith, Christian theology, of course, had much in common with this boundless vision, but so too did communist ideology. This was a grand struggle defined by the historian Odd Arne Westad as the American 'empire of liberty' *versus* the Soviet 'empire of justice'.[35] At a time when the perceived cost of failure was either total subjugation or another total war, neither empire felt it could live in a world with the other.

Taylor's advocacy for an anti-communist alliance was thus perfectly attuned to both Truman's need and desire for geopolitical clarity. In so doing, Taylor launched his own personal crusade with a set of four general principles that changed little over the nearly 6 years, from 1945 to 1951, in which he acted as Truman's personal envoy. First among these was a conviction that Soviet communism was not only anathema in theory to the principles of American democracy, but that it presented an immediate threat to these principles, and thus to American security. Second was the belief that the Soviets were not only godless atheists, but that they were also fundamentally opposed to the principle of the separation of church from state, which made them seem inherently aggressive. Without such separation, the officially atheist Soviet government was able to persecute religion in Eastern Europe, and potentially France and Italy, as well as within the Soviet

Union itself. How, Taylor asked, could the United States live, safely and freely, in a world threatened by such menace?

If the first two principles presented Truman with a diagnosis of the problem, the next two promised a cure. Third came Taylor's successful quest for Truman's support for an anti-communist coalition of religious forces in the United States and Europe, which Taylor himself would rally. And fourth, Taylor wanted to make this coalition as broad as possible, beginning with the Christian churches but eventually extending to all world religions, including Judaism, Islam, Hinduism and Buddhism. While Taylor may have not believed in the tenets of these faiths – or even of Roman Catholicism – he did believe that as religions they were better suited to the desires of humanity than anything the Soviets could offer. While communism was based on a minority forcibly imposing its will on the majority, freely chosen religion represented the majority of people in nations around the world, and thus was inherently more democratic. It was this latent capacity for democracy that offered hope for both humankind and for America's place in the world.

In an almost perfect mirror image, Taylor's vision was as absolutist and uncompromising as the communist ideology he fought. In this polarized ideological climate, which long predated the end of World War II, it would have been virtually impossible for either side to accept the other's terms for post-war peace. During the wartime Roosevelt administration, Taylor's vision had been that of the minority; but by 1947, it had become the majority viewpoint. Indeed, Taylor and other religious officials had promoted containment before Kennan had coined the term and well before Truman had adopted it as official policy. Taylor could never trust the Soviet Union's declarations of peaceful intent because the Soviets had proven themselves untrustworthy with their refusal to separate church from state and tolerate freedom of worship.

The tragedy which tormented Taylor was that America was thought to have possessed the power and morality to bring about world peace and prosperity. Only the expansionist, atheist, totalitarian Soviet communists stood between humanity and peace. The Nazis had been defeated only to see a new threat emerge. After the war, Taylor reminded the Pope, 'new aggressions, direct and indirect, were made under the false doctrines of communism against the peace of the world, the fundamental freedoms of mankind, and the independence of nations'. The Soviets were guilty of committing 'incessant crimes' and the 'retardation of recovery'.[36] Truman concurred. 'The years immediately behind us have been fraught with difficulties', he complained to the Pope in early 1948. The world's 'hopes for an enduring peace have been deferred' due solely to the efforts of 'a totalitarian minority representing a philosophy of retrogression'.[37] He was even more emphatic and explicit later that year. 'I share your apprehension over the threat to Christian civilization', he replied to one of Pius XII's missives. 'All who cherish Christian and democratic institutions should unite against the common enemy. That enemy is the Soviet Union which would substitute the Marxian doctrine of atheistic communism for Revelation'.[38]

Moreover, if religion could identify the problem, it could also provide a solution. Both Taylor and Truman envisioned an international system based on a 'moral world order' to which Americans 'are dedicated by faith, and to which all must rally by destiny'. In contrast to international communism, the 'moral world order' would be based on individual political, religious and economic liberty. Religion was integral to this order because it could alleviate concerns on all three fronts: religious values would make it 'moral', religion's universal appeal would give it force around the 'world', and adherence to the values of peace and justice would provide 'order'. However, communism was such a potent threat because it too claimed to address all three components of the 'moral world order', albeit in a twisted, unrepresentative, fraudulent way. Truman and Taylor believed that communism was so dangerous, in other words, because it also claimed to embody the desires of all humanity. However, if communism was a disease, Christianity, in alliance with Americanism, could provide the cure. 'We are assisting in ways unprecedented in the history of the human race', Truman believed, 'the peoples and governments who share with us the intention to construct a world order of true and enduring peace under God'.[39]

This vision fit neatly into the emerging strategy of containment. If economic and military aid to Europe were two aspects of stemming the advance of communism, religious unity was another. As Truman wrote in a letter to Pius XII that Taylor delivered in the Summer of 1947, 'all persons . . . must unite their efforts in the cause of enduring peace if they are not one by one to be weakened and rendered impotent at the time of their great need'. The challenges 'now confronting us are formidable'. In the face of such gravity, unless 'the moral forces of the world now join their strength, discouragement must inevitably deepen, and the strength and effectiveness which thereby would be lost by these moral forces would be gained by those forces which oppose and seek to destroy them'.[40] American leadership was indispensable because America was the only power capable of stopping communism. 'These hopeless people' in Europe, Taylor told a group of American clergy, 'all look to us to help them, to save them'.[41]

Sensitive to any hint of favouritism of the Catholic church, Protestant clergy in the United States urged Truman to expand Taylor's contacts to the leaders of the Protestant churches.[42] Truman needed little encouragement. In 1947, he expanded Taylor's duties and charged his envoy with gathering together all the religious forces of the Western world, not just the Vatican, under American leadership in a grand anti-communist alliance. Taylor's task, and Truman's goal, was 'to appeal to all *believers in God and human liberty* to join together to bring pressure of a common desire for peace upon the atheistic communistic government of Russia'.[43] In an effort to win the world's hearts and minds, Truman and Taylor aimed to cast their net as widely as possible. 'Looks as if he and I [Taylor] may get the morals of the world on our side', Truman boasted to his wife Bess: 'We are talking to the Archbishop of Canterbury, the bishop at the head of the Lutheran Church, the Metropolitan of the Greek Church at Istanbul', even 'the top Buddhist and the Grand Lama of Tibet'. Religious faith was America's secret weapon in the Cold War. 'If I can mobilize the people who believe in a moral world against the Bolshevik materialists', he felt, 'we can win this fight'.[44]

Following the thought of Roosevelt and Truman, Taylor viewed the end of wartime hostilities with Germany and the beginnings of post-war hostility with the Soviet Union as two parts of the same struggle. The fact that his mission to the Vatican continued after the war with Germany, Taylor wrote Truman in 1950, 'is a part of the history of the struggle for an enduring peaceful world order that the free nations have unflaggingly made in the presence of adverse and discouraging circumstances'. Nobody, Taylor recognized, could have expected a smooth transition from the most severe economic depression and war in world history. However, victory in the war did present an opportunity for what Taylor, like Truman, called 'the moral forces of the world'. It provided an opportunity to rebuild the world system on the principles of justice, freedom and prosperity – on the principles, that is, of Roosevelt's Four Freedoms. American power, and the taming of German and Japanese expansionism, meant that the United States had in its grasp the ability to realize this vision. What blocked the fulfilment of this vision was not depression or war, but the emergence of a new expansionist, illiberal threat, namely, Soviet communism. Depression and war, Taylor believed, were not so much the source of post-war tension as was the Soviet Union's aggressive behaviour, expansionist designs and, above all, ideological threat. Faced with such a threat, the United States had little choice but to respond in kind. After 1945, he noted, these

> deeply disturbing conflicts became manifest in almost all aspects of world affairs. International tension increased, accompanied by widespread and profound concern lest new aggressions, direct and indirect, jeopardize the fundamental freedoms of mankind, the independence of free nations, and the peace of the world. In these circumstances, unparalleled efforts were instituted by the free nations directed toward the preservation of liberty and basic human rights, economic recovery, social advancement, and the safeguarding of the vital moral foundations of civilization.[45]

As the world's last hope for survival and recovery, Americans 'realized that every resource, spiritual and material, was necessary to bring to the troubled world the progress and enduring peace for which most of the world was striving'. Only America could secure 'a peaceful and advancing world in accordance with Christian principles'. Only America could confront 'the new problems of sustaining the hopes of the enslaved victims of communist tyranny'. This had been Roosevelt's mission against German and Japanese fascism, and it now defined Truman's mission against Soviet communism. For Taylor, then, the world war had never ended; it had simply entered a new phase.[46]

To be successful, any special relationship needs to be cemented not just by common national interests and enemies, but also by shared values and morals. Indeed, a common ideology is what makes such relationships 'special' in the first place. To be sure, states pursue their own interests, and when those interests clash with the priorities of a special relationship the national interest almost always prevails in actual decision-making. However, when states form alliances and forge bonds of international solidarity, the most successful ones have a common set of values as their foundation. While the United States and the Soviet Union cooperated to a remarkable degree during World War II, they did so because they shared a common enemy. When that enemy was defeated, their sharply divergent ideological values – which each side felt should exclusively determine the basis for post-war order – could never come together. While policymakers in Washington hoped for the continuation of great power cooperation after the war as the only way to guarantee international peace and stability, activist American Christians, such as Myron Taylor, argued that the United States could never share a common cause with the Soviet Union because of communist atheism and Soviet repression of faith. Furthermore, Taylor – and eventually President Harry Truman himself – deployed religion as an ideological weapon to use against the Soviet Union in the Cold War. Had Washington and Moscow formed a post-war special relationship in the face of such domestic American hostility, it would have been a peculiar relationship indeed.

Notes

1 On this point, see W. F. Kimball, 'The Incredible Shrinking War: The Second World War, Not (Just) the Origins of the Cold War', *Diplomatic History*, 2001, vol. 25, pp. 347–65.

2 J. L. Gaddis, *The United States and the Origins of the Cold War, 1941–1947*, New York: Columbia University Press, 1972, p. 41; W. F. Kimball, *The Juggler: Franklin Roosevelt as Wartime Statesman*, Princeton: Princeton University Press, 1991, pp. 198–99; D. J. Dunn, *Caught between Roosevelt and Stalin: America's Ambassadors to Moscow*, Lexington: University Press of Kentucky, 1998, p. 263. For Roosevelt's vision of an American–Soviet working relationship that would underpin post-war order, see R. Dallek, *Franklin Roosevelt and American Foreign Policy*, 2nd edn., New York: Oxford University Press, 1995, pp. 144–45, 433–39, 471–72, 507–8; M. E. Glantz, *FDR and the Soviet Union: The President's Battles over Foreign Policy*, Lawrence: University Press of Kansas, 2005; D. Reynolds, *From World War to Cold War: Churchill, Roosevelt, and the International History of the 1940s*, Oxford: Oxford University Press, 2006, pp. 237, 272; and W. D. Miscamble, *From Roosevelt to Truman: Potsdam, Hiroshima, and the Cold War*, Cambridge: Cambridge University Press, 2007, pp. 41–43, 48–69, 78–80.

3 Gaddis, *Origins of the Cold War*, pp. 32–62; D. S. Foglesong, *The American Mission and the 'Evil Empire': The Crusade for a 'Free Russia' since 1881*, Cambridge: Cambridge University Press, 2007, pp. 83–106.

4 M. E. Marty, *Modern American Religion*, vol. 3, *Under God, Indivisible, 1941–1960*, Chicago: University of Chicago Press, 1996, pp. 17–112; J. A. Carpenter, *Revive Us Again: The Reawakening of American Fundamentalism*, New York: Oxford University Press, 1997.

5 W. A. Harriman and E. Abel, *Special Envoy to Churchill and Stalin, 1941–1946*, New York: Random House, 1975, p. 103.

6 'Calls for Religion in Soviet', *New York Times*, 13 July 1941, p. 16.

7 'Urge Soviet Aid Hinge on Reforms', *New York Times*, 27 June 1941, p. 8.

8 Dallek, *Franklin Roosevelt and American Foreign Policy*, p. 296.

9 Roosevelt press conference, quoted in Cordell Hull to Moscow Embassy, 2 October 1941, *Foreign Relations of the United States, 1941*, vol. I, *General: The Soviet Union*, Washington, D.C.: Government Printing Office, 1958, p. 1001.

10 'Catholic Leader Assails "Mockery"', *New York Times*, 6 October 1941, p. 4.

11 'Soviet's "Freedom" Defined', *New York Times*, 6 October 1941, p. 4.

12 Both quotations from 'God & Lend-Lease', *Time*, 13 October 1941.

13 On Soviet religious freedom during the war, see S.M. Miner, *Stalin's Holy War: Religion, Nationalism, and Alliance Politics, 1941–1945*, Chapel Hill: University of North Carolina Press, 2003. On American optimism about this development, see Foglesong, *American Mission and "Evil Empire"*, pp. 90–93.

14 Department of State, Division of Special Research, 'Summary of Opinion and Ideas on International Post-War Problems', 4 November 1942, Sumner Welles papers, Box 190, Folder, 1, Franklin D. Roosevelt Library, Hyde Park, NY (hereafter FDRL).

15 F. J. Sheen, 'What This War Is Not And What It Is', *Current Religious Thought*, February 1943, p. 15.

16 R. Niebuhr to W. Van Kirk, 6 November 1944, Record Group 18, Box 40, Folder 8, Archives of the Federal Council of Churches, Presbyterian Historical Society, Philadelphia, PA.

17 M. Taylor, 'The Importance of Religious Cooperation', speech to the National Conference of Christians and Jews, 23 April 1942, Myron C. Taylor papers, Box 22, FDRL.

18 J. S. Conway, 'Myron C. Taylor's Mission to the Vatican, 1940–50', *Church History*, 1975, vol. 44, p. 87; A. J. Badger, *The New Deal: The Depression Years, 1933–1940*, Houndmills: Macmillan, 1989, pp. 129–30.

19 Miner, *Stalin's Holy War*, pp. 174–78.

20 M. C. Taylor, 'Explanatory Note' in *Wartime Correspondence between President Roosevelt and Pope Pius XII*, New York: Macmillan, 1947, p. 57.

21 L. Braun to Taylor, 5 October 1941, Taylor Papers, Box 3, Manuscript Collections, Carl A. Kroch Library, Cornell University, Ithaca, NY. See also L. L. S. Braun, *In Lubianka's Shadow: The Memoirs of an American Priest in Stalin's Moscow, 1934– 1945*, ed. by G. M. Hamburg, Notre Dame: University of Notre Dame Press, 2006.

22 E. Mooney to Taylor, 30 November 1942, Taylor Papers, Box 8, Cornell.

23 G. F. Kennan to Taylor, 2 October 1942, Taylor Papers, Box 8, Cornell.

24 Conway, 'Myron C. Taylor's Mission to the Vatican', p. 98.

25 Quoted in D. Kirby, 'Divinely Sanctioned: The Anglo-American Cold War Alliance and the Defence of Western Civilization and Christianity, 1945–48', *Journal of Contemporary History*, 2000, vol. 35, p. 392. Emphasis in original document.

26 Miscamble, *From Roosevelt to Truman*, pp. 87–123.

27 P. C. Kent, *The Lonely Cold War of Pope Pius XII: The Roman Catholic Church and the Division of Europe, 1943–1950*, Montreal and Ithaca, NY: McGill-Queen's University Press, 2002, pp. 96, 167.

28 On the Atlantic Charter and the Four Freedoms as expressions of America's mission, see E. Borgwardt, *A New Deal for the World: America's Vision for Human Rights*, Cambridge, Mass.: Harvard University Press, 2005.

29 Roosevelt to Pius XII, 23 December 1939, in *Wartime Correspondence between President Roosevelt and Pope Pius XII*, p. 19.

30 Taylor to Pius XII, 19 September 1942, Taylor Papers, Box 1, Cornell.

31 Truman to Taylor, 7 August 1947, Taylor Papers, Box 1, Cornell.

32 A. L. Hamby, *Man of the People: A Life of Harry S. Truman*, New York: Oxford University Press, 1995, p. 474. For an insightful portrait of Truman's religious beliefs and outlook, see E. E. Spalding, *The First Cold Warrior: Harry Truman, Containment, and the Remaking of Liberal Internationalism*, Lexington: University Press of Kentucky, 2006, pp. 205–9.

33 M. Truman (ed.) *Where the Buck Stops: The Personal and Private Writings of Harry S. Truman*, New York: Warner Books, 1989, pp. 120, 210–13.

34 For two accounts that convincingly place the rhetoric of the Truman Doctrine in a tradition of American Puritanism, which explicitly viewed the world as divided between duelling forces of good and evil, see E. S. Rosenberg, 'U.S. Cultural History', in E. R. May (ed.) *American Cold War Strategy: Interpreting NSC 68*, Boston: Bedford Books of St. Martin's Press, 1993, pp. 160–64; and A. Stephanson, 'Liberty or Death: The Cold War as US Ideology', in O. A. Westad (ed.) *Reviewing the Cold War: Approaches, Interpretations, Theory*, London: Cass, 2000, pp. 82–100.

35 O. A. Westad, *The Global Cold War: Third World Interventions and the Making of Our Times*, Cambridge: Cambridge University Press, 2005, pp. 8–72.

36 Taylor to Pius XII, 13 December 1949, Taylor Papers, Box 1, Cornell.

37 Truman to Pius XII, 26 March 1948, Taylor Papers, Box 1, Cornell.

38 Truman to Pius XII, 11 August 1948, Taylor Papers, Box 1, Cornell.

39 Truman to Taylor, 26 March 1948, Taylor Papers, Box 1, Cornell.

40 Truman to Pius XII, 6 August 1947, Taylor Papers, Box 1, Cornell.

41 'Meeting of Protestant Clergymen with Myron C. Taylor at Union Club, New York', 20 October 1947, 16, Taylor Papers, Box 3, Cornell.

42 See, for example, W. Hale to Taylor, 31 May 1947, Taylor Papers, Box 7, Cornell; and G. H. Bechtold to Truman, 20 August 1947, Taylor Papers, Box 3, Cornell. Hale was an Episcopalian minister from Boston and Bechtold was a Lutheran minister from Philadelphia. Like Roosevelt, Truman wanted to elevate the Taylor mission to the Vatican from presidential envoy to official ambassador. Following Taylor's retirement in 1950, Truman moved to appoint Mark Clark, a retired Army general, as the first-ever US ambassador to the Holy See. However, tightening and formalizing official relations with the Catholic Church proved to be so deeply controversial among Protestants, across the political and theological spectrum, that Truman dropped the idea, and the establishment of official relations between Washington and the Vatican would have to wait until 1984. On Truman's problems with Protestant anti-Catholicism, see D. Acheson, *Present at the Creation: My Years in the State Department*, New York: Norton, 1969, pp. 574–75; M. E. Marty, *Under God, Indivisible*, pp. 110, 198–204; P. C. Kent, *Lonely Cold War of Pope Pius XII*, pp. 182–83, 220, 254, 259; and E. E. Spalding, *First Cold Warrior*, pp. 216–17.

43 Taylor, memo for the record, 26 October 1948, Taylor Papers, Box 3, Cornell. Emphasis in original.

44 Truman to Bess Truman, 2 October 1947, in R. H. Ferrell (ed.) *Dear Bess: The Letters from Harry to Bess Truman, 1910–1959*, New York: Norton, 1983, pp. 551–52.

45 Taylor to Truman, 18 January 1950, Taylor Papers, Box 1, Cornell.

46 Ibid.

13 'What Marx, Lenin, and Stalin needed was ... to be born again'
Evangelicals and the special relationship between church and state in US Cold War foreign policy

Axel R. Schäfer

Historians of international relations have long recognized the important role played by business, nonprofits, think tanks, professional organizations and similar societal entities in shaping and implementing American foreign policy. In a liberal polity marked by the separation of powers, checks and balances, and an ideology of limited government and free enterprise, mobilizing society in the name of the 'national interest' generally relies more upon government incentives than state authority. 'Special relationships' between the state and nongovernmental actors thus frequently form the 'corporatist' or 'associationalist' bedrock of US public policy. In the words of historian Michael Sherry, they throw 'a smoke-screen of symbolic anti-statism over deepening government responsibility'.[1]

The Cold War ushered in a dramatic expansion of these state-private networks. Cold War planners sought to attain social and foreign policy objectives by funding and regulating nongovernmental organizations in areas such as higher education, health care, defence and medical research, social services and foreign aid. Rather than creating government agencies and providing services directly, they funnelled billions of dollars of public funds into private and nonprofit organizations via grants-in-aid, vouchers, purchase-of-service agreements, loans and tax exemptions. Legislation such as the 1944 G. I. Bill, the 1946 Hill-Burton Act, and the 1967 Social Security Amendments both facilitated the large-scale expansion of the human service infrastructure and fuelled the growth of nongovernmental agencies.[2]

This large-scale expansion of the 'subsidiarist state' under the auspices of the Cold War liberal consensus dramatically changed the relationship between religious groups and the federal government in the United States. Policymakers, eager to expand the links with voluntary organizations, could hardly ignore the resources of religious charities, which constitute about 40 per cent of the organizations in the nonprofit sector and account for as much as two-thirds of its donations and volunteer labour force. Likewise, many religious charities, remembering the devastating financial impact of the Great Depression, had by the 1940s' relaxed their opposition to public subsidies. Government and religious nonprofits thus became closely intertwined. Indeed, as political scientist Stephen Monsma has pointed out, the 'two characteristics of nonprofit service organizations – their receipt of large amounts of government funds and the religious nature of many of them – overlap'.[3] In the foreign policy arena, government funding for the chaplaincy in the armed forces, donation of surplus land and military facilities to religious charities, and support for overseas mission work undergirded Cold War goals while simultaneously underwriting the expansion of sectarian agencies. Likewise, religious foreign aid agencies constituted the private providers most favoured by the US government in its international relief programmes in the aftermath of World War II.[4]

This support for religious agencies played an important role in shoring up the divergent institutional and ideological underpinnings of the Cold War state. By the same token, it gave religious groups opportunities to reassert their spiritual mission and provided them with new access to the corridors of political power. Nonetheless, the role of religious providers in the subsidiarist state has received little systematic attention in Cold War research.[5] This is indicative of a deeper conceptual limitation of much historical scholarship on religion and politics. While it frequently examines the ideological convergence between church and state during the war and post-war years, it often neglects the institutional and bureaucratic ties between religious organizations and government, and the participation of sectarian groups in public policy implementation.

This essay examines a particular aspect of this special relationship, namely, the integration of evangelicals into these church-state networks in the foreign policy arena. It maintains that the ideological and institutional needs of the Cold War state, in conjunction with the political awakening of evangelicalism, laid the foundation for new political and financial ties between the two. As the Cold War defence-welfare state expanded, evangelicals, driven by their identification with US foreign policy goals, gradually embraced a statist posture in regard to national security. They also largely parted with their traditional rejection to public aid to religion, as agency growth, denominational competition and subsidiarist policies that safeguarded the organizational independence of religious agencies sidelined older evangelical fears about breaches in the 'wall of separation between church and state'. Henceforth, evangelicals made access to funds and the preservation of their faith-based practices within a system of state subsidies the linchpin of their new attitude to public aid. In turn, drawing upon the resources of evangelical entities helped sanctify America's new global role as 'defender of the Free World' and legitimize a Cold War order that uneasily combined the ideology of limited government with the massive expansion of the state's military and welfare components.

Despite these 'statist' and 'subsidiarist' turns, however, the essay shows that evangelicals retained separationist and insurgent elements in their foreign policy profile. They fervently attacked the United Nations by invoking biblical prophesies that linked the rise of the Antichrist to the emergence of world government; their assertion of patriotic conversionism was frequently couched in denunciations of Catholicism and liberalism that were at odds with the pluralistic reality of American life; despite their vocal support for Israel, their biblical demand for the conversion of the Jews and expectation of cataclysmic warfare retained traditional anti-Semitic sentiments; and in the late 1960s and 1970s a resurgent evangelical Left renewed the traditional critique of the corruptibility of secular institutions, denounced the arms race and demanded nuclear disarmament.

The essay concludes by arguing that the new nexus between evangelicals and the federal government, and the need to reconcile traditional church-state separationism with the Cold War state and participation in public funding streams, benefited the Right within in the evangelical movement more than liberal and left-leaning groups. While the Left remained staunchly separationist, conservatives relied on an ideological message that combined a rhetoric of separation and institutional autonomy with an active embrace of the national security state and participation in Cold War subsidiarity. This enabled them to mediate between the movement's internal conflicts and marginalize its left-wing groups, particularly during the period of internal fragmentation in the post-Vietnam era. In the long run, this balancing act formed an important element in the Christian Right's political ideology, which employs the rhetoric of limited government but staunchly supports a hawkish foreign policy and large-scale military spending.[6]

The Cold War, religion and evangelicalism

World War II and the Cold War offered an unexpected ideological windfall for religious groups. The wartime message that the strength of a people in the battle against totalitarianism lay in their moral character bolstered the religious component in American culture and society. While 'Praise the Lord and pass the ammunition' became a slogan in the semantic arsenal of warfare, stories of 'foxhole epiphanies' became staple dramatic components of post-war revivals. The period's atmosphere of anxiety and triumph further synchronized religious themes, nationalism, anti-communism and the American way of life. As influential Presbyterian minister Edward L. R. Elson pointed out in a sermon, the axe of the pioneer 'has become America's gigantic industrial machine, and the world sees that. His gun has become America's powerful armament, and the world knows it well. His Book, by the power of the Person revealed therein, is pouring forth the light of a new spiritual rebirth, and the world must clearly see that'.[7]

Policymakers knew that religious belief in a just cause, a worldview based on a clear distinction between good and evil, adherence to moral principles and strong enemy images were effective tools during the Cold War. By depicting the Cold War as a patriotic battle against an enemy who not only needed to be defeated militarily, but also spiritually and culturally, they tied national security to a renewed commitment to traditional religion and defined Christianity as a natural ally in the anti-communist struggle. FBI Director J. Edgar Hoover pronounced 'the spiritual firepower of the Christian Church' to be 'sufficient to destroy all the Soviet man-made missiles'.[8] 'What is our battle against communism if it is not a fight against anti-God and a belief in the Almighty?', Dwight Eisenhower asked, concluding that 'when God comes in, communism has to go'.[9]

The close link between the constitutional order and Christianity, and between patriotism and religiousness, was given symbolic recognition when the words 'under God' were added to the Pledge of Allegiance in 1954. As William Miller irreverently noted, the pledge henceforth had 'its rhythm upset but its anti-communist spirituality improved'.[10] Moreover, 'In God We Trust' was adopted as a national motto in 1956. Religion in these years was simply seen as a good thing, and even marginal groups, such as fundamentalists, received friendly media coverage. As Eisenhower famously remarked shortly before assuming office, 'Our form of government has no sense unless it is founded in a deeply felt religious faith, and I don't care what it is'.[11]

Meanwhile, religious groups in the 1950s were equally keen to bolster the spiritual component in American society. Many churches embraced the opportunity to counter the long-term trend towards understanding American liberty and democracy as the result of an anticlerical Enlightenment tradition, secular values and pragmatist ethics. They craved putting Judeo-Christian spirituality back into the centre as the template for understanding the post-war totalitarian threats and the moral mission of the redeemer nation to spread American democracy. As Scott Flipse pointed out, 'Pax Americana found wide support among religious people because religious leaders shared the goals and values of US foreign policy leaders'.[12]

Evangelicals did not remain on the sidelines during this renewal of religio-political fervour. In the early 1940s a network of conservative Protestants set out to strip pre-war fundamentalism of its pre-war gloom and doom, to reassert the spirit of revivalism, and to establish a broad interdenominational basis. These neo-evangelicals sought to create a network of evangelical bible institutes, foreign missions, seminaries, colleges, publishing houses, journals and radio stations. Their renewed embrace of social action and their willingness to cooperate with mainline Protestants separated them from traditional fundamentalists. Meanwhile, their espousal of doctrinal orthodoxy and rejection of the social gospel marked their distance from theological liberalism. In the decades after the end of World War II, white evangelical Protestants thus sought a measure of socio-cultural legitimacy, theological authority, internal unity and political influence that they had not achieved since the nineteenth century. They moved away from cultural isolation, social withdrawal and political marginality to become yet again a significant political and cultural force in American society. As Joel Carpenter puts it, 'The postwar evangelical movement reached into the older denominations, the offices of Capitol Hill, the studios of Hollywood, and up the Hit Parade charts as well'.[13]

The neo-evangelical efforts to create a 'third force' in American Protestantism found institutional expression in the formation of the National Association of Evangelicals (NAE) in 1942. The NAE became the main organization of neo-evangelicalism between the 1940s and the 1980s. Under its auspices evangelicals organized lobbying efforts in Washington, set up a clearinghouse for legislative campaigns, coordinated relief and missionary work, spawned the powerful National Religious Broadcasters (NRB) and fostered the training of conservative Christians for positions in government. The most prominent figure in this new generation of evangelicals was Billy Graham. He was not only successful 'in "saving souls" but in making the premillennialist evangelical world view palatable in the mainstream of American culture again'.[14] While William Randolph Hearst told his newspaper editors to 'puff Graham', the famous evangelist helped conservative Protestantism shed its image of religious backcountry bacchanalia. He donned voguish ties, presented a clean-shaven look, and offered a transdenominational, transracial and transethnic alternative to old-style fundamentalism.[15]

A less lofty, but equally important place in the movement was occupied by theologian Carl F. H. Henry. He provided the movement with ideological leadership and set out to show that evangelical Christianity was 'an intellectually viable and vibrant faith and not a suspect cult'.[16] Henry knew that evangelizing alone was not sufficient and that think tanks were needed to provide intellectual guidance and institutional stability. He was instrumental in the founding of Fuller Theological Seminary, which was designed to become the 'Cal-Tech of modern evangelicalism' in the upscale setting of Pasadena, California. Henry also became editor of *Christianity Today*. The magazine was funded by oil magnate J. Howard Pew and other corporate donors, and its editorial offices were set up within view of the White House.[17]

Evangelical foreign policy

The formulation of a distinctive evangelical foreign policy agenda was an integral part of this post-war resurgence of conservative Protestantism. The neo-evangelicals were keenly aware of the political window of opportunity the foreign policy field offered. The transition in the United States from isolationist sentiment and the fear of entangling alliances to the post-war embrace of global superpower status had left an interpretive vacuum. Evangelicals sought to fill this void by promoting eschatological, millennial and prophetic interpretations as plausible patterns for understanding America's new role in world affairs. While most pre-war Americans had been mildly amused by such concepts as the Antichrist, Armageddon and the Apocalypse, the threat of nuclear warfare and the fear of communism, made these biblical prophesies much more real and palpable. As historian Paul Boyer pointed out, 'one cannot fully understand the American public's response to a wide range of international and domestic issues without bearing in mind that millions of men and women view world events . . . through the refracting lens of prophetic belief'.[18]

In the same vein, evangelicals re-legitimized the religious drama of conversion and salvation by linking it to the patriotic embrace of the religious foundations of American society. They presented Christian teachings as the only effective antidote to communism and insisted that traditional evangelical Protestantism was the genuine civil religion of the United States. As Billy Graham exclaimed, 'If you would be a true patriot, then become a Christian. If you would be a loyal American, then become a loyal Christian'.[19] Indeed, Graham later conceded that in the 1950s he had frequently confused the Kingdom of God with the American way of life.[20]

This spiritualization of America's global interests helped integrate conservative Protestants into the Cold War foreign policy consensus. Nonetheless, evangelicals also retained a deeply apocalyptic, premillennialist and anti-liberal view of world events. In the words of Joel Carpenter, they positioned themselves as both effective communicators of the myth of American righteousness and die-hard supporters of conservative piety.[21] Rephrasing the traditional conversion narrative in nationalistic terms, for example, on the one hand associated redemption with American-style democracy and sanctified both the military build-up and liberal capitalism. On the other hand, the conversionist discourse replaced the foreign policy emphasis on order and stability with an emphasis on 'regime change'. As the 'two-star evangelical' William Harrison put it, 'What Marx, Lenin, and Stalin needed was not simply an exposure to the "Christian ethic" but to be "born again"'.[22]

This tension remained at the very core of the evangelical foreign policy agenda and its four main components: support for Israel, opposition to the United Nations, anti-communism and anti-Catholicism. In regard to the Jewish state, evangelicals on the one hand parted with their traditional anti-Semitism and became some of Israel's staunchest allies, since they viewed its founding in 1948 as a sign of the impending return of the Messiah and the fulfilment of scriptural prophesies. On the other hand, anti-Semitic strains remained present in the movement. Evangelicals did not relinquish their active pursuit of converting Jews. They also held on to the notion that the Holocaust was God's punishment for the waywardness of the Jews. Indeed, the uneasy merger of national security-oriented *Realpolitik* with a prophetic attitude continues to shape their contemporary view of the Middle East.[23]

While the pro-Israel stance reflected a new engagement with global politics, evangelical opposition towards the United Nations was indicative of the continuing strength of unilateralist and isolationist sentiment within the movement. This stance was theologically informed by biblical readings that ascribed particular eschatological significance to 'nations' and viewed 'world government' as a sign of the impending advent of the Antichrist. While the ideological basis of the UN was humanistic and secular, evangelicals argued, nations such as the United States were built upon moral and spiritual foundations. In their view, viable international alliances had to be grounded in shared spiritual values.[24] 'Evangelicals consider alliances of nations uncommitted to transcendent justice to be as futile a foundation for future mutuality as premarital promiscuity', Carl Henry declared, concluding that 'as evangelical Christians see it, the vision of One World, or of United Nations, that is built on geographical representation rather than on principal agreement is as socially unpromising as is a lawless home that neglects the commandments of God'.[25] In the 1950s the NAE, therefore, supported a constitutional amendment sponsored by conservative Republican senator John W. Bricker. This amendment, if passed, would have placed severe restrictions on treaties and executive agreements entered into by the US government.

A similar ambivalence characterized evangelical anti-communism. Conservative Protestants on the one hand used anti-communism to give credibility to prophesy belief that identified Russia with the biblical Gog and interpreted communism as a false religion set up by Satan to both mimic and mock God's creation. This 'deep threat' of communism, they contended, could only be counteracted by public declarations of loyalty to the American nation via a renewal of the Christian faith. In its most extreme form, this mindset engendered fears of subversion that provided spiritual legitimacy to the excesses of Hoover's surveillance and intimidation apparatus. Biblically-based anti-communism also explains the nonchalance with which evangelicals were willing to use extreme military force. Hence, Harold John Ockenga, a leading evangelical light, demanded an 'aggressive diplomacy' that 'will maintain access to Berlin whatever come even if this means using atomic weapons'.[26] Despite this fervour, however, evangelicals on the other hand were careful to wield the sword of anti-communism altogether too forcefully. Though avidly anti-communist, they were at pains to disassociate themselves from the militancy of fundamentalist firebrands such as Carl McIntire and Billy James Hargis. Moreover, the short-lived 'brown scare' during the war had impressed upon evangelicals the need to separate themselves from the extreme right wing.[27]

This combination of projecting anti-communist resolve while rejecting fundamentalist extremism was crucial in cementing the political credentials of post-war evangelicalism. Staunch anticommunism opened up the pathway for the coalition of religious and political conservatives. J. Edgar Hoover and Republican Senate leader William Knowland, among others, frequently penned anti-communist tracts for *Christianity Today*. Likewise, the evangelical anti-communist crusade adopted a number of high-profile foreign policy causes, such as staunch opposition to diplomatic recognition of 'Red China'.[28] By the same token, however, evangelicals increasingly shifted the discourse away from tirades against socialism and communism towards attacks on the moral dangers of 'permissiveness', 'secular humanism', and 'big government'. As Paul Peachey noted in *Christianity Today*, 'Communism, which we despise, and the secularism of the West are blood relatives'.[29] In evangelical parlance, church leaders were cast in the role of doctors who 'should appreciate the evil nature of the germ of godlessness' and should be able to 'see beneath the superficial symptoms to the underlying spiritual pathology'.[30] The real danger of this 'ideological disease', they argued, lay in its secularizing tendencies that threatened to undermine the moral fibre of the nation. As George Marsden, Jerome Himmelstein and Lisa McGirr have concluded, this shift from conspiratorial, apocalyptic anticommunism to religio-therapeutic moralism allowed conservative Protestants to move into the respectable mainstream and was a key factor in their broad-based political success.[31]

Finally, evangelicals in the 1950s and 1960s were at least as rabidly anti-Catholic as anti-communist. Ignoring finer differences between Moscow and the Vatican they depicted Catholicism as simply a different side of the same communist coin.[32] The main reason for this virulence was that the Catholic challenge was ultimately closer to home than the communist threat. Even the most avid red-baiter had to admit that incidences of communist subversion remained limited in the United States. In contrast, Catholic institutions had a real and palpable presence in American society. This evangelical antipathy was exacerbated by the wartime and post-war clash of evangelical overseas missionary activities with similar Catholic efforts. In turn, legislative campaigning against perceived Catholic repression abroad became the hallmark of the NAE's lobbying activities. The 'vicious reaction of fanatical Romanism putting government under pressure to harass Protestants' in Columbia, for example, prompted Clyde Taylor, the director of the NAE's Office of Public Affairs (OPA) to ask for a resolution denouncing the 'satanic tactics' that Catholics allegedly employed in calling for the suppression – 'meaning, in general, liquidation' – of Protestants in the country.[33]

Crucially, the NAE's efforts to stymie Catholic abuses generated a new awareness of the benefits of working with government agencies. Taylor triumphantly noted in the mid-1950s that after years of 'giving full cooperation to government agencies we have seen the fruit. Men on the inside of government, knowing the stand of N.A.E. and our specific interests in religious matters, are calling and alerting us when critical matters come up'.[34] As evangelicals combined their efforts to establish new missions with pressure on government to create a stable religious investment climate abroad, a subtle but decisive change took place in their rhetoric. They began to package their campaign in more general terms as the defence of religious liberty, the rights of individual Protestant missionaries overseas, and the separation of church and state, rather than as an anti-Catholic crusade. In the ensuing decades the NAE devoted significant resources to the religious freedom campaign, which eventually culminated in the passage of the International Religious Freedom Act in 1998.[35]

In the long term, phrasing evangelical interests as a religious freedom issue had another important advantage. Though initially spawned by both anti-communist and anti-Catholic sentiments, the emphasis on religious liberty was crucial in enabling evangelicals to form transdenominational coalitions, especially after the Second Vatican Council. While anti-Catholicism lost its raw edge, however, it continued to demarcate post-war evangelicalism as both mainstream and militant. The NAE campaign to prevent diplomatic relations with the Vatican, for example, continued well beyond the 1960 election. In fact, it continued well into the 1980s. 'We have battled this all the way, in keeping with a 1943 NAE resolution, reiterated ten times since', OPA director Robert Dugan reported in 1984 when the Reagan administration appointed an ambassador to the Vatican.[36]

Evangelicals and the Cold War state

On the surface the fledgling evangelical enthusiasm for foreign policy issues in the 1950s and early 1960s had little immediate impact on US policy. The personal and intellectual links between the Eisenhower and Billy Graham, for example, did not translate into significant political influence. As William Miller aptly put it, Eisenhower was 'a fervent believer in a very vague religion'. Indicative of his attitude was that, after declaring Independence Day in 1953 a day of prayer and repentance, he took off to go fishing, play golf and spend the evening at the

Bridge table.[37] There were also no clear indications that Eisenhower's foreign policies were decisively influenced by evangelicalism. Despite the administration's strident anti-communism, NATO's strategy of massive retaliation, and John Foster Dulles' 'roll back' ideology, Eisenhower followed a much more moderate course. He neither believed that the Soviet Union wanted another war, nor did he consider the use of the atomic bomb to be a realistic military option. In contrast to recurrent evangelical demands for 'an aggressive spiritual-moral international policy', his foreign policy focus tended to be on collective security and containment.[38]

Nonetheless, the evangelical political inroads pioneered during the Eisenhower administration were invaluable to the movement. They allowed evangelicals to learn lobbying techniques, engage in political networking, get media attention and acquire *Herrschaftswissen*, i.e., the expertise required for the exercise of power. Moreover, the needs of the Cold War state were not just ideological, but also administrative. The Cold War not only rhetorically revived religious images of the 'redeemer nation' but, more importantly, ushered in new bureaucratic ties between a growing state and religious organizations. In turn, neo-evangelicals managed to gain influence in a number of institutions. In particular, the federal government's efforts to strengthen the anti-communist training of army recruits, its support for the military chaplaincy and evangelization campaigns, and its promotion of church building on military sites were decisive factors in furthering the influence of evangelicals and establishing contacts between church and state. For example, the shared commitment to the Cold War mission was the background on which the career of John C. Broger, one of the most influential evangelicals in the Pentagon, unfolded. Broger was in charge of implementing the Pentagon's programme to fight the 'spiritual illiteracy' of young soldiers and to promote their commitment to his concept of 'militant liberty'. He promoted ties to conservative and patriotic organizations, such as the American Heritage Foundation, as well as to extreme right-wing organizations, such as the John Birch Society. Broger also directed the NAE's Freedom Studies project and his materials were widely distributed via International Christian Leadership (ICL), an evangelical organization led by Abraham Vereide that organized meetings of politicians and bureaucrats and helped set up an effective network of evangelical Christians in politics and the military.[39]

Above all, foreign aid opened up new opportunities for the development of bureaucratic ties and personnel interchange between government and evangelical agencies. As one of the most reliable components of the federal budget, international relief was a quintessential Cold War state-private project that linked the expansion of the state with the growth of religious agencies in the pursuit of the shared goals of humanitarian aid, commercial access, military support and containment. The main church-state funding ties developed in the aftermath of the federal government's decision to fund ocean freight costs in 1947, provide US surplus food distribution abroad under the Agricultural Act of 1949 and the 1954 Food for Peace legislation, and offer international technical assistance under Truman's Point Four proposals, which later developed into the Agency for International Development (AID) and its foreign aid programme for the Third

World AID programme. In 1948, a subcommittee of the House Committee on Foreign Affairs acknowledged that voluntary agencies that 'represent in part the interest of American religious groups' should be seen as 'an essential counterpart of foreign assistance programs'. By the early 1960s, religiously-affiliated voluntary agencies handled 70 per cent of surplus food distribution.[40]

Crucially, Catholic and evangelical Protestant agencies with strong anti-communist heritages in particular were often much less concerned about taking federal funds and being identified with government goals than many secular agencies, who feared that they would become tools of American foreign policy. Nonetheless, the NAE was slow on the uptake and remained an outspoken critic of the foreign aid programme well into the 1950s.[41] The organization faced a dilemma, though. While it was reluctant to participate in government-funded activities, evangelical groups such as the Seventh-Day Adventists and the Salvation Army were using their overseas networks for the distribution of surplus food. What is more, Catholic Relief Services, which had become the largest private relief agency in the world by the 1950s, received over 50 per cent of the relief supplies from the State Department's International Cooperation Agency in 1958 and threatened the survival of Protestant agencies.[42]

By 1954, Clyde Taylor urged his fellow evangelicals to apply pressure on the State Department 'to counterbalance the influence of the Roman heirarchy [sic] and other forces that constantly exert their maximum influence for their own interests regardless of the legality of their action'.[43] Republican congressman Walter H. Judd admonished *Christianity Today* readers that in the fight against communism, the main significance of religious foreign aid was not to replace government efforts, but to 'give meaning to, and put heart and soul into the government programs', which 'administer, but rarely do they minister'.[44] In due course, the NAE's World Relief Commission (WRC) became an avid participant in government foreign aid programmes. As the NAE's international aid agency, it was involved in a wide variety of activities, including agricultural rehabilitation and development, the creation of farming cooperatives, refugee settlement and rehabilitation, literacy programmes and children's clinics. In the 1960s, WRC, later renamed World Relief, was incorporated as NAE-WRC, a nonprofit subsidiary corporation of the NAE. This allowed it to gain separate tax-exempt status and improved its ability to qualify for government funds.[45]

This participation in federally-subsidized foreign aid arrangements helped shift the emphasis in evangelical circles away from orthodox church-state separationism. Ensuring that foreign aid was linked to spiritual mission, and that evangelical agencies had equal access to foreign aid funds and mission fields, became more important than fighting the growing administrative state. While WRC continued to criticize Catholics for linking foreign aid to proselytizing, the organization itself eagerly exploited the lack of overall restraints government funding put on the spiritual mission of religious agencies. A 1973 WRC agenda paper showed that recipients of government surplus food in Korea 'were exposed to the Gospel in many different ways and their compensation and reward was WRC provided surplus food, clothing, vitamins, materials, equipment, and so forth'.[46]

The networks and funding ties pioneered in the 1950s and 1960s laid the foundation for the expansion of government funding for evangelical agencies in the 1970s, particularly in conjunction with the post-Vietnam refugee flow. The growing involvement in Vietnam softened the evangelicals' separationist stance even further as WRC entered the relief effort in the region at the same time as Catholic, mainline, and evangelical peace church agencies were having second thoughts about close ties to the US government. The involvement in Vietnam also eased the pressure to separate mission from aid. Sources indicate that WRC had to fear little interference from American officials who saw tolerating evangelism as a small price to pay for having workers friendly to US policies in the refugee camps. Incidentally, this was also the time when the unwavering support of many evangelicals for the Vietnam War effort helped them become the dominant religious group in the army. However, the involvement in Vietnam-related aid also indicated how dependent the WRC had become on government funds. The organization faced significant financial problems in the 1970s when Congress largely discontinued the surplus food programme.[47]

Despite this retrenchment, subsidiarist relations with evangelical providers continued to characterize international relief. By the 1980s, over 70 per cent of Seventh-Day Adventist and close to 40 per cent of World Relief total agency income came from government sources. Federal grants and contracts had also helped World Vision, a California-based evangelical relief agency established in 1952, become one of the largest international aid providers. Only a quarter of evangelical international aid organizations surveyed in the 1990s received no government funds at all, as opposed to one half of mainline Protestant agencies. The odd man out in the Cold War state was no longer evangelicalism, but 'that assortment of strict separationists, leftist critics, and theological liberationists who from their various perspectives find government funding of religiously grounded activities abhorrent to the best interests of American democracy'.[48]

The politics of evangelical foreign policy

Despite these apparent successes in gaining new political and institutional inroads, foreign policy remained a deeply controversial topic within evangelical ranks throughout the Cold War. The new church-state attitudes emerged only gradually from often heated internal conflicts over political partisanship, militarism and government aid. These debates are altogether too easily ignored in analyses that see the right-wing political alignment of evangelicals as rooted in a natural affinity between religious and secular conservatism. In contrast, throughout the 1950s and 1960s significant groups within the evangelical movement expressed pacifist sentiments, retained a strong aversion to civil religion, rejected the spiritual sanctification of US foreign policy, denounced the arms race and demanded nuclear disarmament. A 1956 *Christianity Today* poll of evangelical clergy, for example, showed significant support for 'world security built on a trusting spiritual level, and less on military spending'. Likewise, a significant minority called for 'less emphasis on bombs and materials for war', more international disarmament negotiations, and even efforts to strengthen international relations through the UN.[49] Even conservatives such as the magazine's editor Harold Lindsell insisted in 1967 that the church should not commit itself to either a free market or a managed economy, and should avoid becoming 'the voice of those who have managed to seize control of the power structures'.[50]

This diversity of opinion remained a salient feature of the NAE in the post-Vietnam period. In 1977, the NAE reaffirmed its 1952 resolution against 'the militarization of the nation in peacetime' and spoke out against universal military training and the proliferation of nuclear weapons.[51] In a confidential 1986 *Christianity Today* poll, subscribers listed 'continuing arms negotiations with the Soviets' as the most pressing foreign policy issue (23 per cent). 80 per cent expressed support or strong support for further talks with Russia. In regard to defence policies, 'pursuing increased nuclear disarmament treaties with the Soviets' and 'making substantial cuts in the overall defense budget' were the top priorities (23 and 21 per cent respectively), with 72 per cent supporting the former and 36 per cent the latter. 13 per cent picked unilateral US disarmament as the most important issue, which won the support of 25 per cent of those surveyed.[52]

Conservatives within the movement were increasingly alarmed about this pacifist drift, which they feared had the potential to derail their project to build up evangelicals as a coherent religious voting block within the Republican party. In his address at the NAE Washington Leadership Briefing in April 1977, Colorado congressman William L. Armstrong, a key figure in engineering links between the NAE and the Republicans, warned about 'the evident decline in the willingness of our people to support an adequate national defense needed to keep the peace'.[53] In the run-up to President Reagan's speech at the 1983 NAE convention, Robert Dugan told Reagan's deputy chief of staff, Michael K. Deaver, that he was 'working behind the scenes to counteract some of the drift toward the nuclear freeze position'.[54] Similarly, he confessed to evangelical theologian Francis A. Schaeffer that he was 'deeply concerned that the public not perceive evangelicals as irretrievably leaning to the left on the issue of national defense'.[55]

It was clearly time for conservatives to act if they wanted to bring evangelical opinion in line with their partisan political aspirations. Their objective was clear: while the NAE had in the past mainly focused on domestic public policy, evangelical concern 'for the moral dimension in all aspects of public life, including international affairs, needed to be transmitted to decision-makers'. The result was the launch of the NAE's Peace, Freedom and Security Studies Program (PFSS) in 1984. Coordinated by OPA intern Brian O'Connell, whom Dugan lauded for knowing both the evangelical leadership and major players in Washington, the ambitious PFSS remit included organizing correspondence courses, study kits, a Sunday school curriculum, a speaker's bureau, a college conference series, a media network, ministry consultations and lunches on foreign policy issues.[56]

Though financial problems continued to beset the organization, the PFSS Leadership Network had by 1989 grown to over 500 and plans were underway to move the thrust 'away from consultations across the nation toward the increase of evangelical influence in the foreign and defense policy arenas'.[57] Yet, the PFSS stance, which largely amounted to a civil religious identification with American-style democracy, was not without its critics even within the upper NAE echelons. Controversies about how to represent the diversity of feelings, ranging pacifism to the 'peace through strength' position, continued throughout the 1980s. 'The American Enterprise Institute, American Heritage Foundation, Institute for Religion and Democracy, Hoover Institute, and the N.A.E. Office of Public Affairs all seem to agree on the same positions', the NAE's Social Action Commission chairman Wilbert Hill complained, 'nowhere do I see organizations like Physicians for Social Responsibility, Beyond War, Center for Defense Information, or Union of Concerned Scientists acknowledged as expressing valid viewpoints'. Criticizing O'Connell for ignoring or misrepresenting left evangelical positions, Hill concluded that 'I hope that the word liberal will not become a bad word in N.A.E.'.[58]

Hill's concerns were indicative of the sidelining of left and liberal sentiments in the NAE. Indeed, PFSS foreign policy advocacy helped separate the evangelical Left from the New Christian Right as left evangelicals continued to adhere to a separationist stance while conservatives aligned themselves with the defense-related 'statist turn' of the secular Right. Nonetheless, conservatives also took on board left evangelical concerns. In effect, they asserted their claim to political leadership within the evangelical fold by forging a distinctive policy profile that combined Cold War intransigence with concerns about human rights and political oppression. Though largely a mouthpiece of conservatism, PFSS aimed to avoid what it regarded as the most conspicuous error of the Right, namely 'unquestioning support of any and all US defense programs', while also sidestepping the most conspicuous error of the Left, i.e., 'seeing America as the source of evil in the international community'.[59] By mediating between left and right in this manner, it connected 'peace' and 'freedom' in ways that anticipated the neoconservative agenda of the late 1990s.

Conclusion

The war years and America's post-war international entanglements provided a crucial impetus for the re-engagement of evangelicals with public policy and the state. Discovering foreign policy as a mission field, evangelicals channelled their renewed desire for political and cultural relevance into efforts to infuse redemptive themes into the public discourse. At the same time, Cold War administrative needs, especially in the foreign aid arena, engineered new personal and institutional ties between evangelicals and government. These made evangelicals a constituent part of the special public–private relationships that underlay Cold War state-building.

In turn, post-war engagement with foreign policy eased the transition for many evangelicals from their traditional misgivings about church-state funding ties and suspicions about civil religion towards the embrace of Cold War state-building in the name of national security and global power. What is more, the transformation of church–state relations influenced the patterns of the conservative political mobilization of evangelicals in the 1970s and 1980s. In particular, it strengthened the conservative wing in the movement and helped cement the right-wing orientation of evangelicalism. Indeed, it formed the backdrop for the ideology of the New Christian Right, which combines an anti-statist self-image with support for big government, particularly in defence and national security matters.

Notes

1　Michael S. Sherry, *In the Shadow of War: The United States Since the 1930s*, New Haven: Yale University Press, 1995, p. 78. On the role of state-private networks during the Cold War, see Michael J. Hogan, 'Corporatism: A Positive Appraisal', *Diplomatic History*, 1986, vol. 10, pp. 363–67; Thomas J. McCormick, 'Drift or Mastery: A Corporatist Synthesis for American Diplomatic History', *Reviews in American History*, 1982, vol. 10, pp. 318–29; Helen Laville and Hugh Wilford (eds) *The US Government, Citizen Groups and the Cold War: The State-Private Network*, London: Routledge, 2006. On the growth of the Cold War state see, for example, Sherry, *Shadow of War*, pp. 71–86; Steve Fraser and Gary Gerstle (eds) *The Rise and Fall of the New Deal Order, 1930–1980*, Princeton: Princeton University Press, 1989; Alan Wolfe, *America's Impasse: The Rise and Fall of the Politics of Growth*, New York: Pantheon, 1981; Robert M. Collins, *More: The Politics of Economic Growth in Postwar America*, New York: Oxford University Press, 2000; Aaron L. Friedberg, *In the Shadow of the Garrison State: America's Anti-statism and Its Cold War Grand Strategy*, Princeton: Princeton University Press, 2000.
2　On public funding of nongovernmental organizations, see Lester H. Salamon, *Partners in Public Service: Government-Nonprofit Relations in the Modern Welfare State*, Baltimore: Johns Hopkins University Press, 1995, pp. 18–28, 45–50; Steven Rathgeb Smith and Michael Lipsky, *Nonprofits for Hire: The Welfare State in the Age of Contracting*, Cambridge: Harvard University Press, 1993, pp. 15–16, 179–80; Peter Dobkin Hall, 'The Welfare State and the Careers of Public and Private Institutions Since 1945', in Lawrence J. Friedman and Mark D. McGarvie (eds) *Charity, Philanthropy and Civility in American History*, Cambridge: Cambridge University Press, 2003, pp. 363–83.
3　Stephen V. Monsma, *When Sacred and Secular Mix: Religious Nonprofit Organizations and Public Money*, Lanham: Rowman and Littlefield, 1996, pp. 9, see also pp. 69–70, 104–5.
4　On public funding for religious nonprofits see, for example, Charles L. Glenn, *The Ambiguous Embrace: Government and Faith-Based Schools and Social Agencies*, Princeton: Princeton University Press, 2000; Robert J. Wineburg, *A Limited Partnership: The Politics of Religion, Welfare, and Social Service*, New York: Columbia University Press, 2000; Ellen F. Netting, 'Secular and Religious Funding of Church-Related Agencies', *Social Service Review*, 1982, vol. 56, pp. 586–604; Paul J. Weber and Dennis A. Gilbert, *Private Churches and Public Money: Church–Government Fiscal Relations*, Westport: Greenwood Press, 1981.
5　On the lack of reliable statistical information, see Robert Wuthnow, 'Improving Our Understanding of Religion and Giving: Key Issues for Research', in Robert A. Wuthnow, Virginia Hodgkinson and Associates, *Faith and Philanthropy in America: Exploring the Role of Religion in America's Voluntary Sector*, San Francisco: Jossey-Bass, 1990, pp. 271–83; Peter Dobkin Hall and Colin B. Burke, 'Historical Statistics of the United States Chapter on Voluntary, Nonprofit, and Religious Entities and Activities: Underlying Concepts, Concerns, and Opportunities', *Working Paper #14*, The Hauser Center for Nonprofit Organizations, Cambridge: Harvard University, 2002, pp. 9, 27–28; Monsma, *Sacred and Secular*, pp. 4, 12–13.

6   This essay forms part of a forthcoming book on the Cold War state and evangelical-
    ism. I have also explored these issues in Axel R. Schäfer, 'The Cold War State and the
    Resurgence of Evangelicalism: A Study of the Public Funding of Religion Since 1945',
    Radical History Review, 2007, vol. 99, pp. 19–50; and Axel R. Schäfer, 'Religious
    Nonprofit Organizations, the Cold War, the State and Resurgent Evangelicalism,
    1945–90', in Laville and Wilford (eds) *The State-Private Network*, pp. 175–93.
7   Quoted in *Christianity Today*, 4 February 1957, p. 38. On religion, World War II
    and the Cold War, see Robert Wuthnow, *The Restructuring of American Religion:
    Society and Faith Since World War II*, Princeton: Princeton University Press, 1988,
    pp. 21, 27–28, 33, 39–43, 47, 50–51, 59–60; Robert S. Ellwood, *The Fifties Spiritual
    Marketplace: American Religion in a Decade of Conflict*, New Brunswick: Rutgers
    University Press, 1997, pp. 18, 38, 48–51, 189; Joel A. Carpenter, *Revive Us Again:
    The Reawakening of American Fundamentalism*, New York: Oxford University Press,
    1997, pp. 178–79; Gerald L. Sittser, *A Cautious Patriotism: The American Churches
    and the Second World War*, Chapel Hill: University of North Carolina Press, 1997.
    See also the essay by Andrew Preston in the present volume.
8   J. Edgar Hoover, 'Communist Propaganda and the Christian Pulpit', *Christianity
    Today*, 25 October 1960, p. 5.
9   Quoted in Richard V. Pierard and Robert D. Lindner, *Civil Religion and the
    Presidency*, Grand Rapids: Academie Books, 1988, pp. 189, 197–98.
10 William Lee Miller, *Piety Along the Potomac: Notes on Politics and Morals in the
    Fifties*, Boston: Houghton Mifflin, 1964, p. 41.
11 On this famous quote and its various uses see Patrick Henry, '"And I Don't Care What
    It Is": The Tradition-History of a Civil Religion Proof Text', *Journal of the American
    Academy of Religion*, 1981, vol. 49, pp. 35–49.
12 Scott Flipse, 'To Save "Free Vietnam" and Lose Our Souls', in Daniel H. Bays
    and Grant Wacker (eds) *The Foreign Mission Enterprise at Home: Explorations in
    American Cultural History*, Tuscaloosa: University of Alabama Press, 2003, p. 209.
13 Carpenter, *Revive Us Again*, p. 233. On post-war neo-evangelicalism see George
    Marsden, *Understanding Fundamentalism and Evangelicalism*, Grand Rapids:
    William B. Eerdmans, 1991, pp. 68–70, 100–101; Joel Carpenter, 'Revive Us
    Again: Alienation, Hope, and the Resurgence of Fundamentalism, 1930–50', in
    M. C. Bradbury and James B. Gilbert (eds) *Transforming Faith. The Sacred and
    Secular in Modern American History*, New York: Greenwood Press, 1989, pp. 111,
    115–16; James Davison Hunter, *American Evangelicalism: Conservative Religion
    and the Quandary of Modernity*, New Brunswick: Rutgers University Press, 1983,
    pp. 41–45; Nathan O. Hatch and Michael S. Hamilton, 'Taking the Measure of the
    Evangelical Resurgence, 1942–92', in D. G. Hart (ed.) *Reckoning with the Past:
    Historical Essays on American Evangelicalism from the Institute for the Study of
    American Evangelicals*, Grand Rapids: Baker Books, 1995, pp. 395–412; Grant
    Wacker, 'Uneasy in Zion: Evangelicals in Postmodern Society', in Hart (ed.)
    Reckoning with the Past, pp. 384–86.
14 Hunter, *Conservative Religion*, p. 44.
15 William Martin, *With God on Our Side: The Rise of the Religious Right in America*,
    New York: Broadway Books, 1996, pp. 29–30; see also Marsden, *Understanding
    Fundamentalism*, pp. 65, 73.
16 Carl F. H. Henry, *Confessions of a Theologian: An Autobiography*, Waco: Word
    Books, 1986, p. 119.
17 Ibid., pp. 181, 141–44; Marsden, *Understanding Fundamentalism*, pp. 62, 72;
    Christian Smith, *American Evangelicalism: Embattled and Thriving*, Chicago:
    Chicago University Press, 1998, p. 11; Carl F. H. Henry, 'Christian Responsibility in
    Political Affairs', *Christianity Today*, 1 August 1960, p. 24.
18 Paul S. Boyer, *When Time Shall Be No More: Prophecy Belief in Modern American
    Culture*, Cambridge: Belknap Press of Harvard University Press, 1992, p. xii; Michael

Lienesch, *Redeeming America: Piety and Politics in the New Christian Right*, Chapel Hill: University of North Carolina Press, 1993, p. 199.

19 Quoted in Anne C. Loveland, *American Evangelicals and the U.S. Military, 1942–1993*, Baton Rouge: Louisiana State University Press, 1996, p. 37.

20 Richard V. Pierard, 'Billy Graham and Vietnam: From Cold Warrior to Peacemaker', *Christian Scholar's Review*, 1980, vol. 10, p. 38.

21 Joel A. Carpenter, 'Youth for Christ and the New Evangelicals', in Hart (ed.) *Reckoning with the Past*, p. 371.

22 William K. Harrison, 'Christianity and Peace in Our Day', *Christianity Today*, 29 October 1956, p. 16. On the tension in fundamentalism between 'positive revivalism and polemics' see Marsden, *Understanding Fundamentalism*, pp. 110–11.

23 On evangelical attitudes toward Jews and Israel see William K. Harrison, 'Reminiscences and a Prophecy', *Christianity Today*, 4 March 1957, p. 14; Discussion of Rutherford L. Decker's message 'How Others Look at Us in Church–State Relations', NAE Conference on Church–State Relations, 6–7 February 1961, p. 4, NAE Records, Wheaton College Archives and Special Collections, Buswell Memorial Library, Wheaton College, Illinois (hereafter cited as NAE Records). At the time of writing the NAE Records were in the process of being moved to the Billy Graham Center Archives, Wheaton, Illinois; Lienesch, *Redeeming America*, pp. 228–33; Boyer, *When Time Shall Be No More*, pp. 185–87, 208–24; John J. Mearsheimer and Stephen M. Walt, *The Israel Lobby and U.S. Foreign Policy*, New York: Farrar, Straus and Giroux, 2007. See also the essay by Lee Marsden in the present volume.

24 On evangelicals and the United Nations see, for example, Walter H. Judd, 'World Issues and the Christian', *Christianity Today*, 23 June 1958, pp. 6–8; E. L. R. Elson, 'Worship in the Life of the Nation', *Christianity Today*, 12 November 1956, pp. 10–11, 19; H. H. Lippincott, 'World Government and Christianity', *Christianity Today*, 3 February 1958, pp.3–5. Numerous editorials dealt with this issue, including 'UN: Town Meeting? Or Tragedy?', *Christianity Today*, 1 April 1957, p. 20; 'Spiritual-Moral Unity Wanes in United Nations', *Christianity Today*, 4 March 1957, p. 22. See also Robert Booth Fowler, *A New Engagement: Evangelical Political Thought, 1966–1976*, Grand Rapids: William B. Eerdmans, 1987, p. 31; Boyer, *When Time Shall Be No More*, pp. 174–76, 248; Lienesch, *Redeeming America*, pp. 195, 198, 201; Pierard and Lindner, *Civil Religion*, pp. 189, 194–99; Carpenter, *Revive Us Again*, pp.149.

25 Carl F. H. Henry, 'Evangelicals in the Social Struggle', *Christianity Today*, 8 October 1965, p. 9.

26 Harold John Ockenga, 'The Communist Issue Today', *Christianity Today*, 22 May 1961, p. 12. On evangelical anti-communism, see also Edgar Hoover, 'Soviet Rule or Christian Renewal', *Christianity Today*, November 7, 1960, pp. 8–11; 'Left Wing Attacks on FBI and House Un-American Activities Group', *Christianity Today*, March 30, 1959, p. 21; Martin, *With God on Our Side*, pp. 29, 34; Lienesch, *Redeeming America*, pp. 214–15, 224; Wuthnow, *Restructuring Religion*, pp. 51–52; Boyer, *When Time Shall Be No More*, pp. 156, 170–71.

27 'What is the Target: Communism or Anti-Communists', *Christianity Today*, 22 May 1961, pp. 22–23; Ron Arnold, 'Communism Report', in 'Minutes of the NAE Staff Retreat in Glen Eyrie', 10–12 January 1961, p. 8, NAE Records. See also Hunter, *Conservative Religion*, pp. 43–45; Leo Ribuffo, *The Old Christian Right: The Protestant Far Right from the Great Depression to the Cold War*, Philadelphia: Temple University Press, 1983.

28 William F. Knowland, 'Admit Red China?', *Christianity Today*, October 29, 1956, pp. 10–11; J. Edgar Hoover, 'The Communist Menace: Red Goals and Christian Ideals', *Christianity Today*, 10 October 1960, p. 3; Martin, *With God on Our Side*, p. 39. On ties between religious and secular conservatives see Lienesch, *Redeeming America*, pp. 195, 211.

29 Paul Peachey, 'Beyond Christian–Communist Strife', *Christianity Today*, 27 October 1958, p. 16.

30 Frederick G. Schwarz, 'Can We Meet the Red Challenge', *Christianity Today*, 13 April 1959, p. 13.

31 Lisa McGirr, *Suburban Warriors: The Origins of the New American Right*, Princeton: Princeton University Press, 2001, pp. 16, 168, 176, 186, 260; Jerome L. Himmelstein, *To the Right: The Transformation of American Conservatism*, Berkeley: University of California Press, 1990, pp. 212–22; Marsden, *Understanding Fundamentalism*, p. 109.

32 'Billy Graham and the Pope's Legions', *Christianity Today*, 22 July 1957, pp. 20–21; 'Bigotry or Smear?', *Christianity Today*, 1 February 1960, p. 20; 'Immigration Bill', *Christianity Today*, 22 July 1957, p. 29.

33 Clyde W. Taylor, 'Watchman in Washington', 1955, p. 8, NAE Records. On the rapid expansion of foreign missionary activities after World War II and its role in generating interest in foreign policy see Carpenter, *Revive Us Again*, pp. 177–80; Lienesch, *Redeeming America*, p. 222; Wuthnow, *Restructuring Religion*, p. 41.

34 Taylor, 'Watchman in Washington', 1955, p. 2.

35 On the campaign for religious liberty see Clyde W. Taylor, 'Religious Liberty in America', paper given at NAE National Conference on Church-State Relations, 6–8 March 1963, p. 1, NAE Records; Robert P. Dugan Jr., 'NAE Office of Public Affairs Report to the Board of Administration', 8–9 October 1985, NAE Records.

36 Robert P. Dugan Jr., 'NAE Office of Public Affairs Annual Report to the Board of Administration', 5 March 1984, NAE Records. On attitudes towards Catholics see also 'Confrontation: A sharp look at the issues facing Evangelicals in 1966', NAE circular, pp. 6–8, NAE Records; Clyde W. Taylor, 'Report of the Evangelical Action Commission and the NAE Office of Public Affairs to the Board of Administration', 14 April 1969, p. 2, NAE Records; Watt, *Transforming Faith*, pp. 65–67; Wuthnow, *Restructuring Religion*, pp. 142–43.

37 Miller, *Piety Along the Potomac*, pp. 34, 42. On the Graham–Eisenhower axis see Richard V. Pierard, 'Billy Graham and the U.S. Presidency', *Journal of Church and State*, 1980, vol. 22, p. 116; Pierard and Lindner, *Civil Religion*, pp. 184–205; Billy Graham, *Just As I Am: The Autobiography of Billy Graham*, San Francisco: Harper, 1997, pp. 188–206. On religion and the presidency in general see Gary Scott Smith, *Faith and the Presidency*, Oxford: Oxford University Press, 2007.

38 'Where Do We Go From Here?', *Christianity Today*, 12 November 1956, p. 17; Miller, *Piety Along the Potomac*, pp. 19, 34, 43; Pierard and Linder, *Civil Religion*, pp. 199, 184. For good discussions of Eisenhower and foreign policy see Robert R. Bowie and Richard H. Immerman, *Waging Peace: How Eisenhower Shaped an Enduring Cold War*, New York: Oxford University Press, 1998; Campbell Craig, *Destroying the Village: Eisenhower and Thermonuclear War*, New York: Columbia University Press, 1998; Fred J. Greenstein, *The Hidden-Hand Presidency: Eisenhower as Leader*, New York: Basic Books, 1982.

39 Loveland, *Evangelicals and the Military*, pp. 10–13, 56–64. On Broger's involvement with the NAE see Clyde W. Taylor, 'Report of the Office of Public Affairs to the Executive Committee, National Association of Evangelicals', 12 June 1962, p. 1, NAE Records; Clyde W. Taylor, 'Report of the Office of Public Affairs to the NAE Board of Administration', 7 October 1963, p. 3, NAE Records.

40 Fowler Hamilton to Clinton P. Anderson, 9 November 1962, NAE Records. Hamilton cites Department of State, Agency for International Development, 'Involvement of Religious Affiliated Institutions in the U.S. Foreign Aid Program', 1962, NAE Records. On foreign aid see also 'The Peace Drive in the Churches', *Christianity Today*, April 13, 1959, p. 20; Bruce Nichols, *The Uneasy Alliance: Religion, Refugee Work, and U.S. Foreign Policy*, New York: Oxford University Press, 1988, pp. 207–8; Flipse, 'Vietnam', pp. 208–9; Gary R. Hess, 'Waging the Cold War in the

Third World: The Foundations and the Challenges of Development', in Friedman and McGarvie (eds), *Charity*, pp. 319–39.

41 'Pressures Rise for Federal Handouts', *Christianity Today*, 12 May 1958, p. 22; 'The Spirit of Foreign Policy', *Christianity Today*, 29 April 1957, pp. 20–22; Monsma, *Sacred and Secular*, p. 79.

42 Nichols, *Uneasy Alliance*, pp. 92–93, 200–206.

43 Clyde W. Taylor, 'Citizens of Heaven and Earth', address given at Winona Lake, Indiana, 8 August 1954, p. 5, NAE Records.

44 Walter H. Judd, 'World Issues and the Christian', *Christianity Today*, 23 June 1958, p. 8.

45 'Executive Committee Minutes', NAE Board of Administration, 6 April 1964, NAE Records. See also Lienesch, *Redeeming America*, p. 222; Wuthnow, *Restructuring*, p. 41.

46 'Agenda – Miscellaneous', Executive Committee of the World Relief Commission, 13–14 November 1973, p. 9, NAE Records. On the shift in evangelical attitudes to foreign aid see also C. N. Hostetter Jr., 'Government Overseas Programs and the Churches', paper given at NAE National Conference on Church–State Relations, 6–8 March 1963, p. 5, NAE Records.

47 Wendell L. Rockey, 'Report of the Executive Director N.A.E. World Relief Commission, Inc. to the Executive Committee and the Board of Administration of N.A.E.', 4 April 1967, NAE Records; 'Minutes of the Executive Committee', World Relief Commission, 14–15 September 1972, p. 4, NAE Records; 'Plans Proposed for the Re-organization of WRC', Executive Committee of the World Relief Commission, 7 February 1974, NAE Records; 'Sectional Reports', World Relief Corporation, NAE Board of Administration, 7 October 1980, p. 5, NAE Records. See also Nichols, *Uneasy Alliance*, pp. 170–71, 203.

48 Nichols, *Uneasy Alliance*, p. 206; see also pp. 92–93, 211; Carpenter, *Revive*, p. 182; Monsma, *Sacred and Secular*, pp. 10, 72–73. See also pp. 65–68, 78.

49 'Where Do We Go From Here?', *Christianity Today*, 12 November 1956, p. 17. On critical voices within the evangelical fold see Marsden, *Understanding Fundamentalism*, p. 97; Fowler, *New Engagement*, pp. 30–31; Augustus Cerillo Jr., 'A Survey of Recent Evangelical Social Thought', *Christian Scholar's Review*, 1976, vol. 5, p. 277.

50 Harold Lindsell, 'An Evangelical Evaluation of the Relationship between Churches and the State in the United States', Consultation on the Church in a Secular World, 11–13 October 1967, pp. 14–15, NAE Records.

51 'Resolutions – The Use of Force', in 'Minutes, NAE General Session, Second Session', 24 February 1977, pp. 5–6, NAE Records.

52 'Christianity Today Confidential Survey of Subscribers: A Political Opinion Poll', 29 April 1986, pp. 1–2, NAE Records.

53 William L. Armstrong, 'Christian Responsibility and Government', address given at the Washington Leadership Briefing, 18–22 April 1977, pp. 1–2, NAE Records.

54 Robert P. Dugan Jr. to Michael K. Deaver, 3 December 1982, NAE Records.

55 Robert P. Dugan Jr. to Francis A. Schaeffer, 23 November 1982, NAE Records.

56 'NAE's Peace, Freedom and Security Studies Program', [c. 1985], NAE Records; Robert P. Dugan Jr., 'NAE Office of Public Affairs Semi-Annual Report to the Board of Administration', 2–3 October 1984, NAE Records; Robert P. Dugan Jr., 'Semi-Annual Report to the Board of Administration', [with marginalia], 6–7 October 1987, p. 2, NAE Records.

57 Robert P. Dugan Jr., 'NAE Office of Public Affairs Annual Report to the Board of Administration', [with marginalia], 6 March 1989, NAE Records.

58 Wilbert Hill to Social Action Commission, 28 September 1988, NAE Records.

59 'NAE's Peace, Freedom and Security Studies Program'; see also Robert P. Dugan, Jr., 'PFSS: "First Steps of NAE Leadership"', handwritten notes, 1989, NAE Records. On the political realignment of evangelicals in general see Geoffrey Layman, *The Great Divide: Religious and Cultural Conflict in American Party Politics*, New York: Columbia University Press, 2001; Robert William Fogel, *The Fourth Great Awakening and the Future of Egalitarianism*, Chicago: University of Chicago Press, 2000.

Index

5 -year plans, India and China 16
9/11: Australia's response 81; effects on
    Canada 67–8; Israel–US relations 186

*A Clean Break: A New Strategy of
    Securing the Realm* 195
A Turning Point in the Nation's History
    (van Wolferen and Sampiemon) 127
Acheson, Dean 97–8
Adams, W.G. 29
Afghanistan 119–21, 141, 164
agriculture, as weakness of
    communism 19
Airey, Willis 100
Allen, George V. 17
alliance network 60, 61
alliance relations, political economy
    of 86–8
American Israel Education
    Foundation 195
American Israel Public Affairs Committee
    (AIPAC) 180–1, 191, 193, 194–5
American Jewish Committee 193
American Jewish Congress 193
American Notes (Dickens) 25–7
Amis, Martin 50
Animal Farm (Orwell) 61
Ansari, Ali 155, 158–9
anti-American feeling: British 51–4;
    expressed in literature 46–51
anti-Catholicism 229–30
anti-communist alliance 216, 217
anti-nuclear movement 101–2, 103, 106
anti-war movements 102
ANZUS Treaty 81–3, 97–9, 101, 103, 104
Arab-Israeli wars 179, 185
Arafat, Yasser 186
Armstrong, Scott 162

Armstrong, William L. 234
Arnold, Matthew 27, 30
Aspe, Pedro 62
Association of Southeast Asian Nations'
    (ASEAN) Treaty of
    Amity and Cooperation 83
Atherton, Alfred 153
Attlee, Clement 35
AusMin talks 88
Australia: discourses of danger and
    uncertainty 88; East Asia as potential
    threat 88; geography and foreign
    relations 80; Iraq invasion 85;
    multilateralism 87; relations with East
    Asian countries 87–8; shifts in foreign
    policy 77–8; significance to US 88;
    weakening of security 84–5
Australia–US Ministerial Consultations 88
Australia–US relations: assessment
    of relationship 88; calculating
    benefits 82–4; closeness 76; evolution
    of strategic relationship 80–4;
    hegemony 77–80; ideational
    consensus 77; information sharing 85;
    political, economic and strategic
    nexus 84–8; political economy of
    alliance relations 86–8; trade 86–7
Australian Labor Party (ALP) 85

Baker, James 135
Baku-Tbilisi-Ceyhan (BTC) pipeline 143
balance of power, US and GB 29
Baldwin, Stanley 33
Balfour, A.J. 30
Balkenende, Jan Peter 117–18, 119
Bauer, Gary 199
Beard, Mary 48
Beeman, William O. 162

Ben Gurion, David 176
Berendsen, Carl 96, 97, 98
Berlijn, Dick 120
Berlin, Isaiah 11–12
Bevin, Ernest 35
bilateralism 87
Bill, James 152, 158
Binational Planning Group (BPG) 65
Bismarck, Otto von 33
Blair government, debate over Iraq
   invasion 84
Blair, Tony 49, 139, 140, 202
Blank, Stephen 142
Blom, Lt. Col. Jan 118–19
'Blue Stream' gas pipeline 143
B'nai B'rith 193
Boer War 31
Bolton, John 49, 146
Bonfire of the Vanities (Wolfe) 49
Borlaug, Norman 12
Bot, Bernard 124, 125, 126
Bourke-White, Margaret 16
Bowles, Chester 16
Boyer, Paul 227
Brash, Rev. Alan 95
Braun, Leopold 212
Bretton Woods, US undermining
   79–80
Britannia 93–4
British colonies, independence 25
British Empire 24–5
Broger, John C. 231
Bullitt, William 14
Burdick, Eugene 17–18
Bush, George W.: characteristics
   49–50; as child 47–8; European
   opinions 56; foreign policy 79;
   legislative record 51; literary expressions
   of hatred for 46–51; misplaced
   complaints against 53–4; personality,
   policy and the Iraq invasion 51; public
   opinion 55; response to anti-American
   feeling 48; UK attitudes 45
Bush (G.W.) administration 147; Christian
   Zionism 199–200;
   Israel–US relations 186–7,
   200–4; Middle East policy 203;
   neoconservatives and Israel 196–7
business, US-GB competition 32

Caccia, Sir Harold 36
Campaign for Nuclear Disarmament 101
Campbell, Alistair 49

Canada: defence spending 70; effects
   of 9/11 67–8
Canada–US relations: armed conflict, as
   unthinkable 62–3; assessment 71–2;
   creation of alliance 64–6; empirical
   differences 72; geography 70;
   latitude 70; as more special 61; special
   as better? 69–72; trade 69
Cárdenas, Lázaro 9, 10
Carpenter, Joel 226, 228
Carter administration, Iran–US
   relations 156–67
Chamberlain, Sir Neville 33
Chapman, Robert 101, 102
charities 223–4
Chase, Stuart 10
Cheney, Dick 144
China 8, 16–17, 18
China–Australia relations 87, 88
Chomsky, Noam 177
Christian Zionism: Bush (G.W.)
   administration 199–200, 201–2;
   Israel–US relations 197–200
Christianity, as antidote to
   communism 227
Christians: attitude to Soviet Union 208,
   209, 210–11; political influence 209–10
Christians United for Israel (CUFI) 199
Christmas island 101
chronology 208
church-state relations 236
Churchill, Sir Winston 33, 65
Civilization in the United States
   (Arnold) 27
Clark, Helen 102, 105, 106
Clarke, Jonathon 196
Cleveland, Grover 31
Clinton, Bill 52, 125, 136–7, 139, 186
Coalition of the Willing 119
Cold War: defining 208; effects of
   ending 78; expansion of
   state-private networks 223–4;
   foreign policy 233–5;
   Netherlands–US relations 117; religion
   and evangelicalism 225–7; religious
   faith as weapon 218–19; revival 105;
   role of New Zealand 96; shift to
   Asia 13; significance of India 17
Cold War state, and evangelicalism 230–3
Colijn, Ko 121
Collective Security Treaty Organization
   (CSTO) 142
Colour Revolutions 143

Commager, Henry Steele 16
communism: Christianity as antidote 227;
   containment policy 218; as post-war
   enemy 217
Conference of Major American Jewish
   Organizations 193
conservatives: and evangelicalism 234–5;
   view of Mexico 11
containment 218
Conventional Forces in Europe
   (CFE) treaty 138
Conway, Stephen 25
Cooperative Threat Reduction
   Program 136, 137–8
copyright 28–9
Corner, Frank 101
Cosgrove, General Peter 81
Crêvecoeur, J. Hector St John de 26
Cuban Missile Crisis 101
cultural relations, UK-US 37
culture 28, 52
Curtin, John 77–8
Cutler, Lloyd 166

Darby, John Nelson 197–8
Davis, James 145
de Hoop Scheffer, Jaap 118, 119, 120, 121
de Soto, Alvaro 202
Democracy in America 29
Depression 11
Desert Fox 56
Development Decade 18
Dickens, Charles 26–7
disarmament 234
Doidge, Frederick 97
Domestic Manners of the Americans
   (Trollope) 26
dos Passos, Katherine 10
Douglas, William O. 16
Downer, Alexander 82–4, 86
Drabble, Margaret 46, 47, 52
Dugan, Robert 234
Dulles, John Foster 12, 15, 97, 98, 174, 231
Dyess, William 123

East Asia 83–4, 87–8
Eban, Abba 174
Efford, Lincoln 95–6
Egypt 184
Eisenhower administration 15–17, 100
Eisenhower Doctrine 184
Eisenhower, Dwight 8, 35, 225, 226,
   230–1
ejidos 10, 12

Elson, Edward L.R. 225
Emerson, Ralph Waldo 27–8
energy, Russia 143–4
English Traits (Emerson) 28
European Economic Community (EEC),
   Britain's entry 103
evangelicalism: ambivalence 228–9;
   anti-Catholicism 229–30; in church-
   state networks 224–5; Cold War
   and religion 225–7; and Cold War
   state 230–3; and conservatives 234–5;
   foreign policy 227–30; influence 231;
   militarism 229; pacifism 234; politics of
   foreign policy 233–5; public policy and
   the state 235–6; support for Israel 228;
   world view 228
extraordinary rendition 125–6

Fahrenheit 9/11 (Moore) 54
Falklands War 36–7
Falwell, Jerry 201–2
financial hegemony, shift to US 32
financial relations, UK and US 32
foreign aid 231–2; to India 14, 16;
   strategic value 14; support for 18; US
   idea of 32
foreign policy: evangelicalism
   227–30, 233–6; role of business 223
Fortuyn, Pim 128
Four Freedoms 214
France-US relations 64
Franks, Tommy 119
Fraser, Malcolm 81–2
Fraser, Peter 93, 94–5, 96–7
Frei, Matt 47, 50

G8, St Petersburg 2006 143
geography, Canada–US relations 70
geopolitics, balance of power US and
   GB 29
Georgia 142–3
Germany, as ally to US 36
'Global Initiative to Combat Nuclear
   Terrorism' 145
global interdependence 139
Global War on Terror, Russia–US
   relations 141–3
Gorbachev, Mikhail 135–6
Graham, Billy 227
Graham, Franklin 200
Green Revolution 12, 19
Greene, Graham 47
Greenpeace III 103
Griffiths, Franklyn 63

Gruening, Ernest 10
Guiana, Anglo-American crisis 30

Hagee, Pastor John 199, 200
Halper, Stefan 196
Hamas 202–3
Hare, David 46
Harper, Stephen 63
Harrison, William 228
hegemonic power 77–8
hegemonic temptation 87
hegemony 32, 79–80
Henry, Carl F.H. 227, 228
Hensley, Gerald 105
Here and Now 99–100
Hezbollah 203
Hill, Wilbert 235
historical documents, problems with
    finding and using 174–5
Holland, Sydney 98–9
Hollywood, view of Mexico 10
Holmes, Sherlock 30
Holyoake, Keith 102, 103
homeland security, and Kingston
    dispensation 66–9
Hoover, Herbert 33
Hoover, J. Edgar 225
House of Commons, debate 18
    March 2003 52–3
Howard, John 80, 81, 82
Hyde Park aide-mémoire 34–5

ideological polarity, Soviet–US
    relations 217, 219–20
images, of specialness 72
independence, British colonies 25
India: aid 14, 16; development
    strategy 15; images of 16; as model
    of development 13–19; as racing with
    China 16–17; strategic importance 13
innocence 48
integration processes 140
intelligence relationship, UK-US 35–6
interdependence, politics and
    economics 84
international aid 231–2
International Christian Leadership
    (ICL) 231
International Criminal Court (ICC) 124–5
international politics, role of Dutch 122–3
international power, US desire for 33
International Religious Freedom Act 230
international threat environment, changes
    to 67

Iran: fragility of Shah's regime 154; Iraqi
    invasion 164; Revolution 158
Iran–US relations: anti-American
    feeling 154; Carter administration
    156–67; CIA networks 162; effects
    of Iranian Revolution 158–65; Great
    Satan 161–3; hostages 160, 163–4,
    165–6; before Iranian Revolution 152–8;
    lack of alternative policies 155–6;
    lessons to be learned 165–7;
    overview 152; US foreign policy
    goals 153
Iraq invasion: Australia's role 79, 81,
    85; effect on Blair government 84; and
    Israeli interests 203; personality and
    policy 51; support for in UK 55
Iraq, Netherlands–US relations 117–19
Islam 200
Israel: attack on Hezbollah in
    Lebanon 203; criticism of 177–8; US
    foreign assistance 200
Israel lobby: activities and
    influence 179–81; effectiveness 183–4;
    overestimation of influence 181–2; and
    US interests 187–8
Israel Lobby thesis 192–3
Israel Policy Forum 193
Israel–US relations: American Jewish
    supporters of Israel 193–5; arms
    supplies 183–4; Bush (G.W.)
    administration 186–7, 200–4; Christian
    Zionism 197–200; complexity 178;
    domestic sources of US policy 192–3;
    as dynamic 179; effect of 9/11 186;
    evangelicalism 228; expansionism 178;
    Israeli view of US 177; lack of
    consensus between Israelis and
    diaspora 176; lack of US consensus 176;
    military assistance 184–5; military
    intervention 179; misperceptions 178,
    188; neoconservatives and
    Israel 195–7; overviews 173, 191, 204;
    Palestinian conflict 178; preserving
    US interests 187–8; problems of
    researching 174–5; shared ideals 192;
    sources of evidence 176; as special 174;
    summary 204; underlying premises 175;
    US balance 186; US coolness 184–5;
    US view of Israel 173–4
Ivanov, Igor 139–40

Japan–Australia relations 87–8
Japan, peace treaty 98
Jewish identity 176

Jewish population, United States 194
Johnson, Lyndon 102, 185
Joint Strike Fighter (JSF) 121–2, 128
Jordan, US arms supplies 184–5
Judd, Walter H. 232

Kamp, Henk 117, 118, 120
Karzai, Hamid 120
Kasyanov, Mikhail 138
Kaufman, Gerald 54
Keillor, Garrison 60
Kennan, George F. 213
Kennedy–Cooper resolution 17
Kennedy, John F. 7, 8, 13, 17, 185
Kilfoyle, Peter 52
King, Mackenzie 66–7
Kingston dispensation, and homeland
    security 66–9
Kirk, Norman 102, 103–4
Kissinger, Henry 17
Knapp, Gary 107
Korea, US intervention 15
Kosovo, Russia–US relations 138–41
Kozyrev, Andrei 137, 138
Kriuchkov, Vladimir 135–6
Kroes, Rob 51
Kuchins, Andrew 141
Kyoto Agreement 87, 88

La Farge, Fr John 210
Laingen, Bruce 165–6
Lake Wobegon 60
Lange, David 93–4, 101, 105, 106
language, power of 33
Latham, Mark 85
Lawrence, D.H. 47
Leaves of Grass (Whitman) 29
Ledeen, M. 154
Lederer, William J. 17–18
leftism, anti-American feeling 52
Lend–Lease 66
Letters from an American Farmer
    (Crèvecoeur) 26
Lewis, Flora 161
Lippmann, Walter 8, 13
literature, British influence 28–9
Lowry, Malcolm 10
Lugar, Richard 137

MacArthur, General Douglas 8
Macmillan, Harold 49
'Mahalanobis model' 18
Maier, Pauline 24–5
Malloch Brown, Mark 49

Manley, John 62, 68
Marquand, David 55
Martin, Chris 50
Martin, Paul 71
Martineau, Harriet 26
'Marx Was a City Boy' (Rostow) 18–19
Maslin, Gen Yevgenii 137
mathematical modelling 9
McCain, John 191
McEwan, Ian 46
McMahon Act 34
Meacher, Michael 54
Mearsheimer, John 180–1, 192
Melman, Yossi 177
Mendelson, Sarah 137
Menzies, Robert 77, 78
Merry, Wayne 140
Metrinko, Michael 159, 161
Mexican Agricultural Program 11,
    12–13
Mexico, as model of development 9–13
Middendorf, William 123
military alliances 71
Military Cooperation Committee
    (MCC) 65
Military Intelligence and Security Service
    (MIVD) 117–18
military intervention, evangelical support
    for 229
Miller, Perry 8
Mitchell, Timothy 9
Moby Dick; or, The Whale (Melville) 29
'model', in vocabulary of development 9
model nations, relationship to US 19
modelling, mathematical 9
modernizing ambition 8
Monroe Doctrine 30
Monsma, Stephen 223
Mooney, Edward 212–13
Moore, Michael 54
moral world order 218, 219
Moran, Theodore 157
Muldoon, Robert 104
multilateralism, Netherlands–US
    relations 122–3, 124–6
multinationals, Netherlands 122–3

Nabucco Project 143
National Association of Evangelicals
    (NAE) 226, 230; World Relief
    Commission (WRC) 232
national missile defence (NMD) 67, 71
nationalism: anti-American feeling 52;
    post-independence US 28

nations, as old and new 7
NATO (North Atlantic Treaty
  Organization) 64, 67, 116, 120–1
Naval supremacy, US-GB
  competition 32–3
Nehru, Jawaharlal 14–15, 17
neoconservatism, fear of 48–9
neoconservatives 195–7, 199
Netherland (O'Neill) 46–7
Netherlands 122–3
Netherlands–US relations:
  Afghanistan 119–21; assessment of
  relationship 126–8; Cold War 117;
  economic relationship 123;
  extraordinary rendition 125–6; 'Hague
  Invasion Act' 124–5; international
  organizations 122–3; Iraq 117–19; Joint
  Strike Fighter (JSF) 121–2;
  NATO (North Atlantic Treaty
  Organization) 115–17; neutrality 115;
  overview 115; security
  policy 117–22; US Unilateralism v.
  Dutch Multilateralism 124–6
New Deal, applied in Mexico 9
'New Look' 15
New Statesman 54
New Zealand: anti-communism 97;
  campaigns for withdrawal from ANZUS
  and SEATO 101; changing nature
  of special relationships 94; changing
  relationship with UK 103; Cold War
  security system 100; criticism of
  relationship with UK 101; ending
  of special relationships 108; foreign
  policy 94, 96, 108; involvement
  in Vietnam 102, 103; loyalty to
  UK 98–9; nationalism 104; nuclear-free
  legislation 107; nuclear issue 104–5;
  post-imperial identity 94; reactions to
  anti-war movement 95; reactions to
  ANZUS Treaty 98–9; relations with
  UK 93–4
New Zealand Campaign for Nuclear
  Disarmament (NZCND) 101–2
New Zealand Day 104
New Zealand Labour Party 103
New Zealand Listener 102–3
New Zealand–US relations: criticism
  from left 99–100; developing
  relationship 95–6; effect of
  anti-nuclear position 105–6;
  post-war security 96
Niebuhr, Reinhold 211
Norrish, Mervyn 105

North American Security
  Community 61–4
North Korea 146
NRC Handelsblad 118
nuclear power, UK 35
nuclear relationship, UK-US 34–5
nuclear weapons 35
Nunn, Sam 137

Obama, Barack 57, 191
Ockenga, Harold John 229
Ogdensburg accord 65
O'Hagan, Andrew 49, 52
oil, US Middle East interests 187–8
Olmert, Ehud 201
Olney, Richard 30–1
On the Beach (Shute) 101
O'Neill, Joseph 46–7
Operation Enduring Freedom 120
Operation Iraqi Freedom, Dutch support
  for 118
opium 120
Orwell, George 61
Oslo Accords 201
Oxford Union debate 106

Pacific pact 97
Pacific war, effects on New Zealand 94–5
pacifism 234
Pahlavi, Mohammad Reza Shah 155–9
Pakistan, US alliance with 15
Palestine Liberation Organization
  (PLO) 186
Palestinian elections 2006 202
Palmer, Geoffrey 106
Pamela, or Virtue Rewarded
  (Richardson) 28
'Paper War' 28
parent–child theme, in UK-US
  relations 47
Parsons, Anthony 159
Partial Test-Ban Treaty 102
patriotism, and religion 226
Paz, Octavio 7
peace activists, New Zealand 95–6, 97
Peace, Freedom and Security Studies
  Program (PFSS) 234–5
Peachey, Paul 229
Permanent Joint Board on Defence
  (PJBD) 65
Perry, William J. 137
Pinter, Harold 46
political economy, of alliance
  relations 86–8

political parties, pro-Israel funding 194
post-war religious renewal 226
post-war world view, possibility of moral
    rebuilding 219
Pound, Ezra 29
power differentials 72–3
power, hegemonic 77–8
Prairie Home Companion (Keillor) 60
Precht, Henry 157
premillennial dispensationalism 197–8
Presidential Decision Directive 39 125
Primakov, Yevgenii 138–9
progress, showcases 8–9
Project for the New American Century
    (PNAC) 196
publishing 28–9
Putin, Vladimir 137, 141, 144–5, 147
Pye, Lucian 19

Ramsbotham, Sir Peter 154
Raviv, Dan 177
Reagan administration: military
    build-up 105; retaliation against New
    Zealand 106
'real *ekonomi*' 144
religious agencies 224
religious liberty 230
religious practice, US growth in 209
religious unity, against communism 218
replacement theology 198
Rice, Condoleezza 52
Roadmap for Peace 202
Rockefeller, Abby 10
Rockefeller Foundation 11, 12
Rockefeller, Nelson 12
Roosevelt, Franklin D. 11, 33, 66, 208–9,
    210–11, 214
Rose Revolution 142–3
Rostow, Walt W. 8, 16, 18–19
Royal Titles Act 99, 104
Ruane, Chris 53
Rubin, Barry 51, 52, 162, 165
Rubin, Joyce 51, 52
Rudd, Kevin 76, 85–6
Rumsfeld, Donald 7, 47, 52
Rushdie, Salman 55
Russell, Robert 17
Russia: economic growth 143; economy
    and foreign policy 144; energy 143–4;
    as Gog 229; North Korea 146; ties with
    Central Asian states 142
Russia–US relations: Afghanistan 141;
    arms treaties 147; assessment
    of relationship 146–8; early to

mid 1990s 135–8; final stages of Bush
    administration 145–6; Global War on
    Terror 141–3; historical context 134–5;
    hostility 146; Kosovo 138–41; national
    sovereignty 140–1; overview 132–4;
    Putin and George W. Bush,
    2006–7 143–6; US National Security
    Strategy 145; view of the other 145

Safire, 164
Salisbury, Lord (Robert Cecil) 30–1
Sampiemon, Jan 127
Saturday (McEwan) 46, 49–50
Saudi Arabia 187–8
Savage, Michael Joseph 93
Scandinavia, security
    community 63
Schieffer, Tom 86
Second Chechen War 140–1
secularism 229
security agreement, Southeast Asia 100
Segev, Tom 177
Seitz, Raymond 24
Sheen, Rev. Fulton J. 211
Sheridan, Greg 85
Shultz, George 105
Shute, Neville 101
Sick, Gary 159, 162, 166
Simpson, Eyler N. 10–11
Sinclair, Keith 100
Sisco, Joseph 164
slavery 26
Slotkin, Richard 10
Smith, Harold P. Jr. 136, 137, 138
Smith, Sydney 28
Sobel, Clifford 128
Society in America (Martineau) 26
soft power 47
Sokolsky, Joel 67, 70
Southeast Asia, security agreement 100
Southeast Asia Treaty Organization
    (SEATO) 100–1, 103
sovereign democracy 143
Soviet Nuclear Threat Reduction Act 137
Soviet Union, US Christian attitudes
    to 208, 209, 210–11
Soviet–US relations: attitude of US
    Christians 208, 209; deterioration 214;
    ideological polarity 217, 219–20;
    moral world order 218; post-war
    world views 215; Truman
    administration 213–20; US popular
    viewpoint 217; during and after World
    War II 208–9, 210

Spanish–American War 31
special relationships: motivations for 24; as problematic concept 24; risks of 101; state and non-governmental bodies 223; use of term 7–8
specialness: defining 61, 132–4; images of 72; and North American Security Community 61–4
Spender, Percy 97–8
stability, East Asia 83–4
Statute of Westminster 96
steel 29
Stikker, Dirk 115
Stowe, Harriet Beecher 27
Stuff Happens (Hare) 46–7
subsidiarist state 223–4
subsidiarity, international aid 233
Sudetenland crisis 66
Suez crisis 36
Sutch, Bill 100
Sweig, Julia 72
symbiosis, US and Israel 174
symbolism, in international relations 17
Syria, withdrawal from Lebanon 203

Taiwan 19
Talbott, Strobe 136, 139
Taylor, Clyde 230, 232
Taylor, Myron C.: advice on Soviet Union 212–13; anti-Soviet crusade 216–17; character and attitudes 211–12; expansion of duties 218–19; objectives of appointment 212; relationship with Truman 215; suspicion of Soviet communism 213; US war aims 214–15
Teicher, Howard 161, 165
Thatcher, Margaret 36–7
The Adventures of Huckleberry Finn (Twain) 29
The Ejido: Mexico's Way Out 10–11
The Israel Lobby and US Foreign Policy (Mearsheimer and Walt) 180–1, 192
The Quiet American (Greene) 47
The Russia Hand: A Memoir of Presidential Diplomacy (Talbott) 136
The Ugly American (Lederer and Burdick) 17–18
think tanks 193–4, 196
Timmermen, Frans 126
Tocqueville, Alexis de 29
trade, Netherlands 122
Trollope, Anthony 29–30

Trollope, Fanny 26
Truman administration: fear of communist expansion 97; relations with India 15; Soviet–US relations 213–20; support for Israel 183
Truman Doctrine 216
Truman, Harry S. 191; attitude to Soviet Union 213, 216; relationship with Myron C. Taylor 215; religiosity 215–16; view of India 13
Twain, Mark 27
Tyler, William 123

UK-US relations: cultural 37; evaluation 37; exasperation 53–4; friendships between leaders 37; Greeks and Romans doctrine 49; hatred of G.W. Bush 56–7; parent–child theme in 47; private curiosity 25–7; structures and uniqueness 56; support for Washington 54–7; as tested 34
UN Office on Drugs and Crime (UNODC) 120
Underhill, Frank 72
unilateralism, Netherlands–US relations 124–6
United Kingdom: borrowing from US 32; colonization 24–5; exclusion from ANZUS Treaty 98, 100; as principal ally 34; settling conflicts with US 31; settling imperial problems 30; US as 'wordy' 33
United Nations, evangelical opposition 228
United States: arms sales 187–8; as defender of the West 36; foreign policy determined by elite 175–6; independence 25; Israel lobby 179–84, 187–8; Jewish population 194; oil policy 187–8; opposition to state of Israel 183; post-war world view 214–15; pro-Israeli organizations 193–4; public opinion 55
United States Information Agency (USIA) 16
US–UK alliance 65–6
US–UK Mutual Defence Agreement 35
Uzbekistan 142

van Middelkoop, Einert 120
van Mierlo, Hans 117
van Staden, Alfred 128
van Wolferen, Karel 127

Vance, Cyrus 157, 164
Vansittart, Sir Robert 33
Venezuela, Anglo-American crisis 30
Verhagen, Maxime 126
Vietnam 102, 103, 233
village communes 10
Volk, Yevgeny 145
Voorhoeve, Joris 122

Wade, Raymond J. 210–11
Waldman, Louis 210
Wallace, Henry 11
Walsh, Rev. Edmund A. 210
Walt, Stephen 65, 180–1, 192
war debts 32
Ward, Barbara 9, 16
Washington, UK support 54–7
Webb, Clifton 100
Weigle, Luther A. 211
Weld, William 62

welfare imperialism 8
Wendt, Alexander 79
Westad, Odd Arne 216
Wilson, Ormond 100
Wilson, Woodrow 7
Wisner, Frank 34
Wolfe, Tom 49
Wolfowitz, Paul 105
Wood, Frederick 93, 94
World War I 31–2
World War II 33–4, 209
writers: Bush-haters 46–51; views of
  UK 27–8; views of US 25–7, 29–30

Yankee at the Court of King Arthur
  (Twain) 27
Yeltsin, Boris 136–7, 140

Zionist Organization of America
  (ZOA) 193